S0-BSB-068

VOLUME 599

MAY 2005

THE ANNALS

of The American Academy of Political
and Social Science

ROBERT W. PEARSON, *Executive* Editor
LAWRENCE W. SHERMAN, *Editor*

Place Randomized Trials: Experimental Tests of Public Policy

Special Editor of this Volume

ROBERT BORUCH
University of Pennsylvania

CABRINI COLLEGE LIBRARY
610 KING OF PRUSSIA ROAD
RADNOR, PA 19087

SAGE Publications Thousand Oaks · London · New Delhi

✱59158734

H
I
.A4
v.599

The American Academy of Political and Social Science

3814 Walnut Street, Fels Institute of Government, University of Pennsylvania,
Philadelphia, PA 19104-6197; (215) 746-6500; (215) 898-1202 (fax); www.aapss.org

Board of Directors
LAWRENCE W. SHERMAN, *President*
STEPHEN B. BURBANK, *Chair*

ELIJAH ANDERSON	KLAUS NAUDÉ
HEIDI HARTMANN	NORMAN H. NIE
JERRY LEE	NELL IRVIN PAINTER
JANICE FANNING MADDEN	JAROSLAV PELIKAN
SARA MILLER McCUNE	LOUIS H. POLLAK
MARY ANN MEYERS	ERIC WANNER

Editors, THE ANNALS

ROBERT W. PEARSON, *Executive Editor*	RICHARD D. LAMBERT, *Editor Emeritus*
LAWRENCE W. SHERMAN, *Editor*	JULIE ODLAND, *Managing Editor*

Origin and Purpose. The Academy was organized December 14, 1889, to promote the progress of political and social science, especially through publications and meetings. The Academy does not take sides in controverted questions, but seeks to gather and present reliable information to assist the public in forming an intelligent and accurate judgment.

Meetings. The Academy occasionally holds a meeting in the spring extending over two days.

Publications. THE ANNALS of The American Academy of Political and Social Science is the bimonthly publication of the Academy. Each issue contains articles on some prominent social or political problem, written at the invitation of the editors. Also, monographs are published from time to time, numbers of which are distributed to pertinent professional organizations. These volumes constitute important reference works on the topics with which they deal, and they are extensively cited by authorities throughout the United States and abroad. The papers presented at the meetings of the Academy are included in THE ANNALS.

Membership. Each member of the Academy receives THE ANNALS and may attend the meetings of the Academy. Membership is open only to individuals. Annual dues: $80.00 for the regular paperbound edition (clothbound, $120.00). For members outside the U.S.A., add $24.00 for shipping of your subscription. Members may also purchase single issues of THE ANNALS for $17.00 each (clothbound, $26.00). Student memberships are available for $53.00.

Subscriptions. THE ANNALS of The American Academy of Political and Social Science (ISSN 0002-7162) (J295) is published six times annually—in January, March, May, July, September, and November— by Sage Publications, 2455 Teller Road, Thousand Oaks, CA 91320. Telephone: (800) 818-SAGE (7243) and (805) 499-9774; FAX/Order line: (805) 499-0871; E-mail: journals@sagepub.com. Copyright © 2005 by The American Academy of Political and Social Science. Institutions may subscribe to THE ANNALS at the annual rate: $544.00 (clothbound, $615.00). Add $24.00 per year for subscriptions outside the U.S.A. Institutional rates for single issues: $96.00 each (clothbound, $108.00).

Periodicals postage paid at Thousand Oaks, California, and at additional mailing offices.

Single issues of THE ANNALS may be obtained by individuals who are not members of the Academy for $33.00 each (clothbound, $36.00). Single issues of THE ANNALS have proven to be excellent supplementary texts for classroom use. Direct inquiries regarding adoptions to THE ANNALS c/o Sage Publications (address below).

All correspondence concerning membership in the Academy, dues renewals, inquiries about membership status, and/or purchase of single issues of THE ANNALS should be sent to THE ANNALS c/o Sage Publications, 2455 Teller Road, Thousand Oaks, CA 91320. Telephone: (800) 818-SAGE (7243) and (805) 499-9774; FAX/Order line: (805) 499-0871. E-mail: journals@sagepub.com. *Please note that orders under $30 must be prepaid.* Sage affiliates in London and India will assist institutional subscribers abroad with regard to orders, claims, and inquiries for both subscriptions and single issues.

Printed on recycled, acid-free paper

THE ANNALS

© 2005 by The American Academy of Political and Social Science

All rights reserved. No part of this volume may be reproduced or utilized in any form or by any means, electronic or mechanical, including photocopying, recording, or by any information storage and retrieval system, without permission in writing from the publisher. All inquiries for reproduction or permission should be sent to Sage Publications, 2455 Teller Road, Thousand Oaks, CA 91320.

Editorial Office: 3814 Walnut Street, Fels Institute for Government, University of Pennsylvania, Philadelphia, PA 19104-6197.

For information about membership° (individuals only) and subscriptions (institutions), address:

Sage Publications
2455 Teller Road
Thousand Oaks, CA 91320

For Sage Publications: Joseph Riser and Esmeralda Hernandez

From India and South Asia, write to:

SAGE PUBLICATIONS INDIA Pvt Ltd
B-42 Panchsheel Enclave, P.O. Box 4109
New Delhi 110 017
INDIA

From Europe, the Middle East, and Africa, write to:

SAGE PUBLICATIONS LTD
1 Oliver's Yard, 55 City Road
London EC1Y 1SP
UNITED KINGDOM

°Please note that members of the Academy receive THE ANNALS with their membership.
International Standard Serial Number ISSN 0002-7162
International Standard Book Number ISBN 1-4129-2582-7 (Vol. 599, 2005 paper)
International Standard Book Number ISBN 1-4129-2581-9 (Vol. 599, 2005 cloth)
Manufactured in the United States of America. First printing, May 2005.

The articles appearing in *The Annals* are abstracted or indexed in Academic Abstracts, Academic Search, America: History and Life, Asia Pacific Database, Book Review Index, CAB Abstracts Database, Central Asia: Abstracts & Index, Communication Abstracts, Corporate ResourceNET, Criminal Justice Abstracts, Current Citations Express, Current Contents: Social & Behavioral Sciences, Documentation in Public Administration, e-JEL, EconLit, Expanded Academic Index, Guide to Social Science & Religion in Periodical Literature, Health Business FullTEXT, HealthSTAR FullTEXT, Historical Abstracts, International Bibliography of the Social Sciences, International Political Science Abstracts, ISI Basic Social Sciences Index, Journal of Economic Literature on CD, LEXIS-NEXIS, MasterFILE FullTEXT, Middle East: Abstracts & Index, North Africa: Abstracts & Index, PAIS International, Periodical Abstracts, Political Science Abstracts, Psychological Abstracts, PsycINFO, Sage Public Administration Abstracts, Social Science Source, Social Sciences Citation Index, Social Sciences Index Full Text, Social Services Abstracts, Social Work Abstracts, Sociological Abstracts, Southeast Asia: Abstracts & Index, Standard Periodical Directory (SPD), TOPICsearch, Wilson OmniFile V, and Wilson Social Sciences Index/Abstracts, and are available on microfilm from ProQuest, Ann Arbor, Michigan.

Information about membership rates, institutional subscriptions, and back issue prices may be found on the facing page.

Advertising. Current rates and specifications may be obtained by writing to *The Annals* Advertising and Promotion Manager at the Thousand Oaks office (address above).

Claims. Claims for undelivered copies must be made no later than six months following month of publication. The publisher will supply missing copies when losses have been sustained in transit and when the reserve stock will permit.

Change of Address. Six weeks' advance notice must be given when notifying of change of address to ensure proper identification. Please specify name of journal. POSTMASTER: Send address changes to: *The Annals* of The American Academy of Political and Social Science, c/o Sage Publications, 2455 Teller Road, Thousand Oaks, CA 91320.

THE ANNALS

OF THE AMERICAN ACADEMY OF POLITICAL AND SOCIAL SCIENCE

Volume 599　　　　　　　　　　　　　　　　　　May 2005

IN THIS ISSUE:

Place Randomized Trials:
Experimental Tests of Public Policy

Special Editor: ROBERT BORUCH

Quick Read Synopsis

FORCHOMING

The Use and Usefulness of the Social Sciences:
Accomplishments, Disappointments, and Promise

Special Editors: LAWRENCE W. SHERMAN
and ROBERT W. PEARSON

Volume 600, July 2005

The Science of Voter Mobilization

Special Editors: DONALD P. GREEN
and ALAN S. GERBER

Volume 601, September 2005

PREFACE

Better Evaluation for Evidence-Based Policy: Place Randomized Trials in Education, Criminology, Welfare, and Health

By
ROBERT BORUCH

Phrases such as "evidence-based policy" are seductive and are used promiscuously in some quarters. Here, we take the phrase and its intent seriously, as others have. In the international sector, for instance, the Campbell Collaboration was created to generate systematic reviews of dependable evidence on the effects of policies, programs, and practices. This is in the arenas of crime and justice, education, and social services. The Cochrane Collaboration, Campbell's older sibling, was created to achieve a similar aim in health care. Their reviews of evidence are intended to assist people in making decisions.

Executing the Campbell Collaboration's and the Cochrane Collaboration's mission requires specifying what high-quality evidence is. The Campbell Collaboration's focus is similar to that of the Cochrane Collaboration. It is on randomized controlled trials that are designed to evaluate the relative effects of different interventions. See http://www.campbellcollaboration.org and http://www.cochrane.org.

One important and emerging vehicle for generating dependable evidence falls under the rubric of place randomized trials. In fact, one activity that led to this *Annals* volume was a U.S. trial in which entire housing developments were randomly assigned to the Jobs Plus program or to control conditions to generate high quality of evidence on the program's effect on wage rates, employment, and other outcomes. The Rockefeller Foundation and other organizations contributed resources for this trial. More pertinent here, the Rockefeller Foundation also pro-

Robert Boruch is University Trustee Chair Professor at the University of Pennsylvania.

NOTE: Research and development work on this topic has been supported by the Rockefeller Foundation and was organized under the auspices of the Campbell Collaboration. Dorothy de Moya, executive officer of the Collaboration, organized the Bellagio meetings and assisted in the organization of the New York meetings on this topic.

DOI: 10.1177/0002716205275610

vided support for a broadened view of place randomized trials under Campbell Collaboration auspices.

The Campbell Collaboration initiative was actualized partly through commissioning papers that appear in this *Annals* volume. The papers were vetted in conferences organized by the Campbell Collaboration and at which authors presented briefings on their papers in Bellagio, Italy, and in New York. The Campbell initiative also involved developing an internet accessible register of randomized trials in which places, groups, clusters of individuals, and entities are the target of studies to understand what works.

The articles in this issue of the *Annals* are diverse in some respects. They also have some remarkable commonalities. This introduction covers both and lays out some important dimensions of the topic of place randomized trials. It also identifies new issues and questions that ought to be addressed in further research and some recent efforts to enhance the quality of reporting and in designing such trials.

Recent History:
Evidence-Based Policy and Randomized Trials

A variety of organizations have undertaken substantial efforts to understand whether and how randomized trials can be used to inform evidence-based policy.

During 2000 to 2005, for instance, the World Bank's Operations Evaluation Division laid on workshops (at Carleton University) and conferences (Washington, D.C.) in which randomized trials were considered seriously as a vehicle for generating better evidence. The most pertinent of recent proceedings of the conference are given in Pitman, Feinstein, and Ingram (2005); see especially the paper by Rawlings (2005) on randomized trials in Central and South American countries.

During 2000 to 2005, the U.S. Institute of Education Sciences (IES) was created and began to invest money in place randomized trials to understand how to improve children's learning, character education, and teacher development. During the same period, various federal agencies in the United States began to cooperate with one another in developing standards of evidence and producing better evidence. The U.S. Office of Management and Budget, for instance, has invested intellectual and organization resources in harmonizing the language used to describe research designs, including randomized trials.

The Organization for Economic Cooperation and Development (OECD), until recently, had invested mainly in passive surveys. The OECD-IES Conference on Evidence suggests a shift toward better evidence based on fair comparisons, especially randomized trials.

Within countries, the push toward better evidence has led to both quarrels and to defensible evidence from randomized trials. The U.K. Cabinet Office's evaluation unit (Davies 2004) has fostered the development of new randomized trials to evaluate programs for low-income families, for instance. In the health sector, at least one special issue of *Statistics in Medicine* is dedicated toward cluster (place) randomized trials (Campbell, Donner, and Elbourne 2001).

In the crime arena, the U.S. National Academy of Sciences has reiterated collective ignorance about information on firearms and their use in crime in the United States. The report also reiterates the need for controlled trials, including place randomized trials, on what works to reduce the misuse of firearms (Wellford, Pepper, and Petrie 2005).

Flay and Collins, in this *Annals* volume, give a recent history on school-based prevention research. Sikkema also does so for one strand of work on AIDS prevention work. Earlier, Boruch and Foley (2000) identified influential groups with serious interests in evidence and that have contributed notably to the development of research policy on trials in which places, organizations, and other charters are the target of randomization.

Places That Are Randomized: Theory and the Units of Randomization

The rudimentary theory underlying all of these *Annals* articles is that one must change entire places to enhance the well-being of people in those places or to decrease the risks that confront them. The "places" vary considerably in character.

In the health care sector, for instance, Grimshaw and his colleagues randomly allocated medical family practices to different interventions. Leviton and Horbar randomly allocated willing and eligible tertiary care facilities and neonatal intensive care units within hospitals to different regiments to learn whether better practices could be introduced and whether the practices would have a discernible effect on outcomes of patients.

Sikkema and her colleagues randomly allocated eligible and willing housing developments to different regimens to learn whether a particular opinion leader-based intervention, tested earlier in other trials and sustained by coherent theory, produced a detectable and substantial effect on women's health behavior. Although the particular focus was AIDS, the work has implications for other arenas.

In the Jobs-Plus trials, Bloom and Riccio and their colleagues also randomized housing developments but for a different purpose: understanding the effects of this form of increasing social capital on wage and employment rates, and other outcomes. Sikkema depends on a long history of research on the effects of diffusion strategies, including opinion leader approaches. Bloom and Riccio depend more on what could be loosely construed as a theory of developing human capital. A theory of diffusion of innovation and change is implicit, rather than explicit, in their work.

Flay appears to be the first social scientist to have succeeded in executing a well-designed trial that involved randomizing entire schools to different health risk reduction interventions. This was in Waterloo, Canada. He and his colleagues in the United States and Canada have depended on and have advanced the theory of change to understand how to develop the interventions and to test a theory that posits that changing individual behavior depends on changing school conditions including group processes within the school. Cook's article in this volume depends on similar theory that is implicit. Porter et al. provide more concrete information on training the trainer approach in trials on a teacher professional development program.

Weisburd's study focused on high crime geographic areas within cities—hot spots—as opposed to specific institutions such as housing developments or schools or hospital units. The broad theory posits that redistributing police resources to hot spots will reduce crime. This is in counterpoint to a theory that says it will not have an effect and, furthermore, that focusing police resources on hot spots will lead to the migration of criminal activity to neighboring areas.

Entire villages and other geopolitical jurisdictions were randomly assigned to different interventions in the studies in Mexico that Parker and Teruel describe and a complex study in China that Smith describes. In Mexico's Progresa trial, the theory was that changing village behavior, notably through financial incentives that would increase the rate at which children stayed in schools rather than working in the fields, would lead to better outcomes at the village level on account of local economies. In the fertility control trials in China that Smith describes, the implicit theory is that people will change if given the opportunity to do so but that the change depends on local circumstances and place-based influences.

Each of these articles educates us. Each invites further questions. For instance, how can we develop better theory about what should happen at various levels of the units being considered in a place randomized trial: province or county, and city or village within province, and institution or housing development within village or city, and catchment area or hot spot within city? Each article also invites a question about how to learn more easily about other trials of this sort, involving yet other units of allocation and analysis.

Relationships and Agreements

How have people gotten place randomized trials off the ground? Part of the answer to this question hinges on the development of agreements between the trialist's team and the prospective participants in the place based trial. "Participants" here mean individuals or groups whose cooperation is essential in deploying both the intervention and the trial.

In their article on prevention research trials, for example, Flay and Collins emphasize written agreements signed by people who are authorized to represent their organizations' interest in testing ways to improve. In their case, this includes the school principal and the school superintendent. Given the mobility (turnover) of school administrators and teachers in some parts of the United States, at least, one or the other signatory might disappear before the end of the trial. Having both kinds of school administrators as signatories to an agreement helps reduce the obstacles to running a fair trial to completion. Elsewhere, Robert Slavin and his colleagues take a similar but different tack in their tests of Success for All. They demand that a large fraction of teachers in a school agree on testing his program at a point in time. For Kellam and Van Horn (1997), developing long-term relationships is essential to generating evidence over long periods of time. Porter et al. in this volume remind us about the practical matter that agreements are essential but substantial changes in the places (in leadership for instance) may abrogate agreements and that this prospect has to be considered in such trials.

[O]ne must change entire places to enhance the well-being of people in those places or to decrease the risks that confront them.

In some areas of the health sector, agreements have been able to depend on an overarching theme and organization. Leviton and Horbar's work in this volume of the *Annals*, for instance, depends partly on the Vermont Oxford Network. Health care institutions commit in advance to be willing to engage in research, including perhaps randomized trials at times in the interest of contributing to the accumulation of knowledge about what works. At least part of the Grimshaw et al. effort described here also depends on formal networks of people and institutions whose interest lies in collaborating on studies that help us understand what works better.

The Bloom and Riccio trials on Jobs-Plus depended on identifying entities and people who wanted to develop a relationship in the interest of a place randomized trial and for reasons that were more important. The process of identifying prospective partners, inviting proposals, and reaching agreement on willingness and capacity to participate that the authors describe is instructive. The relationships were formalized through written agreements at the level of agencies within city, such as departments responsible for public housing, as well as with federal and other entities. Very complex, and requiring time and industry.

Weisburd emphasizes the need to develop personal relationships that lead to trust and willingness to experiment on innovations that may work better than conventional practice. His description of the Jersey City effort and others is refreshing.

Relationships involve reputation, of course, a reputation that must be developed at different levels to get a place randomized trial off the ground. The principal authors of each of the articles in this *Annals* volume, and the institutions to which they belong, are graced with high reputations. The reputations reflect authors' high productivity, stamina, and willingness to recognize their own ignorance and to reduce their own and others' ignorance. Their reputations are high and, more important, give them access to relationships that permit good research to be done.

Relationships and agreements have been important in mounting high-quality trials. These authors' handling of the topic invites attention to questions for the future: How do we develop better contracts and agreements with organizations, public and private, that permit us to generate better evidence about the effects of an innovation? And how do we make the specific contents of agreements and changes in these agreements more accessible to other trialists and the people who might collaborate with trialists so that they can learn and contribute?

Incentives and Justifications

For Weisburd, an expert in criminological research, an important condition for mounting a randomized trial on police patrolling crime hot spots is that conventional practice, policy, or program was under attack. Cops are local theorists, and they disagree about what might work. Crime experts have also disagreed about what might work in high-crime areas. Weisburd's position accords with ethics of trials in the medical arena. Neither the Salk vaccine trials on polio nor trials on streptomycin for treating tuberculosis would have been mounted had the purported effects of conventional treatments not been suspect and under attack, for instance.

For Leviton and Horbar, the "quality chasm" between what constitutes good health care based on dependable evidence and contemporary medical procedures in hospital units constitutes the justification for running a trial. Grimshaw and colleagues' work in medical practices is similarly justified.

In considering the prospects of the Progresa/Oppotunidad income support program in Mexico that Parker and Teruel describe, economists disagreed about whether an incentive program such as Progresa would keep Mexican children away from working in the agricultural fields and increase the likelihood that they would stay in schools. The disagreements were important because they made plain the uncertainty. A place randomized trial was mounted to appreciably reduce this uncertainty.

The United States has a long history of attempting to reduce poverty, much of which depends on community-based efforts. To judge from the Jobs-Plus effort described by Bloom and Riccio, the incentive for people in local departments of housing and other government agencies to participate in the trial include their interest in reducing the problem.

In trials of a teacher development program that Porter et al. describe here, justifications for the research and development effort lay in U.S. interests in improving mathematics and science education in the middle-school grades, especially in large urban school districts. Justifications lay also in the fact that, prior to the Porter et al. work, no sizeable controlled trials on the effects of any professional development had ever been run.

The scientific justification for such trials is of course the assurance that, if the trial is carried out properly, (1) there are no systematic differences between groups of places randomized and (2) a legitimate statistical statement of one's confidence in the results can be made. This justification holds for all the articles in this volume. Furthermore, as Weisburd, Grimshaw et al., and Smith point out, the simplicity and transparency of the idea of fair comparison through a randomized trial has strong appeal for policy people and decision makers who cannot understand and do not trust complex model-based analyses of data from nonrandomized studies.

Empirical evidence on the vulnerability of nonrandomized trials in comparison to the strength of randomized trials has been building since at least the 1950s. None of the articles in this *Annals* volume refer directly to this body of literature simply because the articles have different aims. See Boruch (2005) for a brief list of other studies on such comparisons and examples that range from pigs to astronomy and econometrics. Virtually all such methodological studies involve data from randomized trials in which individuals rather than places are the units of random allocation and analysis and related quasi-experiments. The biases in estimating an intervention's effect based on the quasi-experiments can be very large. Evidence on whether and by how much estimates of the effect of a nonrandomized trial differ from those of a randomized trial, when individuals are the units of random assignment and analysis (as in most medical trials), are important.

It remains to be seen whether similar methodological studies on aggregate-level analyses (cluster, place, group) yield similar results, that is, serious biases, but it is reasonable to expect biases here also. Bertrand, Duflo, and Mullainathan (2002), for instance, focused on biases in estimates of the standard error of effects assuming no effect at all using "differences in differences" methods that are conventional in some economic analyses. They found Type I error rates that were nine times the error rate presumed (.05) in using conventional statistical tests. This was partly on account of serial correlation. More methodological research, however, needs to be done on the quasi-experimental approaches to estimating effects at the place (aggregate) level to understand when the biases in estimates of effect appear, when the biases in estimates of their standard errors appear, and how large these are, relative to estimates based on place randomized trials.

The incentives and justifications that are identified in these articles are important in the near term. In the long term, it would be good to understand what the incentives are and to make these explicit at different levels and in different areas: policy (crime, health, education, and social services), institution (government and nongovernment agencies), and individual service providers.

Deploying the Intervention: Implementation, Dimensionalization, and Measurement

Incentives are essential for assuring that places, and the influential people in them, are willing to participate in a randomized trial. Understanding how to deploy a new program or practice in each place requires more than willingness, of course. It also demands experience.

Achieving this understanding is no easy matter, one that is apart from the challenge of executing the randomized trial in which the places are embedded. Jobs Plus, for instance, required research teams to engage and guide coordination of the local housing authority, welfare department, workforce development agency, and

---

In the long term, it would be good to understand what the incentives are and to make these explicit at different levels.

---

public housing residents within each site. The challenge of getting these agencies to work together more closely than any had in the past was piled on top of other challenges to implementation including getting housing development residents involved as full partners despite inexperience and distrust, integrating services across providers (to meet housing needs and encourage employment in complex welfare environments), and generating job search and acquisition processes that fit the place.

For school-based trials, the implementation challenges are different insofar as school bureaucracies differ from housing department bureaucracies, labor departments, and so on. Nonetheless, consider the way that Porter et al. dimensionalize one class of implementation. They do so by developing indices of people's participation in meetings and teams that were major ingredients for change. For the DEC (Data on Enacted Curriculum) trials, one such index set includes counting training sessions in which at least one team member participated and computing the average number of participants per session, the proportion of sessions to which local leaders (school principals) contributed, and the consistency of people's participation over time. This also included qualitative reconnaissance on factors that impede participation, such as the limited time that schools allow for teachers to meet during work hours.

The challenges to Sikkema, in deploying an AIDS risk reduction program to women in U.S. housing developments, is similar to others in some respects but differs in others. She and her team developed three different intervention models prior to the trial and, using focus groups, reconnoitered the virtues and vulnerabilities of each model relative to local standards of acceptability. It involved identifying opinion leader cadres, selecting them, and providing workshops to support them. Sikkema, as others, relies on basic count data to index level of participation in workshops and community events. As in the Jobs-Plus effort, learning how to negotiate agreements with different influential entities in housing developments, and documenting this, was an essential part of implementation. More interesting, Sikkema relies on explicit and tentative theory of change, as does Flay. The theory is implicit, rather than explicit, in articles by other authors in this *Annals* volume.

All of the authors rely to a greater or lesser extent on nonnumerical information to understand the deployment of the programs being tested, as well as on numerical information. Quarrels between the qualitative and quantitative tribes have no substantial role here, partly because place-based trials cannot be black box studies. Indeed, Bloom and his colleagues have won an award from the Association for Policy Analysis and Management for the Jobs-Plus trials partly because of the interesting coupling of methods for research.

These articles are informative but necessarily brief about deploying programs. The brevity invites broad questions about how the authors' experience *in detail* can be shared with others, for example, Web-based journals, or reports without page limits, workshops, and so on. It invites more scientific attention to the question of how one can dimensionalize the implementation of programs across different sectors and within them. They invite attention to the engineering questions of how to measure implementation level better and how to enhance it in different places.

Technical Vernacular and Technical Resources

Here, we use the phrase "place randomized trial" because it seems easy for some readers, scientists and public administrators and otherwise, to understand. The vernacular in the statistical and social science literature that is related includes phrases such as "cluster randomized trials," "group randomized trials," "saturation trials," and others.

The important technical references include Donner and Klar (2001) on cluster randomized trials. This is a fine and blessedly brief book that considers technical approaches and examples from different countries, mainly in the health arena. The important references include Murray's (1998) book on group randomized trials, which is more detailed and considers examples from the United States. Bloom's (forthcoming) monograph is excellent on account of its clarity and use of examples in the United States. Bryk and Raudenbush's (1992) text directs detailed attention to analysis of multilevel statistical data that may or may not have been generated by cluster/group/place randomized trials.

Following the Campbell Collaboration conferences on place randomized trials in 2001 and 2002, the William T. Grant Foundation initiated efforts to enhance the technical capacity of researchers to design such trials and to analyze results. Raudenbush and his colleagues have developed software for estimating the statistical power of a trial under various assumptions. This is given at the foundation's Web site, http://wtgrantfdn.org. The foundation also supported a pilot consulting service, through its Web site on design of the trials, and convened a special institute on the topic at the University of Michigan. Bloom, a contributor to this volume, and Raudenbush, a participant in one of the Campbell conferences on the topic, co-led the institute.

A big technical issue in design of the trial includes ensuring that the size of the sample of places or institutions that are randomized is large enough to permit one to detect relative effects of interventions with confidence and that other features of the design, especially covariates, can be exploited to increase statistical power. Bloom and Riccio, Leviton and Horbar, and Grimshaw et al. consider the matter of sample size briefly in this *Annals* volume. See the references cited earlier on technical issues, and see Boruch, Wortman, and Cordray (1981) for another handling of the topic. Bloom and Riccio advance the state of the art in one important respect: coupling conventional comparison of randomized places with time series analyses of data from the places. This approach permits one to also take into account the changing composition of individuals within the places (housing developments).

How Do People Find Out about Trials? International Registers of Place Randomized Trials, Standards of Reporting, and Other Resources

Until recently, people could go to no single source to learn about place (cluster, group) randomized trials that have been completed or that are under way. The authors of studies in this *Annals* volume, for instance, cover undertaken work in China, Canada, England, the United States, and Mexico. It is work that is reported piecemeal, in diverse scientific journals, Web sites, and limited circulation reports.

This diversity in publication venues makes searching the literature difficult. For instance, relying on Web-based searches such as ERIC and PsychInfo is imprudent, at best, relative to hand searches of the research literature, at least in regard to locating randomized trials. The industrious hand searcher can uncover three times as many randomized trials in a full-text search relative to depending on current search engines (Turner et al. 2003).

The difficulty in identifying randomized trials has been reduced with the creation of the international Cochrane Collaboration in health care in 1993 and the international Campbell Collaboration in 2000. Both organizations, which rely heavily on voluntary participation, have developed registers on randomized trials and possibly randomized trials that can be accessed through the relevant Web sites. Both rely heavily on hand searches (full-text readings) of peer-reviewed journals rather than on conventional machine-based searches.

For instance, the Campbell Collaboration Social, Psychological, Educational, and Criminological Trials Register (C-SPECTR) contains about thirteen thousand entries on randomized and possibly randomized trials, and includes more than two hundred references to place randomized trials. They are coded as "CRT" in indexed or nonindexed fields in the register, so searching for them is easy. Most references are supported by abstracts, many of which are standardized. In C2 SPECTR, one can find entries on place randomized trials involving schools and classrooms in Kenya, El Salvador, and India; brothels in Thailand; factories in Russia; barrio segments in Colombia; neighborhoods areas in Taiwan; and bars in England and Canada, among others.

Standards for reporting on randomized trials that involve individuals as the unit of random allocation and analysis are a relatively recent initiative. In the health arena for instance, the CONSORT statement gives guidance on the ingredients that a good report on a randomized trial in the health arena should contain (Moher et al. 2001). The CONSORT statement has been extended to include standards for reporting on place/group/cluster randomized trials. This extension, given in Campbell, Elbourne, and Altman (2004), depends on the ingredients of other kinds of trials, of course, but pays special attention to important topics embedded in a place randomized trial. This includes, for instance, consideration of the rationale for this research design and the fact that there are at least two levels of inference: the cluster (place) level and the individual (person within place) level. There are usually two levels of sampling and sample sizes associated with each level, different levels of attrition and measurement, and so on.

Most contemporary standards for reporting include no requirement that microrecords from the trials be made available for secondary analysis. Such reanalysis is often essential to verify the appropriateness and correctness of original analyses of the data, to test new hypotheses or explore new relationships, to entertain different assumptions about the structure underlying the data, and for other reasons (Boruch, Wortman, and Cordray 1981). As the state of the art in running place randomized trials advances, and as it becomes obvious that resultant data are a valuable resource and deserve secondary analysis, the standards for reporting trials are likely to change. Furthermore, readier Internet access to the data generated in such trials is likely to lead to changes in standards for reporting meta-analyses (Moher et al. 1999) as well as to improvements in the conduct of the trials and to productive exploitation of the resultant data.

Organizations that attempt to evaluate the published statistical evidence on relative effects of large-scale interventions, and that publish the results of their reviews, are also a resource. Many, not all, put randomized trials, including place randomized trials, at a high priority. These organizations identify the trials, review them, and make results accessible through the Internet and in other ways. The Campbell and Cochrane Collaborations illustrate international efforts. In the United States, the Institute of Education Sciences' What Works Clearinghouse focuses heavily on trials in education (2005, http://whatworks.ed.gov), as does the Office of Justice Programs for drug abuse and violence prevention (http://www.colorado.edu/cspv/blueprints). Federal efforts to bring uniformity to standards of evidence and that attend to the trustworthiness of randomized trials are reflected in the products of the Federal Collaboration on What Works (2005) and the Agency for Healthcare Research and Quality (2005, http://ahrq.gov), among others. The Coalition for Evidence Based Policy (2005, http://www.excelgov.org) provides routine updates on such efforts and has been a contributor to them. None thus far attends to or depends on access to microrecords for reanalysis of data from trials. But this may change for reasons given earlier.

Concluding Remarks

The shift in science policy in many countries, toward fair comparisons and toward randomized trials on the effects of an intervention, has had a choppy history at times. Progress has been relatively steady in the health sector. This is partly on account of precedents such as the Salk vaccine and streptomycin trials.

In the social sector, progress has been choppier and less obvious. But the progress depends on some of the same ingredients as the health sector. Good precedents are also effective, for instance. The Tennessee Class Size Trial in the United States, the Waterloo Trial in Canada, Progresa in Mexico, and the police hot spots trials in Jersey City were remarkable in setting precedent.

One of the challenges to progress lies in the need to enhance people's capacity to learn about place randomized trials and how to do them. This issue of the *Annals* was developed with Rockefeller Foundation support and under Campbell Collaboration auspices to meet part of the challenge. The authors of articles in this *Annals* issue are experienced and, more important, have been able to mount such trials with reasonable success. The augmentation and public access to information on place (cluster) randomized trials in the Campbell Collaboration's register is another important product.

Evidence-based policy requires resources. The resources required for place randomized trials described here were supplied, at times, by private foundations. Some foundations have assisted notably or have served as the catalyst in running place randomized trials. The larger and sustained resources, of course, come from countries in which government and the people it represents are interested in evidence about what works, what does not, what is inconclusive, and what is harmful. When the countries, or their governments, are unwilling or unable to care about work issues, we will make no progress. When the countries and the government do care, we will enhance people's lives.

References

Bertrand, M., E. Duflo, and S. Mullainathan. 2002. How much should we trust differences in differences estimates? Working Paper 8841. Cambridge, MA: National Bureau of Economic Research.

Bloom, H. Forthcoming. *Learning more from social experiments: Evolving analytic approaches*. New York: Russell Sage Foundation.

Boruch, R. F. 2005. Comments on the papers by Rawlings and Duflo and Kremer. In *Evaluating development effectiveness*, ed. G. K. Pitman, O. N. Feinstein, and G. K. Ingram 232-39. New Brunswick, NJ: Transaction Books.

Boruch, R. F., and E. Foley. 2000. The Honestly Experimental Society: Sites and other entities as the units of allocation and analysis in randomized trials. In *Validity and social experimentation: Donald Campbell's legacy*, ed. L. Bickman 193-238. Thousand Oaks, CA: Sage.

Boruch, R. F., P. M. Wortman, and D. Cordray, eds. 1981. *Reanalyzing program evaluations: Policies and practices for secondary analysis of social and educational programs*. San Francisco: Jossey-Bass.

Bryk, A. S., and S. W. Raudenbush. 1992. *Hierarchical linear models*. Newbury Park, CA: Sage.

Campbell, M. J., A. Donner, and D. Elbourne, eds. 2001. Design and analysis of cluster randomized trials. *Statistics in Medicine: Special Issue* 20 (1): 329-496.

Campbell, M. K., D. R. Elbourne, and D. G. Altman. 2004. CONSORT statement: Extension to cluster ran-
    domized trials. *BMJ* 328:702-8.
Davies P. 2004. Evidence-based policy. The Jerry Lee Lecture, annual colloquium of the Campbell Collabo-
    ration, Washington DC.
Donner, A., and N. Klar. 2001. *Design and analysis of cluster randomized trials in health research.* London:
    Arnold.
Federal Collaboration on What Works. 2005. *Draft report of the working group: The what works repository.*
    Washington DC: Office of Justice Programs.
Kellem, S. G., and Y. V. Van Horn. 1997. Life course development, community epidemiology, and preventive
    trial. *American Journal of Community Psychology.* 25:177-87.
Moher, D., D. J. Cook, S. Eastwood, I. Olkin, D. Rennie, and D. Stroup, for the QUORUM Group. 1999.
    Improving the quality of reports of meta-analysis of randomized controlled trials: The quorum statement.
    Lancet 354:1896-1900.
Moher, D., K. F. Shulz, M. Egger, F. Davidoff, D. Elbourne. 2001. The CONSORT statement: Revised rec-
    ommendations for improving the quality of reports on parallel group randomized trials. *Lancet* 357:1191-
    2004.
Murray, D. M. 1998. *Design and analysis of group randomized trials.* New York: Oxford University Press.
Pitman, G. K., O. N. Feinstein, and G. K. Ingram, eds. 2005. *Evaluating development effectiveness.* Vol. 7 of
    World Bank Series on Evaluation and Development. New Brunswick, NJ: Transaction Books.
Rawlings, L. 2005. Operational reflections on evaluating development programs. In *Evaluating development
    effectiveness*, ed. G. K. Pitman, O. N. Feinstein, and G. K. Ingram 193-204. New Brunswick, NJ: Transac-
    tion Books.
Turner, H., R. Boruch, A. Petrosino, J. Lavenberg, D. de Moya, and H. Rothstein. 2003. Populating an inter-
    national web-based randomized trials register in the social, behavioral, criminological, and education sci-
    ences. *Annals of the American Academy of Political and Social Science* 589:203-25.
Wellford, C. F., J. V. Pepper, and C. V. Petrie, eds. 2005. *Firearms and violence: A critical review.* Washington,
    DC: National Research Council.

Using Place-Based Random Assignment and Comparative Interrupted Time-Series Analysis to Evaluate the Jobs-Plus Employment Program for Public Housing Residents

By
HOWARD S. BLOOM
and
JAMES A. RICCIO

This article describes a place-based research demonstration program to promote and sustain employment among residents of selected public housing developments in six U.S. cities. Because all eligible residents of the participating public housing developments were free to take part in the program, it was not possible to study its impacts in a classical experiment, with random assignment of individual residents to the program or a control group. Instead, the impact analysis is based on a design that selected matched groups of two or three public housing developments in each participating city and randomly assigned one to the program and the other(s) to a control group. In addition, an eleven-year comparative interrupted time-series analysis is being used to strengthen the place-based random assignment design. Preliminary analyses of baseline data suggest that this two-pronged approach will provide credible estimates of program impacts.

Keywords: place-based research; impact analysis; interrupted time-series analysis; Jobs-Plus Community Revitalization Initiative for Public Housing Families; community-focused employment intervention

The Policy Problem

The Jobs-Plus Community Revitalization Initiative for Public Housing Families is a place-based saturation-level employment demonstration program being tested in six cities across the United States. It was launched to learn important lessons about addressing the problem of geographically concentrated joblessness and poverty. Although it focuses on public housing residents, the process through which the Jobs-Plus intervention was designed and implemented, how it is being evaluated, and certain features of the intervention itself point to a num-

NOTE: This article was originally prepared as a paper for a conference on Place-Based Randomized Trials held in Bellagio, Italy, during November 2002 and sponsored by the Rockefeller Foundation and the Campbell Collaboration.

DOI: 10.1177/0002716205274824

ber of general lessons relevant to other community-based initiatives and institutional reforms.

The basic Jobs-Plus model was designed jointly by MDRC and the demonstration's two core funding partners: the Rockefeller Foundation and the U.S. Department of Housing and Urban Development (HUD).[1] MDRC and other experts have provided extensive technical assistance to each participating city on the design and operation of its particular local approach. MDRC is also conducting a comprehensive evaluation of the program's implementation and effectiveness.

The demonstration began in 1996 and concluded in 2004. Participating sites have been operating the program since 1998. This article summarizes the theory and policy relevance of the project, the sites' experiences in implementing the Jobs-Plus model, and the strategy being used to assess the intervention's effectiveness in improving residents' employment and quality-of-life outcomes and in helping to transform their public housing developments into better places to live. More detail on all of these issues can be found in the collection of evaluation reports and papers on Jobs-Plus that have been completed to date (see Riccio 1999; Kato and Riccio 2001; Miller and Riccio 2002; and Kato 2002). A final report on the project will be available in mid-2005 (Bloom, Riccio, and Verma 2005).

Theory and Design of the Intervention

As the planners of Jobs-Plus set out to craft a new vision for combating high rates of joblessness and poverty in public housing, they sought to build upon lessons learned from past carefully researched welfare-to-work and other employment programs for low-income populations. In addition, they tried to apply key principles from the growing number of comprehensive community initiatives being launched to improve the quality of life in poor urban neighborhoods. And like all community initiatives, Jobs-Plus hoped to achieve broad improvements in the quality of residents' lives. It differs from the more typical approach, however, in

Howard S. Bloom is chief social scientist at MDRC and has the lead role in developing and applying new experimental and quasi-experimental methods for measuring the impacts of social programs. He has written numerous articles and several books on research designs and statistical methods for evaluating public programs, and he has conducted large-scale multisite evaluations of programs in the fields of employment, welfare, education, housing, and criminal justice. Before joining MDRC, he taught research methods, program evaluation, and applied statistics at Harvard University and New York University.

James A. Riccio is director of MDRC's Low-Wage Workers and Communities policy area. He specializes in the study of work-related programs and policies for welfare recipients, public housing residents, and other low-income populations. His methodological expertise spans implementation analysis, benefit-cost analysis, and the integration of implementation and impact findings. He currently directs or codirects large-scale random assignment evaluations of employment retention and advancement programs in the United Kingdom and the United States as well as the quasi-experimental evaluation of the Jobs-Plus work initiative in public housing.

that instead of attempting to achieve a variety of community change goals simultaneously, it focuses on a single goal: improving employment outcomes. This is the
driving force around which all program elements are organized. It is hypothesized
(drawing on the work of William Julius Wilson and others) that by dramatically
increasing employment, other improvements in residents' quality of life will follow,
such as reductions in poverty and material hardship, crime, substance abuse, and
social isolation; increased general satisfaction with living in the community; and
improved outcomes for children.[2]

Drawing on lessons from past employment programs

At the time Jobs-Plus was being designed, employment programs usually included several core features. Typical programs offered job search assistance (i.e.,
instruction and guidance in how to look for work, apply for jobs, and conduct

---

*Jobs-Plus [was planned to] rely not just on
professional caseworkers "doing things" to or
for residents; it would also involve neighbors
helping neighbors in ways that might improve
their employment outcomes.*

---

oneself in job interviews); classroom-based education and training; and, to some
extent, unpaid work experience or on-the-job training. Case management and subsidies for child care and transportation to help recipients participate in programs
were also common. In addition, most programs operating within the welfare system included participation mandates under which recipients faced possible reductions in their welfare grants if they failed to participate without "good cause."

A number of subsequent initiatives adopted a broader vision of what it takes to
help welfare recipients succeed in the labor market. Recognizing that leaving welfare for work at a low-paying job would not necessarily make recipients better off
financially, most states in the United States, as part of their Temporary Assistance
for Needy Families (TANF) welfare reforms, have changed the way they calculate
welfare grants to "make work pay." Specifically, they allow more of a recipient's
earnings to be "disregarded" when the amount of the welfare grant is calculated.
This means that more recipients are able to continue to receive welfare while working and, thus, come out ahead financially by choosing to work. As its designers laid
out Jobs-Plus, emerging results from a test in Minnesota of a program that com-

bined such incentives with participation mandates and employment services looked promising, especially for a subgroup of urban welfare recipients who live in subsidized housing. Other tests of interventions that incorporated financial incentives to "make work pay" were also under way in Canada and Milwaukee, Wisconsin.[3] These and other new strategies and their early evaluation results encouraged the designers of Jobs-Plus to incorporate a financial work incentives component into the Jobs-Plus model. But as discussed below, the Jobs-Plus model goes even further.

Drawing on community-building principles

Conceiving of Jobs-Plus as a place-based intervention with the goal not only of changing individuals but also of transforming the communities in which they live, the demonstration's designers looked for further guidance to the efforts of a growing number of community change initiatives. The past several decades have seen the rise of numerous community efforts to revitalize poor urban neighborhoods and improve their residents' quality of life. The earliest examples launched in the late 1980s by the Annie E. Casey Foundation (New Futures), Ford Foundation (Neighborhood and Family Initiative), and the Rockefeller Foundation (Community Planning and Action Program) helped inspire the emergence of an estimated fifty foundation-funded projects that have come to be known as "comprehensive community initiatives."[4] Although their goals and tactics differ in the details, these initiatives tend to share a common set of "community-building" principles, which stress local control; collaborative decision making; resident empowerment; building on residents' and communities' existing physical, economic, and social assets; and strengthening the capacity of residents and local institutions to promote and sustain positive changes in their communities.[5]

Aware of the potentially powerful role that social networks might play in promoting—or thwarting—economic opportunities for residents of public housing, the Jobs-Plus designers added a third major component, which they called "community support for work." Although they offered no blueprint specifying what forms this feature of Jobs-Plus should take, they did envision that, among other things, it would include involving the residents themselves in becoming sources of work promotion, encouragement, information, advice, and support to each other. In other words, Jobs-Plus would rely not just on professional caseworkers "doing things" to or for residents; it would also involve neighbors helping neighbors in ways that might improve their employment outcomes.

The planners of Jobs-Plus also saw value in the emphasis that community-building initiatives place on enlisting and empowering community stakeholders in designing, funding, and operating the project. The principles of local collaboration, including resident involvement, call for key stakeholders to share the decision-making authority that controls the direction of the initiative and for residents to play a central role, given their special knowledge of their own communities. But residents must work collaboratively with institutional stakeholders (such as social service agencies, schools, community-based organizations, banks, businesses, hospitals, churches, the mayor's office, and public housing authorities) that control resources and broader political influence affecting what can be accomplished. More generally, the joint efforts of a variety of institutions and systems, this view holds, can be much more effective than individual systems working independently, and local funding may contribute to a sense of local ownership necessary to sustain such interventions over a long period of time, if they prove successful.

The Jobs-Plus intervention

Based on these lessons, Jobs-Plus was planned to be an unusually comprehensive and intensive community-focused employment intervention.

Three program components

As indicated in the previous section, the program's designers conceived of a broad, three-component intervention. One component focused on employment-related activities and support services such as instruction in job search skills, education and training, and assistance with child care and transportation. Some of these services could be offered on site at the public housing developments, but the great diversity in residents' job readiness and service needs also required access to broader networks of existing services. The second main program component involved financial incentives to "make work pay." These comprised mainly new public housing rent rules that reduced the extent to which earnings gains would be offset by rent increases. The program's third component, called community support for work, involved strengthening residents' work-supporting social capital through means such as work-related information sharing, peer support, and mutual aid among residents.

Saturation approach

Jobs-Plus is also distinctive because of its attempt to implement all program components at saturation levels. That is, it was to be targeted toward *all* working-age residents living in public housing developments selected to participate in the demonstration. Thus, at the very least, all such residents are to be exposed to new work-promoting "messages" from program staff and neighbors. Furthermore, the families who participate can benefit from the new financial incentives and take advantage of a diverse array of services and supports.

Providing the components of Jobs-Plus at saturation levels is fundamental to the program's theory of change—the vision of how it is expected to produce unusually large impacts on employment and earnings. According to this theory, targeting the intervention toward the entire working-age population of a public housing development will produce a critical mass of employed residents (reaching a "tipping point")[6] whose experiences will generate momentum for change across the development. As these vanguard workers grow in number, their visibility and role-model influence will be enhanced. Their own success will signal to others the feasibility and benefits of working, elevate and strengthen social norms that encourage work, foster the growth of work-supporting social networks, and ultimately contribute to still more residents getting and keeping jobs.

Collaborative process

From the outset, the demonstration's planners decided not to attempt to make detailed design choices centrally. Instead, they chose to leave these decisions to local collaboratives to be formed for this purpose. By requiring that each participating city tap a reservoir of local knowledge, technical expertise, and resources, the planners hoped that what emerged would stand a much greater chance of success than if any single local partner were to design and operate the program alone, or if it were to be designed centrally by the national demonstration team.

Each local collaborative was expected to include a broad group of actors, but four partners were considered to be absolutely essential: the public housing authority, resident representatives, the welfare department, and the workforce development system (represented by the agency operating since 1998 under the Workforce Investment Act, or WIA).

Implementing the Intervention

To implement Jobs-Plus required recruiting and choosing a group of eligible, capable, and willing sites (cities); developing and maintaining a collaborative organization at each site; and building each of the three local program components.

MDRC and the project's core funders—HUD and the Rockefeller Foundation—chose the sites from among a pool of interested and eligible cities. MDRC also deployed special "site representatives" and other experts to provide ongoing operations-related technical assistance to each collaborative to help it plan and implement the specific features of its Jobs-Plus program.

Building local collaboratives and implementing new programs from the ground up are complicated, time-intensive enterprises, and the Jobs-Plus sites' experiences were no exception. It took several years—much longer than had been hoped—for the program to evolve into a mature intervention that reflected the designers' original vision. This long gestation period resulted in part from the slowness of the collaborative decision-making process; the challenges of meeting funding, staffing, and space demands; and the challenges of designing and integrating all the elements of the complex program model.

Recruiting and selecting sites

The planners of Jobs-Plus did not attempt to recruit cities and local housing authorities that, as a group, were nationally representative. Instead, they recruited a diverse set of sites where joblessness in public housing was a serious problem and where there appeared to be a good opportunity to build and test a large-scale, well-managed employment initiative.

Eligibility criteria

Jobs-Plus sites were chosen through a national competition. Only large housing developments—defined as having at least 250 family-occupied units, not counting those occupied only by people sixty-two years old or older—could qualify.[7] In addition, no more than 30 percent of families living in these developments could have an employed member, and at least 40 percent had to be receiving Aid to Families with Dependent Children (AFDC). These criteria were meant to ensure that Jobs-Plus would be tested in places where the need for an employment intervention was great and where the scale of the intervention could be substantial.[8] Across the continental United States, 442 housing developments managed by fifty-three local housing authorities met these criteria.[9]

Five of the seven developments are located in census tracts with poverty rates at the time ranging from 49 to 74 percent, which is well above the 30 or 40 percent threshold commonly used to designate "high-poverty" areas.

The quality of local public housing authority (PHA) management was also important. Because Jobs-Plus was a complex and untried intervention, even the most effective housing authorities would be challenged by it. Thus, an effort was made to screen out PHAs that were having difficulty managing basic housing services.

Furthermore, cities eligible for the demonstration had to be willing to adopt a collaborative strategy for designing and operating the intervention, and at least some of the key local partners had to have collaborated successfully in the past. The core role anticipated for the housing authority and the welfare and job training systems made their commitment essential. Cities also had to show a willingness to include residents as full partners, and existing resident organizations had to have a reasonable capacity to play that role.

Finally, the local partners had to be willing and able to meet the demands of a rigorous research design. In particular, the housing authority had to have at least two—preferably three or more—developments that would qualify for Jobs-Plus, and (as discussed later) MDRC had to be allowed to determine randomly which one of these would be selected to operate the program. One or two of the other developments would become part of a comparison group where research would be conducted but Jobs-Plus would not be operated.

Candidate cities

In June 1996, an invitation to submit a statement of interest in the demonstration was sent to fifty of the fifty-three cities where, according to nationally available data, the PHA had the types of developments being sought. Attesting to the importance that housing authorities and other city agencies ascribed to the project, positive responses were received from forty-one cities.

After several rounds of information-gathering, in-depth site assessments, and internal reviews, the Rockefeller Foundation, HUD, and MDRC chose fifteen cities by August 1996 to begin several months of preliminary program planning. During that period, these semifinalists received technical assistance from MDRC and other groups, in anticipation of submitting a formal application for the demonstration.[10] Of the fifteen semifinalists, six chose not to continue or were encouraged not to do so.

Jobs-Plus developments

In March 1997, seven cities—Baltimore, Maryland; Chattanooga, Tennessee; Cleveland, Ohio; Dayton, Ohio; Los Angeles, California; St. Paul, Minnesota; and Seattle, Washington—were selected to participate in the demonstration. At that point, the Jobs-Plus and comparison developments were selected randomly from the pool of candidate developments for each city, and the main demonstration planning stage began.

In 1999, due to a shift in local priorities, Cleveland left the demonstration by mutual agreement between its housing authority and the national Jobs-Plus team. In addition, Seattle subsequently left the full demonstration because its housing authority received a federal HOPE VI grant to fund major renovations that will displace many residents of its Jobs-Plus development. Seattle continues to run its Jobs-Plus program, but this program is now being evaluated separately from the program in other sites (although there continue to be many points of overlap). In sum, the full Jobs-Plus research demonstration is operating in five of its seven original cities. In four of these cities the program is operating in one public housing development and in the fifth city, Los Angeles, it is operating in two housing developments.

Census data from 1990 indicate that the areas in which the Jobs-Plus developments are located are similar to those featured in the literature on high-poverty communities. As shown in Table 1, these are primarily census tracts populated by people of color. They are also tracts in which a high proportion of households are headed by single parents, many are living in poverty, and large numbers of adults do not have a high school diploma. Five of the seven developments are

TABLE 1
SELECTED 1990 CHARACTERISTICS OF THE CENSUS TRACTS
IN WHICH THE JOBS-PLUS HOUSING DEVELOPMENTS ARE LOCATED (IN PERCENTAGES)

Characteristic	Baltimore	Chattanooga	Dayton	Los Angeles		St. Paul	Seattle
	Gilmor Homes	Harriet Tubman Homes	DeSoto Bass Courts	Imperial Courts	William Mead Homes	Mt. Airy Homes	Rainier Vista
Race/ethnicity							
Black, non-Hispanic	98	97	97	62	34	10	19
White, non-Hispanic	0	3	1	1	18	17	25
Hispanic	1	0	1	37	42	3	4
Asian	0	0	2	0	5	69	50
Single-parent households	43	62	52	58	37	36	21
Adult high school graduates	53	49	58	37	59	34	71
Household poverty rate	24	58	52	59	49	74	20
Unemployment rate	18	19	26	27	10	26	6

SOURCE: Tabulations for MDRC by the Center for Urban Research of the City University of New York, using the Atlas Select CD, a collection of 1990 census data.

NOTE: The sample in each city includes residents of the census tract in which the Jobs-Plus development is located. Distributions may not total 100 percent because of rounding. Before rounding, the zero percentages ranged from 0.1 to 0.4 percent. Adult high school graduate rates are for persons age twenty-five or older.

located in census tracts with poverty rates at the time ranging from 49 to 74 percent, which is well above the 30 or 40 percent threshold commonly used to designate "high-poverty" areas.

Table 2 briefly describes the types of households that were living in the Jobs-Plus developments when the sites were selected. As can be seen, they mirror the demographic composition of the neighborhoods in which they are located. In addition, they comprise mainly female-headed households, with one adult member, plus several children. Perhaps most striking, however, is the very low percentages (15 to 25 percent) of households receiving income from wages and the very high percentages (69 to 93 percent) receiving income from welfare (according to local PHA records).

Launching and supporting the local collaboratives

All sites included the four mandated Jobs-Plus partners in their collaboratives: the local PHA, the welfare department, the workforce development agency, and public housing residents.[11] They also included other local actors such as community foundations, nonprofit social service and employment and training providers, substance abuse treatment agencies, child care agencies, and transportation agencies. Although selection of the lead partner was left to each local collaborative, all sites chose their housing authority. The degree to which the housing authority has been the "driving force" behind the initiative has varied across sites, however.

In each site, some of these partners had worked together before, but rarely, if ever, had they all joined forces in pursuit of such an ambitious employment goal. Thus, how well the partnerships would function was uncertain. As it turned out, collaboration for Jobs-Plus has been a long and bumpy journey, with many challenges and setbacks. Early on, some partners left the collaboratives, seeing no concrete role for their organizations. Others continued but expressed frustration at the slow pace of progress.

These problems (among others) contributed to the slow implementation of Jobs-Plus. Indeed, it took the collaboratives until the year 2000 or later to get elements of all three program components in place—several years after the sites were selected for the demonstration. Despite these difficulties, the collaboratives persevered and made important (if uneven) progress in jointly funding and shaping the Jobs-Plus program and in coordinating services across agencies.

Collective decision making

The collaboratives initially structured themselves as formal governance bodies for making authoritative decisions over Jobs-Plus. In practice, the degree to which this occurred depended on the local housing authority's willingness to share decision making, the other partners' desire to play a governing role, and the project director's commitment to shared decision making.

TABLE 2

SELECTED CHARACTERISTICS OF HOUSEHOLD HEADS AND HOUSEHOLDS IN THE JOBS-PLUS HOUSING DEVELOPMENTS WHEN THE SITES WERE SELECTED (IN PERCENTAGES)

Characteristic	Baltimore Gilmor Homes	Chattanooga Harriet Tubman Homes	Dayton DeSoto Bass Courts	Los Angeles Imperial Courts	Los Angeles William Mead Homes	St. Paul Mt. Airy Homes	Seattle Rainier Vista
Household heads							
Race/ethnicity[a]							
Black, non-Hispanic	99	94	98	78	6	24	42
White, non-Hispanic	0	3	1	2	1	5	12
Hispanic	0	3	0	20	80	3	0
Asian	0	0	0	0	13	65	43
Female	79	85	88	89	60	65	74
Elderly[b]	16	12	8	8	15	8	16
Disabled	30	27	22	16	17	27	31
Households							
Adults							
One	83	89	89	71	44	46	63
Two or more	17	11	11	29	56	54	37
Children							
None	56	35	32	23	34	10	34
One	22	22	29	25	20	13	29
Two	14	23	22	25	21	17	18
Three or more	8	20	17	27	24	59	18
Any income in past year from							
Wages	25	20	19	15	42	16	20
Aid to Families with Dependent Children (AFDC)	46	73	56	70	46	NA	52
Welfare[c]	85	90	82	93	75	87	85

SOURCE: Findings for the characteristics of household heads and the composition of households were obtained from MDRC calculations based on data from tenant rosters provided by housing authorities in October 1997. Findings for household income sources were obtained from housing authority data reported to MDRC in 1996 as part of their Jobs-Plus application.

NOTE: Distributions may not total 100 percent because of rounding.

a. Distribution may not total 100 percent because other groups are not reported.

b. Persons sixty-two years of age or older.

c. Includes AFDC, state General Assistance (GA) payments, and Supplemental Security Income (SSI).

Involving residents as partners

Residents were much more than "token" partners, but ensuring that they were involved in productive ways was a complex effort. Resident leaders had a particularly important role in identifying the service needs of their community and proposing useful service approaches that were not obvious to professional staff operating under agency views of "what can be done." Such leaders' active support was critical in fostering residents' trust and participation in the program.

Integrating services across providers

The collaboratives in a number of sites took actions that improved the ways in which many different agencies worked together to deliver their services to residents of public housing. Although interagency service coordination for Jobs-Plus falls short of constituting a seamless, well-integrated network of services, the collaboratives helped to make changes in standard intake procedures and restructured the roles of frontline workers in key agencies to generate a more sensible division of labor among staff in jointly serving Jobs-Plus participants.

The emerging shape of the program

Designing and implementing a new package of job search, education, training, and support services for all working-age residents in a housing development would have been challenge enough. However, adding the two other components of Jobs-Plus—financial work incentives and community supports for work—increased the challenge several-fold.

Employment-related activities and services

The sites vary considerably in the specific kinds of employment-related services they offer and in the kinds of education and training providers they utilize. However, across the sites residents have tended to want and have been given assistance by Jobs-Plus to try to find work as quickly as possible. Individualized job search guidance is a core program feature at all sites. Some sites have also provided or referred residents to group-based job clubs, which teach job-hunting and interviewing techniques. Instruction (directly or through referral to other organizations) is also offered in "soft" employment skills, such as understanding employers' expectations and appropriate workplace behavior. In addition, sites are trying to make job listings easily available to residents, such as by providing access to computers in Jobs-Plus resource centers to help residents search for jobs posted on the Internet.

To supplement residents' individual job-search efforts, local programs offer assistance from professional job developers who identify employers who are looking for workers in positions for which Jobs-Plus participants would be suitable.

They also try to generate special employment opportunities by encouraging employers to recruit from the Jobs-Plus program when future vacancies occur.

Although Jobs-Plus encourages quick employment, it also helps residents participate in education and training activities—in ways that do not keep them out of the labor market for long. Higher priority is thus given to short-term training and to combining work with education or training concurrently (e.g., working during the day and attending classes at night or on weekends). Because this is easier to do if training is located at the Jobs-Plus development, some programs are offering part-time, on-site basic education classes outside normal business hours.

In addition, Jobs-Plus offers a broad range of support services to help residents participate in program activities as well as find and keep jobs. Most common among these services are child care, transportation, substance abuse treatment, and domestic abuse assistance.

Financial incentives to make work pay

To encourage residents to take jobs and remain employed, Jobs-Plus includes new rent policies that limit how much residents' rent will increase when their incomes rise due to earnings. Under traditional rent policies, residents must pay 30 percent of their household's countable income in rent, up to a maximum amount tied to the cost of operating public housing. Under Jobs-Plus, working residents pay less of their overall income in rent. Depending on how many people are induced by Jobs-Plus to work, it is possible for the housing authority to lose revenues as a result of the program. Recognizing that few housing authorities would be willing to take this risk, HUD agreed to hold them harmless for any extra costs that resulted from approved new Jobs-Plus rent policies.[12]

Current Jobs-Plus incentive packages center primarily on two main strategies, with different sites taking different approaches: (1) flat rents, which specify a fixed rental payment regardless of earnings; and (2) reductions in the percentage of income to be paid in rent.[13] Residents must participate in other Jobs-Plus activities to qualify for these rent benefits.[14]

Another important feature of the Jobs-Plus work incentives approach is a concerted effort by sites to educate their residents about the other financial programs for low-income working families and individuals that exist under current law (such as earnings disregards available under TANF, assistance with the cost of child care and Medicaid that welfare recipients can continue to receive after leaving welfare, child care disregards under public housing rent rules, and the Earned Income Tax Credit or EITC). Each site has developed a strategy to help residents take advantage of these incentives in addition to those available through Jobs-Plus.

Community support for work

As noted earlier, the third main component of Jobs-Plus is an explicit attempt to increase "community support for work." Because this concept is imprecise and means different things to different people, it was no surprise that sites chose to implement the other two program components first. However, as those components began to take shape, it became possible to link community support for work to them. The centerpiece of the sites' efforts was focused on the establishment of a network of resident "community coaches." These residents, who function as outreach workers, engage in a process of "neighbor-to-neighbor" information sharing and support that is focused explicitly on work. This includes disseminating throughout the development information about concrete job openings and about opportunities available through the Jobs-Plus program.

Design and Implementation of the
Impact Evaluation

Given the complex, multifaceted nature of the Jobs-Plus intervention and its implementation, there is no single simple evaluation strategy capable of measuring its impacts.

Measuring impacts from two perspectives:
People and place

A central feature of the Jobs-Plus evaluation design is its focus on impacts from two different perspectives: (1) with respect to specific individual public housing residents (people) and (2) with respect to specific public housing developments (place).

The individual perspective relates to a particular group of persons who were living in Jobs-Plus developments at a specific point in time. Thus, it focuses on a single resident cohort. From this perspective, the Jobs-Plus impact analysis will address the question, "How did the demonstration program affect the future experiences of its target individuals, whether or not they moved away?"

The housing development perspective relates to groups of different persons who were living in Jobs-Plus developments at different points in time. Thus, it focuses on a series of consecutive, partly overlapping resident cohorts. From this perspective, the Jobs-Plus impact analysis will address the question, "How did the demonstration program affect conditions in its target developments, given that different people were living there at different times?"

The distinction between these two perspectives is key to any evaluation of a place-based initiative because sample members can move into and out of its target area. For example, students can move into and out of schools that are implementing whole-school reforms, families can move into and out of communities that are implementing health education programs, and employees can move into and out of firms that are implementing worker retention programs.[15] In these ways, mobility drives a conceptual and operational wedge between people and place. For example, during 1998, when Jobs-Plus was being launched, between 13 and 36 percent of the working-age, nondisabled household heads moved out of its program developments.[16]

Randomly assigning housing developments:
An approach to measuring average impacts across sites

In the field of employment and training research, random assignment experiments are now widely regarded as the best way to estimate program impacts. In the words of one prominent researcher, this approach is "a bit like the nectar of the

---

[A]necdotal evidence suggests that at least some local residents felt that random selection of the participating housing development would be fairer than selection by the PHA [public housing authority]—
which was not always trusted.

---

gods: once you've had a taste of the pure stuff it is hard to settle for the flawed alternatives."[17] However, Jobs-Plus is not a program to which individuals or households can be assigned randomly. Instead, it is a place-based initiative to which all eligible residents of participating public housing developments may be exposed and in which all eligible residents can take part if they desire.

It was possible, however, to select an approximately matched group of two or three candidate housing developments for each Jobs-Plus site and then randomly choose (using computer-generated random numbers) the development that would launch the intervention. The remaining developments could thus serve as a comparison group. As noted earlier, the ability for MDRC to make this choice randomly was an eligibility requirement for each site, and all fifteen cities that became semifinalists accepted this requirement. Although explaining the need for the requirement took considerable time and effort, it was generally recognized that Jobs-Plus represented a scarce resource whose allocation by lottery was ethical and fair. In addition, anecdotal evidence suggests that at least some local residents felt that random selection of the participating housing development would be fairer than selection by the PHA—which was not always trusted.

Table 3 lists the Jobs-Plus and comparison developments for each site. As can be seen, four sites have a randomly selected Jobs-Plus development plus two compar-

TABLE 3

JOBS-PLUS AND COMPARISON HOUSING DEVELOPMENTS, BY SITE

Site	Jobs-Plus Development(s)	Comparison Development(s)
Baltimore	Gilmor Homes	Perkins Courts; Somerset Courts
Chattanooga	Harriet Tubman	College Hill; Emma Wheeler
Dayton	DeSoto Bass	Arlington Courts; Parkside Courts
St. Paul	Mount Airy	McDonough; Roosevelt
Seattle	Rainier Vista	Yesler Courts
Los Angeles	William Mead	Dana Strand
	Imperial Courts	None

NOTE: Cleveland, which is no longer in the demonstration, had one randomly selected Jobs-Plus development (Woodhill Homes) plus two comparison developments (Garden Valley and Riverside Park). Imperial Courts, in Los Angeles, was chosen to implement a Jobs-Plus program but did not have a randomly assigned comparison development.

ison developments; one site has a randomly selected Jobs-Plus development plus one comparison development; and one site (Los Angeles) has two Jobs-Plus developments, one of which has no comparison development and will not be part of the program impact analysis.

It thus will be possible to estimate impacts for each site by comparing outcomes for its Jobs-Plus and pooled comparison groups. In addition, it will be possible to pool these impact estimates across sites by taking their average. For both types of impact estimates, random assignment of Jobs-Plus and comparison developments protects against the possibility of "stacking the deck" by consciously or inadvertently choosing Jobs-Plus developments that are more likely or less likely than others to improve their future outcomes without the intervention. Other than this protection (which is not trivial), site-specific impact estimates are nonexperimental or quasiexperimental, and thus subject to the methodological threats inherent in such designs.

Random assignment of housing developments can produce unbiased (internally valid) estimates of average impacts pooled across the demonstration sites. This means that the long-run expected value of the impact estimator (a theoretical property) equals the "true" average value of the impacts. At the same time, this type of random assignment of groups (often referred to as "cluster" random assignment) produces impact estimates that have less statistical power—and, thus, greater uncertainty—than those based on individual random assignment of the same number of persons.

Although these theoretical properties are well documented,[18] just how much statistical power is lost when moving from individual-level to group-level random assignment is an empirical question. This loss of power depends on three factors: (1) the degree to which individual outcomes vary within versus across groups (measured by their intraclass correlation), (2) the number of groups being randomly assigned (fewer groups produce less power), and (3) the extent to which the variance of the outcome within and across groups is reduced by statistical controls for preexisting individual-level or group-level characteristics. Bloom, Bos, and Lee (1999) provided a detailed empirical analysis of these conditions for the random assignment of schools and found that

> if a good measure of past individual or school performance is available, it might be possible to detect a 3- to 6-percentile improvement in average student performance with cluster assignment of 40 schools . . . (half to the program group and half to the control group) . . . and 60 students per school (2,400 students overall). This implies an effect size of roughly 0.10 to 0.20, which by most existing standards suggests adequate statistical power. (p. 464)

In addition, they found that school-level measures of past student performance are almost as effective as individual-level measures with respect to statistical power.

The Jobs-Plus impact analysis will have six program developments and ten comparison developments (including Seattle for parts of the follow-up period). This small number suggests that impact estimates based on simple or regression-adjusted outcome contrasts for the Jobs-Plus and comparison groups may have limited statistical power. On the other hand, baseline and follow-up data are available for certain outcome measures, which will make it possible to control statistically for preexisting variation within and between developments. This suggests potentially greater statistical power. One final factor, which also suggests greater statistical power, is that developments were approximately matched and blocked by city before they were randomly assigned. This eliminates city-level outcome differences from subsequent impact estimates and thereby increases statistical power.

Comparative interrupted time-series analysis: An approach to measuring site-specific impacts

To produce rigorous site-level estimates of Jobs-Plus impacts (and thereby further enhance corresponding pooled estimates), we are implementing a comparative interrupted time-series analysis. Interrupted time-series analysis is a quasi-experimental design that has been used successfully to evaluate programs in many fields.[19] It is based on multiple baseline observations of an outcome before a program is launched plus one or more follow-up observations after the program is launched. Our application of the approach will proceed in two steps: (1) we will measure the extent to which the follow-up outcome measure (e.g., the employment rate) in a Jobs-Plus development deviates from its baseline trend, and (2) we will compare the observed deviation from trend in the Jobs-Plus development with its counterpart for the comparison group. The first step in this process addresses the question, "To what extent was there an improvement in the experiences of residents at the program development?" The second step addresses the question, "To what extent did Jobs-Plus improve these experiences?"

FIGURE 1
ILLUSTRATION OF AN INTERRUPTED TIME SERIES FOR A
SINGLE JOBS-PLUS DEVELOPMENT

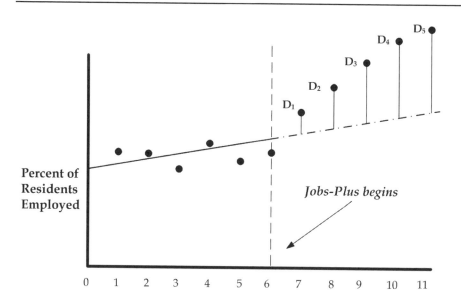

Results During the Follow-Up Period

Year	Predicted Outcome (percent)	Actual Outcome (Percent)	Deviation from Trend (percentage-points)
7	51	54	+3
8	53	60	+7
9	56	68	+12
10	55	70	+15
11	57	74	+17

Estimating the Jobs-Plus deviation from trend

The simplest interrupted time-series analysis involves a single Jobs-Plus development with multiple periods of data before and after the intervention was
launched. Figure 1 illustrates how to use the analysis to estimate shifts in the percentage of residents employed.

With at least six years of baseline data on this measure, it is possible to fit a pre–
Jobs-Plus baseline trend line. A linear trend may be adequate for many outcomes,
but a curvilinear trend can be fit, under some conditions, if the curvature of the
baseline pattern is pronounced. Extrapolation of the baseline trend provides the

best available estimate of what the outcome would have been without any major economic or policy changes.[20]

The deviation from the baseline trend in the first year after Jobs-Plus begins (line D_1 in the figure) provides an estimate of the "shift" in the outcome for that year. Deviations from trend in subsequent years (lines D_2 through D_5) provide corresponding estimates of the shifts for these years. Estimating the shift for each follow-up year provides an easy way to describe the pattern of unpredicted change over time (whether it is constant, it decays, or it grows). One can then average these estimates to summarize them for the follow-up period.[21]

For example, the hypothetical results in the bottom panel of Figure 1 indicate that there was a 3-point increase in the percentage of residents who were employed in the first year after Jobs-Plus began (i.e., year seven of the data collection period), a 7-point increase in the second year, and so on, ending with a 17-point increase in the fifth year after the program began. Hence, the outcome was about 11 percentage points higher than predicted, on average, during the following period.

The following regression model can be used to estimate the shifts in the figure:

$$Y_t = \alpha + B_0 t + B_1 P_t + e_t, \tag{1}$$

where Y_t = the value of the outcome variable in year t, P_t = one if year t is after Jobs-Plus began and zero otherwise, t = the year, e_t = a random error term, B_0 = the slope of the baseline trend, B_1 = the deviation from trend after Jobs-Plus began, and α = the intercept of the baseline trend.

If only years zero through seven are included in the analysis, the coefficient B_1 equals the deviation from trend in year seven (line D_1 in the figure), and the t-statistic for this coefficient provides a test of its statistical significance. To include all five follow-up years in the analysis and allow each to have a separate deviation from trend, one can replace P with a separate dummy variable for each follow-up year. The coefficient for each dummy variable equals the deviation from trend for the follow-up year that it represents (lines D_1 through D_5), and the t-statistic for each coefficient provides a test of its statistical significance. Note that the actual analysis for Jobs-Plus will use quarterly data and thus will reflect information that is more detailed than that in the illustrative example.

For an interrupted time-series analysis to be most effective, there must be a stable baseline trend and a pronounced deviation from this trend. The more stable the baseline trend is (the less the points vary around the trend line), the more confidence one can place in the forecast or extrapolation for the follow-up period. The larger and more abrupt the deviation from trend is, the easier it will be to identify.

Comparing the Jobs-Plus and comparison group deviations from trend

A logical extension of the preceding approach is to conduct a separate interrupted time-series analysis for the comparison group where Jobs-Plus was not implemented (pooling the samples of residents for the two comparison developments for each site where there are two). Figure 2 illustrates how this time-series analysis can be used to produce estimates of the impacts of Jobs-Plus (the shift in outcomes that it caused). The approach is applicable regardless of how the comparison development was chosen (with or without random assignment and/or matching).

The top panel of Figure 2 repeats the time-series analysis for the hypothetical Jobs-Plus development in Figure 1. The bottom panel presents findings during the same period for its comparison group. The interrupted time-series analysis for the comparison group yields deviations from trend in years seven, eight, and nine equal to E_1, E_2, and E_3, respectively. If the comparison group and the Jobs-Plus development were chosen from the same local environment, then the comparison group's deviation from its trend provides an estimate of what the deviation from trend would have been for the Jobs-Plus development without Jobs-Plus (the counterfactual for our impact estimates). Hence, $D_t - E_t$ provides an estimate of the impact of Jobs-Plus in year t. The variance of this difference equals the sum of the variances of D_t and E_t.[22] Thus, one can readily test the statistical significance of the difference.

The slow implementation of Jobs-Plus described in earlier sections of this article—particularly the fact that not all features of the program model were in place until several years after site selection—means that an immediate deviation from the baseline employment trend in the Jobs-Plus developments is unlikely. It is thus fortunate that the follow-up period for the impact evaluation will extend a full five years after program operations began. However, impacts are likely to emerge gradually over time, rather than abruptly. This will make it difficult for the interrupted time-series analysis to clearly identify them because they may not reflect pronounced deviations from the baseline trend. Nevertheless, if these impacts are experienced at all or most of the Jobs-Plus sites, pooling site-specific findings will improve our chances of accurately detecting them.

Pooling site-specific findings

Once site-specific impact estimates have been obtained using the preceding approach, we will pool them across sites by taking their mean. This will produce estimates of the average Jobs-Plus impact for the study sites. These core evaluation findings will have the combined methodological protection of the random assignment of housing developments (which produces unbiased impact estimates) and the comparative interrupted time-series analysis (which provides further protection against bias and most likely also increases statistical power).

Data sources

Given the focus of Jobs-Plus on resident employment, the primary outcomes for its impact analysis will be employment, earnings, and welfare receipt. For each of these outcomes, a comparative interrupted time-series analysis will be used to estimate program impacts. For this purpose, quarterly data on employment and earnings will be obtained from the administrative records of state unemployment insur-

FIGURE 2
ILLUSTRATION OF AN INTERRUPTED TIME-SERIES ANALYSIS
FOR A JOBS-PLUS DEVELOPMENT AND A COMPARISON DEVELOPMENT
DURING THE JOBS-PLUS BASELINE PERIOD

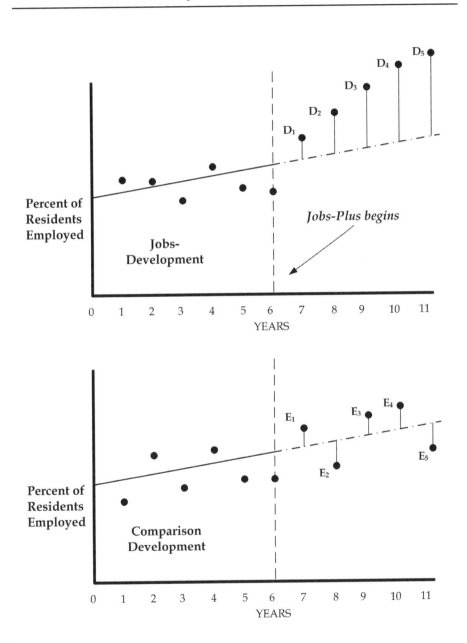

ance (UI) agencies for a baseline period of roughly six years before Jobs-Plus was launched and a follow-up period of roughly five years thereafter. These data, which are reported quarterly by employers in all states to their state UI agency, cover well over 90 percent of all jobs in the formal labor market and have been found in past research to provide adequate information for measuring program impacts.[23] In addition, monthly data on the receipt of AFDC/TANF payments and food stamps during the same period will be obtained from the administrative records of state and local welfare agencies. This type of data has been used for many past evaluations of welfare-to-work and employment programs and is generally thought to be accurate and complete.

Local PHA records will be used to obtain a limited set of background characteristics on residents, such as age, gender, race/ethnicity, how long they have lived in their current development, whether they move from it subsequently, and whether their household is receiving welfare. This information will be used to construct selected subgroups for the impact analysis. We refer to information obtained from UI wage records, welfare payments records, and local PHA records as administrative data.

In addition to this information, a baseline survey has been conducted and a follow-up survey will be conducted in the Jobs-Plus and comparison developments. Information from the surveys includes measures of (1) community life, (2) outcomes and activities for children, (3) residents' employment and the characteristics of their jobs, (4) family income and material well-being, (5) individual physical and mental health, (6) individual background characteristics, and (7) individual participation in education, training, and employment-related activities.

The baseline survey was administered in the spring and summer of 1998 to a representative sample of household heads living in the Jobs-Plus and comparison developments. The follow-up survey was administered in 2003 to a representative sample of household heads who lived in these developments at that time. Hence, the survey data will provide a comparative before-after analysis from the housing development perspective.[24]

Preliminary Assessment
of the Impact Evaluation Strategy

Although the impact evaluation was still in progress when this article was written and final judgments about its methodology could not yet be made, it was possible at the time to offer a brief preliminary assessment using data from the baseline survey and UI wage records.

Evidence from the baseline survey

Perhaps the single most important key to the success of the Jobs-Plus impact estimates is the initial comparability of the Jobs-Plus and comparison samples. One important source of information to assess this comparability is the baseline survey conducted at all of the housing developments in our sample. Early tabulations of these findings were quite promising, indicating that the Jobs-Plus and comparison samples are similar in many important ways.[25]

[M]easuring Jobs-Plus impacts from the individual perspective addresses the question, "How did the program affect the future experiences of a specific group of people who were living in a program development at a particular time?"

Table 4 illustrates this similarity for the overall pooled sample of sites. Given the focus of Jobs-Plus on promoting resident employment, the table lists comparisons in terms of employment-related baseline characteristics.

On average, it appears that the Jobs-Plus group and comparison group are quite comparable in terms of baseline characteristics related to their likely future labor market success. The percentage of sample members that were employed full-time when the baseline survey was administered is identical for the two groups (43 percent), the percentage of the two groups whose household had received Food Stamps during the previous twelve months was almost identical (67 versus 66 percent), and the percentage whose household had received welfare during the past twelve months was very similar (51 to 49 percent). In terms of education level, a key factor related to future job market success, the two groups look quite similar (40 versus 42 percent had a high school diploma).

Evidence from UI wage records

Baseline data from UI wage records were available when this article was written for three Jobs-Plus sites: Baltimore, Dayton, and Los Angeles. Thus, it was possible to compare the baseline employment and earnings trends for their Jobs-Plus and comparison groups from the individual perspective and the housing development perspective. In addition, it was possible to compare the baseline trends for their corresponding pooled Jobs-Plus and comparison groups. To keep the discussion brief, we focus only on employment trends. Corresponding results for earnings (not reported) yield virtually the same results.

TABLE 4

SELECTED MEAN BASELINE CHARACTERISTICS OF
HEADS OF HOUSEHOLD FOR THE POOLED SAMPLE OF
JOBS-PLUS AND COMPARISON DEVELOPMENTS (IN PERCENTAGES)

Characteristic	Jobs-Plus Developments	Comparison Developments
Currently employed full-time (thirty-plus hours per week)		
Yes	43	43
No	57	57
Household received Food Stamps during past twelve months		
Yes	67	66
No	32	33
Household received welfare during past twelve months		
Yes	51	49
No	49	51
Educational attainment		
GED certificate	13	15
High school diploma	40	42
Neither	48	43

SOURCE: MDRC calculations from baseline survey data for each housing development that
was randomly assigned at the six sites in the Jobs-Plus sample (including Seattle).
NOTE: Distributions may not total 100 percent because of rounding.

Baseline experience from the individual perspective

As noted earlier, measuring Jobs-Plus impacts from the individual perspective
addresses the question, "How did the program affect the future experiences of a
specific group of people who were living in a program development at a particular
time?" This requires observing the experience of the same persons over time,
regardless of where they live. Thus, to estimate impacts on employment and earnings from the individual perspective requires choosing a cohort of residents to
track backward and forward in time, acquiring their quarterly UI wage records to
do so, constructing their baseline and follow-up histories, measuring the follow-up
deviation from their baseline trend, and comparing this deviation for the Jobs-Plus
and comparison samples.

For our current analysis, we chose a cohort of individuals who were (1) recorded
by their local housing authority as living in a Jobs-Plus or comparison development
during October 1998, (2) not identified by housing authority records as being disabled, and (3) between twenty-one and sixty-one years of age in October 1998.

This 1998 cohort was chosen because Jobs-Plus began program operations (in
varying degrees) at each site during the middle to latter part of the year. Disabled
persons were excluded from the analysis because their employment problems are

often far more extreme than those of nondisabled persons and they are not
included in the main target group for Jobs-Plus. Persons older than sixty-one years
of age were excluded because they would reach retirement age soon after the follow-up period for the analysis began. Last, persons younger than twenty-one years
of age were excluded because they were teenagers during most of the Jobs-Plus
baseline period, and thus, much of their employment history is not relevant to their
future labor market success.

Based on this definition, there were 349, 334, and 379 members of the 1998
cohort from the Baltimore, Dayton, and Los Angeles Jobs-Plus developments,
respectively. In addition, there were 539, 582, and 453 cohort members from each
of their comparison groups (the sample from the one or two comparison developments for each site).

The pattern of employment over time for the 1998 cohort is described in terms
of its quarterly employment rates. These rates were computed using data from
state UI wage records. Each sample member was considered employed during a
quarter if his or her UI wage records indicated that he or she had received some
earnings during that quarter. If no earnings were recorded for the quarter, the sample member was considered not employed. A quarterly employment rate was thus
computed for a group as the percentage of its members with some UI-reported
earnings for the quarter.

Figure 3 presents the quarterly employment histories of the 1998 Jobs-Plus
cohort and comparison cohort from Baltimore, Dayton, and Los Angeles for a
baseline period that begins in the first quarter of 1992 and ends in the latter part of
1998.[26] Figure 4 presents corresponding findings for the pooled groups from the
three sites. Several striking results emerge from the figures.

*Employment rates rose dramatically for all of the groups during their baseline
period.* In Baltimore, these rates increased from about 20 to 40 percent; in Dayton,
they increased from about 30 to 60 percent; and in Los Angeles, they increased
from about 30 to 45 percent.

One likely explanation for part of this shift is that many public housing
residents—just like many other Americans—probably responded positively to the
jobs created by the strong U.S. economy. This challenges existing negative stereo-
types about public housing residents being unwilling to work.

The Jobs-Plus and comparison groups are matched very well. For each site, the
baseline histories for the Jobs-Plus group and the comparison group are very similar. In fact, they practically "sit on top of each other." In very few quarters is there a
noticeable difference between their employment rates, and in even fewer quarters
is the difference statistically significant (results of these significance tests are not
shown).

Furthermore, the Jobs-Plus and comparison group match should be even
tighter for analyses that pool findings across sites. This is because pooled results
benefit directly from the statistical properties of random assignment. Figure 4
presents such a pooled analysis of quarterly employment rates for the 1998 cohort

FIGURE 3
QUARTERLY PERCENTAGE EMPLOYED DURING THE JOBS-PLUS BASELINE
PERIOD FOR NONDISABLED ADULTS, AGES TWENTY-ONE TO SIXTY-ONE,
FROM A 1998 COHORT OF PROGRAM AND COMPARISON DEVELOPMENTS

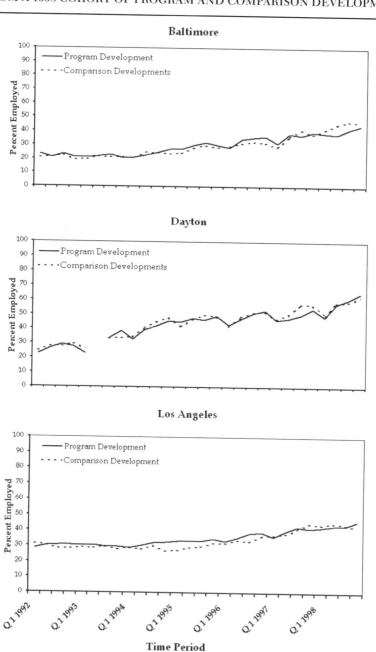

FIGURE 4
**QUARTERLY PERCENTAGE EMPLOYED DURING THE JOBS-PLUS BASELINE
PERIOD FOR NONDISABLED ADULTS, AGES TWENTY-ONE TO SIXTY-ONE,
FROM THE 1998 COHORT OF THE BALTIMORE, DAYTON, AND LOS ANGELES
PROGRAM AND COMPARISON DEVELOPMENTS (POOLED)**

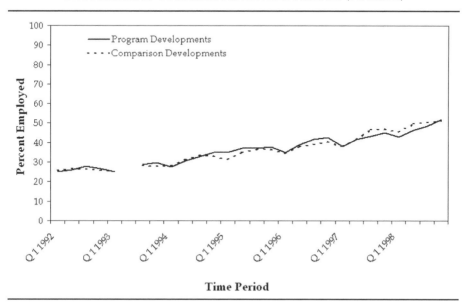

from Baltimore, Dayton, and Los Angeles. As can be seen, its baseline trend is even more stable than that for a single site, because of the larger sample for the pooled analysis. In addition, the baseline trends for the Jobs-Plus and comparison groups are even more similar to each other for the pooled analysis, because random differences for any single site tend to be offset by countervailing differences at other sites.

The pronounced increase in employment rates experienced by public housing residents reduced the margin for Jobs-Plus to "make a difference" in this outcome, although considerable room for improvement still remained when Jobs-Plus was launched. Because employment rates for public housing residents had been rising rapidly for some time before Jobs-Plus began, the margin for it to increase these rates had diminished appreciably. This situation was most pronounced in Dayton, where employment rates had reached 60 percent by the time Jobs-Plus program operations had gotten under way. It was less pronounced in Baltimore and Los Angeles.

Baseline experience from the housing development perspective

As noted earlier, measuring Jobs-Plus impacts from the housing development perspective addresses the question, "How did the program affect levels of work and welfare receipt in its target developments?" To answer this question requires comparing the experiences of persons who were living in the Jobs-Plus and comparison developments each quarter. Thus, to accomplish this task involves determining who lived in each development each quarter, acquiring residents' UI wage records, using these wage records to compute baseline and follow-up employment rates for the Jobs-Plus and comparison developments, and comparing their follow-up deviations from their baseline trends.

Figure 5 illustrates the baseline pattern of quarterly employment rates for the Jobs-Plus and comparison developments from each site, and Figure 6 illustrates the composite results for the pooled sites. To help distinguish this analysis from its counterpart for the individual perspective, we present it as a time series of bar graphs instead of a line graph. The black bars in each figure represent quarterly employment rates for a Jobs-Plus development; the white bars represent corresponding findings for its pooled comparison developments.

These findings indicate that employment conditions in each development changed over time in a way that was very similar to the results presented earlier for individual members of the 1998 cohort. Basically, (1) employment rates for all groups increased throughout the baseline period; (2) the baseline trends were virtually the same for the Jobs-Plus and comparison groups, especially for the pooled sites; and (3) employment rates were higher than expected when Jobs-Plus began program operations.

Concluding Thoughts

From our experiences with Jobs-Plus, we have learned a number of important lessons about using place-based random assignment to evaluate a comprehensive community initiative.

- *It was possible to put such a research design into effect.* When Jobs-Plus was being planned, it was not at all clear whether random assignment of public housing developments would be possible. However, given the widely acknowledged importance of the policy problem being addressed, there was a strong desire by many potential sites to participate in the initiative, even with its research requirements. As noted earlier, forty-one of the fifty cities contacted about Jobs-Plus stated an interest in participating, and all fifteen of the cities chosen to submit a project application expressed a willingness to abide by its research requirements. Thus, it was possible to conduct place-based random assignment in the seven cities chosen to launch the initiative (including Cleveland, which left the project for reasons unrelated to random assignment).
- *It was necessary (and possible) to keep the research design in place for many years.* Given the many difficulties and delays confronted when implementing Jobs-Plus (a common feature of all comprehensive community initiatives), it took a number of years for the program to materialize in full form. Thus, it was

FIGURE 5
QUARTERLY PERCENTAGE EMPLOYED DURING
THE JOBS-PLUS BASELINE PERIOD FOR NONDISABLED ADULTS,
AGES TWENTY-ONE TO SIXTY-ONE, WHO WERE RESIDENTS (AT THE TIME)
OF THE PROGRAM AND COMPARISON DEVELOPMENTS

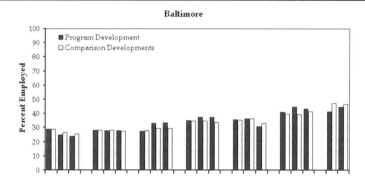

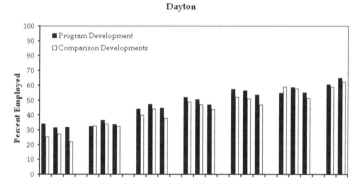

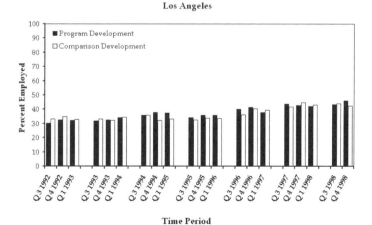

FIGURE 6
QUARTERLY PERCENTAGE EMPLOYED DURING
THE JOBS-PLUS BASELINE PERIOD FOR NONDISABLED ADULTS,
AGES TWENTY-ONE TO SIXTY-ONE, WHO WERE CURRENT RESIDENTS
(AT THE TIME) OF THE BALTIMORE, DAYTON, AND LOS ANGELES PROGRAM
AND COMPARISON DEVELOPMENTS (POOLED)

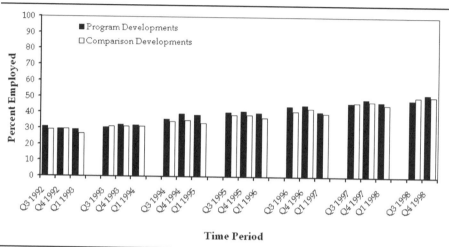

necessary to maintain the Jobs-Plus research design in the field for seven
years.

- *A sustained and intensive effort was required to keep the research design in place and to maintain its integrity.* Fending off threats (often successfully and sometimes not) to the existence or integrity of the Jobs-Plus program and its research design was a full-time, long-term job that required constant vigilance and rapid response. This, in turn, required the organizational capacity and resources needed to keep abreast of what was happening in the field; provide the technical assistance necessary for sites to design, launch, and operate their programs within the constraints of the Jobs-Plus research design; interact frequently and effectively with local decision makers; and contend in real time with a wide range of anticipated and unanticipated problems.

- *Where feasible, embedding a comparative interrupted time-series analysis within a place-based random assignment design can improve estimates of program impacts appreciably.* These improvements can manifest themselves in at least three ways. First, adding an interrupted time-series component makes it possible to produce rigorous site-specific impact estimates, which is not possible with place-based random assignment alone. Second (and relatedly), since the time-series component improves the impact estimate for each site, it also improves the pooled impact estimate for all sites. This feature is particularly important for evaluations with a small number of sites where the strength of random assignment is limited by the small number of units randomized. Third, the time-series component makes it possible to bridge the methodological gap between people and place. This gap, which is created by residential mobility, is a major problem for all evaluations of place-based initiatives.[27] However, by framing an interrupted time-series analysis from two different perspectives (for specific individuals over time and for specific places over time) one can obtain a rich understanding of program impacts.

Notes

1. Other major funders are the U.S. Departments of Health and Human Services and Labor; the Joyce, James Irvine, Surdna, Northwest Area, Annie E. Casey, Stuart, and Washington Mutual Foundations; and BP.

2. Wilson (1996).

3. In Wisconsin, the New Hope Program operated outside the existing public assistance system and was tested on a demonstration basis in two areas of Milwaukee. It included an earnings supplement, child care subsidies, and affordable health insurance for eligible low-income people taking full-time jobs, and access to a temporary subsidized job for those who could not find full-time work in the unsubsidized labor market. An evaluation of the program found that it had positive effects on the employment, earnings, and income of people who were not working full-time when they entered the program and some positive effects on participants' children, particularly boys (e.g., improved behavior in school and higher educational and occupational expectations; see Bos et al. 1999). For a description and final results of the Canadian experiment, see Michalopoulos et al. (2002).

4. Aspen Institute (1997); Walsh (1997).

5. Aspen Institute (1997); Kingsley, McNeely, and Gibson (1997); Walsh (1997).

6. Gladwell (2000).

7. A saturation strategy targeting all working-age residents would be considerably easier to implement in much smaller settings but would be less valuable from a policy perspective.

8. The sample-size needs of the demonstration's evaluation design were another consideration.

9. This estimate is based on MDRC calculations using 1993 data from the U.S. Department of Housing and Urban Development's (HUD's) Information Services Division of Public and Indian Housing.

10. MDRC staff and consultants visited each of these fifteen cities and also sponsored a cross-site conference attended by key collaborative partners from each city, offering workshops and training sessions to help them think boldly and creatively about their initial program designs. After that conference, the sites were required to submit detailed, written applications in which they described their collaboratives, gave evidence of local funding and resource commitments, and described their early vision of a Jobs-Plus program.

11. This section draws heavily on Kato and Riccio (2001), who provided a detailed analysis of the process of collaboration in Jobs-Plus and offered guidance on this topic for other initiatives.

12. Issues arose however, between HUD and the U.S. congressional committee that oversees its departmental budget over how to cover these costs (though not over the "hold-harmless" concept), leading to several months of negotiations and, consequently, delays in sites' ability to implement their incentive plans. The funding problem was eventually solved, and a final agreement between Congress and HUD was reached in May 1999.

13. Miller and Riccio (2002) provided a detailed description of the incentive package offered by each site.

14. Public housing rent reform continues to be of great interest in the United States. For example, the federal Quality Housing and Work Responsibility Act of 1998 requires local housing authorities to introduce certain new rent policies that are more favorable for working families. Hence, the Jobs-Plus experience with rent incentives is directly relevant to housing policy more broadly.

15. See Bloom (2003) and Bloom, Bos, and Lee (1999) with respect to evaluating whole-school reforms. See Murray et al. (1994) with respect to evaluating a health education initiative. Last, note that MDRC is currently evaluating an employer-based worker retention program in Cleveland, Ohio, but written documentation on the project is not yet available.

16. Verma (2002, Figure 1).

17. Hollister and Hill (1995, 134).

18. Raudenbush (1997) presented a clear exposition of these properties.

19. Shadish, Cook, and Campbell (2002) provided a comprehensive review of the interrupted time-series literature. Campbell and Stanley (1966) and Cook and Campbell (1979) are perhaps the most widely read sources about the approach. Bloom (2003) described how to use it to measure the impacts of whole-school reforms on student performance.

20. This implies that the best predictor of future behavior is long-term past behavior, which is the case for many outcomes.

21. If there are at least three follow-up observations, it is possible, in theory, to estimate the impact of the program on the intercept and slope of the original trend line. We do not take this approach, however, because it does not focus on the actual annual impacts and, hence, is more difficult to interpret.

22. This simple formulation is possible because the two developments comprise independent samples.

23. Kornfeld and Bloom (1999).

24. The original survey sampling plan had a longitudinal component that would have followed up baseline survey respondents who moved away. This component was dropped, however, because so many baseline respondents moved before Jobs-Plus began and thus before they could be meaningfully exposed to it.

25. MDRC (1999, vols. I and II).

26. Unemployment insurance wage records were not available for quarter 3 of 1993 in Dayton.

27. Mobility also creates major problems for the programs themselves since it limits the potential exposure of their target populations.

References

Aspen Institute. 1997. *Voices from the field: Learning from the early work of comprehensive community initiatives*. Washington, DC: Aspen Institute.

Bloom, Howard S. 2003. Using "short" interrupted time-series analysis to measure the impacts of whole-school reforms: With applications to a study of accelerated schools. *Evaluation Review* 27 (1): 3-49.

Bloom, Howard S., Johannes M. Bos, and Suk-Won Lee. 1999. Using cluster random assignment to measure program impacts: Statistical implications for the evaluation of education programs. *Evaluation Review* 23 (4): 445-69.

Bloom, Howard S., James A. Riccio, and Nandita Verma. 2005. *Promoting work in public housing: The effectiveness of Jobs-Plus*. New York: MDRC.

Bos, Johannes M., Aletha C. Huston, Robert C. Granger, Greg J. Duncan, Thomas W. Brock, and Vonnie C. McLoyd. 1999. *New hope for people with low incomes: Two-year results of a program to reduce poverty and reform welfare*. New York: MDRC.

Campbell, Donald T., and Julian Stanley. 1966. *Experimental and quasi-experimental designs for research*. Chicago: Rand McNally.

Cook, Thomas, and Donald T. Campbell. 1979. *Quasi-experimental design and analysis issues for field settings*. Chicago: Rand McNally.

Gladwell, Malcolm. 2000. *The tipping point: How little things can make a big difference*. Boston: Little, Brown.

Hollister, Robinson G., and Jennifer Hill. 1995. Problems in the evaluation of community-wide initiatives. In *New approaches to evaluating community initiatives: Concepts, methods, and contexts*, ed. James P. Connell, Anne C. Kubisch, Lisbeth B. Schorr, and Carol H. Weiss. Washington, DC: Aspen Institute.

Kato, Linda Y. 2002. *The special challenges of offering employment programs in culturally diverse communities: The Jobs-Plus experience in public housing developments*. New York: MDRC.

Kato, Linda Y., and James A. Riccio. 2001. *Building new partnerships for employment: Collaboration among agencies and public housing residents in the jobs-plus demonstration*. New York: MDRC.

Kingsley, Thomas G., Joseph B. McNeely, and James O. Gibson. 1997. *Community building: Coming of age*. Washington, DC: Development Training Institute, Inc., and the Urban Institute.

Kornfeld, Robert, and Howard S. Bloom. 1999. Measuring program impacts on earnings and employment: Do unemployment insurance wage reports from employers agree with surveys of individuals? *Journal of Labor Economics* 17 (1): 168-97.

MDRC. 1999. *Jobs-Plus baseline survey: Data resources book*, Vol. I (site-by-site findings) and Vol. II (cross-site information). New York: MDRC.

Michalopoulos, Charles, Doug Tattrie, Cynthia Miller, Philip K. Robins, Pamela Morris, David Gyarmati, Cindy Redcross, Kelly Foley, and Reuben Ford. 2002. *Making work pay: Final report on the Self-Sufficiency Project for Long-Term Welfare Recipients*. Ottawa, Canada: Social Research and Demonstration Corporation.

Miller, Cynthia, and James A. Riccio. 2002. *Making work pay for public housing residents: Financial-incentive designs at six Jobs-Plus demonstration sites*. New York: MDRC.

Murray, D. M., P. J. Hannan, D. R. Jacobs, P. J. McGovern, L. Schmid, W. L. Baker, and C. Gray. 1994. Assessing intervention effects in the Minnesota Heart Health Program. *American Journal of Epidemiology* 139 (1): 91-103.

Raudenbush, Stephen W. 1997. Statistical analysis and optimal design in cluster randomized trials. *Psychological Methods* 2 (2): 173-85.

Riccio, James A. 1999. *Mobilizing public housing communities for work: Origins and early accomplishments of the Jobs-Plus demonstration*. New York: MDRC.

Shadish, William R., Thomas D. Cook, and Donald T. Campbell. 2002. *Experimental and quasi-experimental designs for generalized causal inference*. Boston: Houghton Mifflin.

Verma, Nandita. 2002. Residential mobility of public housing residents: Who moves and who stays? Implications for programs and evaluations of place-based initiatives. Manuscript, New York, MDRC.

Walsh, Joan. 1997. *Stories of renewal: Community building and the future of urban America*. New York: Rockefeller Foundation.

Wilson, William Julius. 1996. *When work disappears: The world of the new urban poor*. New York: Knopf.

HIV Prevention among Women in Low-Income Housing Developments: Issues and Intervention Outcomes in a Place-Based Randomized Controlled Trial

KATHLEEN J. SIKKEMA

The scope and urgency of the HIV epidemic requires the development and evaluation of community-level behavior change intervention strategies. A randomized, multisite community-level HIV prevention trial was undertaken with women living in eighteen low-income housing developments in five U.S. cities. In the nine experimental condition developments, an intervention was undertaken that included identifying opinion leaders to attend risk reduction workshops and to form Women's Health Councils to carry out community events to reach all residents and support risk reduction efforts. Baseline and twelve-month follow-up risk characteristics were assessed by surveying 690 women at both time points. In comparison to women in the control condition developments, women in the community intervention developments reported significant reductions in frequency of any unprotected intercourse and increases in the percentage of condom-protected intercourse occasions. Community-level interventions that engage women in neighborhood-based HIV prevention activities can bring about reductions in HIV risk-related sexual behavior.

Keywords: HIV prevention; women; community intervention

Worldwide, HIV/AIDS has become the leading cause of mortality and the single most important contributor to burden of disease among adults aged fifteen to fifty-nine years (WHO 2003). Global estimates of the epidemic indicate that 38 million adults and children were

Kathleen J. Sikkema, Ph.D., associate professor of psychiatry (and of psychology as well as epidemiology and public health) at Yale University School of Medicine, is a clinical psychologist specializing in health/community psychology and behavioral medicine. Her expertise is in the conduct of randomized controlled HIV prevention and mental health intervention outcome trials. She is the director of HIV Prevention and Mental Health Research at the Consultation Center in the Department of Psychiatry and the director of the Community Research Core in the Center for Interdisciplinary Research on AIDS (CIRA) in the Department of Epidemiology and Public Health.

DOI: 10.1177/0002716205274516

living with HIV/AIDS at the end of 2003, and more than 20 million have died. During 2003, almost 5 million people became newly infected with HIV, the greatest number in any year since the beginning of the epidemic (Joint United Nations Programme on AIDS [UNAIDS] 2004). Women accounted for nearly half of all people living with HIV worldwide, with nearly 2 million newly infected with HIV during 2003 alone (UNAIDS 2004).

HIV prevention efforts must be implemented to reduce the effect and spread of HIV/AIDS. It has been boldly stated that if the HIV prevention successes achieved in some countries were expanded to a global scale by 2005, about 29 million new infections could be prevented by 2010 (Stover et al. 2002). Otherwise, 45 million new infections were estimated to occur by 2010. The immediate implementation of a comprehensive set of interventions could greatly alter the course of the AIDS epidemic, and potentially reverse it (Stover et al. 2002).

Since the onset of the HIV/AIDS epidemic in the United States, rates of HIV/AIDS among women have steadily increased. Women accounted for 26 percent of all new AIDS diagnoses and 29 percent of all newly reported HIV diagnoses (CDC 2002). Minority women have been particularly affected. African American and Latina women, together, account for almost 81.5 percent of all cases among women (CDC 2002).

The scope and urgency of the HIV epidemic requires the development and evaluation of behavior change intervention strategies directed toward communities and large community segments at risk for increased incidence of new infections. While a number of previous studies had shown the efficacy of cognitive-behavioral interventions offered to motivated volunteers participating in individual or small-group programs, the prevention of HIV infection urgently requires the evaluation of larger-scale trials that could reach larger numbers of people. Following the implementation of a successful multicity randomized intervention trial, testing a social diffusion model that identified, trained, and engaged popular opinion leader (POL) gay males in sixteen small U.S. cities to serve as behavior change agents to their peers (Kelly et al. 1997), we sought to determine whether this norm change intervention could be modified to address cultural and social issues related to behavior change among communities of low-income women living in urban housing developments.

NOTE: Portions of this article draw from a previously published journal article: Sikkema et al. (2000). Reprinted with permission from the American Public Health Association. Copyright 2000. This research was supported by Grant R01-MH42908 from the National Institute of Mental Health (NIMH) and by NIMH center grants P30-MH522776 and P30-MH62294. I gratefully acknowledge the contributions of my colleagues in the conduct of this research: Jeffrey A. Kelly, Ph.D.; Richard A. Winett, Ph.D.; Eileen S. Anderson, Ed.D.; Laura J. Solomon, Ph.D.; Victoria A. Cargill, M.D.; Roger A. Roffman, D.S.W.; Timothy L. McAuliffe, Ph.D.; Timothy G. Heckman, Ph.D.; David A. Wagstaff, Ph.D.; Ann D. Norman, Ph.D.; Melissa J. Perry, Sc.D.; Denise A. Crumble; and Mary Beth Mercer, M.P.H.

Theoretical Basis Underlying the Community-Level Approach for Initiation and Maintenance of HIV Risk Reduction

In the mid- to late 1990s, and to a certain extent to date, the state of the science in HIV prevention interventions was the use of risk reduction and skills training in small-group programs based on social cognitive or cognitive behavioral change principles (e.g., Bandura 1986; Fishbein and Ajzen 1975; Fisher and Fisher 1992).

The conceptual foundation for some of these community interventions suggests that skill training is the first component of a larger process necessary to promote meaningful and sustained risk behavior change.

These approaches incorporate such elements as skills training in condom use, sexual assertiveness and negotiation, risk behavior self-management, and risk reduction personal problem solving; exercises to strengthen behavior change intentions and self-efficacy for enacting change; and reinforcement of behavior change efforts. Numerous studies have provided convincing evidence that theoretically based, culturally tailored interventions can produce significant reductions in high-risk behavior practiced across many populations (e.g., DiClemente and Wingood 1995; Jemmott, Jemmott, and Fong 1992). Thus, these HIV prevention approaches are now being disseminated for implementation by community-based organizations and AIDS service organizations.

However, these models—by focusing primarily on individual rather than social environmental change—may have limited long-term effectiveness, especially if peer group norms, peer models, and social reinforcement do not also function to support the individual's behavior change efforts, and may reach limited numbers of people. More recently, community-level interventions (Kegeles, Hays, and Coates 1996; Kelly et al. 1997; Sikkema et al. 2000; Lauby et al. 2000; CDC AIDS Community Demonstration Projects Research Group 1999) that are based on the assumption that HIV prevention outcomes will be most successful when individuals' behavior change efforts are systematically supported by peer group norms consistent with risk reduction and reinforcement in one's social environment have been successfully undertaken. The conceptual foundation for some of these community interventions suggests that skill training is the first component of a larger process necessary to promote meaningful and sustained risk behavior change. From a social cognitive perspective, behavior change is best initiated, and is only likely to be well-maintained, under conditions where it is also supported by the presence of change models, peer norms, and expected positive social reinforcement contingencies (Bandura 1986; Winett, Altman, and King 1990; Winett et al. 1995). To the extent that peer and social environmental factors and models serve to support and reinforce behavior change efforts, changes should maintain and perhaps strengthen over time. If we teach and encourage persons to make HIV risk reduction behavior changes through structured small-group programs, but then "return" people to a social environment unlikely to support change, HIV prevention efforts will not have their maximum long-term impact. Clearly, to develop better ways to intervene, we need not only to change the behavior of individuals but also to change social networks and communities so that natural influence networks function in ways that reinforce the risk avoidance efforts of population members (Kelly 1999).

Diffusion of innovation theory

There has been a resurgence of interest in social diffusion theory as a potential means to induce changes in communities and population member behavior. Most of this research can be traced to work in the 1970s and 1980s by Rogers and his colleagues, who postulated that novel trends in a population typically occur when an innovation is first initiated by opinion leaders, adopted by "early adopters," and then diffuses in predictable fashion through the population under study (Rogers 1983). Mechanisms by which diffusion produces behavior change include modeling and observational learning, personal influence, induction of beliefs that the innovative change will bring about benefits, and creation of new social norms (Bandura 1986; Rogers 1983). How efficiently innovations diffuse depends upon the nature of the innovation, characteristics of the early-adopting innovators, and population characteristics. Diffusion occurs most readily when trend setters exhibiting the innovation are well liked, credible, and regarded positively by population members and when there are a sufficient number of early-adopting trend setters and sufficient social/communication connectedness in population social networks to facilitate the diffusion process (Bandura 1986; Rogers 1983). With respect to HIV prevention, innovative trends that one seeks to produce among presently high-risk population members include increased communication between sexual partners about AIDS and health concerns, adoption of safer sex practices and condom use, and deferral of sexual activity under risk-producing circumstances or at times when an individual does not want to have sex. In contrast to such highly visible innovations as clothing fashions, haircut styles, and public exercise regimens, sexual behaviors typically occur in private and are rarely directly observed by others. For that reason, innovative trends concerning HIV risk reduction are communicated primarily by conversation and description of behavior, although personal experience with sexual partners undoubtedly also influences normative perceptions.

Social cognitive theory

Social cognitive theory also provides a useful conceptual framework for understanding principles that can support the risk reduction efforts of population members. Modeling processes have long been known to influence behavioral learning and performance in a wide variety of areas. While models can be live, symbolic, or portrayed, peers who are liked, admired, and viewed as competent exert a particularly strong influence on observer behavior (Bandura 1986). Perceptions about whether members of one's social reference group adopt or have not adopted, encourage or discourage, and support or oppose risk avoidance steps such as condom use or refusal to have sex can also influence one's own sexual behavior practices (DiClemente 1991; Kelly et al. 1995; Sikkema et al. 1995, 1996). Social cognitive theory posits the importance of expected reinforcing consequences on behavioral enactment (Bandura 1986). To the extent that risk avoidance is expected to be socially reinforced—and actually is reinforced—HIV preventive behavior changes will be more sustainable. External social reinforcement can strengthen individuals' intentions, skills, and willingness to enact steps to avoid risk. Over time, externally delivered reinforcement can lead to internalized patterns of self-reinforcement and self-instruction related to behavior change.

Background on the
Community Intervention Trial Development

Interventions for gay men based on social diffusion theory. The initial study, in our series of HIV prevention community-level intervention projects, focused on men patronizing gay bars in sixteen small U.S. cities (Kelly et al. 1997). The gay bars were well-defined social communities with stable and relatively nontransient populations. Based on social diffusion theory, POLs were identified and recruited from among different social networks of bar patrons. The cadres of POLs were trained over four weekly sessions to model and endorse safer sex behavior change recommendations to their peers to change the social norms related to HIV risk behavior. Eight matched city pairs were identified and randomly assigned to receive the opinion leader norm change community intervention or a control condition of HIV educational brochures and condom availability. Risk behavior surveys were conducted with all men entering the bars during three-night periods at baseline and at one-year follow-up. Population-level rates of risk behavior decreased significantly in the intervention cities compared with the control cities at one-year follow-up, after exclusion of surveys completed by transients and men with exclusive sexual partners. In a city-level analysis, we found a reduction in the mean frequency of unprotected anal intercourse during the previous two months (baseline/follow-up, respectively: intervention 1.68/0.59 occasions; control 0.93/1.29; p = .04) and an increase in the mean percentage of occasions of anal intercourse protected by condoms (intervention 44.7-66.8 percent; control 62-58.7 percent; p = .02) in the intervention cities. Increased numbers of condoms taken (increase of 65 percent from baseline to follow-up) from dispensers in intervention city bars corroborated risk behavior self-reports. Popular and well-liked members of a community who systematically endorse and recommend HIV risk behavior can influence the sexual risk practices of others in their social network. This study is believed to have been the first randomized, controlled trial of a community-level intervention to reduce HIV sexual risk behaviors.

Intervention research with communities of at-risk women. An important next question was whether this community-level HIV prevention intervention would have a similar effect with different and more disadvantaged populations, and in settings other than bars. We extended the community-level HIV prevention models to impoverished and predominantly minority women who live in low-income, inner-city housing developments (Sikkema et al. 2000). In addition to serving as a venue to reach women at risk for HIV, housing developments were selected as the site for the community-level intervention for two methodological reasons: (1) based on residents' demographic characteristics and size and type of development, we planned to identify pairs of matched sites that would allow to us to randomize to condition and analyze findings at the level of housing development; and (2) the total number of female residents could be ascertained, thus providing a "denominator" for determining the extent to which we assessed representation of the housing development community. The project was conducted with women in eighteen low-income housing developments in Milwaukee, Wisconsin; Cleveland, Ohio; Tacoma, Washington; Rochester, New York; and Roanoke, Virginia.

In the work with gay men, risk reduction followed an intervention in which opinion leaders were engaged to model and endorse safer sex behavior change recommendations to their peers. However, gay men constituted a population already quite sensitized to the threat of HIV, often with strong intentions to enact change, considerable experience in safer sex practices, and relatively few life stressors related to disadvantage. For a population such as this, relatively high in "readiness to change" (Prochaska and DiClemente 1983), the induction of improved normative supports for behavior change was "enough" of an intervention to bring about reductions in risky behavior. In the study involving communities of minority women in low-income housing developments, results of formative and baseline survey studies revealed a different pattern. As reported in a series of recent publications, many disenfranchised women had low levels of risk sensitization, weak behavior change attitudes intentions and efficacy beliefs, little experience in condom use, weak perceived norms concerning risk avoidance, and competing life stressors (Heckman et al. 1996; Sikkema et al. 1995; Wagstaff et al. 1995). In this context, simply enlisting opinion leaders in the housing developments to endorse risk avoidance norms in conversations with friends seemed an overly narrow and insufficient approach unlikely to produce substantial behavior change. An effective intervention for disenfranchised women would need to include multiple elements and components, derived from both social cognitive and diffusion of innovation theory, to help women acquire AIDS preventive skills, attitudes, intentions, and efficacy beliefs and provide normative and social supports.

Intervention Design, Development, and Implementation

Intervention development

A series of formative research activities, including elicitation interviews and focus groups with women and men, were conducted to identify potential risk reduction motivations and attitudes, perceived barriers to behavior change, and

---

While we were able to ascertain that HIV/AIDS was a concern for the women, daily life stressors had greater salience, power-imbalanced relationships were a significant barrier to risk reduction, and concern was expressed related to discussing personal and sexual matters with other women in the housing development who were not within women's social and familial networks.

---

other personal and situational characteristics relevant to intervention planning. The nature of the intervention also required that we identify social interaction and social influence patterns within the community. While we were able to ascertain that HIV/AIDS was a concern for the women, daily life stressors had greater salience, power-imbalanced relationships were a significant barrier to risk reduction, and concern was expressed related to discussing personal and sexual matters with other women in the housing development who were not within women's social and familial networks. Based on the information gathered, three intervention models were developed and presented to women in focus groups to gather feedback on the most appropriate and socially acceptable approach. Each model varied on the level of assistance from research staff, involvement of female residents in implementing the intervention, and extent to which women initiated detailed risk reduction conversations with other residents. Interestingly, the selection of the intervention model was unanimously agreed on across housing developments in various U.S. cities and is the multicomponent intervention described below.

Intervention design and implementation

Intervention condition procedures. A twelve-month community-level intervention was undertaken in the experimental intervention condition developments. The intervention had three overlapping phases: (1) inviting women regarded as opinion leaders to attend a focus group to provide input on the planned intervention and a four-session risk reduction workshop conducted in the development (two months); (2) encouraging these women to form Women's Health Councils (WHCs) and to recruit female friends and neighbors to participate in the risk reduction workshop series (two months); and (3) assisting each WHC to carry out community events to reach all women tenants and to strengthen behavior change intentions, attitudes, and normative perceptions concerning risk reduction (nine months). Condoms and HIV/AIDS educational materials were made available to all women in the intervention condition developments.

Opinion leaders were identified in each intervention condition housing development at the time of the baseline survey by asking each female resident to name up to five women living in the same development that she liked most and trusted for advice. The cadre of key opinion leaders in a given experimental condition housing development was composed of women who received the greatest number of peer nominations. The opinion leader cadre in a given housing development ranged in size from nine to fourteen women; approximately 12 percent of all the adult women who lived in each development were recruited as opinion leaders.

Risk reduction workshops for opinion leaders. Two female facilitators trained by the investigational team led each series of four 90-minute workshops. Workshop content areas included HIV and STD risk education, women's reproductive health and sexuality issues, male and female condom use, sexual assertiveness and negotiation skills regarding condom use, risk behavior self-management, and skills training to talk with family and friends about HIV and sexual behavior. The workshops also stressed the important role that can be played by women who take leadership in HIV prevention efforts in their community. Women received $15 for participating in each workshop.

Recruitment by opinion leaders of neighbors to attend risk reduction workshops. The cadres of opinion leader women were the first to complete the workshops and then formed a WHC to undertake AIDS prevention outreach activities targeting other women who lived in their development. As their first activity, WHC members began talking with other women to encourage them to attend additional iterations of the risk reduction workshop. In addition, posters and brochures placed in the housing development announced the availability of the workshops. The workshops were attended by an average of 48 percent (range = 40-57 percent) of all adult female residents. Workshop attendees were demographically similar to all residents.

WHC AIDS awareness community events for women. The WHC in each intervention condition development met at least monthly to develop and implement HIV/AIDS education community events tailored for women and families in the development. Each WHC undertook at least three major community events over a nine-month period. Examples of events included tenant picnics that featured presentations made by local HIV prevention resource speakers, a family carnival with contests for women based on the theme of safer sex, musical events interspersed with HIV prevention messages, and a potluck dinner with HIV-positive women. These events were attended by an average of fifty-five (range = fifteen to two hundred) members of each housing development community, representing from 20 percent to more than 90 percent of family units. Each WHC also conducted six smaller-scale activities such as the distribution of safe-sex materials, a WHC HIV/AIDS newsletter, conversations focused on HIV risk reduction, and local AIDS Day walks.

Research staff provided logistical and organizational support for each WHC. WHC members were not compensated for their efforts in carrying out community events, but they received an incentive payment of $15 for attending monthly event-planning meetings. Following completion of the study, research staff worked with WHCs for three months to develop collaborations with organizations to continue HIV prevention activities.

Managerial, political, and ethical issues

A variety of cooperation-building activities were conducted to enhance community collaboration and to reduce misunderstanding or potential conflict. Key informant interviews were conducted with a variety of individuals familiar with the housing developments and related community concerns. These system representatives included members of the tenant management organizations; health care professionals knowledgeable about service delivery to residents in the housing development; management or staff members of the housing development; socially influential residents; and neighborhood residents recognized as civic, social, or political leaders. The key informant interviews provided further information on the social networks in the housing development community and on other social and health programs under way in the community, recommendations concerning logistics of intervention implementation, and perceptions of health and social problems affecting residents.

Support and approval was initially sought from local Housing and Urban Development (HUD) local offices. Public housing authority records were reviewed to identify single female head-of-household housing developments in each city with similar tenant demographic characteristics. Upon selection of matched pairs of housing developments, collaborative discussions were initiated with management to seek support and approval for the intervention trial. While most managers and staff were supportive, some expressed concern on topics ranging from reporting of illegal behaviors (e.g., illicit drug use, additional family members/male partners living in the household) to a desire to influence the intervention content (e.g., restriction on sexuality content to adhere to religious beliefs). To ensure privacy and encourage honesty among participants regarding sexual and substance use behaviors, anonymous surveys were administered and site-specific data summaries were not provided to the housing management or reported in data analyses. Community acceptance of the "research" aspect of the study was enhanced by our willingness to offer HIV risk reduction workshops to women in the control condition developments (who also received educational brochures and condoms) following completion of the study. Finally, we utilized research staff members who were familiar with issues faced by community members to facilitate community-based collaborative research and enhance cultural competence to the greatest extent possible.

Success of the
Design, Implementation, and Analysis

Study design

This research was conducted between 1994 and 1996 in eighteen low-income, inner-city housing developments in five geographically diverse U.S. cities: Milwaukee, Wisconsin; Roanoke, Virginia; Cleveland, Ohio; Rochester, New York; and Tacoma, Washington. Nine demographically matched pairs of housing developments were identified. Each development was composed primarily of single female heads of households and ranged in size from 56 to 170 apartment units. To minimize contamination of experimental conditions, study housing developments in a city were located two or more miles apart. Women eighteen years or older in all of the developments were asked to complete anonymous but unique identifier-linked baseline risk assessment surveys. Over a four-month baseline survey period, a total of 1,265 women (representing 82 percent of all adult women living in the developments) completed baseline surveys. The baseline assessment included demographic characteristics, HIV risk behavior knowledge, sexual behavior, HIV risk level of male sexual partners, estimation of personal risk, availability of condoms, and conversations with male partners about condoms and AIDS concerns.

After the baseline survey data were collected, the two developments composing each pair were assigned to either the intervention or the comparison condition, so that nine housing development populations received the experimental intervention and nine served as comparisons. Within each pair, assignment of developments to one or the other condition was random, except in the case of one pair where the availability of meeting space and environmental constraints necessitated assigning one of the developments to the comparison condition. These two developments did not differ from one another in population risk behavior characteristics at baseline.

All households (in both the experimental and control conditions) with women older than eighteen were mailed packets that offered HIV/AIDS brochures and a coupon that could be returned to receive ten free condoms. The return forms were coded to determine the housing development from which it came. An additional "order" form was included with the free condoms.

Follow-up assessments of risk behavior. One year after the workshop intervention and two months following the last community events undertaken in the experimental condition housing developments, women in all eighteen housing developments in the study were resurveyed to establish HIV risk behaviors and risk-related characteristics. Survey procedures used in the twelve-month follow-up were identical to those used at baseline, except that the follow-up questionnaire also included several items used to assess the respondent's exposure to the intervention. We sought to determine whether, between the baseline survey assessment and the one-year follow-up, the intervention produced changes in sexual HIV risk behavior among women in the nine experimental condition housing developments relative to those in the control condition housing developments. Primary outcomes were the percentage of women reporting any occurrence of unprotected intercourse, the percentage of acts of intercourse protected by condoms, and the mean frequency of unprotected acts of intercourse in the past two months. We also examined corroborative changes in risk characteristics, including (1) rates of condom coupon redemption, (2) women's reports of talking about AIDS concerns and condoms with their sexual partners, (3) the number of women at each survey site who reported that they were carrying a condom or had a condom at home, and (4) other psychosocial risk-related variables.

Statistical methods

Housing developments within each city were the units of randomization by which intact social groups were allocated to intervention and comparison conditions. The cohort of participants living in the study housing developments and surveyed at both baseline and twelve-month follow-up formed the study population used to analyze the impact of the intervention. Methods of analysis that account for intact social groups as the unit of randomization and the interdependence of data from members of these social groups have been developed for examining the effects of community-level prevention trials (Donner and Donald 1987; Feldman and McKinley 1994; Murray and Hannan 1990).

The analyses of response data were based on the use of housing developments as the unit of analysis and a mixed-model generalized linear model approach for hypothesis testing (Littell et al. 1996). The model describing response Y_{ijklm} of individual m within development $l(k)$ in city k and condition i at survey time point j is as follows:

$$Y_{ijklm} = m + G_i + T_j + GT_{ij} + C_k + D_{l(k)} + DT_{jl(k)} + S_{m[l(k)]} + ST_{jm[l(k)]}.$$

The above model, a nested cohort design model for an individual's response, includes the grand mean component and terms for the effects attributable to the study condition (G_i), the survey time (T_j), the city (C_k), development $[D_{l(k)}]$ within condition, and subject within development $\{S_{m[l(k)]}\}$, along with the interaction terms for condition and time (GT_{ij}), development and time $[DT_{jl(k)}]$, and subject and time $\{ST_{jm[l(k)]}\}$. The effect attributable to city, development, and subject and the interaction effects of development and subject with time are random effects. Of primary interest for assessing the effectiveness of an intervention is the presence of an interaction effect due to the study condition by survey time (GT_{ij}), indicating that one study condition group changed patterns of sexual practices related to HIV risk more than the other study condition group over time. The SAS (Statistical Analysis System, version 6.12) procedure Proc MIXED and the SAS macro GLIMMIX30 were used for estimating and testing in the generalized linear mixed model framework. This macro, which uses iteratively reweighted likelihoods, fits the specified model by the method of restricted maximum likelihood estimation (REML) for parameter estimation. The SAS macro GLIMMIX enables the use of non-Gaussian residual error distributions in model specification. For study end points that represent frequency of an occurrence, such as the number of unprotected acts of sexual intercourse, the negative binomial model was used. For study end points that represented binary data, such as any unprotected sexual intercourse during the past two months, a logit model was used.

Results

Study cohort

A total of 1,265 women in the eighteen housing developments were surveyed at baseline, representing 82 percent of all women living in the housing developments. At the twelve-month follow-up (two months after the last community events were undertaken in experimental condition housing developments), 83 percent of all women in the same developments were surveyed. Completion rates by development ranged from 66 to 94 percent, but they did not differ by condition or assessment point. Of the 1,265 women who completed baseline surveys, 690 were still living in the housing developments and completed the assessment at the twelve-month follow-up; this included 351 women surveyed at both baseline and follow-up in intervention condition developments (51 percent of the baseline sample) and 339 women in comparison condition developments (49 percent). This group of 690 women constituted the study cohort used to analyze intervention outcomes. Before analyzing the intervention outcomes, we compared the baseline character-istics of the cohort of 690 women with those of all 1,265 women who had com-pleted a baseline survey. The women in the cohort did not differ from the other women in education, ethnicity, income, or characteristics of sexual relationships,

---

With the goal of enhancing sustainability of the community intervention, we worked with WHCs [Women's Health Councils] in all nine of the experimental condition housing developments following the completion of the study to assist in planning and decision making regarding continuation of their efforts.

---

although they were somewhat older (35.9 vs. 31.4 years) and had lived in the devel-opments longer. The study cohort was composed primarily of ethnic minority women (75 percent African American, 20 percent white, 3 percent Hispanic, and 2 percent of other ethnicities), and their mean educational level was 11.6 years.

Effects of the intervention on sexual risk behavior

Table 1 presents the means for sexual risk behavior characteristics in the past two months among women in each study condition at each survey point, as well as the results of the analysis of variance for the time-by-condition interaction, with housing developments used as units for statistical analysis. Almost identical per-centages of women in the intervention condition developments (50.0 percent) and comparison developments (49.5 percent) reported at baseline that they had engaged in unprotected intercourse in the past two months. At follow-up, the per-centage of women who reported any unprotected intercourse in the past two months showed little change (46.2 percent) in the comparison developments, but it declined to 37.6 percent among women in the intervention developments, $F(1, 16) = 5.44, p = .03$.

TABLE 1

SEXUAL RISK BEHAVIOR CHARACTERISTICS AT BASELINE AND TWELVE-MONTH FOLLOW-UP AMONG WOMEN IN INTERVENTION AND COMPARISON HOUSING DEVELOPMENTS

	Comparison Developments				Intervention Developments			Interaction of Time and Condition		Intervention Development Women Who Attended at Least Two Workshop Sessions			Interaction of Time and Condition	
	Baseline Mean (95% CI)	Follow-Up Mean (95% CI)		Baseline Mean (95% CI)	Follow-Up Mean (95% CI)			F^a	p	Baseline Mean (95% CI)	Follow-Up Mean (95% CI)		F^b	p
Mean percentage of women reporting any unprotected intercourse in the past two months	49.5 (43.4, 55.6)	46.2 (40.1, 52.4)		50.0 (44.0, 56.1)	37.6 (31.9, 43.7)			5.44	.03	50.2 (43.8, 56.6)	36.9 (30.9, 43.3)		5.98	.03
Mean percentage of women's acts of intercourse in the past two months protected by condoms	33.9 (26.7, 41.1)	36.3 (29.1, 43.5)		30.2 (27.0, 37.4)	47.2 (40.0, 54.4)			9.66	.007	29.8 (22.0, 37.7)	48.5 (40.7, 56.3)		10.50	.005
Mean frequency of unprotected acts of intercourse in the past two months	5.2 (3.8, 7.1)	5.1 (3.7, 7.0)		5.8 (4.3, 7.8)	4.5 (3.3, 6.3)			0.90	n.s.	6.0 (4.5, 8.1)	4.0 (2.9, 5.7)		3.71	.07

SOURCE: Sikkema et al. (2000). Reprinted with permission from the American Public Health Association. Copyright 2000.

NOTE: 95% CI = 95 percent confidence interval; n.s. = not significant.

a. F-test for condition-by-time interaction between comparison housing development women ($n = 351$) and intervention housing development women ($n = 339$), with 1 and 16 degrees of freedom.

b. F-test for condition-by-time interaction between comparison housing development women ($n = 271$) and intervention housing development women who attended at least two workshop sessions ($n = 339$), with 1 and 16 degrees of freedom.

With respect to condom use, at baseline the mean percentage of acts of intercourse in the past two months protected by condoms was 30.2 percent among women in intervention developments and 33.9 percent among women in comparison developments. At twelve-month follow-up, little change in condom use was found among women in comparison developments (36.3 percent); however, among women in intervention developments, the percentage of protected intercourse rose to 47.2 percent, $F(1, 16) = 9.66, p = .007$. Women in comparison developments reported a similar mean number of unprotected acts of intercourse in the past two months at baseline (mean = 5.2 occurrences) and follow-up (mean = 5.1 occurrences), while women exposed to intervention activities tended to report lower frequencies at follow-up (mean = 4.0) than at baseline (mean = 6.0). Condom redemption rates were nearly twice as high in the populations that received intervention. These changes were corroborated by changes in other risk indicators, such as increased HIV knowledge, increased risk perception, condom-carrying behavior, and conversations with male partners about condom use (Sikkema et al. 2000).

Management, political, and ethical issues

With the goal of enhancing sustainability of the community intervention, we worked with WHCs in all nine of the experimental condition housing developments following the completion of the study to assist in planning and decision making regarding continuation of their efforts. This form of continued collaboration is relatively rare in the conduct of research trials. The WHCs varied in the direction taken, as well as in the success of their endeavors. Examples of the focus of continued activities from several different WHCs included

- seeking and successfully receiving support from a foundation and the state to continue HIV prevention efforts over a two-year period;
- focusing efforts to programs related to adolescent health, including prevention of HIV, STDs, and unwanted pregnancy (one WHC member became employed through these efforts);
- maintaining other relationships with university-based prevention and care programs;
- emphasizing a broader array of health concerns, including exercise and nutrition; and
- forming a tenant council (in a development where one did not exist) to serve as an advocacy-type group to address daily problems encountered by residents.

It is likely that none of the above activities, which developed following the formation of the WHCs to reduce HIV risk among women in the neighborhood, would have occurred without the support and encouragement of our research staff after completion of the research trial. These efforts, along with our offering the HIV risk reduction to women in the control condition housing developments following study completion, contributed positively to longer-term university-community research collaboration.

This multisite collaboration was maintained as our research team planned for the development and implementation of a community-level intervention trial for adolescents living in low-income housing developments, which is described below. The collaborative research relationships—spanning more than ten years, in some instances—were maintained through effective communication, leadership, and respect and were critical to the successful implementation of this series of studies on community-level HIV prevention intervention trials.

Application of the POL
Community Intervention Model to Other Populations

The effectiveness and appeal of this community-level approach, including its cost-effectiveness (Holtgrave, Qualls, and Graham 1996; Johnson-Masotti et al. forthcoming; Pinkerton et al. 1998), has resulted in a variety of ongoing research projects, including interventions with adolescents and adults with severe mental illness (SMI) living in supportive housing settings (SHPs).

As a continuation of this community-level intervention research project, a multiple component community-level intervention was implemented with adolescents aged twelve to seventeen in urban housing developments (Sikkema et al. 2004). In the study with women, we evaluated the effects of a multicomponent intervention in relation to an educational brochure and condom distribution comparison intervention. A number of studies (e.g., Jemmott, Jemmott, and Fong 1992; Rotheram-Borus et al. 1991; St. Lawrence et al. 1995) have reported the outcomes of small-group risk reduction interventions undertaken with adolescents. Significant effects on sexual risk behavior have established this approach as the current "state of the science" in HIV prevention among adolescents. Thus, similar to the study with at-risk minority women, the purpose of the community intervention study with adolescents was to determine the effect of adding social and environmental norm support elements to individually focused risk reduction workshops.

To determine the effectiveness of the community-level intervention, fifteen housing developments (five sets of demographically matched development triads) were randomly assigned in equal number to education-only control waiting intervention, state-of-the-science skills training workshops only, or the experimental community-level intervention consisting of workshops plus sustained HIV risk avoidance community norm change intervention. The community-level intervention was shown to be effective in delaying the onset of first intercourse and increasing condom use among adolescents (Sikkema et al. 2004).

Second, a pilot intervention trial was conducted to determine the feasibility of an HIV prevention community intervention among adults with SMI in SHPs (Sikkema et al. forthcoming). A multicomponent community-level trial was implemented in two SHPs with a total of twenty-eight residents. Participants completed assessments at three time points: prior to the intervention (baseline), following skills training (postassessment), and following the four-month community intervention (follow-up). Results demonstrated significant improvements in psychosocial risk factors at both postassessment and follow-up assessment, with indications of sexual behavior change at follow-up. The community-level intervention appeared to reduce the risk of HIV among persons with SMI living in SHPs, and supports the importance of conducting larger-scale intervention trials.

Dissemination of Research Findings

Given the scope and urgency of the HIV pandemic, it is important to quickly develop strategies for disseminating research findings and transferring evidence-based HIV prevention interventions to those providing services in community-based and nongovernmental organizations. Further research is needed to identify innovative strategies to effectively transfer findings from research into prevention services, and improved efforts are needed to establish the support of their implementation in at-risk communities.

References

Bandura, Albert. 1986. *Social foundations of thought and action: A social cognitive theory*. Englewood Cliffs, NJ: Prentice Hall.

Centers for Disease Control (CDC). 2002. Cases of HIV infection and AIDS in the United States, 2002. *HIV/ AIDS Surveillance Report* 14:12-14.

Centers for Disease Control (CDC) AIDS Community Demonstration Projects Research Group. 1999. Community-level HIV intervention in 5 cities: Final outcome data from the CDC AIDS community demonstration projects. *American Journal of Public Health* 89:336-45.

DiClemente, Ralph J. 1991. Predictors of HIV-preventive sexual behavior in a high-risk adolescent population: The influence of perceived peer norms and sexual communication on incarcerated adolescents' consistent use of condoms. *Journal of Adolescent Health* 12:385-90.

DiClemente, Ralph J., and Gina M. Wingood. 1995. A randomized controlled trial of an HIV sexual risk reduction intervention for young African American women. *Journal of the American Medical Association* 274:1271-76.

Donner, Allan, and Alan Donald. 1987. Analysis of data arising from a stratified design with the cluster as unit of randomization. *Statistics in Medicine* 6:43-52.

Feldman, Henry A., and Sonja M. McKinley. 1994. Cohort versus cross-sectional design in large field trials: Precision, sample size, and unifying model. *Statistics in Medicine* 13:61-78.

Fishbein, Martin, and Icek Ajzen. 1975. *Belief, attitude, intention, and behavior: An introduction to theory and research*. Reading, MA: Addison-Wesley.

Fisher, Jeffrey D., and William A. Fisher. 1992. Changing AIDS risk behavior. *Psychological Bulletin* 111:455-74.

Heckman, Timothy G., Kathleen J. Sikkema, Jeffrey A. Kelly, R. Wayne Fuqua, Mary Beth Mercer, Raymond G. Hoffman, Richard A. Winnett, Eileen S. Anderson, Melissa J. Perry, Roger A. Roffman, Laura J. Soloman, David A. Wagstaff, Victoria Cargill, Ann D. Norman, and Denise Crumble. 1996. Predictors of condom use and HIV test seeking among women living in inner-city public housing developments. *Sexually Transmitted Diseases* 23:357-65.

Holtgrave, David R., Noreen L. Qualls, and John D. Graham. 1996. Economic evaluation of HIV prevention programs. *Annual Review of Public Health* 17:467-88.

Jemmott, John B., Loretta S. Jemmott, and Geoffrey T. Fong. 1992. Reductions in HIV risk-associated sexual behaviors among black male adolescents: Effects of an AIDS prevention intervention. *American Journal of Public Health* 82:372-77.

Johnson-Masotti, Ana P., Steven D. Pinkerton, Jeffrey A. Kelly, David A. Wagstaff, and Kathleen J. Sikkema. Forthcoming. Cost-effectiveness of a community-level HIV risk reduction intervention for women living in low-income housing developments. *Journal of Primary Prevention.*

Joint United Nations Programme on AIDS (UNAIDS). 2004. *Report on the global HIV/AIDS epidemic: July 2004.* Bangkok, Thailand: UNAIDS.

Kegeles, Susan M., Robert B. Hays, and Thomas J. Coates. 1996. The Empowerment Project: A community-level HIV prevention intervention for young gay men. *American Journal of Public Health* 86:1129-36.

Kelly, Jeffrey A. 1999. Community-level interventions are needed to prevent new HIV infections. *American Journal of Public Health* 89:299-301.

Kelly, Jeffrey A., Debra A. Murphy, Kathleen J. Sikkema, Timothy L. McAuliffe, Roger A. Roffman, Laura J. Solomon, Richard A. Winett, Seth C. Kalichman, and the Community HIV Prevention Research Collaborative. 1997. Randomized, controlled community-level HIV prevention intervention for sexual-risk behavior among homosexual men in U.S. cities. *Lancet* 350:1500-1505.

Kelly, Jeffrey A., Kathleen J. Sikkema, Richard A. Winett, Laura J. Solomon, Roger A. Roffman, Timothy G. Heckman, L. Yvonne Stevenson, Melissa J. Perry, Ann D. Norman, and Laurie L. Desiderato. 1995. Factors predicting continued high HIV risk behavior among gay men in small cities: Psychological, behavioral, and demographic characteristics related to unsafe sex. *Journal of Consulting and Clinical Psychology* 63:101-7.

Lauby, Jennifer L., Philip J. Smith, Michael Stark, Bobbie Person, and Janet Adams. 2000. A community-level HIV prevention intervention for inner-city women: Results of the woman and infants demonstration trial. *American Journal of Public Health* 90:216-22.

Littell, Ramon C., G. A. Miliken, Walter W. Stroup, and R. D. Wolfinger. 1996. *SAS system for mixed models.* Cary, NC: SAS Institute Inc.

Murray, David M., and Peter J. Hannan. 1990. Planning for the appropriate analysis in school-based drug use prevention studies. *Journal of Consulting and Clinical Psychology* 58:458-68.

Pinkerton, Steven D., David R. Holtgrave, Wayne J. DiFranceisco, L. Yvonne Stevenson, and Jeffrey A. Kelly. 1998. Cost-effectiveness of a community-level HIV risk reduction intervention. *American Journal of Public Health* 88:1239-42.

Prochaska, James O., and C. DiClemente. 1983. Stages and processes of self-change of smoking: Toward an integrative model of change. *Journal of Consulting and Clinical Psychology* 51:287-305.

Rogers, Everett M. 1983. *Diffusion of innovations.* New York: Free Press.

Rotheram-Borus, Mary Jane, Cheryl Koopman, C. Haignere, and M. Davies. 1991. Reducing HIV sexual risk behaviors among runaway adolescents. *Journal of the American Medical Association* 26:1237-41.

Sikkema, Kathleen J., Eileen S. Anderson, Richard A. Winett, C. Gore-Felton, R. G. Hoffmann, Jeffrey A. Kelly, Roger A. Roffman, Michael J. Brondino, and Timothy G. Heckman. 2004. Community-level HIV prevention intervention outcomes among low-income adolescents. Paper presented to the American Psychological Association Annual Convention, Honolulu, Hawaii, July.

Sikkema, Kathleen J., Timothy G. Heckman, Jeffrey A. Kelly, Eileen S. Anderson, Richard A. Winett, Laura J. Solomon, David A. Wagstaff, Roger A. Roffman, Melissa J. Perry, Victoria Cargill, Denise A. Crumble, R. Wayne Fuqua, Ann D. Norman, and Mary Beth Mercer. 1996. Prevalence and predictors of HIV risk behaviors among women living in low-income, inner-city housing developments. *American Journal of Public Health* 86:1123-28.

Sikkema, Kathleen J., Jeffrey A. Kelly, Richard A. Winett, Laura J. Solomon, Victoria A. Cargill, Roger A. Roffman, Timothy L. McAuliffe, Timothy G. Heckman, Eileen A. Anderson, David A. Wagstaff, Ann D. Norman, Melissa J. Perry, Denise A. Crumble, and Mary Beth Mercer. 2000. Outcomes of a randomized community-level HIV prevention intervention for women living in 18 low-income housing developments. *American Journal of Public Health* 90:57-63.

Sikkema, Kathleen J., Jeffrey J. Koob, Victoria C. Cargill, Jeffrey A. Kelly, Laurie L. Desiderato, Roger A. Roffman, Ann D. Norman, Michelle Shabazz, Crystal Copeland, Richard A. Winett, Susan Steiner, and Audie L. Lemke. 1995. Levels and predictors of HIV risk behavior among women living in low-income public housing developments. *Public Health Reports* 110:707-13.

Sikkema, Kathleen J., Christina S. Meade, Jhan D. Doughty, Susan O. Zimmerman, B. Kloos, and David L. Snow. Forthcoming. Community-level HIV prevention for persons with severe mental illness living in supportive housing programs: A pilot intervention study. *Journal of Prevention and Intervention in the Community*.

St. Lawrence, Janet S., Ted L. Brasfield, Kennis W. Jefferson, et al. 1995. Cognitive-behavioral intervention to reduce African American adolescents risk for HIV infection. *Journal of Consulting and Clinical Psychology* 63:221-47.

Stover, John, Neff Walker, Geoff P. Garnett, Joshua A. Salomon, Karen S. Stanecki, Peter D. Ghys, Nicholas C. Grassly, Roy M. Anderson, and Bernhard Schwartländer. 2002. Can we reverse the HIV/AIDS pandemic with an expanded response? *Lancet* 360:73-77.

Wagstaff, David A., Jeffrey A. Kelly, Melissa J. Perry, Kathleen J. Sikkema, Laura J. Solomon, Timothy G. Heckman, Eileen S. Anderson, Roger A. Roffman, Victoria Cargill, Ann D. Norman, Richard A. Winett, Mary Beth Mercer, Denise A. Crumble, and R. Wayne Fuqua. 1995. Multiple partners, risky partners, and HIV risk among low-income urban women. *Family Planning Perspective* 27:241-45.

World Health Organization (WHO). 2003. *Global health: Today's challenges*. Geneva, Switzerland: World Health Organization. http://www.who.int/whr/2003/chapter1/en/index3.html.

Winett, Richard A., David G. Altman, and Abby C. King. 1990. Conceptual and strategic foundations for effective media campaigns for preventing the spread of HIV infection. *Evaluation and Program Planning* 13:91-104.

Winett, Richard A., Eileen S. Anderson, Laurie L. Desiderato, Laura J. Solomon, Melissa Perry, Jeffrey A. Kelly, Kathleen J. Sikkema, Roger A. Roffman, Ann D. Norman, David N. Lombard, and Tamara N. Lombard. 1995. Enhancing social diffusion theory as a basis for prevention intervention. *Applied and Preventive Psychology* 4:233-45.

Cluster Randomized Trials of Professional and Organizational Behavior Change Interventions in Health Care Settings

By
JEREMY GRIMSHAW,
MARTIN ECCLES,
MARION CAMPBELL,
and
DIANA ELBOURNE

Individual patient randomized trials are the gold standard for assessing the effects of health care evaluations. However, individual randomization may not be possible for practical, logistical, ethical, or political reasons, for example, when evaluating health care professional and organizational behavior change interventions. Under such circumstances, cluster randomized trials are commonly used. This article discusses the practical and ethical issues in the design, conduct, and analysis of cluster randomized trials of professional behavior and organizational change strategies using examples from two primary studies evaluating health care provider behavior change strategies. Cluster randomized trials are commonly used in health care. They raise distinct ethical and methodological issues that have rarely been adequately addressed in studies to date.

Keywords: cluster randomized trials; implementation research; interventions; dissemination and implementation interventions; COmputerised Guidelines Evaluation in the NorTh of England (COGENT)

Background

Biomedical and health services research are constantly generating new evidence that has the potential to improve patient outcomes and health services delivery. For example, around 10,000 new randomized trials are included in Medline each year (Chassin 1998), and more

NOTE: The COGENT study was funded by the UK NHS R&D Programme on Methods to promote the uptake of research findings with additional funding from EMIS Computing and the Department of Health for England and Wales. The NEXUS study was funded by the NHS R&D Primary Secondary Interface Programme. The Health Services Research Unit, University of Aberdeen, is funded by the Chief Scientist Office of the Scottish Executive Health Department. The Centre for Health Services Research, University of Newcastle upon Tyne and the Health Services Research Unit, University of Aberdeen, are part of the UK MRC Health Services Research Collaboration. The views expressed are those of the authors and not necessarily those of the funding bodies.

DOI: 10.1177/0002716205274576

than 350,000 trials have been identified by the Cochrane Collaboration (2002). However, these findings will not change population outcomes unless patients, health services, and health care professionals adopt them in practice (Grimshaw, Ward, and Eccles 2001). Unfortunately, one of the most consistent findings in health services research is that the transfer of research findings into practice is unpredictable and can be a slow and haphazard process. For example, in 1988 the results of the ISIS-2 (Second International Study of Infarct Survival) trial were published, which provided (perhaps) the most robust evidence available about the effectiveness of a health care intervention ("thrombolysis"—clot-busting drugs in heart attacks). However, a series of international studies in the 1990s observed that many eligible patients failed to receive thrombolysis: the European Secondary Prevention Study Group (1996) observed that the eligible proportion of patients receiving thrombolysis in eleven European countries varied between 13 and 52 percent with a median of 36 percent; McLaughlin and colleagues (1996) observed that only 72 percent of eligible patients received thrombolysis in North American settings, with less compliance for elderly patients. The McLaughlin study also observed that 20 percent of ineligible patients received lidocaine despite its potentially harmful effects (Antman et al. 1992).

Traditional approaches to promoting the uptake of research findings have emphasized publication within scientific journals and continuing professional edu-

Jeremy Grimshaw is director of the Clinical Epidemiology Program of the Ottawa Health Research Institute and a full professor in the Department of Medicine, University of Ottawa. He holds a Canada Research Chair in Health Knowledge Transfer and Uptake. His research focuses on the evaluation of interventions to disseminate and implement evidence-based health care. He has been involved in more than twenty cluster randomized trials of a wide range of such interventions (for example, educational meetings, educational outreach, organizational interventions, computerized guidelines) relating to a wide range of professional behaviors in a wide range of settings (including community pharmacy settings, family medicine settings, and secondary- and tertiary-care-level settings).

Martin Eccles is a professor of clinical effectiveness and the William Leach Professor of Primary Care Research at the Centre for Health Services Research, School of Population and Health Sciences, University of Newcastle upon Tyne, United Kingdom, where he runs the Clinical Effectiveness research program. He has a long-standing interest in the design and conduct of cluster randomized trials of strategies to change health care professionals' behavior. He is also a practicing general practitioner in mid-Northumberland.

Marion Campbell is deputy director of the Health Services Research Unit in the University of Aberdeen and a professor of health services research. She is an experienced medical statistician, and her main research interests are in the methodology of evaluative research, especially the design, conduct, and analysis of individual and cluster randomized trials.

Diana Elbourne works in medical statistics and in the social sciences. She is a professor of healthcare evaluation in the Medical Statistics Unit of the London School of Hygiene and Tropical Medicine (where she conducts applied and methodological research in randomized controlled trials and systematic reviews). She is also a professor of evidence informed policy and practice in education at the EPPI Centre, which is part of the Social Science Research Unit in the Institute of Education, University of London (where she coordinates a program of systematic reviews in education). Her long-standing interest in cluster trials spans both these sectors.

cational lectures and seminars. This model assumes that health care professionals (providers) and managers have the time, energy, and skills to find and appraise primary research and the willingness and ability to introduce new practices in their working environment. However, providers and managers have limited time to read the ever-growing mountain of primary research, the quality of published research is highly variable, and many providers and managers have not been trained to appraise published research. Furthermore, providers and managers encounter a range of potential barriers that may prevent them from introducing new practices. These barriers may occur at a variety of levels, including structural (e.g., financial disincentives), organizational (e.g., inappropriate skill mix, lack of facilities or equipment), peer group (e.g., local standards of care not in line with desired practice), individual (e.g., knowledge, attitudes, skills), information overload within busy work settings leading to acts of omission, or patient expectations. Thus, it is not surprising that the uptake of research findings into health care appears slow and haphazard.

Increased recognition of the failure of this traditional dissemination model has led to increased policy, managerial, clinical, and research interest in more active dissemination and implementation strategies. However, to date, decision makers have often adopted a simplistic and opportunistic approach to choosing implementation strategies, largely based on individual beliefs of different stakeholders (Grol 1997).

Implementation Research

Implementation research is the scientific study of methods to promote the systematic uptake of clinical research findings into routine clinical practice (Foy, Eccles, and Grimshaw 2001). It aims to inform policy decisions about how best to use resources to improve the uptake of research findings by testing approaches to change professional and organizational behavior. Implementation research is a relatively new area of health services research with a distinctive perspective and specific methodological challenges.

While there are a range of dissemination and implementation interventions available (e.g., audit and feedback, educational outreach, reminders, organizational interventions), systematic reviews have demonstrated that there are "no magic bullets" (Oxman et al. 1995). The effectiveness of interventions varies across different clinical problems, contexts, and organizations. Grol (1997) argued, "Evidence based medicine should be complemented by evidence based implementation." In other words, we should expect the same strength of evidence when considering which dissemination and implementation strategies to use when attempting to improve uptake of research findings as we do when considering which antibiotic to use when faced with a patient with an infection.

Randomized controlled trials (RCTs) are considered the gold standard methodology for evaluating clinical interventions (Cochrane 1979). Randomization is the best way of ensuring that both known and unknown factors that may independently affect the outcome of an intervention do not differ systematically between the trial groups. As a result, differences observed between groups can be more confidently ascribed to the effects of the intervention rather than to other factors. The same arguments that are used to justify RCTs of clinical interventions are as salient to the evaluation of dissemination and implementation strategies, namely, the effects of the interventions are likely to be modest, the potential for bias is substantial, and our poor understanding of competing explanations for an observed effect relating to organizational or professional performance makes it more difficult to adjust for these in nonrandomized designs. Furthermore, most health care professionals and organizations have limited resources to support implementation initiatives, and there are significant opportunity costs if ineffective or inefficient strategies are used.

Implementation research is a relatively new area of health services research with a distinctive perspective and specific methodological challenges.

The majority of RCTs in health care have randomized individual patients to different interventions. However, when evaluating health care professional or organizational behavior change, individual patient randomization is problematic. There is a risk that the care provided to patients in the control group could be affected by an organization's or professional's experience of applying the intervention to patients in the experimental group (known as "contamination") resulting in an underestimate of the true effects of strategies. For example, Morgan and colleagues (1978) used an individual patient randomized trial to evaluate the use of computerized reminders for antenatal care. Patients were randomized to a control or an experimental group (where any noncompliance by the doctor generated an automatic reminder from the computer-based medical record system). Any one doctor managed the care of both control and experimental patients. Compliance for experimental patients rose from 83 to 98 percent over six months, while compliance for control patients rose from 83 to 94 percent in twelve months. This suggests that the intervention had a significant, although delayed, effect on the management of control patients. To avoid this problem, cluster randomized trials, which randomize intact social units or clusters of individuals rather than individuals[1] (Donner and Klar 2000), are considered the optimal design in implementation research (Grimshaw et al. 2000).

In this article, we highlight some methodological and practical issues that were faced during the design, conduct, and analysis of cluster randomized trials of professional and organizational behavior change interventions in health care settings. We use two cluster randomized trials of different professional behavior change strategies targeting family practitioners within U.K. family practice settings to illustrate these issues (see Tables 1 and 2 for summaries of both projects). The NEXUS (North East X-Ray Utilisation Study) study demonstrated that educational reminder messages reduced X-ray requests for lumbar and knee by around 20 to 30 percent, whereas the provision of peer audit and feedback was ineffective (Eccles et al. 2001). The COGENT study demonstrated that computerized decision support did not improve management of chronic diseases by family physicians (Eccles et al. 2000; Eccles, McColl, Steen, Rousseau, Grimshaw, Parkin, and Purves 2002; Eccles, McColl, Steen, Rousseau, Grimshaw, Parkin, Purves, and Newton 2002; Rousseau et al. 2003).

Design Issues

Choice of study design

The simplest randomized design is the two-arm trial where subjects are randomized to study or control groups. Such trials are relatively straightforward to design, and they maximize statistical power (half the sample is allocated to the intervention group and half to the control group). However, they only provide information about the effectiveness of a single intervention compared to control (or the relative effectiveness of two interventions without reference to a control). Within implementation research, we frequently are interested in establishing the relative effectiveness of different interventions in different settings; under these circumstances extensions of the two-arm trial to multiarm trials or factorial designs may be useful (see Grimshaw et al. 2000 for further discussion).

For example, we used a 2×2 factorial design in the NEXUS study (Eccles et al. 2001). Participating family practices were randomized twice, first to receive educational reminders or control and then to receive audit and feedback or control. This resulted in four study groups: one receiving both educational reminders and control, one receiving educational reminders only, one receiving audit and feedback only, and one receiving neither reminders nor audit and feedback (control) (Table 3) (Pocock 1983; Shaddish, Cook, and Campbell 2002). This allowed us to estimate the main effects of two interventions within the same setting and test for any interaction effect.

In contrast, in the COGENT study, we were interested in the effects of computerized guidelines for the management of two chronic conditions (an extension to an available acute prescribing computerized decision support system) in U.K. family medicine (Eccles, McColl, Steen, Rousseau, Grimshaw, Parkin, and Purves 2002). We used a 2×2 balanced incomplete block design (Eccles et al. 2000). Participating practices were randomized into two groups: one received computerized guidelines for one chronic condition (asthma) and provided control data for a second chronic condition (angina); the second group received computerized guide-

TABLE 1

COMPUTERISED GUIDELINES EVALUATION IN THE
NORTH OF ENGLAND (COGENT)

Objectives: To evaluate the use of a computerized decision support system in implementing evidence-based clinical guidelines for the primary care management of asthma in adults and angina.

Design: A 2 × 2 balanced incomplete block cluster randomized controlled trial.

Setting: Sixty family practices in northeast England.

Participants: Family practitioners and practice nurses in the study practices and their patients aged eighteen years or older and with angina or asthma.

Main outcome measures: Data were collected twelve months before and twelve months following the intervention on adherence to the guidelines based upon case note review and patient-reported generic and condition-specific outcome measures.

Results: There were no significant effects on consultation rates, process of care measures (including prescribing), or any quality of life domain for either condition. Levels of use were low.

Conclusions: The study did not demonstrate any effect of evidence-based clinical practice guidelines delivered via a computerized decision support system. This is probably due to low levels of use of the software, despite optimizing the system as far as was technically possible. Even if it is possible to solve the technical hardware and software problems of producing a system that fully supports chronic disease management, there remains the challenge of integrating computerized decision support systems into clinical encounters where busy practitioners manage patients with complex, multiple conditions.

TABLE 2

NORTH EAST X-RAY UTILISATION STUDY (NEXUS)

Objectives: To evaluate the use audit and feedback and educational reminder messages in the number of requests for lumbar spine and knee X-rays.

Design: A 2 × 2 factorial cluster randomized controlled trial.

Setting: 247 family practices served by six radiology departments in the northeast of England and Scotland.

Participants: Family practitioners in the study practices.

Main outcome measures: Data on the number of X-ray requests were collected twelve months before and twelve months after from the reporting software systems of the participating radiology departments.

Results: The effect of educational reminder messages (expressed as X-ray requests per one thousand patients) was an absolute change of –1.53 (95 percent confidence interval (CI): –2.5, –0.57) lumbar spine requests and of –1.61 (95 percent CI: –2.6, –0.62) knee X-ray requests, relative reductions of about 20 percent. Similarly, the effect of audit and feedback was an absolute change of –0.07 (95 percent CI: –1.3, 0.9) lumbar spine X-rays requests and an absolute change of –0.04 (95 percent CI: –0.95, 1.03) for knee X-rays requests, relative reductions of about 1 percent. Educational reminder messages were cost saving; audit and feedback was more expensive and provided fewer referrals avoided.

Conclusions: While feedback of audit data is ineffective, the routine attachment of educational reminder messages to the results of X-rays is both an effective and cost-saving strategy and does not affect the overall quality of referrals. Any department of radiology within the U.K. National Health Service (NHS) could deliver this intervention to good effect.

TABLE 3

2 × 2 FACTORIAL DESIGN

(a) Simple factorial design			
R	X_{A1B1}		O_{Post}
R	X_{A1B2}		O_{Post}
R	X_{A2B1}		O_{Post}
R	X_{A2B2}		O_{Post}
(b) Factorial design with pretest			
R	O_{Pre}	X_{A1B1}	O_{Post}
R	O_{Pre}	X_{A1B2}	O_{Post}
R	O_{Pre}	X_{A2B1}	O_{Post}
R	O_{Pre}	X_{A2B2}	O_{Post}

NOTE: R = group formed by randomization; X = treatment group (X_{A1B1} = group receives interventions A and B, X_{A1B2} = group receives intervention A only, X_{A2B1} = group receives intervention B only, X_{A2B2} = group receives neither intervention [control]); O = observation (O_{Pre} = preintervention data collection, O_{Post} = postintervention data collection).

TABLE 4

2 × 2 BALANCED INCOMPLETE BLOCK DESIGN

R	O_{PreMN}	X_{M1N2}	O_{PostMN}
R	O_{PreMN}	X_{M2N1}	O_{PostMN}

NOTE: R = group formed by randomization; X = treatment group (X_{M1N2} = group receives intervention for condition M, X_{M2N1} = group receives intervention for condition N); O = observation (O_{PreMN} = preintervention data collection for conditions M and N, O_{PostMN} = postintervention data collection for conditions M and N).

lines for the second condition and provided control data for the first condition (Table 4) (Cochran and Cox 1957). Such designs are useful because they equalize the level of intervention and nonspecific effects across both groups and also provide a replication of the intervention in a second condition (Grimshaw et al. 2000). However, due to the 2 × 2 balanced incomplete block design, it was important to choose interventions whose management did not influence each other (i.e., that the management of patients with a control condition was not influenced by the introduction of the guidelines for a intervention condition). The elements of care for the asthma and angina in this trial are discrete with no overlap in terms of actions performed. This might not be the case with conditions such as diabetes and angina.

Level of randomization

Implementation researchers need to consider at what level to randomize units. This often involves considering the trade-off between reducing the number of units available to randomize if higher-level units are randomized against the risk of contamination if lower-level units are randomized. Consider a trial to evaluate professional behavior change strategies within hospital settings. Potential levels of randomization include the individual clinician, the ward, the clinical service or directorate, and the hospital. Randomization at the level of the hospital will minimize the risk of contamination but dramatically increase the number of hospitals required. This could have substantial logistical implications, limiting the feasibility of the study. In contrast, randomization at the level of the individual ward will decrease the number of hospitals required but potentially increase the risk of contamination to an unacceptable level because of regular contact by professionals working within the same ward environment. In our two case studies, we could have randomized at the level of the town, the health care center (where more than one family practice might be based), the family practice (most U.K. family practitioners work in group practices), or the individual family practitioner. We chose to randomize at the level of the family practice, reasoning that the risk of contamination within a practice was high but that the risk of contamination across practices sharing the same premises was sufficiently low based upon our own clinical experiences and experiences of previous trials that had not demonstrated contamination at this level.

Sample size issues

Within individual patient randomized trials, responses of patients are considered to be independent from each other. The primary implication of adopting a cluster randomized design is that patients within any one cluster are often more likely to respond in a similar manner and thus can no longer be assumed to act independently. This lack of independence in turn leads to a loss of statistical power in comparison with a patient randomized trial. To achieve the equivalent power of a patient randomized trial, standard sample size calculations (for a completely randomized design) need to be inflated by a factor based upon consideration of the degree of clustering (known as the intracluster or intraclass correlation coefficient [ICC]) and the average cluster size (Donner 1998). The inflation factor is relatively straightforward to calculate: $1 + [(\text{average cluster size} - 1) \times \text{ICC}]$.

To achieve the increased sample size required, it is possible either to increase the number of clusters to be recruited to the study or to increase the number of subjects included from each cluster. Compared with increasing the number of clusters to be included within a study, however, the effect of increasing the cluster size on power is minimal (Diwan et al. 1992). While increasing the number of clusters is theoretically more effective in redressing the loss of efficiency caused by clustering, this is not always feasible. Practical considerations, such as the cost of recruiting extra clusters and extra staffing costs to deliver the intervention and data collection, have to be taken into account (Flynn, Whitley, and Peters 2002). A further problem often faced by implementation researchers is a fixed number of clusters available. This is often seen in regional studies of primary care interventions, where there is, for example, a set number of family practices available within a health region. A public domain sample size calculator that allows researchers to explore the trade-offs between increasing the number of clusters and patients per cluster is available from http://www.abdn.ac.uk/hsru/epp/cluster.shtml (correct as of February 9, 2005).

Reliable estimates of ICCs are required for robust sample size calculations to be made. At the time of the COGENT study, there were few external estimates of ICCs available to inform the sample size calculation. Fortunately, we had access to a data set reporting process and outcome measures for family practitioners' management of pediatric problems derived from a previous trial in the study area (Anonymous 1992a, 1992b). Process of care variables relate to what that health care professional does to or for the patient (for example, prescription of medication), whereas outcomes of care relate to the resulting changes in the health of that patient (for example, improved quality of life) (Donabedian 1966). This data set suggested that the majority of process of care ICCs were usually less than .1, and outcome of care ICCs were usually less than .05. (Further data sets have since confirmed that these estimates are realistic for U.K. primary care; Campbell, Grimshaw,

---

In implementation research studies, baseline measures of performance are also useful in that they provide an initial estimate of the magnitude of the problem. Low baseline performance may indicate that performance is poor and that there is much potential for improvement. High baseline performance may indicate, however, that there is little potential for improvement and that a trial may not be needed.

---

and Steen 2000.) See also http://www.abdn.ac.uk/hsru/epp/cluster.shtml (correct as of February 9, 2005) for further estimates of ICCs in implementation research and Ukoumunne et al. (1999) for ICCs relevant to health indices at different population levels. Assuming a type 1 error of .05, an ICC of .06, and power of 80 percent, using these data in our sample size calculation suggested that we would need to recruit fifty-seven patients per condition from sixty practices to detect a 10 percent difference in a dichotomous process of care measure (from 45 to 55 percent) and thirty-five patients from sixty practices to detect an effect size of .22 standard deviation in a continuous outcome of care measure.

The sample size calculation was easier for the NEXUS study as we planned to calculate the annual X-ray referral rate for each participating family practice. We had access to historical data from a single radiology department that suggested that 55 practices in each of two groups would give 80 percent power to detect a 15 percent difference in X-ray requests assuming a type 1 error of .05. In a factorial design with four groups, this gave a total sample size requirement of 220 practices. In the absence of any interaction effect, the estimate of the main effects would be based on a comparison of two groups of 110 practices. This would give 80 percent power to detect a difference of 11 percent in the number of X-rays requested.

In both studies, we anticipated that the sample size calculations would be conservative as they did not take into account the availability of baseline data (see below). However, they would be "liberal" in assuming no important interactions.

Collecting pretest data

Relatively few clusters are allocated to control and study groups in cluster trails in implementation research. As a result, there is increased danger of imbalance in baseline performance of study and control groups. By adopting a pre-post design, where baseline measurements are undertaken in addition to postintervention measurements, the imbalance due to adequacy of the allocation process can be examined (Shaddish, Cook, and Campbell 2002). Baseline performance may also be used as a stratifying or matching variable to ensure balance across the trial groups (Shaddish, Cook, and Campbell 2002). In addition, adjusting for baseline performance in the analysis stage can also increase statistical power if the premeasure is expected to be a good predictor of postperformance (Duffy, South, and Day 1992). In implementation research studies, baseline measures of performance are also useful in that they provide an initial estimate of the magnitude of the problem. Low baseline performance may indicate that performance is poor and that there is much potential for improvement. High baseline performance may indicate, however, that there is little potential for improvement and that a trial may not be needed.

In our case studies, we chose to collect baseline data to assess the adequacy of the randomization process and to adjust for baseline performance in the data analysis. The pretest data showed that despite randomizing a relatively large number of units in the NEXUS trial ($n = 242$), minor imbalances in baseline performance remained. There was an additional reason for including pretest data in the COGENT study (Eccles et al. 2000). The patients in the trial had chronic illnesses that may worsen with time. Therefore, patients would be expected to be more ill at the end of the study than they were at the start. To compensate as far as possible for this natural deterioration, the study evaluated change over two periods of twelve months before and after the intervention.

Other design issues

Schwartz and Lellouch (1967) made a distinction between explanatory and pragmatic studies. Explanatory studies aim to test whether an intervention is efficacious, that is, whether the intervention is beneficial under ideal conditions. Contextual factors (e.g., clinical expertise) and other effect modifiers are equalized between study groups. Typically, they are conducted in highly selected groups of subjects under highly controlled circumstances. Patients withdrawing from such a study may be excluded from analysis. The narrow inclusion criteria and rigid conduct of explanatory studies limit the generalizability of the results to other subjects and contexts.

In contrast, pragmatic studies aim to test whether an intervention is likely to be effective in routine practice by comparing the new procedure against the current regimen; as such, they are the most useful trial design for developing policy recommendations. Such studies attempt to approximate normal clinical conditions and do not attempt to equalize contextual factors and other effect modifiers in the intervention and study groups. In pragmatic studies, the contextual and effect-modifying factors therefore become part of the interventions. Such studies are usually conducted on a predefined study population and withdrawals are included within an "intention-to-treat" analysis; all subjects initially allocated to the intervention group would be analyzed as intervention subjects irrespective of whether they received the intervention. For example, in an evaluation of an educational seminar, some professionals may not be able to attend the intervention. In an intention-to-treat analysis, data from all professionals would be included in the analysis irrespective of whether they attended the seminar; as a result, the estimates of effect would more likely reflect the effectiveness of the intervention in real-world settings.

Ideally, within a pragmatic evaluation of a professional or organizational behavior change strategy, participants would only be aware of being invited to receive the intervention with all other aspects of the study being opaque to the participants. However, this is not always possible. In the COGENT study, we chose to include only practices that had medium to high computer usage. This required us to undertake a survey of the levels of computerization across our sampling frame prior to recruitment to identify eligible practices. Furthermore, we used the practice register and computerized prescribing systems to identify potentially eligible patients and asked practices to screen the resulting lists of patients to avoid approaching patients inappropriately (for example, approaching patients who had a terminal illness). In contrast, all primary endpoint data (number of X-rays requested) in the NEXUS study were abstracted from routine data sources (reporting software of the X-ray departments) independently of the participating family practices. Both studies were analyzed on an intention-to-treat basis.

Study Settings, Conditions, and Interventions

Implementation research aims to develop a generalizable evidence base to support the choice of professional and organizational behavior change strategies. It is likely that the effects of different interventions are moderated by many different factors including the study contexts (for example, primary or hospital care), types of participants (for example, family practitioners or nurses), study conditions, and characteristics of the targeted behaviors. Across the area of implementation research, it is important to ensure that these moderators are represented to allow exploration of their influence on the effectiveness of different interventions.

Study conditions

Our work has focused on areas where there is evidence of suboptimal professional performance when compared against a robust evidence base or strong professional consensus about what to do or not do. COGENT aimed to evaluate providing computerized guidelines for chronic disease. The conditions were chosen for both clinical and methodological reasons. The conditions (asthma in adults and angina) were chosen as chronic illnesses, predominantly cared for in primary care and important because of their associated morbidity and mortality. For both conditions, there was evidence of underuse of effective treatments (Neville et al. 1996; Griffiths et al. 1997; Woods et al. 1998). In addition, due to the 2×2 balanced incomplete block design, it was important to choose interventions whose management did not influence each other, that is, the management of patients with a control condition was not influenced by the introduction of the guidelines for a intervention condition. The clinical management of asthma and angina is discrete with no overlap in terms of actions performed. This would not be the case with conditions such as diabetes and angina. At the time of planning the study, there were no available evidence-based guidelines for asthma and angina, so we developed these (North of England Stable Angina Guidelines Development Group 1996; North of England Asthma Guidelines Development Group 1996).

In contrast, there were well-accepted guidelines for the referral of patients for radiological investigations within the United Kingdom (Royal College of Radiologists 1998). In the NEXUS study, we chose to focus on lumbar spine and knee X-rays. These are common referrals where X-rays are rarely informative unless patients have specific indications. Further lumbar spine X-rays have the potential for harm; each investigation involves a significant radiation dose.

Rationale for interventions

Choice of experimental interventions. Experimental interventions may be selected for a variety of reasons, including the judgment of the researcher based upon a formal or informal assessment of the barriers to adopting an evidence-based practice, empirical evidence about the effectiveness of the intervention under similar (or different) conditions, theoretical considerations, or a proposed change in policy.

The intervention in COGENT, computerized guidelines for management of chronic diseases, was chosen as an extension to a well-established acute prescribing computerized decision support (Purves 1998). Furthermore, there was substantial evidence that computerized decision support systems were effective for changing a wide range of behaviors, although these had not been well tested for complex chronic diseases (Hunt et al. 1998). The COGENT decision support system was integrated into the two leading electronic family practice management systems in the United Kingdom. The decision support system anticipated clinicians' requirements by using information contained in a patient's computerized record to trigger the guideline and present a patient scenario to the clinician (e.g., for asthma: review of stable patient, and acute exacerbation). Based on the scenario chosen, the system offered management suggestions informed by the content of the patient's record and requested the entry of relevant information, which was subsequently stored in the patient's record. Further information (to the level of the text of the full guideline) could be viewed or printed. Immediately prior to the intervention period, each practice was invited to send up to two practice members, physicians or other health care professionals, to a one-day training workshop where the system was demonstrated and they received training materials. Every clinician (doctor or practice nurse) in the study received a paper copy of the summary version of both guidelines, and each practice received one paper copy of the full version of both guidelines.

To minimize the intrusiveness of data collection, process of care data were collected from patients' clinical records once, at the end of the intervention period, for the twenty-four months from twelve months before to twelve months after the introduction of the computerized decisision support system.

The audit and feedback intervention of the NEXUS study was chosen because radiology departments were planning to provide this to family practices to encourage appropriate use of X-ray departments. Audit and feedback is a commonly promoted intervention within the U.K. National Health Service (National Institute for Clinical Excellence 2002), though the evidence about its effectiveness is variable (Thomson O'Brien et al. 2002a, 2002b). The feedback, prepared by the research team from routine data provided by the radiology departments, covered the preceding six-month period and was delivered on two occasions during the study. It provided practice-level information relating the number of lumbar spine and knee radiograph requests made by the whole practice relative to the number of requests made by all general practitioners in the study.

The choice of a 2×2 factorial design also gave us the opportunity to evaluate a further intervention. Educational prompts and reminders have been found to be effective for changing a number of different behaviors (Hunt et al. 1998). Ideally, these should be delivered within consultations at the time of a decision. However, retrospective prompts have also been found to be effective at influencing future decisions (Tierney, Hui, and McDonald 1986). Family practitioners request X-rays using written forms. While redesign of test-ordering forms have been found to be effective, it was not practical to redesign forms for each individual targeted test. We therefore chose to provide educational reminder messages on the report of every knee and lumbar spine X-ray ordered during the twelve-month intervention period. The messages were developed by a multidisciplinary consensus group (including family practitioners and radiologists) based upon the Royal College of Radiologists (1998) guidelines. These were short (less than thirty-word) messages that provided general guidance about appropriate use of the test. For example, the lumbar spine message stated, "In either acute (less than 6 weeks) or chronic back pain, without adverse features, x-ray is not routinely indicated." These messages were generated automatically by the reporting software in three radiology departments and manually by attaching colored stickers to the X-ray report in two departments. We also provided copies of the relevant Royal College of Radiologists guidelines to all practices.

Choice of control interventions. Experiments may include a no-intervention control or an intervention control. A no-intervention control will provide the best evidence about the likely counterfactual in the absence of the experimental intervention. However, this may not be informative if there is a well-established existing policy or intervention. In both of the case studies, we chose to provide the control practices with paper copies of the targeted guidelines. We reasoned that any experimental intervention would need to be more effective than this relatively cheap intervention that was common practice at the time of planning the studies. Available evidence at that time suggested that dissemination of printed educational materials was unlikely to lead to improvements in performance (Freemantle et al. 1996).

Ethical Issues

While ethical issues have been well elucidated in individual patient randomized trials of health care interventions, less attention has been paid to ethical issues arising in cluster randomized trials (Hutton 2002). In patient randomized trials, patients often consent to study participation and data collection when they are recruited into the trial. However, in implementation research, we often randomize professionals to educational interventions and collect data about the care of individual patients. At the time of recruitment, it is possible to seek professionals' consent but difficult to seek consent from all relevant patients who may come under the care of participating physicians during the course of the study. In our experience, it is helpful to distinguish between ethical consent for study participation (intervention allocation) and consent for data collection. Edwards and colleagues (1999) distinguished between *cluster-patient trials*, where the unit of allocation is the cluster but the level of intervention is the individual patient, and *cluster-cluster trials*, where the unit of allocation and intervention is the cluster. While individual patient consent for the intervention can be sought in cluster-patient trials, this is not the case for cluster-cluster trials. Implementation research trials tend to be cluster-cluster trials due to the contamination issues mentioned above. Under such circumstances, the health care organization or professional acts as the "guardian" for their patients choosing to participate in the trial if they think it is in the best interests of their patients. This would raise concerns if the intervention promoted care that was not necessarily in the best interests of all patients and participating physicians slavishly followed the intervention (for example, failing to order a lumbar spine X-ray if a physician considered that a patient may have a malignancy but the patient did not fulfill the criteria suggested in the guidelines). Under such circumstances, professionals' usual ethical responsibilities to do the best for their patients should override the effects of any interventions promoting care that the professional may consider harmful for an individual patient. It is important for researchers to make this explicit in the information sheet provided to prospective participants in any trial.

While it may not be possible to seek individual patient consent for study participation, it is possible to seek consent for nonanonymized data collection. Until relatively recently within the United Kingdom, confidential case note review by a researcher without patient consent was considered acceptable. More recent policies on confidentiality have emphasized the need for individual patient consent for case note review. The practical and scientific implications of this are as yet unclear. Baker and colleagues (2000) sought consent to collect data from patients' clinical records from 5,069 patients in 81 U.K. family practices. Approximately two-thirds of surveyed patients responded, and 9.8 percent of responders refused consent. They recommended that all future studies should seek such consent. However, Woolf et al. (2000) observed that patients consenting to case note review in a U.S. primary care setting varied systematically from patients who did not consent. Further seeking of individual patient consent will increase the cost and length of large-scale studies. Within the COGENT study, we planned to undertake case note review of patients with the two clinical conditions. In the patient survey, we highlighted this and sought patients' consent for the case note review. In the NEXUS study, we were using routine anonymized data for the primary outcome and did not therefore seek individual patient consent.

Data Collection Issues

What to measure

Commonly, researchers have measured performance by asking the professional involved what they have done or intend to do in a specific set of circumstances (for example, At what level of hypertension would you initiate pharmacological treatment?). However, there is empirical evidence that self-reports of activity tend to overestimate actual performance (Adams et al. 1999). It could be argued that in experimental studies of guideline implementation strategies, this would not be important if the professionals in the experimental and control groups inflated their estimate by the same degree. However, there is a danger that the intervention may sensitize the professionals in the experimental group about desired practice, potentially leading to an imbalance in the degree to which the experimental and control groups report their behavior. This could lead to an overestimate of the effect of the intervention: given these concerns, implementation researchers should measure actual performance and not rely on self-report. In both case studies, we collected data on actual physician performance.

Minimal intrusiveness of data collection

Researchers also need to be aware that the methods of data collection may sensitize professionals about desired practice. For example, de Dombal, Dallos, and McAdam (1991) observed that the introduction of structured collection of clinical data by professionals improved performance. If the data collection methods are intrusive, they may lead to improved performance in both the experimental and control groups, potentially leading to an underestimate of the effect of an intervention. Within the NEXUS study, data were abstracted from the reporting software systems in the participating radiology department. In COGENT, we needed to collect process of care data by case note review and electronic query of the family practices' computer systems. To minimize the intrusiveness of data collection, process of care data were collected from patients' clinical records once, at the end of the intervention period, for the twenty-four months from twelve months before to twelve months after the introduction of the computerized decision support system. Prescribing data were abstracted electronically from computerized clinical records. Trained data collectors, blinded to practice allocation, manually abstracted nonprescribing data from the patients' written and computerized records.

Analytical Issues

There are three general approaches to the analysis of cluster randomized trials: analysis at cluster level, the adjustment of standard tests, and advanced statistical techniques using data recorded at both the individual and cluster level (Donner 1998; Murray 1998). No consensus exists as to which approach should be used to analyze all cluster randomized trials. The most appropriate analysis option will depend on a number of factors, including the research question, the unit of inference, the study design, whether the researchers wish to adjust for other relevant variables at the individual or cluster level (covariates), the type and distribution of outcome measure, the number of clusters randomized, the size of cluster and variability of cluster size, and statistical resources available in the research team. Mollison et al. (2000) presented worked examples comparing these different analytical strategies.

In NEXUS, the number of requests per one thousand patients registered with the practice was determined for each practice, for each year (preintervention/postintervention). These repeated measures were then analyzed using the multilevel modeling package MLwiN (Goldstein et al. 1998) assuming that the rates were normally distributed. Variation between practices and variation between occasions were modeled as random effects. Treatment effects (audit and feedback, and reminder messages) were then included as fixed effects. To allow for rate estimates being more precise for larger practices, a weighted least squares procedure (with practice list size as the weight) was used to estimate the models.

In COGENT, each data set was analyzed in Stata using generalized linear modeling procedures appropriate for hierarchical data. Binary variables, data in the form of counts, and continuous outcome variables were analyzed using binary, Poisson, and normal error structures, respectively. Variation between practices and variation between patients (nested within practices) were modeled as random effects. The effect of decision support software was included as a fixed effect.

In both case studies, the primary analysis was by intention to treat. In COGENT, we also undertook an explanatory analysis of process of care data restricted to those patients who consulted following implementation of the computerized decision support system and for whom there was thus an opportunity for the intervention to influence their management.

Economic Evaluation

Professional and organizational behavior change interventions are not without costs, and it is increasingly being recognized that the effectiveness of a particular strategy must be balanced against the resource consequences. In some circumstances, it may even be more efficient to adopt a less costly but less effective strategy. The most informative evaluations to policy makers are, therefore, those that incorporate concurrent economic evaluations of the relative efficiency of different implementation strategies in addition to their relative effectiveness. Economic evaluation involves identifying, measuring, and valuing the resource consequences (including savings) associated with the development and implementation of an intervention. These can then be used to judge whether (1) costs are reduced overall and benefits increased, in which case a decision about the implementation inter-vention is straightforward; or (2) costs are increased but benefits have also increased, in which case a decision will have to be made if the benefits are worth the extra costs. While relatively little attention has been given to the development of eco-nomic evaluations alongside implementation trials, there are an increasing num-ber of papers highlighting issues to be considered (Mason, Wood, and Freemantle 1999; McIntosh 1999; Sculpher 2000), reporting estimates of economic intraclass correlations (Campbell, Mollison, and Grimshaw 2001), and providing a frame-work using worked examples for considering the cost-effectiveness of strategies (Mason et al. 2001).

Within both case studies, we included concurrent economic evaluations. The economic evaluation within COGENT took a health service perspective but also covered costs to patients and their families. Three types of cost data were collected. The costs of development and implementation were measured by questionnaires to, and interviews with, key participants in collaboration with finance departments of relevant organizations. Changes in the costs of care were measured by linking process of care data to unit cost data. Changes in costs to patients and their families were assessed by incorporating appropriate questions in the outcome and process data sets. We initially planned to undertake both cost-effectiveness and cost-utility analyses; however, these plans were abandoned given that the study failed to ob-serve any effects of the intervention.

A more limited economic evaluation analysis was undertaken in NEXUS. A cost analysis was conducted from the perspective of the radiology departments. This sought to determine the costs required to deliver the interventions, together with the costs associated with the delivery of X-rays before and after implementation. The limited scope of the economic evaluation reflected the limited resources avail-able to the project given the substantial task of conducting a broader-based analysis.

Process Evaluations

Randomized trials inform us about whether an intervention does more good than harm, but unless they are designed to do so, they provide little information about the likely causal mechanisms of interventions and modifying factors. Within our two case studies, we undertook process evaluations to explore further these issues. Within COGENT, the computerized system routinely generated a guide-line usage log that recorded when the guidelines were used and by whom. This demonstrated that one possible explanation for the observed lack of effect was the lack of usage of the computerized system by providers (Eccles, McColl, Steen, Rousseau, Grimshaw, Parkin, Purves, and Newton 2002). In addition, we under-took a nested longitudinal qualitative study in five family practices involving nine-teen semistructured interviews with thirteen respondents (Rousseau et al. 2003). This found that while respondents had generally positive attitudes about the potential of computerized decision support in family practice settings, they had found that the system tested was difficult to use within routine settings and rarely provided useful information when required. These process evaluations provide insights into why the intervention was unsuccessful.

Within the NEXUS trial, we were concerned that the effects of the educational reminder messages may decay over time. Data were abstracted from the routine reporting systems of the participating radiology departments making it possible to plot monthly X-ray requests following the introduction of the intervention. This demonstrated that the reduction in X-ray requests appeared within one to two months of the introduction of the intervention and that there was no evidence of a decay effect over the following twelve months (Ramsay et al. 2003). These two examples demonstrate that embedding process evaluations alongside randomized trials can enrich our understanding of the effects of interventions and modifying factors.

Reporting Issues

Commonly, evaluations of professional and organizational behavior change strategies are poorly reported with inadequate detail of methods used and of the intervention. In part, this is due to journal space requirements. One of our colleagues described how he had to argue with the editor of a prestigious medical journal to allow a paragraph-and-a-half description of key aspects of the intervention. We have also been requested to remove estimates of intraclass correlations from journal manuscripts despite the importance of these for interpretation of the presented studies and planning future studies. The need for clear reporting of randomized trials has been widely recognized. This has been highlighted through the publication of the Consolidated Standards of Reporting Trials (CONSORT) statement, an influential international consensus statement that outlines the common standards for the reporting of trials (Moher, Schultz, and Altman 2001). The introduction of the CONSORT statement has been instrumental in improving the standards of reporting in clinical trials (Moher, Jones, and Lepage 2001). It has been widely adopted by medical journals worldwide including both general and disease-specific journals. Elbourne and Campbell (2001) have proposed an extension to the CONSORT statement specifically for cluster randomized trials, which we used in reporting the COGENT trial (Eccles, McColl, Steen, Rousseau, Grimshaw, Parkin, and Purves 2002; Eccles, McColl, Steen, Rousseau, Grimshaw, Parkin, Purves, and Newton 2002). This extension has recently been updated (Campbell, Elbourne, and Altman 2004). We believe that this initiative should make journal editors and researchers more responsive to clear reporting of cluster randomized trials.

Conclusions

In this article, we have highlighted a number of methodological and practical issues faced during the design, conduct, and analysis of cluster randomized trials of professional and organizational behavior change interventions in health care settings. This is a relatively new area of health services research with distinct methodological challenges that have not yet been adequately elucidated.

Note

1. Commonly, these are place-based randomized trials; however, some cluster trials have randomized professionals or groups of professionals within the same organizational setting.

References

Adams, A. S., S. B. Soumerai, J. Lomas, and D. Ross-Degnan. 1999. Evidence of self-report bias in assessing adherence to guidelines. *International Journal of Quality in Health Care* 11:187-92.

Anonymous. 1992a. Medical audit in general practice. I: Effects on doctors' clinical behaviour for common childhood conditions. North of England Study of Standards and Performance in General Practice. *British Medical Journal* 304:1480-84.

———. 1992b. Medical audit in general practice. II: Effects on health of patients with common childhood conditions. North of England Study of Standards and Performance in General Practice. *British Medical Journal* 304:1484-88.

Antman, E. M., J. Lau, B. Kupelnick, F. Mosteller, and T. C. Chalmers. 1992. A comparison of results of meta-analyses of randomized control trials and recommendations of clinical experts: Treatments for myocardial infarction. *Journal of the American Medical Association* 268:240-48.

Baker, R., C. Shiels, K. Stevenson, R. Fraser, and M. Stone. 2000. What proportion of patients refuse consent to data collection from their records for research purposes? *British Journal of General Practice* 50:655-56.

Campbell, M. K., D. R. Elbourne, and D. G. Altman, for the CONSORT Group. 2004. The CONSORT statement: Extension to cluster randomized trials. *British Medical Journal* 328:702-8.

Campbell, M. K., J. M. Grimshaw, and I. N. Steen. 2000. Sample size calculations for cluster randomized trials. *Journal of Health Services and Policy Research* 5:12-16.

Campbell, M. K., J. A. Mollison, and J. M. Grimshaw. 2001. Cluster trials in implementation research: Estimation of intracluster correlation coefficients and sample size. *Statistics in Medicine* 20:391-99.

Chassin, M. 1998. Is health care ready for Six Sigma Quality? *Milbank Quarterly* 76:565-91.

Cochran, W. G., and G. M. Cox. 1957. *Experimental design*. New York: Wiley.

Cochrane, A. L. 1979. *Effectiveness and efficiency: Random reflections on health services*. London: Nuffield Provincial Hospitals Trust.

Cochrane Collaboration. 2002. *Cochrane controlled trials register*, 3rd ed., in *The Cochrane Library*, iss. 4. Oxford: Update Software.

de Dombal, F. T., V. Dallos, and W. A. McAdam. 1991. Can computer aided teaching packages improve clinical care in patients with acute abdominal pain? *British Medical Journal* 302:1495-97.

Diwan, V. K., B. Eriksson, G. Sterky, and G. Tomson. 1992. Randomization by group in studying the effect of drug information in primary care. *International Journal of Epidemiology* 21:124-30.

Donabedian, A. 1966. Evaluating the quality of medical care. *Milbank Memorial Fund Quarterly* 44:166-206.

Donner, A. 1998. Some aspects of the design and analysis of cluster randomization trials. *Applied Statistics* 47:95-113.

Donner, A., and N. Klar. 2000. *Design and analysis of cluster randomization trials in health research*. London: Arnold.

Duffy, S. W., M. C. South, and N. E. Day. 1992. Cluster randomization in large public health trials: The importance of antecedent data. *Statistics in Medicine* 11:307-16.

Eccles, M. P., J. M. Grimshaw, N. Steen, D. Parkin, I. Purves, E. McColl, and N. Rousseau. 2000. The design and analysis of a randomized controlled trial to evaluate computerised decision support: The COGENT Study. *Family Practice* 17:180-86.

Eccles, M., E. McColl, N. Steen, N. Rousseau, J. Grimshaw, D. Parkin, and I. Purves. 2002. A randomized controlled trial of computerized evidence based guidelines for angina and asthmas in UK primary care. *British Medical Journal* 325:941-44.

Eccles, M., E. McColl, N. Steen, N. Rousseau, J. Grimshaw, D. Parkin, I. Purves, and J. Newton. 2002. *An evaluation of computerised guidelines for the management of two chronic conditions*. Newcastle upon Tyne, UK: Centre for Health Services Research.

Eccles, M. P., I. N. Steen, J. M. Grimshaw, L. Thomas, P. McNamee, J. Souter, J. Wilsdon, L. Matowe, G. Needham, F. Gilbert, and S. Bond. 2001. Effect of audit and feedback, and reminder messages on primary-care referrals: A randomized trial. *Lancet* 357:1406-9.

Edwards, S. L., D. A. Braunholtz, R. J. Lilford, and A. S. Stevens. 1999. Ethical issues in the design and conduct of cluster randomized controlled trials. *British Medical Journal* 318:1407-9.

Elbourne, D., and M. K. Campbell. 2001. Extending the CONSORT statement to cluster randomized trials: For discussion. *Statistics in Medicine* 20:489-96.

European Secondary Prevention Study Group. 1996. Translation of clinical trials into practice: A European population-based study of the use of thrombolysis for acute myocardial infraction. *Lancet* 347:1203-7.

Flynn, T. N., E. Whitley, and T. J. Peters. 2002. Recruitment strategies in a cluster randomized trial—Cost implications. *Statistics in Medicine* 21:397-405.

Foy, R., M. P. Eccles, and J. M. Grimshaw. 2001. Why does primary care need more implementation research? *Family Practice* 18:353-55.

Freemantle, N., E. L. Harvey, F. Wolf, J. M. Grimshaw, R. Grilli, and L. A. Bero. 1996. Printed educational materials to improve the behaviour of health care professionals and patient outcome (Cochrane Review). In *The Cochrane Library*, iss. 4. Oxford: Update Software.

Goldstein, G., J. Rasbash, I. Plewis, et al. 1998. *A user's guide to MLwiN: Multilevel Models Project (version 1.0)*. London: Institute of Education, University of London.

Griffiths, C., P. Sturdy, J. Naish, R. Omar, S. Dolan, and G. Feder. 1997. Hospital admissions for asthma in east London: Associations with characteristics of local general practices, prescribing, and population. *British Medical Journal* 314:482-86.

Grimshaw, J. M., M. K. Campbell, M. P. Eccles, and I. N. Steen. 2000. Experimental and quasi-experimental designs for evaluating guideline implementation strategies. *Family Practice* 17:S11-S18.

Grimshaw, J. M., J. Ward, and M. P. Eccles. 2001. Getting research into practice. In *Oxford handbook of public health*, ed. D. Pencheon, J. A. Muir Gray, C. Guest, and D. Melzer. Oxford: Oxford University Press.

Grol, R. 1997. Beliefs and evidence in changing clinical practice. *British Medical Journal* 315:18-21.

Hunt, D. L., R. B. Haynes, S. E. Hanna, and K. Smith. 1998. Effects of computer-based clinical decision support systems on physician performance and patient outcomes. *Journal of the American Medical Association* 280:1339-46.

Hutton, J. L. 2002. Are distinctive ethical principles required for cluster randomized trials? *Statistics in Medicine* 20:473-88.

ISIS-2 (Second International Study of Infarct Survival) Collaborative Group. 1988. Randomized trial of intravenous streptokinase, oral aspirin, both or neither among 17,187 cases of suspected acute myocardial infarction: ISIS-2. *Journal of the American Medical Association* 268:240-48.

Mason, J., N. Freemantle, I. Nazareth, M. Eccles, A. Haines, and M. Drummond. 2001. When is it cost effective to change the behaviour of health professionals? *Journal of the American Medical Association* 286:2988-92.

Mason, J., J. Wood, and N. Freemantle. 1999. Designing evaluations of interventions to change professional practice. *Journal of Health Services Research and Policy* 4:106-11.

McIntosh, E. 1999. Economic evaluation of guideline implementation studies. In *Changing professional practice: Theory and practice of clinical guidelines implementation*, ed. M. Makela and T. Thorsen. Copenhagen, Denmark: Danish Institute for Health Services Research and Development.

McLaughlin, T. J., S. B. Soumerai, D. J. Willison, J. H. Gurwitz, C. Borbas, E. Guadagnoli, B. McLaughlin, N. Morris, S. C. Cheng, P. J. Hauptman, E. Antman, L. Casey, R. Asinger, and F. Gobel. 1996. Adherence to national guidelines for drug treatment of suspected acute myocardial infarction: Evidence for undertreatment in women and the elderly. *Archives of Internal Medicine* 156:799-805.

Moher, D., A. Jones, and L. Lepage, for the CONSORT Group. 2001. Use of CONSORT statement and quality of reports of randomized trials: A comparative before-and-after evaluation. *Journal of the American Medical Association* 285:1992-95.

Moher, D., K. Schultz, and D. G. Altman, for the CONSORT Group. 2001. The CONSORT statement: Revised recommendation for improving the quality of reports of parallel-group randomized trials. *Lancet* 357:1191-94.

Mollison, J. A., J. A. Simpson, M. K. Campbell, and J. M. Grimshaw. 2000. Comparison of analytical methods for cluster randomized trials: An example from a primary care setting, *Journal of Epidemiology and Biostatistics* 5:339-46.

Morgan, M., D. R. Studney, G. O. Barnett, and R. N. Winickoff. 1978. Computerized concurrent review of prenatal care. *Quality Review Bulletin* 4:33-36.

Murray, D. M. 1998. *The design and analysis of group randomized trials*. Oxford: Oxford University Press.

National Institute for Clinical Excellence. 2002. *Principles for best practice in clinical audit*. Oxford, UK: Radcliffe Medical Press.

Neville, R. G., G. Hoskins, B. Smith, and R. A. Clark. 1996. Observations on the structure, process and clinical outcomes of asthma care in general practice. *British Journal of General Practice* 46:583-87.

North of England Asthma Guidelines Development Group. 1996. North of England evidence based guidelines development project: Summary version of evidence based guideline for the primary care management of asthma in adults. *British Medical Journal* 312:762-66.

North of England Stable Angina Guidelines Development Group. 1996. Evidence based guideline for the primary care management of stable angina: Summary version. *British Medical Journal* 312:827-32.

Oxman, A. D., M. A. Thomson, D. A. Davis, and R. B. Haynes. 1995. No magic bullets: A systematic review of 102 trials of interventions to improve professional practice. *Canadian Medical Association Journal* 153:1423-31.

Pocock, S. J. 1983. *Clinical trials: A practical approach*. New York: Wiley.

Purves, I. N. 1998. PRODIGY: Implementing clinical guidance using computers. *British Journal of General Practice* 48:1552-53.

Ramsay, C., M. Eccles, J. Grimshaw, and N. Steen. 2003. Assessing the long term effect of educational reminder messages on primary care radiology referrals. *Clinical Radiology* 58:319-21.

Rousseau, N. R., E. McColl, J. Newton, J. Grimshaw, and M. Eccles. 2003. A qualitative study of computerised evidence based guidelines for angina and asthma in primary care. *British Medical Journal* 326:1-8.

Royal College of Radiologists. 1998. *Making the best use of a department of clinical radiology: Guidelines for doctors*. 4th ed. London: Royal College of Radiologists.

Schwartz, D., and J. Lellouch. 1967. Explanatory and pragmatic attitudes in clinical trials. *Journal of Chronic Diseases* 20:637-48.

Sculpher, M. 2000. Evaluating the cost-effectiveness of interventions designed to increase the utilisation of evidence-based guidelines. *Family Practice* 17:S26-S31.

Shaddish, W. R., D. T. Cook, and D. T. Campbell. 2002. *Experimental and quasi experimental designs for generalized causal inference*. Boston: Houghton Mifflin.

Thomson O'Brien, M. A., A. D. Oxman, D. A. Davis, R. B. Haynes, N. Freemantle, and E. L. Harvey. 2002a. Audit and feedback: Effects on professional practice and health care outcomes (Cochrane Review). In *The Cochrane Library*, iss. 3. Oxford: Update Software.

———. 2002b. Audit and feedback versus alternative strategies: Effects on professional practice and health care outcomes (Cochrane Review). In *The Cochrane Library*, iss. 3. Oxford: Update Software.

Tierney, W. M., S. L. Hui, and C. J. McDonald. 1986. Delayed feedback of physician performance versus immediate reminders to perform preventive care. Effects on physician compliance. *Medical Care* 24:659-66.

Ukoumunne, O. C., M. C. Gulliford, S. Chinn, J. A. C. Sterne, and P. G. J. Burney. 1999. Methods for evaluating area-wide and organisation based interventions in health and health care: A systematic review. *Health Technology Assessment* 3:iii-92.

Woods, K. L., D. Ketley, A. Lowy, A. Agusti, C. Hagn, R. Kala, N. B. Karatzas, A. Leizorowicz, A. Reikvam, J. Schilling, R. Seabra-Gomes, D. Vasiliauskas, and L. Wilhelmsen. 1998. Beta-blockers and antithrombotic treatment for secondary prevention after acute myocardial infarction. *European Heart Journal* 19:74-79.

Woolf, S. H., S. F. Rothemich, R. E. Johnson, and D. W. Marsland. 2000. Selection bias from requiring patients to give consent to examine data for health services research. *Archives of Family Medicine* 9:1111-18.

Cluster Randomized Trials for the Evaluation of Strategies Designed to Promote Evidence-Based Practice in Perinatal and Neonatal Medicine

By
LAURA C. LEVITON
and
JEFFREY D. HORBAR

This article makes a case for cluster-randomized trials to encourage evidence-based practice in medical care. The case rests on theoretical, empirical, and methodological grounds. To illustrate, we describe two recent studies. The first trial, with participation by 27 tertiary care hospitals, concerned methods to encourage a relatively simple, low-cost therapy for women in premature labor. A significant effect was seen in intervention hospitals on the primary outcome variable: increase in the proportion of eligible patients receiving antenatal corticosteroid therapy. The second trial, with participation by 114 neonatal intensive care units, aimed to close the gap between evidence and practice in the use of early and prophylactic surfactant therapy for premature infants. It achieved one of the largest effects seen in the literature on changing medical care practices. Using the two illustrations, the authors discuss some of the theoretical, methodological, and practical issues when using cluster randomized designs in this field of inquiry.

Keywords: cluster randomized trials; evidence-based practice; antenatal; neonatal; therapeutic interventions; multilevel analysis

Scientific knowledge about the best medical care is not routinely or consistently applied in daily practice (Institute of Medicine 2001). Despite a large and growing body of evidence, the overuse, underuse, and misuse of therapeutic interventions are commonplace, resulting in dramatic variations in both practice and out-

NOTE: Originally prepared for the Campbell Collaboration Conference on Place-Based Randomized Trials Sponsored by the Rockefeller Foundation, November 11-15, 2002, in Bellagio, Italy. The article presents two studies supported by the United States Agency for Healthcare Research and Quality (AHRQ): *Dissemination Study of Practice Guidelines on Antenatal Corticosteroid Administration*, AHCPR/DHHS 282-92-0055; and *Evidence-Based Surfactant Therapy for Preterm Infants*, AHCPR/DHHS R01HS10528. The authors would like to acknowledge the contributions of our coinvestigators on these studies, including (for the corticosteroid study) Drs. Goldenberg, Freda, Fish, Baker, Cliver, Rouse, Chazotte, Merkatz, and Raczynski; and (for the surfactant study) Drs. Carpenter, Buzas, Soll, Suresh, Bracken, Plsek, and Sinclair.

DOI: 10.1177/0002716205274742

comes among providers (Institute of Medicine 2001). New strategies designed to promote evidence-based practice must therefore be identified, tested, and implemented.

A valuable tool for testing these strategies is the cluster randomized trial, medicine's term for the place-based randomized experiment (Donner and Klar 2000). Hospitals, long-term care settings, group practices, health insurance plans, and health care markets all offer potential as the unit of assignment and intervention. Yet cluster random assignment and multilevel analysis are still relatively uncommon in studies of intervention to increase uptake of evidence-based practices in medicine (Loeb 2002). To illustrate its value, we will discuss two cluster randomized trials testing strategies to change medical practices for preterm infants. We highlight some issues that arose during the conduct of the studies that are most pertinent to the use of cluster randomized designs.

Gaps between evidence and practice in the care of premature infants

The two illustrative studies concern an intervention to increase antenatal corticosteroid therapy for women in preterm labor (Leviton et al. 1995, 1999) and an intervention to increase early and prophylactic (preventive) use of surfactant in preterm infants (Horbar et al. 2004a, 2004b). Both of these studies identified a gap between prevalent practices and evidence-based medicine. Both used multifaceted intervention strategies to increase the uptake of evidence-based practice.

Preterm infants have a high risk of disease, death, and long-term disabilities such as brain damage.[1] There has been a great deal of progress in the effective treatment of these babies. In particular, systematic reviews indicate that both corticosteroid therapy and early surfactant therapy reduce infant disability, disease, and death (summarized in our primary papers: Horbar et al. 2004a, 2004b; Leviton et al. 1999). Perinatal-neonatal medicine has a strong track record of

Laura C. Leviton, Ph.D., is a senior program officer of the Robert Wood Johnson Foundation (RWJF). She has overseen evaluations in most of the areas of focus for the foundation, and now works primarily on foundation initiatives in preventing childhood obesity and in serving vulnerable populations. Before joining RWJF in July 1999, she was a professor of public health at the University of Alabama at Birmingham and, before that, on the faculty of the University of Pittsburgh School of Public Health. She is a leading writer on evaluation methods and practice, in particular for disease prevention. She received the 1993 award from the American Psychological Association for Distinguished Contributions to Psychology in the Public Interest.

Jeffrey D. Horbar, MD, is a board-certified neonatologist and clinical scientist with extensive experience in clinical research and its application to the improvement of neonatal care. He is currently a professor of pediatrics at the University of Vermont, College of Medicine; chief executive and scientific officer of the Vermont Oxford Network; consulting editor for Pediatrics electronic pages; and coeditor of the Neonatal Review Group of the Cochrane Collaboration. He has been responsible for the Oxford Network Database, which is used by more than four hundred neonatal intensive care units around the world to monitor and improve outcomes for very low birth weight infants.

patient-level randomized trials and an early and continuing interest in systematic overviews of the evidence through the Cochrane Collaboration (Chalmers, Enkin, and Keirse 1989; National Perinatal Epidemiology Unit 1985; Sinclair et al. 1997). In spite of this record, and perhaps because the evidence is evolving so quickly, it is a continuing challenge to speed the uptake of evidence-based practice for preterm infants.

The problem of medical practice improvement

The two cluster randomized trials borrowed from the literature on "what works" in practice improvement. It is a major challenge to alter medical care practice to be consistent with the evidence (Agency for Health Care Policy and Research [AHCPR] 1992; Institute of Medicine 2001). There are many likely causes for the gap between evidence and practice. Most obvious is that evidence continues to develop while practice changes less rapidly. To make practitioners aware of changes in the evidence, information is shared through print, electronic, and organizational strategies (Institute of Medicine 2001). However, with the exception of drug companies' information, these strategies do not change practices very much (Mittman, Tonesk, and Jacobson 1992). Purely didactic presentations, such as continuing medical education, achieve only small effects (Thomson O'Brien, Freemantle, et al. 2002).

Organizational interventions offer more promise. For example, decision and administrative supports enable the physician to change practice (Bodenheimer, Wagner, and Grumbach 2002). An example of such supports might be hiring staff to counsel patients on self-management of chronic illness. Another such support is the presence of a reminder in the medical chart, which provides a cue to action and can increase the use of therapies or other practices as much as five-hundred-fold (Burns et al. 1993).

Several strategies mix influences on the individual practitioner and the practice group or organization. For example, local opinion leaders help to diffuse medical innovations; therefore, efforts to introduce evidence-based practices have identified such local leaders and recruited them to champion a new practice. However, tests of this strategy reveal mixed effects (Thomson O'Brien, Oxman, et al. 2002). Another example is performance feedback (at both individual provider and group levels), which increases attention to a practice and facilitates comparisons among individual practices, group practices, and evolving standards of care (Soumerai et al. 1998).

A promising development in translating evidence into practice is the rapid cycle collaborative improvement process (Berwick, Godfrey, and Roessner 1991). Quality improvement teams first identify an overall measurable aim, then develop a measurement plan. Then teams develop a list of potential change ideas. The method relies on trial and learning cycles (Plan, Do, Study, Act) that introduce and test relatively small changes. If successful, the small changes are instituted and a new cycle begins. Featured in the process are multidisciplinary teams within practice settings and meetings to facilitate collaboration across settings (Plsek 1997).

Our study of early and preventive surfactant therapy is among the first randomized experiments testing this strategy.

The multifaceted interventions tested in our two illustrative studies borrowed from these techniques. However, we did not merely combine them in a "kitchen sink" approach. Instead we sequenced them, in line with an underlying theory of the adoption of medical innovations described in the final section.

The Antenatal Corticosteroid Trial

Details of the study's rationale, methods, and results can be found in the primary research papers (Leviton et al. 1995, 1999). In overview, the design was a two-arm, randomized controlled trial with hospitals as the unit of assignment. Patient-level data were collected from the medical charts: the primary outcome measure was the proportion of patients receiving corticosteroid therapy prior to delivery. Patient-level data were collected from medical records for the twelve-month period before implementation started and for the twelve-month period after start-up of implementation (and corresponding period for control hospitals).

Context and opportunity

The aim of this trial was to test an intervention to encourage obstetricians and maternal-fetal medicine specialists to adopt a practice guideline. The practice guideline, based on a Consensus Conference of the National Institutes of Health, recommended the use of antenatal corticosteroid therapy when women went into labor prematurely. The therapy is cheap, effective, and safe for use with eligible women.[2] Although strong evidence of effectiveness dated from the early 1970s, by the 1990s obstetricians were only using the therapy in 26 percent of eligible cases, from available data (Bronstein and Goldenberg 1995).

We chose this therapy for study because of its simplicity, trialability, and observability (Rogers 1995). To craft a more powerful intervention, we conducted focus groups with obstetricians in four cities and interviewed eight leading maternal-fetal medicine specialists and eight leading neonatologists (Leviton et al. 1995). We shared our insights about the forces at work with the Consensus Conference, which used them to craft a strong and simple recommendation. Because the Consensus Conference released its findings at the beginning of our study intervention year, the study became a test of dissemination strategies. The usual dissemination methods, such as word of mouth, journal articles, and professional meetings, would be contrasted with a more active effort to encourage adoption of the therapy. In essence, the hypothesis was that active dissemination would lead to uptake of the evidence-based practice more quickly than would usual dissemination.

The American College of Obstetricians and Gynecologists published its endorsement of the Consensus Conference recommendations. Change takes place more quickly when professional societies endorse a practice guideline (Mittman, Tonesk, and Jacobson 1992). For obstetricians, who are highly vulnerable to medical malpractice lawsuits, such endorsement is important because it represents a change in the accepted standard of care.

In summary, the conditions existed for the corticosteroid guideline to be adopted fairly rapidly. First, the therapy itself is simple; second, the message was simple; and obstetricians could not afford to ignore an endorsement by their professional society. At the same time, this set of conditions clearly impaired the chances that the cluster randomized trial would find a significant difference between the active dissemination and usual dissemination hospitals. On balance, however, our decision to facilitate an effective Consensus Conference recommendation was clearly the right and ethical one.

Active dissemination intervention

Treatment hospitals were exposed to an active, low-cost dissemination effort designed to increase the effects of the Consensus Conference practice guideline. The components included (1) designation of a lead physician and nurse coordinator at each hospital; (2) grand rounds by an eminent clinician associated with the study; (3) group discussion of hypothetical cases indicating the range of conditions for which the therapy might be considered; (4) chart reminders and inserts on the practice guideline in the medical record; and (5) performance feedback at the hospital level, concerning extent of implementation, extent to which therapy was used in eligible cases, and median time to administration of the therapy.

Design and sampling choices

We anticipated conducting hierarchical logistic regression on the principal outcome variable, the proportion of patients who received the therapy (Goldstein 1995). We were conscious that there were four potential levels of analysis: patients as units were nested within the physicians who cared for them; physicians were nested within hospitals where women delivered their babies, which were nested within localities and regions. We chose only the patient and hospital levels for data collection and analysis. *Patients* receive treatment, in part, based on their characteristics. Physician behavior could be expected to vary in response to patient characteristics, and patient-level data were easily gathered from the medical record and other sources. *Physicians* would be the primary targets for educational intervention, but getting an adequate response rate from physicians is notoriously difficult. In contrast, the patient-level information in the medical record was a by-product reflecting physician behavior. Also, physicians vary greatly in terms of the number of high-risk pregnancies they treat. In many tertiary care centers, the large majority are seen by relatively few perinatologists, making for very peculiar distributions of cases across institutions. Most important, some institutions would participate in the study only on the condition that individual physicians would not be studied.

To detect change sensitively, we restricted the settings we sampled to *tertiary care centers*. These centers had most of the eligible cases and would likely be the first to adopt the practice guideline. These centers often reflect the forces at work in local practitioner networks and health care markets since they get referrals of high-risk pregnancies from the surrounding area. Moreover, tertiary care centers are often the easiest health care settings to study. They more often participate in research and would be amenable to random assignment. However, the choice of the tertiary care hospitals also limits external validity, that is, the ability to generalize the results to other settings and populations.

Data collection was relatively unobtrusive, because we abstracted medical records after the study period ended.

To ensure adequate statistical power, we required at least twenty hospitals, and to gain their cooperation we worked with two existing research networks. Nineteen institutions were members of the National Perinatal Information Center (NPIC), while an additional eight were hospitals affiliated with the Albert Einstein College of Medicine (AECOM). In all, thirty hospitals were invited to participate; twenty-eight agreed to do so, and one hospital dropped out before intervention began. We aimed to sample 150 patients from each hospital at baseline and again in the post-conference year.

Sampling was complicated by several changes in health care referral patterns and hospital census from the baseline to the postconference year. These issues do not appear to have introduced any serious selection bias, as described in Results, below. However, to maintain the sampling plan, it became necessary in some hospitals to collect information on the entire population of preterm births, while in others, the actual sample was increased to make up the difference and achieve the planned number of total cases.

Data collection and analysis

Data collection was relatively unobtrusive, because we abstracted medical records after the study period ended. NPIC and AECOM supervised and maintained quality control of the abstracting process at their member institutions. To identify the eligible cases, abstractors relied initially on the logs kept by hospital labor and delivery units. Then, records were inspected and ineligible cases were discarded. This strategy introduced a potential difficulty because the percentage of records we retained as eligible differed between NPIC hospitals (94.2 percent) and AECOM hospitals (74.5 percent), and the range was from 0 to 52.6 percent. There were serious problems with the quality of three labor and delivery logs, all at hospitals in New York City. At these hospitals, many cases appeared eligible on labor and delivery logs but were ineligible according to the medical records. In these hospitals, between 8 and 13 percent of the medical records could not be found; two had been randomized to usual dissemination and one to active dissemination.

Fortunately, AECOM and NPIC hospitals were generally comparable, and the data collection issues did not appear to affect results. However, this issue does point to a potential challenge when cluster randomized trials depend on data being generated by the organizations themselves. We will pursue this point in the final section because our second study provides an interesting contrast.

The primary analysis was based on a two-level logistic regression model, with patients as the units of analysis at level one, and hospitals at level two. Patient-level variables included in the study are as follows: administration of steroid before delivery (the dependent variable); study year (baseline or postconference); diagnosis of preterm; premature rupture of membranes (PROM, an important patient characteristic in obstetrics); and gestational age (GA) of twenty-four to twenty-eight weeks, and GA of twenty-nine to thirty-two weeks, both contrasted with GA of thirty-three to thirty-four weeks. The hospital-level variable is study condition, usual or active dissemination.

Results

To summarize, the two-level logistic regression revealed a significant effect of study year ($p < .01$). Controlling for other variables in the model, the odds of corticosteroid use after the consensus conference (compared with baseline) is 3.16. Thus, although Consensus Conferences rarely have much effect, this one produced a powerful effect, probably due to its simple message, tailored to obstetricians' concerns, and to the endorsement of their professional association. With active dissemination, the odds of administering corticosteroids during the postconference year was 1.63 ($p < .01$). Thus, the intervention gave a statistically significant "boost" to the effect of the postconference study year, increasing use of the therapy more than one-third again as much as in the control hospitals. (Significant effects of patient-level characteristics on use of the therapy did not interact with treatment and are not reported here.)

Two other issues are relevant to the challenges of cluster randomized designs. First, in the postconference year, the participating hospitals saw changes in their case mix, which had potential to bias the results. Based on hospital census information (not on the sample we obtained from the hospitals), treatment hospitals had a significantly larger proportion of the lowest GA cases in the postconference year. Three of the control hospitals reduced their proportion of such cases, and one treatment hospital increased its proportion of these cases. Furthermore, all hospitals saw an increase in PROM cases, but the increase was greater in treatment than in control hospitals. To determine whether these changes biased our results, we undertook two analyses. First, we established that corticosteroid use due to being in the treatment condition was not significantly associated with use due to either PROM or GA. If case mix had affected the test of the dissemination treatment, we would have seen such an association. Second, we also analyzed the data separately by various levels of GA and presence/absence of PROM and obtained the same results as the overall study.

The second issue presents a puzzle, more than a challenge. Hospitals varied greatly in their baseline rate of corticosteroid use, consistent with prior findings. Hospitals also showed extreme and statistically significant variation in their *changes* in corticosteroid use. This variation is not explained by the treatment or by patient-level characteristics. Across the hospitals, the absolute increase in the rate of corticosteroid use ranged from 5 to 62 percent. Moreover, baseline level appeared to be unrelated to the amount of increase: for example, some hospitals began with fairly high use of the therapy and showed marked increases, while other hospitals began with fairly high use and changed hardly at all. Finally, the hospitals changed their use of the therapy in response to individual patient characteristics, in markedly different ways. The sources of this variation remain a mystery. Based on qualitative data collection and content analysis, we have conducted some exploratory work to understand patterns. To date, however, this has not been informative.

Some implications of the corticosteroid study

Previous studies had indicated how difficult it was to change physicians' practices in line with research evidence. The study results were useful to demonstrate some conditions under which marginal increases in uptake of evidence-based practice could be achieved for relatively low cost. However, it is clear that the operative word is "marginal." In addition to the Consensus Conference and professional association endorsement, other forces were already producing uptake of the therapy by the time of our intervention in spring 1995. Figure 1 illustrates how the percentage of cases receiving therapy increased in the Vermont Oxford Network hospitals (which may be early adopters compared to others). Given the "sea change" in use of the therapy, as well as the strong effect of the Consensus Conference, it is a wonder that an effect of active dissemination emerged at all. Yet such changes take time to become institutionalized. The intervention speeded these changes, getting many more babies treated and likely preventing disability and death.

During our planning for the surfactant study, we used the experience of the corticosteroid study in several ways. It confirmed the choice of a cluster randomized trial and provided some assurance that direct study of the practitioner level was unnecessary. Inferences could be made from the patient-level data. It confirmed the usefulness of a multifaceted approach informed by an underlying theory of medical practice adoption. The value of focus groups was also made clear: to understand practitioners' beliefs and practice patterns. Four were conducted to inform the multifaceted strategy of our second study.

FIGURE 1
ANTENATAL STEROIDS 1991 TO 2001

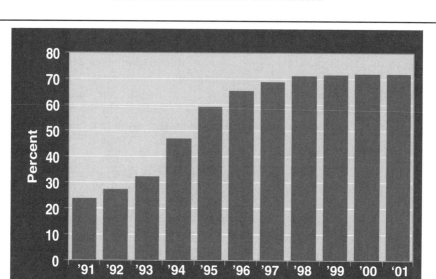

SOURCE: Vermont Oxford Network 175,000 very low birthweight infants at more than four hundred hospitals. Figure courtesy of the Vermont Oxford Network, Burlington.

A Trial of Evidence-Based Surfactant Therapy

Details of the study's rationale, methods, and results can be found in the primary research papers (Horbar et al. 2004a, 2004b). In overview, the design was a two-armed randomized controlled trial with neonatal intensive care units as the unit of assignment. The primary outcome measures were the proportion of infants in each hospital receiving surfactant in the delivery room, the proportion of infants receiving surfactant more than two hours after delivery, hospitals' median time from delivery until administration of surfactant, proportion of infants dying before discharge, and pneumothorax (leakage of air into the chest cavity). Patient-level data were abstracted by the participating hospitals and forwarded to the investigators for a twelve-month baseline period and a twelve-month intervention year.

Context and opportunity

The aim of this trial was to evaluate a coordinated, multifaceted intervention designed to close a gap between research and practice in the use of early surfactant therapy for preterm infants. The intervention aimed to promote the translation of research into practice, a translation that must occur at both the individual physician level (consideration of the evidence and gap in practice) and the institution level (through a shared standard of care, agreed-upon goals, and changes in the processes of care).

The intervention speeded these changes, getting many more babies treated and likely preventing disability and death.

Introduced in the early 1990s, surfactant is a highly effective therapy to prevent disease and death from Respiratory Distress Syndrome (RDS).[3] From meta-analysis, we concluded that surfactant is most effective when it is delivered early, before symptoms of RDS develop. Early surfactant therapy is given in the delivery room to infants at high risk for developing RDS, usually within ten to fifteen minutes of birth. However, analysis of Vermont Oxford Network data from 1998 demonstrated a significant gap between the practices supported by research and those in routine use for high-risk infants (Horbar et al. 2004b). Of the infants treated with surfactant, only 19 percent received the first dose within fifteen minutes of birth, and 27 percent received their first dose more than two hours after birth. Relatively few infants received delivery room treatment, yet 79 percent of them were intubated in the delivery room and 90 percent ultimately received surfactant.

A public-private consortium conducted the study, formed by the University of Vermont and the Vermont Oxford Network. The network is a private nonprofit corporation dedicated to improving the effectiveness and efficiency of medical care for newborn infants and their families through a coordinated program of randomized trials, outcomes research, education, and quality improvement projects. The network is supported by membership fees, grants, and contracts. The basic philosophy of the network is to integrate research into daily practice by designing simple, pragmatic studies that are compatible with the demands of busy health professionals and relevant to questions that arise in daily practice. Member institutions are located in several countries, with the majority located in the United States. Member hospitals had participated in patient-level randomized trials, observational research, and quality improvement efforts through the network in the past. For many reasons, therefore, the institutional members were receptive to the activities and guidance of the network.

This receptivity was helpful to plan the management of the trial as it surely influenced the successful accrual of hospitals and the credibility of the intervention to participants. Of the 300 member hospitals in North America in 2000, 178 were eligible for the trial and 114 participated—this indicates substantial advantages of working with an existing research and quality improvement network.

Member hospitals were also accustomed to providing patient-level data to the network. The network maintains a database including information on preterm infants and very-low-birthweight infants, born at member institutions or admitted to them within twenty-eight days of birth. Member institutions submit information to the network on standardized paper data forms using uniform definitions included in the Manual of Operations. No personal patient identifiers are included. Upon receipt of the data forms, items are submitted to a series of range, logic, and consistency checks using customized software developed by the network. Forms with errors are returned for correction. Because data collection and management were already routinized, the study's cost of data collection was greatly reduced, and reasonable quality was assured. The accuracy and reliability of the database have been documented (Horbar and Leahy 1995).

The intervention

The intervention included three components, sequenced carefully. First, hospitals in the intervention group received confidential, individualized feedback on their surfactant use. The reports included both site-specific practice information and peer comparisons related to the timing of surfactant treatment. Following the workshop, hospitals in the intervention group received quarterly feedback reports. None of these reports were available to hospitals in the control group. We asked the staff selected for workshop participation to share this information with their colleagues at the hospital and discuss it prior to the meeting. The confidential reports included data on the proportion of infants who received surfactant, the proportion who received the first dose within fifteen minutes of birth, the proportion who received the first dose more than two hours after birth, and the proportion intubated in the delivery room. Data were provided for the individual center as compared to all 335 network centers participating in the database for 1998 and 1999.

Second, we generated a review of the evidence on early surfactant therapy. We paid for two participants per hospital in the intervention group to attend a two-day workshop. We first presented the evidence review on early surfactant, and then facilitated their discussion about the gap between evidence and practice at their hospitals. Unlike the corticosteroid study, we chose not to present a specific guideline or one "best practice" for surfactant therapy. Based on our literature review and focus group experience, we chose to assist practitioners to understand and critically evaluate the primary evidence on which surfactant treatment decisions are based and to allow them to review their own practices in light of the evidence.

Third, the workshop focused on evidence-based quality improvement. The workshop, as well as follow-on work, utilized the rapid cycle collaborative improvement approach. The workshop applied four key habits for clinical improvement to the problem of early surfactant therapy. These key habits are integrated into all clinical practice improvements of the Vermont Oxford Network: change, evidence-based practice, practice as process, and collaborative learning (Horbar

1999; Plsek 1997). Following the workshop, collaboration among participants in the intervention group was fostered through a series of quarterly conference calls and a dedicated e-mail listserv.

Study design, methods, and analysis

Sample size calculations require an estimate of outcome variability. We were able to use the Vermont Oxford Network Database to obtain realistic and reliable estimates of outcome variability. Based on the 1998 Vermont Oxford Network Database, the average proportion of infants receiving delivery room surfactant at hospitals eligible for the trial was 16.4 percent where the proportion is computed by averaging across hospitals. The minimum clinically meaningful increase we were interested in detecting was 20 percent (from 16.4 to 36.4 percent). The interhospital standard deviation of proportion of delivery room surfactant administration, estimated from the 1998 database, was .21. Lee and Dubin (1994) described a method for computing sample size for clustered binary data that was applicable to our situation. Using their method with our estimated standard deviation, we calculated that twenty-four hospitals were needed in each treatment arm to achieve 90 percent power for detecting a 20 percent increase in delivery room surfactant for a two-sided, level .05 test. With fifty-five hospitals per treatment arm, the power to detect a 20 percent difference was near 100 percent, and a 12 percent difference could be detected with 90 percent power.

We also wanted to detect whether mortality declined as a result of increased delivery room surfactant administration. Based on previous studies of surfactant efficacy, we calculated that mortality would decrease by 4 percent for infants of twenty-three to twenty-nine weeks GA if the proportion of delivery room surfactant administration increased by 60 percent in the intervention group over the control group. Using the network database to estimate the interhospital variability in mortality (standard deviation = .075), we calculated that fifty-five hospitals per group were needed to detect a 4 percent difference in mortality with 80 percent power using a two-sided, level .05 test. Based on these calculations we planned to enroll fifty-five centers per group. However, we actually enrolled fifty-seven per group.

In May 2000, the enrolled hospitals were randomly assigned to either the intervention or control group using customized software. The team leader at each hospital was notified in writing of the assignment. Those in the control group were instructed to continue collecting and submitting routine Vermont Oxford Network data as usual. No additional data collection was required from either group, although we did administer a poststudy, follow-up questionnaire on surfactant therapy to leaders at all institutions.

The analyses were performed by intention to treat. The analysis of primary outcomes was performed with the analyst masked to the group assignments. The statistical methods account for the cluster randomization used in this trial. We tested the hypothesis of differences between intervention and control groups on the primary outcomes via a logistic regression model, using treatment received as the covariate (SAS PROC: GENMOD). Intrahospital correlation was accounted for using the generalized estimating equation approach (Donner and Klar 2000, 98).

An adjusted odds ratio was computed and tested using several covariates for adjustment: GA and ethnicity of the infant, whether the infant was transferred from another hospital or born at the participating hospital, type of neonatal intensive care unit, teaching/nonteaching hospital, and the annual volume of infant patients. The proportional hazards model was used to model time to first surfactant administration using treatment received as the covariate (equivalent to log-rank test). The effect of intrahospital correlation was accounted for by adjusting the standard error of the hazard ratio for treatments as described in Donner and Klar (2000, 135) and Lin (1994). Infants who did not receive surfactant by the seventh day were censored at seven days. To have adequate power for detecting differences in surfactant administration that occur early, the weighted log-rank test (also referred to as the generalized Wilcoxon test), adjusted for clustering, was also used. The tests were augmented by a plot of the Kaplan-Meier estimates for the distribution of time to surfactant administration.

Results

Treatment and control hospitals were generally similar at baseline, although more of the control hospitals were at the lowest technological level for neonatal intensive care (14 versus 7 of the intervention hospitals), and the proportion of white babies was greater in the intervention hospitals.

After the intervention, a significantly greater proportion of infants in the intervention hospitals received surfactant in the delivery room, compared to control hospitals. The adjusted odds ratio is 5.38 and translates into a 37 percent increase in early surfactant use across hospitals, one of the largest effect sizes we can find in the research literature on medical practice improvements. By way of comparison, eight other multifaceted interventions have reported practice improvements ranging from 2.6 to 9.0 percent (Grimshaw et al. 2004).

A significantly smaller proportion of infants in the intervention hospitals received the first dose more than two hours after birth, and the median time until they received the first dose was twenty-one minutes in intervention hospitals, compared to seventy-eight minutes in control hospitals. These effects were larger for infants born in the participating hospitals than for infants transferred to a participating hospital after birth.

However, there were no significant differences in the primary patient–level outcomes, infant mortality, and pneumothorax. There could be many reasons for this, but among them is the fact that the power calculations assumed a 60 percent increase in early surfactant use, and 37 percent was obtained. Also, the relative risk of death we employed for power calculations derived from the systematic reviews contrasting early surfactant use to use of surfactant once the baby had RDS. Two "sea changes" in practice may have led us to expect too large an effect on mortality.

First, the average time until administration of surfactant has been greatly reduced since the original studies were conducted. Second, the increased use of antenatal corticosteroids has led to a reduction in the mortality rate of preterm infants since the original studies were conducted.

Implications and Challenges

The case for cluster randomized study of medical practice improvement

Our case rests on theoretical, empirical, and methodological considerations. *The theory* behind these interventions relies largely on Rogers's (1995) framework to understand diffusion of innovations. From the very start, medical practice adoption utilized this framework. Medical practices diffuse through organizations and through local professional networks (AHCPR 1992). A medical practice setting is an aggregate of health care providers, some of whom may already have adopted the innovation and others who may do so soon, but all of whom interact with each other to some degree. One way to frame the outcome measures for these studies, therefore, is to track uptake of the practice at specific time points, as seen in the hypothetical examples of Figure 2. Can intervention speed up the adoption of innovation, producing a greater proportion of clinicians who have adopted the practice at an earlier point in time? Features of the organization or network can facilitate or delay diffusion. By taking these features into account, we gain insight for more powerful interventions.

The empirical argument for cluster random assignment is that medical care practices vary substantially across organizations and localities. This issue is crucially important for understanding medical care quality. It is now widely understood that medical care practices vary from one organization to another (Keller et al. 1990). Much of the variation occurs at the level of small geographic areas, often defined by hospital market areas and their corresponding professional networks (Tedeschi, Wolfe, and Griffith 1994). A related empirical point is that powerful forces, beyond individual beliefs and knowledge, enable or prevent practice changes. Within a practice setting, change is best accomplished when systems and processes of care are retooled to enable practitioner changes (Institute of Medicine 2001; Bodenheimer, Wagner, and Grumbach 2002). Outside the practice setting itself, forces known to affect medical practice include the local standard of care, the influence of peers, hospital admitting privileges, liability concerns, and the incentives and requirements of dominant health insurance plans and purchasers.

Practitioners are embedded in organizations and networks that have strong influence on their behavior. Innovations are more likely to be adopted if they are observable and trialable and if they can be adapted or "reinvented" (Rogers 1995).

FIGURE 2
**SPEEDING THE UPTAKE OF EVIDENCE-BASED PRACTICE:
EXAMPLE CUMULATIVE DISTRIBUTIONS**

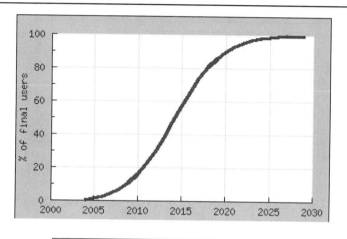

Without Intervention

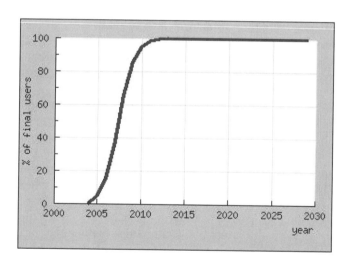

With Intervention

SOURCE: Curves were generated based on a predictive model of the diffusion of innovations described by Jordi Robert-Ribes and Phillip Wing at http://www.andorraweb.com/bass/index.php.

Observability and trialability are part of practitioner interactions, both within an organization and in professional networks (AHCPR 1992). Practitioners may observe or hear about a medical innovation, try it, perhaps discuss and evaluate it as a group, then determine whether it should be made permanent. The rapid cycle collaborative improvement strategy formalizes these natural interactions to achieve a practice improvement aim (Langley et al. 1996). "Reinvention" of the innovation often occurs in medical practice because of the need to address logistics of the local situation—the very basis of the rapid cycle improvement strategy. Such logistical issues are a feature of the larger setting, not the individual practitioner. Can we afford to ignore this level of analysis under the circumstances?

"Reinvention" of the innovation often occurs in medical practice because of the need to address logistics of the local situation—the very basis of the rapid cycle improvement strategy.

Concerning method, physicians and other health care providers are "nested within" organizations such as hospitals and group practices. Cluster random assignment minimizes the potential for contaminating treatment and control groups (Shadish, Cook, and Campbell 2001), an important concern since physicians rely on local networks of colleagues for information. By including multiple settings for study, one can also minimize the effects of local extraneous events (Shadish, Cook, and Campbell 2001), such as a change in referral patterns due to the pressures of managed care.

Multilevel analysis helps one to understand both individual practitioner and group-level responses to an intervention. This is important because statistically significant variation in effect sizes can appear at the *group* level, across the clusters or individual settings. This variation in response to intervention was reported both in our study of antenatal corticosteroid therapy and by Burack et al. (1996). Hypothetical adoption curves, drawn from the diffusion literature, are seen in Figure 3. Assume that an intervention occurs in 1990: baseline data are obtained in 1990 and follow-up data in 1995. Hospitals or group practices may have already begun to adopt the intervention at different time points and at different rates, thus affecting the proportion of adopters at baseline. Moreover, the various barriers and facilitators inherent in the setting may cause a relatively quick or slow uptake of the practice, regardless of baseline levels. The variation in effect sizes makes more sense when framed in terms of the underlying adoption curves.

FIGURE 3
SIGNIFICANT VARIATION IN UPTAKE AMONG SITES:
EXAMPLE CUMULATIVE DISTRIBUTIONS

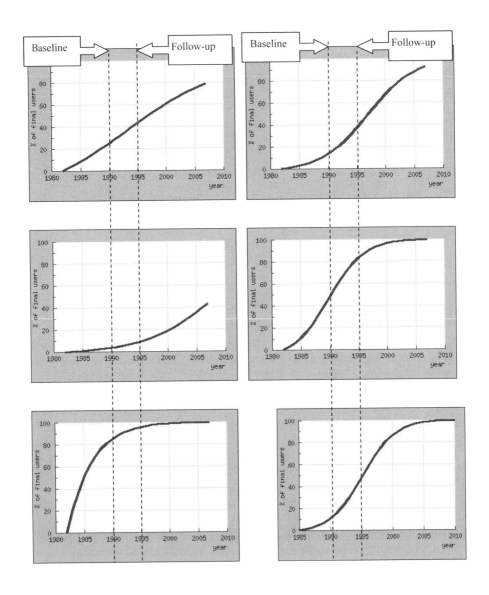

SOURCE: Curves were generated based on a predictive model of the diffusion of innovations described by Jordi Robert-Ribes and Phillip Wing at http://www.andorraweb.com/bass/index.php.

Understanding these barriers and facilitators to adoption is a fruitful area for further inquiry. In line with recommendations by Campbell et al. (2000), the two studies presented here aimed to explain setting-level variation by collecting both quantitative and qualitative data as a by-product of the multifaceted intervention. For the corticosteroid study, these were too limited to explain much variance. For the surfactant study, they are under active investigation. Other projects may eventually cast light on the important mediators and moderators of medical practice changes: for example, the survey of health care organizational factors in improving chronic illness care (Rundall et al. 2002) or qualitative work on primary care improvements (Crabtree, Miller, and Stange 2001).

Practicalities and trade-offs in the use of this design

Preexisting research networks may offer important economies of scale in conducting cluster randomized studies. This can be seen in comparing both the cost and quality of data collection in the corticosteroid and the surfactant trials. Data collection was the major expense for the antenatal corticosteroid trial. In the Vermont Oxford Network, by contrast, data collection was a routinized by-product of a preexisting relationship. This lowered the expense of data collection substantially, and permitted a greater number of hospitals to be studied for the price, in the surfactant trial.

We can also speculate about the potential impact of a preexisting research network on data quality. The corticosteroid trial encountered problems of missing data. These problems may have arisen in part from the ad hoc nature of the collaboration. In contrast, the Vermont Oxford Network hospitals rely on the network to interpret for them the data that they provide. In other words, they use and value their own data as well as providing it to the network. They are provided with feedback and interpretation about their performance over time and are able to contrast their own performance with that of other institutions.

Both trials present trade-offs between internal validity and external validity or generalizability (Shadish, Cook, and Campbell 2001). An obvious advantage of cluster randomized trials is the increased number of settings in which they occur and our ability to control for features of the setting in analysis. At the same time, settings self-select for participation in randomized trials, which limits generalizability. The corticosteroid trial recruited tertiary care centers, an appropriate choice given the sheer volume of eligible patients seen in these centers and the better prospects for high-quality data collection. But do the results generalize to other settings? Certainly, the overall trend in antenatal corticosteroid use generalizes, as seen in Figure 1. The available research on the components of active dissemination leads us to believe that these generalize, as well.

It may be easier to establish how far the surfactant trial results can be generalized, given the sheer size of the Vermont Oxford Network. Participants in the study can be compared to other network members: more than four hundred hospitals at the present time. The sheer number of units permits a look at setting-level variation both within the trial and subsequently, within the network, to discover types of hospitals that had greater uptake, or quicker uptake of the evidence.

Generalization depends on both time and place, however (Shadish, Cook, and Campbell 2001). In both studies, we observed background trends in treatment practices that were unrelated to the trial interventions but that affected the results in a variety of ways. Between 1993 and 1995, the time of the corticosteroid trial, the proportion of women treated with antenatal corticosteroids in the general population increased steadily. Similarly, between the early 1990s and 2001, the end of the surfactant trial, practice for both surfactant therapy and corticosteroid therapy had greatly improved. This may have lowered the overall mortality rate among preterm infants and possibly led to the lack of effect on infant mortality.

Others have noticed how secular trends can reduce or even wash out the effects of intervention (e.g., Murray 1998). By the time a problem in health is recognized and a study is funded, the larger field may already be changing. Several approaches are emerging to address the problem of secular trends. One is to determine, to the best of one's ability, how far the trend has gone at the time intervention begins— ideally, one might choose a study's focus and outcome measures based on background trends and the prospects for detecting significant changes (Murray 1998). Another approach in the case of medical practices is to study the generic "tools of the trade" (such as rapid cycle collaborative improvement), apart from their isolated use to close any specific gap between evidence and practice.

Notes

1. Preterm or premature infants are those born before thirty-seven weeks gestational age (GA). GA is defined as the number of weeks from the first day of the mother's last menstrual cycle before conception until the baby is delivered or reaches full term of forty weeks.

2. Corticosteroid therapy matures the organs of the fetus, preventing severe complications and death.

3. Surfactant in human lungs prevents the tiny air sacs (alveoli) from collapsing and clinging together. However, preterm infant lungs may not have matured enough to produce surfactant, causing Respiratory Distress Syndrome (RDS). Infants with RDS are intubated through the trachea to allow air to get into their lungs, and one or more doses of surfactant are given through the tube.

References

Agency for Health Care Policy and Research (AHCPR). 1992. *Annotated bibliography: Information dissemination to health care practitioners and policymakers.* Rockville, MD: AHCPR.

Berwick, D. M., A. B. Godfrey, and J. Roessner. 1991. *Curing health care: New strategies for quality improvement.* San Francisco: Jossey-Bass.

Bodenheimer, T., E. H. Wagner, and K. Grumbach. 2002. Improving primary care for patients with chronic illness: The Chronic Care Model, Part 2. *Journal of the American Medical Association* 288:1909-14.

Bronstein, J. M., and R. L. Goldenberg. 1995. Practice variation in the use of corticosteroids: A comparison of eight datasets. *American Journal of Obstetrics and Gynecology* 173:296-98.

Burack, R. C., P. A. Gimotty, J. George, M. S. Simon, P. Dews, and A. Moncrease. 1996. The effect of patient and physician reminders on use of screening mammography in a health maintenance organization. Results of a randomized controlled trial. *Cancer* 78:1708-21.

Burns, D. M., S. Cohen, E. R. Gritz, and T. E. Kottke, eds. 1993. *Tobacco and the clinician: Intervention for medical and dental practice*. Smoking and Tobacco Control Program Monograph no. 5. Bethesda, MD: National Cancer Institute.

Campbell, M., R. Fitzpatrick, A. Haines, A. L. Kinmonth, P. Sandercock, D. Spiegelhalter, and P. Tyrer. 2000. Framework of design and evaluation of complex interventions to improve health. *British Medical Journal* 321:694-96.

Chalmers, I., M. Enkin, and M. J. N. C. Keirse, eds. 1989. *Effective care in pregnancy and childbirth.*. Oxford: Oxford University Press.

Crabtree, B. F., W. L. Miller, and K. C. Stange. 2001. Understanding practice from the ground up. *Journal of Family Practice* 50:881-87.

Donner, A., and N. S. Klar. 2000. *Design and analysis of cluster randomisation trials in health research*. London: Hodder Arnold.

Goldstein, H. 1995. *Multilevel statistical models: Applications and data analysis methods*. Thousand Oaks, CA: Sage.

Grimshaw J. M., R. E. Thomas, G. MacLennan, C. Fraser, C. R. Ramsay, L. Vale, P. Whitty, M. P. Eccles, L. Matowe, L. Shirran, M. Wensing, R. Dijkstra, and C. Donaldson. 2004. Effectiveness and efficiency of guideline dissemination and implementation strategies. *Health Technology Assessment* 8:iii-iv, 1-72.

Horbar, J. D. 1999. The Vermont Oxford Network: Evidence-based quality improvement for neonatology. *Pediatrics* 103:350-59.

Horbar, J. D., J. H. Carpenter, J. Buzas, R. F. Soll, G. Suresh, M. B. Bracken, L. C. Leviton, P. E. Plsek, and J. C. Sinclair. 2004a. A cluster randomized trial of a multifaceted intervention for promoting evidence-based surfactant therapy. *British Medical Journal* 329:1004-1100.

——— (for the Vermont Oxford Network). 2004b. Timing of initial surfactant treatment for infants 23 to 29 weeks gestation: Is routine practice evidence-eased? *Pediatrics* 113:1593-1602.

Horbar J. D., and K. Leahy (for the Investigators of the Vermont-Oxford Trials Network). 1995. An assessment of data quality in the Vermont-Oxford Trials Network Database. *Controlled Clinical Trials* 16:51-61.

Institute of Medicine. 2001. *Crossing the quality chasm: A new health system for the 21st century*. Washington, DC: National Academy Press.

Keller, R. B., D. N. Soule, J. E. Wennberg, and D. F. Hanley. 1990. Dealing with geographic variations in the use of hospitals: The experience of the Maine Medical Assessment Foundation. *Journal of Bone and Joint Surgery* 72-A:1286-93.

Langley, G., K. Nolan, T. Nolan, C. L. Norman, and L. P. Provost. 1996. *The improvement guide: A practical approach to enhancing organizational performance*. San Francisco: Jossey-Bass.

Lee, E., and N. Dubin. 1994. Estimation and sample size considerations for clustered binary responses. *Statistics in Medicine* 13:1241-52.

Leviton, L. C., C. S. Baker, A. Hassol, and R. L. Goldenberg. 1995. An exploration of opinion and practice patterns affecting the use of antenatal corticosteroids. *American Journal of Obstetrics and Gynecology* 173:312-16.

Leviton, L. C., R. L. Goldenberg, C. S. Baker, M. Freda, L. J. Fish, S. P. Cliver, D. J. Rouse, C. Chazotte, I. R. Merkatz, and J. M. Raczynski. 1999. Randomized controlled trial of methods to encourage the use of antenatal corticosteroid therapy for fetal maturation. *Journal of the American Medical Association* 281:46-52.

Lin, D. Y. 1994. Cox regression analysis of multivariate failure time data: The marginal approach. *Statistics in Medicine* 13:2233-47.

Loeb, M. B. 2002. Application of the development stages of a cluster randomized trial to a framework for valuating complex health interventions. *BMC Health Services Research* 2:13-21.

Mittman B. S., X. Tonesk, and P. D. Jacobson. 1992. Implementing clinical practice guidelines: Social influence strategies and practitioner behavior change. *Quality Review Bulletin* 18:413-22.

Murray, D. 1998. Coping with secular trends in health promotion and disease prevention. Presented at "Public Health in the 21st Century," a joint meeting of the American Psychological Association and the Centers for Disease Control and Prevention, May, in Atlanta, GA.

National Perinatal Epidemiology Unit. 1985. *A classified bibliography of controlled trials in perinatal medicine 1940-1984*. Oxford: Oxford University Press.

Plsek, P. E. 1997. Collaborating across organizational boundaries to improve the quality of care. *American Journal of Infection Control* 25:85-95.

Rogers, E. M. 1995. *Diffusion of innovations*. New York: Free Press.

Rundall, T. G., S. M. Shortell, M. C. Wang, L. Casalino, T. Bodenheimer, R. R. Gillies, J. A. Schmittdiel, N. Oswald, and J. C. Robinson. 2002. As good as it gets? Chronic care management in nine leading US physician organizations. *British Medical Journal* 325:958-61.

Shadish, W. R., T. D. Cook, and D. T. Campbell. 2001. *Experimental and quasi-experimental designs for generalized causal inference*. New York: Houghton Mifflin.

Sinclair, J. C., M. B. Bracken, J. D. Horbar, and R. F. Soll. 1997. Introduction to neonatal systematic reviews. *Pediatrics* 100:892-95.

Soumerai, S. B., T. J. McLaughlin, J. H. Gurwitz, E. Guadagnoli, P. J. Hauptman, C. Borbas, N. Morris, B. McLaughlin, X. Gao, D. J. Willison, R. Asinger, and F. Gobel. 1998. Effect of local medical opinion leaders on quality of care for acute myocardial infarction. *Journal of the American Medical Association* 279:1358-63.

Tedeschi, P., R. Wolfe, and J. Griffith. 1994. Micro-area variation in hospital use. *Health Services Research* 24:729-40.

Thomson O'Brien, M. A., N. Freemantle, A. D. Oxman, F. Wolf, D. A. Davis, and J. Herrin. 2002. Continuing education meetings and workshops: Effects on professional practice and health care outcomes (Cochrane Review). In *The Cochrane Library*, iss. 3. Oxford: Update Software.

Thomson O'Brien, M. A., A. D. Oxman, R. B. Haynes, D. A. Davis, N. Freemantle, and E. L. Harvey. 2002. Local opinion leaders: Effects on professional practice and health care outcomes (Cochrane Review). In *The Cochrane Library*, iss. 3. Oxford: Update Software.

Historical Review of School-Based Randomized Trials for Evaluating Problem Behavior Prevention Programs

By
BRIAN R. FLAY
and
LINDA M. COLLINS

The authors provide a historical review of developments in the methods of school-based evaluations of problem behavior prevention interventions. The design and statistical methodologies used in school-based intervention research have advanced tremendously over the past twenty years. Methods have improved for approaches to the randomization of whole schools, the choice of appropriate comparison or control groups, solutions when randomization breaks down, limiting and handling of variation in integrity of the intervention received, limiting biases introduced by data collection, awareness of the effects of intensive and long-term data collection, limiting and analysis of subject attrition and other missing data, approaches to obtaining parental consent for children to engage in research, design and analysis issues when only small numbers of schools are available or can be afforded, the choice of the unit of analysis, phases of research, optimizing and extending the reach of interventions, and differential effects in subpopulations. The authors conclude that sequential planning, timing, keeping up with methodological advances, publication of results, and accumulation of knowledge are all important in conducting high-quality school-based intervention research, and that the devil is in the details.

Keywords: school-based randomized trial; prevention research; educational research; health behavior; intervention development; causal statements; parental consent

Prevention researchers have conducted school-based randomized trials of prevention programs routinely since the early 1980s. We provide a brief review of theoretical developments in prevention research during the past twenty years, then discuss many of the methodological issues with conducting randomized trials with schools. We identify many methodologi-

Brian R. Flay is distinguished professor of community health sciences (public health) and psychology at the University of Illinois at Chicago (UIC). He has conducted a series of experimental studies of programs for the prevention of cigarette smoking, substance use, AIDS, and violence in Canada, California, Hawaii, and Chicago. He is currently conducting four school-based randomized trials of the Positive Action program, a K-12 character education program that appears to change

DOI: 10.1177/0002716205274941

cal improvements over the past two decades that put prevention research at the forefront of school-based research and some areas that still need improvement.

A. The Problems

Health-compromising and high-risk behaviors such as smoking, alcohol abuse, drug use, violence, unsafe sexual practices, and delinquency are the problems addressed by school-based prevention trials. These behaviors occur at problematic levels among our youth and are highly correlated (Flay 2002; Jessor and Jessor 1977).

B. The Science and Theory: A Short History of Prevention Research

Many school-based programs have been evaluated during the past thirty years, enough to allow for multiple meta-analyses (Derzon and Wilson 1999; Durlak and Wells 1997; Rooney and Murray 1996; Tobler 1986, 1992; Tobler et al. 2000;

---

school climates, improve class management skills and time on task by teachers, and increase learning and improve behavior of students. He is a fellow of the Society for Behavioral Medicine, the Society for Community Research and Action, and the American Academy of Health Behavior. He received recognition for outstanding research from the Research Council of the American School Health Association (1993), the American Academy of Health Behavior (Research Laureate Award, 2001), and Current Contents ISI (recognized as a Highly Cited Researcher—in the top one-half percent—for 1981-2000).

Linda M. Collins is director of the Methodology Center and professor of human development, Penn State University. Her work has centered on design, measurement, and statistical methodology for research in the behavioral, biomedical, and prevention sciences. She is particularly interested in methods for longitudinal research and for intervention design and evaluation. She has numerous publications in both methodological and substantive outlets and has edited several books and special issues of journals devoted to applied research methods. Awards include the Cattell Award for outstanding early career contributions to multivariate behavioral research, Pennsylvania State University's Faculty Scholar Medal in the Social and Behavioral Sciences, and the President's Award from the Society for Prevention Research. She is a past president of the Society of Multivariate Experimental Psychology, and she is a fellow of the American Psychological Association and the American Psychological Society.

NOTE: This article was originally prepared for the conference on "Progress and Prospects for Place-Based Randomized Trials" convened by the Campbell Collaboration at the Rockefeller Foundation Study and Conference Center, Bellagio, Italy, November 11-15, 2002. Preparation of this article was supported in part by grants from the National Institute on Drug Abuse (DA13474 and P50 DA10075). Some of the work described herein was supported by the Ontario Ministry of Health (CHS R26), the National Cancer Institute (CA38268, CA35596, CA44907), the National Institute on Drug Abuse (DA03046, DA03976, DA11019), the National Institutes of Mental Health (MH45470), the Office for Research on Minority Health through the National Institute of Child Health and Human Development (HD30078), the Centers for Disease Control and Prevention (CCR505025, CCU509661), and the Robert Wood Johnson Foundation.

Tobler and Stratton 1997). Historically, the focus of prevention programs has moved from (1) information to (2) affective approaches to (3) social skills and correction of normative beliefs. They have also changed in terms of the domains of influence, from being largely classroom based to including parents, using the mass media, and involving community. Recent programs tend to be comprehensive, addressing multiple behaviors and/or their precursors. Each of these changes has, on the whole, been accompanied by improved prevention effectiveness.

In the first generation of preventive approaches, information about the properties and consequences of drugs (sometimes laced with fear, e.g., "Reefer Madness") was shown to change knowledge but little else. Indeed, some informational programs led to increased drug use because the information led to increased curiosity and, in some cases, increased knowledge about how to identify, where to get, and how to use substances (Glasgow et al. 1981; Goodstadt 1978; Green 1979; Thompson 1978).

In the second generation, affective approaches (values clarification and decision making) were used. They were not very effective, largely because, like the informational approaches, they focused on only one small part of the complex set of influences on substance use.

The third generation of prevention research utilized McGuire's social inoculation and persuasive communications theories (McGuire 1964, 1985) and Bandura's (1977) social learning theory. These programs provided students with skills to resist peer pressure (Evans 1976), including the now-infamous "Just say 'no'" approach popularized by Nancy Reagan. These approaches reported more consistent, though still relatively small effects on cigarette smoking (Flay 1985) and substance use (Tobler 1986). Most early social influences programs included little, if any, information on consequences of substance use; it was assumed that adolescents did not want to use substances, but they did not have the skills to resist social pressures. One major exception was Gil Botvin's Life Skills Training (LST) program, a more general social skills approach to substance abuse prevention that included a wider array of both personal and social skills than most other programs, as well as some informational content designed to motivate students to want to avoid substance use (see Botvin [2000] for a review). In recent years, secondary analyses of variables that mediate the effects of prevention programs on substance use behavior has suggested that, for some programs at least, the correction of normative beliefs may be more important than skills development (Dielman et al. 1985; Hansen and Graham 1991; MacKinnon et al. 1991).

In smoking prevention (see Flay [1985, 1987] and Best et al. [1988] for reviews), a series of preexperimental and quasi-experimental studies led to initiating the first school-based randomized trial (SBRT), the first of the Waterloo smoking prevention studies, in 1979 (Best et al. 1984; Flay et al. 1983, 1985, 1989). At the University of Southern California, Johnson and colleagues expanded the application of the social influences approach to the prevention of drug abuse (Graham et al. 1990; Hansen et al. 1988; Hansen 1992; Rohrbach et al. 1995; Weber et al. 1989). At about this time, Gilbert Botvin started his long series of SBRTs of his LST program (Botvin and Griffin 2001). Several meta-analyses have established that these social influences and social skills approaches to prevention of substance use are effective, with those approaches involving interactive learning having an average effect size of .24 (Tobler and Stratton 1997).

Most, if not all, of these randomized trials were funded by the National Institutes of Health, particularly the National Cancer Institute (NCI) and the National Institute on Drug Abuse (NIDA), which also held several workgroups and expert meetings during the 1980s to set the stage for these improved studies. This started a long series of methodological papers aimed at improving the quality of prevention research.

We identify many methodological improvements over the past two decades that put prevention research at the forefront of school-based research and some areas that still need improvement.

Many studies in the 1990s and up to the present have an expanded focus to assess the generalizability of interventions; expand the targeted behaviors to include violence and unsafe sexual behavior; and involve mass media, families, and communities (Flay 2000). Current SBRTs focus most on making programs more comprehensive, considering not only the health-compromising behaviors discussed so far, but also including general child developmental tasks, mental health, and general positive youth development (Flay 2002; Gottfredson, Gottfredson, and Skroban 1996; Hawkins et al. 1999).

Meta-analysis of substance use prevention program results (Tobler et al. 2000) supported the conclusions reached above in more traditional reviews and early meta-analyses. They divided programs into noninteractive and interactive. Noninteractive programs tend to be didactic, with little or no student interaction, and emphasize informational and affective approaches.[1] Interactive programs, on the other hand, tended to be dialectic or Socratic, with a high degree of student activity and interaction, and also included more skills training. High-quality studies[2] of noninteractive programs (informational and affective) had a mean effect size of 0. High-quality studies of interactive programs had a mean effect size of .19 for social influences/skills programs and .24 for comprehensive life skills programs. Effect sizes were not different for different substances (tobacco, alcohol, marijuana, illicit substances), outcomes (behavior and attitudes), or different providers (teachers, peer leaders, and others). A valuable result is that programs delivered in high-minority schools were equally or slightly more effective than programs delivered in mostly white schools. However, effects from large-scale implementations were significantly smaller than effects from small-scale implementations (.16 and .5, respectively), suggesting a need for more research on how to take effective programs to scale.

C. Intervention Development and Implementation

Most programs tested in SBRTs had previously been tested in small-scale nonexperimental and quasi-experimental pilot studies. Most often, these were conducted by the group developing the program that then went on to conduct the SBRT. Managerial issues for most of these studies were minimized because the interventions were designed and developed by researchers on the basis of explicit theory, risk/protective factors derived from epidemiological or social etiological research, and/or adaptations of others' interventions. Few involved the eventual program implementers (e.g., teachers and other school staff) or the targets of the intervention (students, parents, school staff, other community members) at the design stage.

The use of theory has been explicit in most prevention intervention development (Sussman et al. 1995). The studies cited above relied on a broad array of theories from education, psychology, and sociology (Sussman and Ames 2001; Petraitis and Flay 2002; Petraitis, Flay, and Miller 1995; see Flay and Petraitis [1994] for an integrative view). Many studies also assess and demonstrate intervention effects on the presumed mediating variables, and an increasing number have tested and demonstrated partial or complete statistical mediation (MacKinnon and Lockwood 2003).

Most prevention studies have been efficacy trials (conducted under ideal, investigator-controlled circumstances) rather than effectiveness trials ("real-world" implementation) (Flay 1986). They have been conducted within the framework of one or another of the models of Phases of Research for intervention development promulgated by the NCI (Greenwald and Cullen 1984); the National Heart, Lung and Blood Institute (NHLBI 1983); and others that were, in turn, derived from the Federal Drug Administration's approach to the development of new pharmaceutical drugs. Many recent papers have bemoaned the lack of effectiveness trials, or other kinds of studies to assess the effects of proven interventions under "real-world conditions" (Biglan et al. 2003). This is an issue of current concern given the demands by federal agencies (e.g., U.S. Department of Education, Center for Substance Abuse Prevention) that only programs of "proven effectiveness" be supported with federal funds.

Most SBRTs of prevention programs also have involved program implementation/delivery by research staff. For example, the first Waterloo project employed two graduate students, who helped develop and deliver the program. For most of the University of Southern California and University of Illinois at Chicago studies in which the present authors were involved, the interventions were delivered by extensively trained health educators, employed by the investigators. Some of these health educators were involved in curriculum development. Of course, as the field moves to engaging in more effectiveness trials, we will have to either develop methods of teacher/staff training that lead to implementation with fidelity and integrity or develop programs that are more robust to implementation variability.

Gil Botvin's studies of his LST program were an exception in this respect. After a series of small-scale studies for which his staff delivered the curriculum, for most of his large studies he and his staff trained regular classroom teachers to deliver the curriculum. This has the potential advantage of teachers integrating the philosophy and ideas of the program into the rest of the school day. It has the disadvantages that the program is less standardized and not all teachers will implement the program equally well. As a result, most of the reports of tests of the LST program include a report of the effects for those classrooms or students who received all or most of the program, or for those teachers who delivered the program with the greatest integrity.

D. Methodological Issues and Considerations

School-based prevention research faces many significant methodological challenges. Flay and Best (1982, hereafter referred to as FandB) published an early review of methodological issues in school-based prevention research, drawn largely from the challenges they faced when designing the first SBRT of smoking prevention. In this section, we discuss methodological considerations related to design and implementation of SBRTs, measurement of important variables, statistical analysis, and optimizing and extending the reach of interventions being evaluated in SBRTs. We take a fresh look at many of the recommendations made by FandB and discuss how the field has (or has not) advanced in the intervening twenty years. We also raise a few new issues not included in FandB.

1. Design and implementation

1a. Need for randomization of whole schools
Random assignment to research conditions is the cornerstone of scientific inference and is an indispensable part of SBRTs. In most research endeavors, individuals can be assigned to conditions. However, most prevention or health promotion programs are provided to intact groups, usually classrooms or schools. This frequently means that random assignment must be carried out at the classroom or school level. Most often in prevention research, schools are used rather than classrooms. Students from different classrooms within a school talk to each other, and this may contaminate experimental conditions because students in the control classrooms may learn of the intervention components from students in interven-

tion classrooms. Furthermore, some programs have a schoolwide component, demanding school-based randomization.

1982 recommendations. The desirability of randomized trials had already been made clear by others (Boruch 1975; Campbell and Boruch 1975; Campbell and Stanley 1967; Cook and Campbell 1979; Riecken and Boruch 1978). FandB recommended the use of randomized studies at either the classroom level for tests of small-scale programs or the school level for tests of larger-scale interventions where contamination between classrooms within schools was highly likely.

FandB recommended that randomization take place at the smallest unit possible that does not compromise the program or contaminate across conditions (Shadish, Cook, and Campbell 2002). In some instances, this may be at the classroom level; however, in most instances it should be at the school level. In some instances, programs are targeted to the whole age range of students, K-12. In such instances, whole school complexes (for example, a high school and all middle or junior high and elementary schools that feed into it) or communities will need to be randomized to conditions (see Peterson et al. [2000] for an example).

History. During the 1980s, dozens of NIH-supported SBRTs, mostly in the areas of smoking or drug abuse prevention, were conducted. These were funded initially by NCI, NIDA, and NHLBI; and later by the National Institutes of Alcohol and Alcoholism (NIAAA), the National Institute of Mental Health (NIMH), the National Institute of Child Health and Human Development (NICHHD), the Centers for Disease Control and Prevention (CDC), and the National Institute of Allergy and Infectious Diseases (NIAID).

In the late 1980s, partly as a result of a National Academy of Science Committee report (Turner, Miller, and Moses 1989), SBRTs were applied to youth-focused AIDS prevention and pregnancy prevention (Frost and Forrest 1995; Kirby 2001; Kirby and DiClemente 1994). In the 1990s, it extended to violence prevention (Tolan and Guerra 1994).

The U.S. Department of Education (DE), and educational research in general, was a different matter, with few randomized trials being funded (Cook 1999; Cook and Payne 2000). Fortunately, this is currently changing. For example, in 2002, the DE even encouraged Local Educational Agencies (LEAs, i.e., school districts) to add a high-quality quasi-experimental or a randomized trial component to their request for "Partnerships in Character Education" grant proposals. Of 266 proposals, 39 were funded, all of which proposed high-quality quasi-experimental or randomized trials.

1b. Resistance to randomization

Ethical concerns with randomizing people or groups of people to conditions are sometimes raised. Resistance to randomization often blinds people to the many alternative possibilities for randomization (Boruch 1975; Cook and Campbell 1979; Shadish, Cook, and Campbell 2002).

1982 recommendation. In general, the ethical arguments *for* conducting randomized studies are stronger than the arguments against them. In many cases, it would be more unethical to provide intervention or education that has unknown or possibly negative effects than it would be to assign people or schools randomly to find out which programs are most effective.

History. Over the years, researchers have successfully convinced many school districts, schools, school boards, parents, and institutional review board (IRB) members of the need for randomization. Results from randomized trials that proved counterintuitive (such as women's hormone replacement therapy, e.g., Cushman et al. 2004) serve a useful purpose in educating consumers. Indeed, the argument that randomization is unethical is rarely heard these days, and when it is, it is easily reversed.

Approaches to random assignment of schools. There has been wide variation over the years in how researchers go about randomization and with what success. Prior to 1983, most smoking prevention studies had assigned only one or two schools per condition or were entirely nonrandom. These small sample sizes lead to lack of comparability, even after randomization. The first Waterloo study (Flay et al. 1983) was the first smoking or substance abuse prevention study to randomly assign sufficient schools to be a valid randomized trial.

Two examples of approaches to randomization in SBRTs are discussed here. One approach is to recruit schools into the study on the condition that they then agree to be randomly assigned to condition. Another approach is to conduct the random assignment from matched pairs or strata first, and then recruit pairs or sets of schools into the condition into which they have been preassigned. We describe one example of each approach here.

The first approach (recruit then assign) was taken by Flay et al. (1983) for the first Waterloo smoking prevention study and by Flay and colleagues (1988, 1995) for the Television, School and Family Project (TVSFP). The latter study involved testing the effects of televised (in Los Angeles) and classroom-based (in Los Angeles and San Diego) programs for smoking prevention. We utilized the Graham et al. (1984) multiattribute utility measurement approach, which uses data from presumed risk factors or predictors of the dependent variable to create a single scale of risk on which to stratify, to randomly assign schools who had already agreed to participate in the study to conditions from risk-based strata. We assigned thirty-five schools from four school districts in Los Angeles County to five conditions, and twelve schools from two school districts in San Diego County to two of the same (but not exposed to the TV) conditions. Some schools assigned to the control conditions would have preferred to receive the program—that is, it was harder to retain schools in the control conditions—but assignment was never altered.

A second approach to randomization is to identify a large sample of schools, randomly assign them in advance, and then recruit them into their assigned condition. The Aban Aya Youth Project was a longitudinal efficacy trial of three interventions to reduce violence, risky sex, and drug use among African American students in grades five through eight in Chicago Metropolitan area schools that started in the fall of 1994 (Flay, Graumlich, et al. 2004). School report card data, which the majority of states now report, was used to stratify schools with 90 percent or more African American students in and around Chicago into "risk" strata based on poverty level (percentage free/reduced lunch), mobility rates, enrollment, attendance/truancy, and achievement test scores. Three schools at a time were then randomly selected from each stratum, randomly assigned to one of the three conditions, and then recruited into the condition to which they had been assigned.

In general, the ethical arguments for conducting randomized studies are stronger than the arguments against them. In many cases, it would be more unethical to provide intervention or education that has unknown or possibly negative effects than it would be to assign people or schools randomly to find out which programs are most effective.

Only one school refused to participate, and it was replaced with another randomly selected school from the same stratum. Despite only four schools per condition, this procedure ensured a high level of pretest comparability. Schools signed an agreement to participate in the study for four years and agreed not to participate in another prevention initiative during that time, for which they received the assigned program (research staff delivered all lessons—about twenty per year) and up to $1,000 per year. All schools stayed in the study for the full four years and five waves of data collection. Providing a program to every school (one program was the control for the others) eliminated the difficulty of having to recruit schools to a no-intervention control condition.

1c. Choice of appropriate comparison or control groups

In general, no-intervention comparison/control conditions are inadvisable for both ethical and scientific reasons. If a standard intervention is in place, it may be unethical to replace it with a no-intervention condition; instead, the standard intervention can be used as a comparison condition. The scientific argument against no-intervention conditions is that they do not control for factors such as the amount of attention received (known as the "Hawthorne effect") or the perceived value of the intervention. For this reason, in medical settings the best randomized controlled trials (RCTs) use either a standard treatment or an attention-placebo as a control. In behavioral or educational research, an attention-placebo might be a program that provides equal attention or subject involvement (to rule out Hawthorne effects) and that leads subjects to have equal expectations about program success or outcomes (Flay, Graumlich, et al. 2004; Sussman et al. 1995).

Another common element of RCTs in medicine is blinding. That is, both the subject of the intervention and the provider of the intervention are blinded to the condition that the subject is in. In group-process programs, it often is impossible to make intervention providers (e.g., teachers) blind to what they are providing, or the target audience blind to what they are receiving. However, comparison of alternative interventions, with providers and recipients blind to the comparisons to be made, might sometimes be possible.

Lack of attention-placebo or blinding may lead to overestimates or underestimates of intervention effects. Demand characteristics (Rosnow 2002) in the intervention condition or demoralization in the control condition can artificially inflate intervention-control differences. Underestimation of intervention effectiveness can occur when, for example, schools assigned to the control condition perceive that they are underserved because they are not in the intervention condition and then take steps to compensate, such as adopting other programs (Cook and Campbell 1979).

1982 recommendations. FandB recommended that to draw credible causal inferences about intervention effects, attention-placebo or alternative intervention comparison conditions, preferably with intervention providers blinded to the comparisons, should be used. This is important because otherwise any detected intervention effects could be due to difference in attention or outcome expectancies rather than to the actual intervention. They also recommended the use of process evaluation to assess what actually happens in control schools.

History. Very few prevention researchers have followed these recommendations. One exception was the TVSFP study, for which attention-placebo activities were developed that led to equal outcome expectancies. In another example, in the Aban Aya project for inner-city African American schools, a Health Enhancement Curriculum (designed to improve diet, physical activity, and health care behaviors) was developed as a control for a Social Development Curriculum (designed to reduce violence, unsafe sex, and drug use). Both programs were Afrocentric, and both taught some of the same cognitive/affective and social skills, but related them to the different behavioral outcomes. In both cases, it was demonstrated that teachers and students exposed to these programs reported equal levels of involvement and outcome expectancies (Flay, Graumlich, et al. 2004; Sussman et al. 1989).

Very few prevention studies have included precise measurement of what actually happens in control schools. The lack of appropriate control schools is an ever-increasing problem, with schools today reporting that they have an average of fourteen special programs (Hallfors and Godette 2002). It is imperative that programs in both intervention and control schools be assessed to determine whether there is any change in the interventions implemented related to assignment to condition. For example, are intervention schools ceasing their use of an alternative program because they are receiving the research intervention free of charge? Are control schools adopting a new intervention to address the same problem because they were denied the research intervention?

1d. Breakdown of design

In field-based trials, randomization may fail, conditions may be contaminated, or the intervention may not be fully implemented in some of the intervention schools (or attrition may be differential or biased—see below). Cook and Campbell (1979) advocated careful thought about the "fallback" quasi-experimental design that would result in the event of such failure.

1982 recommendation. Following Cook and Campbell (1979), FandB recommended that posttest-only designs be avoided—because posttest-only designs cannot be salvaged if randomization breaks down.

History. Few researchers report breakdown of randomization. The first Waterloo prevention trial did suffer a partial breakdown. Flay et al. (1995) conducted analyses to suggest that nonrandomization of three of the eleven pairs did not affect pretest comparability or results.

It is a common recommendation and common practice in medical, economic, and psychological research to analyze data according to "intention to treat," regardless of variations in the level of intervention actually received or consumed. For example, in medical trials, patients are not excluded from analysis if they do not complete a course of treatment. A secondary analysis may be conducted to determine the effects of the treatment on those who completed it versus those who did not—but this is acknowledged to be secondary to the primary analysis.

An example concerns Botvin and colleagues' reports of results of a large (fifty-five schools) randomized trial of the LST. Botvin et al. (1990) presented results only for those 75 percent of classrooms that received the program with a 60 percent or better implementation score (the control group was not adjusted for likely participation). In a long-term follow-up (Botvin et al. 1995), they reported results both for the complete and for the reduced sample. However, it is the results from the high implementation subsample that are promulgated widely.

Breakdown of design can lead to lack of pretest comparability. Most researchers who subset their sample for analysis do not report on the pretest comparability of the resulting subsets. Many journal articles do include a section establishing pretest comparability on the outcome variable (and some include pretest comparability on matching variables) for the original design, but not for the revised analysis design. Clearly, failure of full program implementation, failed results in subsets of schools or students, and negative effects in some subsets of students or schools need to be reported fully in future publications.

1e. Variation in intervention received

A related issue concerns variation in intervention received that occurs because of some form of self-selection at the individual student level. This can arise because of different rates of attendance at school, transfers out of or into the study schools, or differential participation or involvement in the program. Students absent more often and students who transfer between schools more often are overwhelmingly likely to be those most at risk of problem behavior.

1982 recommendations. This issue was not addressed by FandB. At this time, we would recommend conducting analyses to assess the extent of differential exposure to intervention and determine its effects on estimates of intervention effectiveness (Boruch and Foley 2000).

History. Though most researchers assess attrition from studies over time (see section 3a below), few have assessed differential attendance at school, transfers in or out of study schools, or participation in program activities. Clearly, this is an issue that needs to be addressed—though secondarily to the primary intent-to-treat analysis.

In most cases, absenteeism or transfers are similar in intervention and comparison schools, and the results of the primary analysis are valid—and represent what would happen in the real world. If, however, absenteeism or transfers are differential across experimental conditions, then further careful analyses are called for.

In some cases, different students participate at different levels in the program activities, either in the classroom or outside it (e.g., on the playground or at home). What effects does this differential self-selection have on estimates of program effects? Clearly, this is an exact parallel to the compliance issue in medical trials. The intent-to-treat analysis must be the primary analysis (Little and Yau 1996, 1998). Secondarily, one may then investigate how those students who choose to participate at different levels differ from each other and whether this self-selection has any effect on the estimated program effects (MacKinnon and Lockwood 2003). A major concern has to be with whether it is those students most in need of the program who elect to participate less. Such a finding would suggest that observed effects can only be generalized to lower-risk students, or that potential program effects might be greater than found in the intent-to-treat analysis, and that future versions of the program might include some way of motivating such students to participate at higher levels (MacKinnon and Lockwood 2003).

2. Measurement

2a. Bias introduced by data collection

In educational studies, students are often surveyed by the same people who delivered the intervention to them, or by their regular classroom teachers. These approaches may compromise the honesty of student responses (e.g., they may be subject to demand characteristics) and the actual and perceived confidentiality of student responses (e.g., they may underreport illegal behavior). By contrast, in medical studies, data are often collected by treatment providers who are blind to the assigned condition of any particular subject. In educational studies, maintaining blindness of data collectors would require that third parties, rather than intervention staff or teachers, collect the data from students in schools. In practice, due to funding limitations, this is often not done.

1982 recommendation. FandB recommended the use of third-party data collectors who are blind to all conditions being compared in the study. Of course, they recognized the extreme difficulties involved in doing this in practice. They also suggested greater use of unobtrusive measures (Webb et al. 1966).

History. Researchers have rarely followed the recommendation of using third-party data collectors who know nothing of the research project, especially not the interventions being evaluated or tested. In practice, it is often too expensive to hire third-party data collectors. In addition, keeping even third-party data collectors blind is extremely difficult. Most school-based interventions have many materials, such as posters, that immediately make it clear to a visitor that a particular intervention is present at the school. One would have to ask for these materials to be removed or hidden during data collection, or for the data collection to take place in a location where intervention materials are not displayed. Neither of these suggestions is practical in schools, where even scheduling the data collection can be a major headache. Moreover, the surveys themselves sometimes provide clues as to the interventions being tested. One way of overcoming this is to have all questions that refer to the intervention (for example, questions that are about the process of intervention delivery, receipt, and involvement) be in a separate survey from the survey that asks about outcome behaviors and have it administered separately by different people. The main survey of outcome behaviors could then be administered without the survey administrators seeing any reference to the intervention(s) being evaluated.

Despite the relative inability to remain blind to conditions, the desirability of using as data collectors people who do not know the students and whom the students do not know has been accepted by prevention researchers for many years. This at least maintains actual and perceived confidentiality of student responses at a high level. Most SBRTs use data collectors different from intervention providers and insist that classroom teachers not be present or remain seated during survey administration.

Future studies may be able to utilize Web-based surveys to eliminate or reduce the problems incurred when data collectors are not blind to condition. However, many surveys of young students will still require an on-site proctor to help students understand the questions or navigate the survey—and it will be difficult to keep proctors totally blinded.

Prevention researchers have rarely followed the recommendation to use unobtrusive measures (see Sussman et al. [1993] for an exception). This is due to a perceived lack of viable measures.

2b. Intensive measurement and long-term follow-up

Most modern-day health behavior change/prevention programs are complex and are expected to have both short-term and long-term effects. Therefore, both short-term and long-term evaluations are imperative. Moreover, complex programs have a complex set of outcomes and mediators (and potential moderators), all of which need to be assessed in comprehensive evaluations. When this much assessment is necessary, questions about reactivity naturally arise.

1982 recommendations. Prior to the 1980s, there was great concern about the possible reactivity of intensive measurement, even of pretesting. The concern was that measurement by itself might alter behavior. If only it were so easy to alter behavior! So FandB recommended designs that would enable researchers to disentangle the effects of measurement from the effects of programs. They also recommended that researchers plan evaluations of health behavior change programs to last at least five years, preferably longer.

History. Pretest reactivity is no longer believed to be of real concern, so Solomon four-group designs are not even considered. Similarly, intensive measurement is rarely brought up as a potential problem in evaluation trials of school-based programs.

A related issue, however, concerns the reporting of results from studies that collect measures of many different constructs. Many journals cannot handle articles long enough to report on all available outcomes in one article. Therefore, researchers publish multiple papers from the same study, with different papers reporting results on different constructs. Sometimes, this leads to difficulties of interpretation because slightly different samples may be utilized in different analyses. Also, because of the difficulty of publication, splitting of results into multiple reports sometimes leads to nonreporting of data on some measured constructs because of rejected papers. In other cases, results on some constructs may deliberately not be reported because they were nonsignificant or negative. This can lead to misinterpretation of future meta-analyses because study reports are incomplete. Clearly, full publication of results needs to be encouraged so that inconsistent, nonsignificant, and negative results are known to the field and reviewers.

For many years, the validity of self-reports of sensitive behaviors was questioned. After a series of studies of the use of biochemical validation or the collection of biochemical samples for use in a "bogus pipeline" procedure (Aguinis, Pierce, and Quigley 1993; Presti, Ary, and Lichtenstein 1992; Roese and Jamieson 1993), methods for surveying adolescents that ensure confidentiality were developed that seem to ensure the validity of self-reports of sensitive behaviors (Murray and Perry 1987; Patrick et al. 1994; Stacy et al. 1990).

If we are to understand the processes underlying risky behavior and its prevention, then careful consideration must be given to the choice of measurement occasions, as well as the potential reactivity and subject burden associated with more frequent measurement.

In the 1980s, we were not cognizant of the types of effects that could or could not be expected to last over time. In retrospect, it was never realistic to expect the effects of a six-session smoking prevention program in grade six or seven to last for several years without any other smoking prevention education or without large-scale changes to the environments (and/or the behavior of others in those environments) in which students live and learn. The influences on behavior are widespread and pervasive, ranging from intrapersonal factors such as personality or biological vulnerability, to interpersonal or social influences of families and peers, to broader sociocultural influences of the mass media and other societal-level informational and values-based systems (e.g., economic, political, religious) (see Flay and Petraitis [1994] for one integrative perspective).

More distal causal factors will influence multiple behaviors; hence, the high correlations between adolescent problem behaviors (Flay 2002; Jessor and Jessor 1977). Recognition of this fact has led to proposals for more complex programs that might influence the development of multiple behaviors, both positive and negative (Flay 2002; Flay, Allred, and Ordway 2001).

An important related issue is the dynamic nature of the constructs of interest in SBRTs. Collins and Graham (2002) argued that the nature of the change over time in the constructs being measured should determine the choice of timing and spacing of measurement occasions in a longitudinal study. If a construct is expected to change rapidly and this change is of scientific interest, then frequent measurement is called for. If change is expected to occur more slowly, less frequent measurement is sufficient. If an effect is expected to unfold over time, for example, several years after implementation of a program, then measurement should not end prior to this. If there are certain key developmental points, then measurement should be timed accordingly. In general, most SBRTs have chosen the timing and spacing of measurement occasions on logistical rather than scientific grounds. Many SBRTs obtain measures approximately yearly, which is not frequently enough to be informative about rapidly changing variables. If we are to understand the processes underlying risky behavior and its prevention, then careful consideration must be given to the choice of measurement occasions, as well as the potential reactivity and subject burden associated with more frequent measurement.

3. Analysis

3a. Attrition and other missing data issues

All longitudinal studies suffer from attrition to varying degrees. Most common is attrition of individuals. Less common, but even more devastating, is attrition of entire schools (see section 1d above). In a meta-analysis of eighty-five substance abuse prevention studies, average attrition of students ranged from 19 percent after three months to 33 percent after three years (Hansen, Tobler, and Graham 1990). Studies have shown that absentees, transfers, and dropouts are disproportionately likely to occur among higher-risk populations who are most in need of the intervention (Pirie, Murray, and Jacobs 1988).

Attrition may affect SBRTs in several ways. The loss of subjects may reduce statistical power. If subjects with certain characteristics are more likely to drop out, the external validity of the study is reduced. If attrition is related to experimental condition, the internal validity of the study may be compromised.

1982 recommendations. FandB recommended the use of a blocked design, where if one member of a block or pair drops out, its matched counterpart(s) is dropped as well. They also recommended the use of historical or population-level data as alternate controls.

History. The approach of dropping matched pairs/sets is difficult to implement, either for individuals or for schools (and we know of only one study where it has been done at the school level—see section 1d above). Most researchers do not attempt to match students at the individual level. The approach makes eminent sense at the school level, especially if the number of pairs/sets of schools is relatively small. However, given the expense, in terms of statistical power, of dropping a pair/set of schools from a study, this is an approach that is unlikely to be used very often. It also leads to limiting the generalizability of study findings to the types of schools that remain in the study.

Attrition of individuals was considered a very serious problem as long as statistical analysis occurred at the individual level. Great efforts were made to (1) include schools in studies that had minimal turnover, (2) minimize attrition from measurement due to student absenteeism, and (3) assess the impact of student attrition on results (Biglan et al. 1987; Ellickson 1994; Ellickson, Bianca, and Schoeff 1988; Hansen et al. 1985). From the current perspective, it is interesting to note that researchers typically did not include students in the analysis who entered the school during the course of a study.

When statistical analysis was at the level of the school, attrition of students over time was thought to be less important. It was argued that the unit to be changed was the school, even though most interventions were still designed to change the behavior of individual students, with little attention to altering the school environment, except insofar as it would be altered if many students changed their behavior. However, researchers quickly realized that nonrandom attrition of students from schools, for different reasons, could still have serious repercussions on estimates of intervention effects.

About the same time, multilevel analytical techniques became available, so that data from all students in the school at each wave of data collection could be included in analyses. One common belief is that normal student turnover involves students at the same level of risk leaving and entering the school, and so no special attention need be given to student attrition issues. However, this ignores the fact that students entering the school during the course of the study, although at the same risk level as students leaving the school, are not exposed to the intervention as much as students who remain in the school. At one level, though, this is a sensible perspective—after all, in the real world, programs must be demonstrably effective at the school level despite student turnover.

The modern missing data perspective. Previously, it was not possible to make effective use of partial data from a subject. Therefore, statistical analyses involving any variables for which a particular subject was missing had to eliminate that subject's data entirely. This often introduced severe bias in results, reduced the generalizability of findings, eroded statistical power, and also meant that different analyses performed on the same data set could be based on different subsets of subjects.

Today, the issue of subject attrition has been reframed as a missing data problem (Collins, Schafer, and Kam 2001; Schafer 1997; Schafer and Graham 2002). Maximum likelihood and multiple imputation procedures allow the researcher to include all available data in analyses, without the need to eliminate subjects who may not have been present for a wave of data collection or were present but chose not to respond to some questions (Laird 1988; Hedeker and Gibbons 1997; Hedeker and Rose 2000). These procedures also adjust for biases introduced by differential nonresponse, provided that certain key assumptions are met. Even when these assumptions are not met, modern missing data procedures are greatly preferable to casewise deletion and other ad hoc approaches (Graham, Cumsille, and Elek-Fiske 2003).

Although modern missing data procedures are a huge advance in dealing with attrition, they do not eliminate the associated problems completely. Statistical power is improved with the use of modern missing data procedures as compared to ad hoc procedures, but it is generally not as good as the statistical power associated

with complete data. Furthermore, if the assumptions of the missing data procedures are not met, some bias may remain, albeit greatly reduced in most cases
(Collins, Schafer, and Kam 2001). Resources devoted to minimizing attrition and
other missing data are well spent; complete data are still the best.

Parental consent. One type of "attrition" can occur before a study starts. Students enrolled in a school and participating in a program may not be involved in the
measurement process because they do not have parental consent to do so. There
are two methods to obtain parents' consent for their child to participate in the measurement process: (1) "passive" parent consent, where students are excluded only
if parents return a signed form indicating that they do not want their child to participate; and (2) "active" signed parental consent, where students may only participate in studies if parents return a signed consent form granting permission for their
child to participate (Ji, Pokorny, and Jason 2004). Many studies involving students
are required by federal agencies and IRBs to obtain active rather than passive
parental consent (Protection of Human Subjects 2001; Protection of Pupil Rights
Amendment 2002; U.S. Department of Health and Human Services 1991; see
Brooks-Gunn and Rotheram-Borus [1994] and Tigges [2003] for reviews).

Active consent form return rates (30 to 60 percent; Tigges 2003) are usually
lower than passive consent return rates (93 to 100 percent; Tigges 2003). The lower
return rate, as well as differences between parents who give or deny consent, often
result in a sampling bias, where students who have returned a parent consent form
or whose parents provided consent tend to be less "at risk" for problem behaviors
than students who have not returned a consent form (Dent et al. 1993; Ellickson
and Hawes 1989; Severson and Biglan 1989). Procedures to increase active consent rates require multiple methods at great cost and resources (e.g., monetary,
staff, and time costing $20 to $32 per student—Tigges 2003). For example, we
recently achieved a 98 percent response rate from parents of third graders in Chicago; but it took a special visit and presentation to each classroom, daily visits to
each classroom teacher, an incentive for the teacher, and a pizza party for each
classroom when they achieved a 90 percent return. Twenty percent of the respond-
ing parents denied consent for their child to participate in our study, demonstrat-
ing that although the incentives improved return rates, they did not appear to
coerce active consent. However, this also demonstrates that even high rates of
return may still result in biased samples (Ellickson and Hawes 1989; Ji, Pokorny,
and Jason 2004; Moberg and Piper 1990; O'Donnell et al. 1997). Biased samples
clearly limit the generalizability of research results.

Despite the apparent tightening of government regulations regarding parental
consent, many researchers can still use passive consent procedures (Tigges 2003).
They do this by meeting the "exceptions" that are written into the regulations.
Even with DE funding, it is legally allowable to survey students without signed
parental consent if questions about sensitive topics are not asked, or if students are
not required to participate in the survey or answer all questions (Society for Ado-

lescent Medicine 1995). A recent Institute of Medicine (IOM) report provides the latest views on ethical research with children (Field and Berman 2004).

3b. Small numbers of schools

Randomizing large numbers of large units like schools, school complexes, or communities to multiple conditions is expensive and difficult to coordinate/ manage. But reliance on small numbers of schools limits statistical power, particularly power associated with school-level effects, and also makes it difficult to achieve pretest comparability.

1980s recommendations. One recommended approach was to work in districts where schools are small—one to three classrooms per grade. This was the case for the first Waterloo study. Another recommended approach was to stratify schools on key predictor variables, then randomize from within strata (Graham et al. 1984). This approach has two advantages. First, it helps to ensure statistical comparability even when the sample size is small. Second, if schools are sampled from a wide enough range of strata, it helps to ensure selection of a sample of schools representative of a specified range of "risk" and consequent generalizability of findings (or specification of a narrow range of risk strata within which the program is effective) (Shadish, Cook, and Campbell 2002).

History. Many reports of SBRTs did not report how they minimized statistical differences between conditions, even when small *N*s were involved. Some followed the Graham et al. (1984) recommendations of stratification before randomization, at least in concept. Stratification before randomization should reduce the probability of "unhappy randomization" where there are important chance differences at baseline. The Graham et al. recommendations involved a multiattribute utility measurement approach that used data from presumed risk factors or predictors of the dependent variable to create a single scale of risk on which to stratify. Most researchers have used a simplified version of the approach, stratifying on some combination of presumed correlates of the outcome behavior or related risk factors.

Stratification utilizing pretest data on the dependent variable would probably lead to improved statistical comparability with small sample sizes. To date, very few school-based studies have done this. Usually, this is because schools will not agree to be in a study without knowing their condition (see above). So randomization has to occur before baseline data are available. With the increasing availability of student behavior and achievement data in computerized records, more accurate stratification may be possible for future studies.

3c. Choice of unit of analysis

Students within a group (classroom or school) are not independent, in the statistical sense, of other students within the same group. Thus, students within classrooms are more like each other than they are like students in other classrooms or schools. This dependence affects statistical properties and impacts analytical strategies. This leads to questions about the unit of analysis. The question used to be phrased in terms of at which level or unit to analyze the data, the individual, or the unit of assignment (e.g., school) or something in between (e.g., classroom).

1982 recommendation. FandB's recommendation was to be aware of the issue and conduct analyses at multiple levels in an attempt to estimate the true level of intervention effect and a confidence interval. The conservative approach was presumed to be to conduct the analysis at the level of the unit of assignment. FandB suggested hierarchical analytical approaches; however, such methods were not widely known or available at that time.

History. During the 1990s, the issue of intraclass correlations in school-based research came to the fore (e.g., Murray et al. 1994; Siddiqui et al. 1996; Murray 1998) and multilevel analyses were recommended (Koepke and Flay 1989; Murray 1998). However, until methods appeared that made such analyses easier (Bryk and Raudenbush 1992; Goldstein 1987, 1995; Hedeker, Gibbons, and Flay 1994), few researchers attempted them. These days it would be almost impossible to publish data from a SBRT that was not analyzed using one of the well-established approaches to multilevel analysis (Bloom, Bos, and Lee 1999).

There is one conceptual point we wish to emphasize. Because SBRTs take place within a multilevel structure, research questions may be posed at any of several levels or may even involve more than one level. For example, consider the following three research questions pertaining to a hypothetical intervention administered at the school level: (1) Is the intervention effective for high-risk individuals? (2) Is the intervention as effective for high-risk schools? (3) Are individuals at high- and low-risk statuses differentially affected by the intervention in high- as opposed to low-risk schools? In (1), the effect is defined at the individual level; in (2), the effect is defined at the school level; (3) involves an interaction between individual- and school-level characteristics. These are distinct questions requiring different analyses that may yield different answers about intervention effectiveness. It follows that analyses to address them are not interchangeable; in other words, analyses performed on school means may address (2) but do not address (1).

4. Optimizing and extending the reach of preventive interventions

4a. Phases of research: Understanding complex program packages

School-based prevention programs have always been multiple-session curricula. Over the years, they have become longer and more complex as the list of target behaviors, the corresponding mediating variables, and the targeted ecologies (classrooms, schools, families) increased in number and scope. Many programs now take place over multiple years, consist of multiple components (e.g., information, correction of social norms, development of social skills, and many others), and involve whole schools, families, and communities.

1982 recommendation. FandB suggested that where possible, experimental studies to determine the separate contributions of different program components should be conducted.

History. Very few researchers have adopted the recommended approach of experimentally manipulating program components. There are two related approaches: dismantling and constructive research strategies (MacKinnon et al. 2002; West and Aiken 1997). Hansen and Graham (1991) conducted a dismantling study in which one condition provided only information, one provided information plus social skills training, and one provided information plus education on correcting normative beliefs. The constructive approach has been used to find intervention components that have significant effects on presumed mediator variables, which are then combined into one program (Sussman et al. 1995).

Another approach to determining which program components produce behavioral effects is to attempt to determine whether some components have the immediate effects expected of them and to then determine whether those immediate effects actually lead to (i.e., mediate) program effects on the final behavioral outcomes of interest. This approach has been tried with mixed results. For example, in a review of reports of program effects on mediators in early tobacco prevention studies, McCaul and Glasgow (1985) found inconsistent findings across studies. For example, Botvin and his colleagues have assessed intervention effects on a wide range of presumed mediators but reported positive results on different mediators from different studies. What do we make of such a pattern of findings? Other mixed results have been reported. For example, several researchers (Donaldson, Graham, and Hansen 1994; Hansen et al. 1998; MacKinnon et al. 1991) found that changes in normative beliefs mediated intervention effects on substance use, but improved resistance skills did not. Others have found that improved resistance skills did mediate program effects on behaviors (Botvin et al. 1999). These mixed results suggest either that different programs have their effects in different ways or that current research designs or mediation analytical methods are still inadequate for understanding complex programs.

The use of another, very different approach to developing programs with effective components, called the Multiphase Optimization Strategy (MOST) has been suggested recently by Collins et al. (forthcoming). The objective of MOST as applied in prevention research is to identify active components and their most appropriate doses and combine them into an optimized intervention, which is then subjected to an experimental evaluation. This approach was inspired by methods originally developed in engineering and agriculture, and owes much to Box (e.g., Box, Hunter, and Hunter 1978). MOST divides the program development and evaluation process into three phases, called screening, refining, and confirming. In the screening phase, an array of candidate program components is identified, and a series of rapid experiments is conducted to sort through them to identify the effective ones. In the refining phase, the program components that make it through the screening phases are examined further. In this phase, interactions with other components and with characteristics of the individual or delivery setting are examined, and the optimal dose of each component is determined. The goal of the screening and refining phases is to arrive at an optimized intervention, containing only active components set to the most appropriate doses. This optimized intervention is then tested for efficaciousness or effectiveness in the confirming phase. One notable aspect of the MOST approach is that, in contrast to the approaches used in much of prevention science, MOST rests heavily on randomized experiments rather than on results of observational analyses of secondary data from prior SBRTs. Although MOST calls for a greater up-front investment in the screening and refining phases than the standard approach, there is a payoff later in terms of fewer, simpler, and more powerful full-blown SBRTs.

4b. Efficacy and effectiveness

Before the 1980s, there was little recognition of the desirability of a carefully designed sequence of studies to inform the development, testing, and adoption of effective prevention programs. It was also quite common to confound formative and summative evaluation, and efficacy and effectiveness studies, or not recognize the difference between them (see explanation below). Often, a short intervention developed to test theory in a real-world setting (classroom or school) was converted into a "program" with the belief that this program could be adopted in a widespread way and delivered to many classrooms or schools with positive outcomes. Many early prevention research projects involved developing short programs (two to ten lessons for one particular grade level) delivered by research staff to test a broad hypothesis that a particular approach to prevention could be effective or could be more effective than another approach. When found to be effective in the context of a study, these programs were then often promoted as effective programs, not just as promising strategies ready for further development or ready to be incorporated into a more comprehensive program.

1982 recommendations. FandB advocated a careful distinction between formative and summative research, with the idea that interventions developed for early phases of research would not necessarily translate into effective programs in the real world. They also suggested the necessity of engaging in a thoughtful sequence of phases of research during the development of prevention programs, an idea later elaborated in Flay (1986).

History. Despite much attention to the idea of phases of research during the 1980s (Flay 1986; Greenwald and Cullen 1984; McKinlay 1981; NHLBI 1983; Office of Technology Assessment 1978), only a few researchers have pursued a careful sequence of studies during program development. Most notable is Steve Sussman (Sussman et al. 1995). Some researchers have conducted multiple efficacy studies and a few effectiveness studies to demonstrate generalizability of program effects to different populations, most notably Gil Botvin. Harold Holder and others have written on a modified sequence of studies that can accommodate programs developed outside of the research context (Holder et al. 1995, 1999).

Effectiveness trials are called health care trials by some health care researchers (Sechrest et al. 1979; Spitzer, Feinstein, and Sackett 1975) and are similar to what program evaluators call outcome/impact evaluations. However, some key differences between the health care and evaluation approaches have important implications. When health care researchers conduct an effectiveness evaluation, they usually have already determined the efficacy (effects under controlled conditions) of the treatment or program being tested. The effectiveness evaluation is then concerned with whether more good than harm is done by the efficacious treatment when delivered via a program in the real-world setting. An efficacious treatment may still have differential effects because of differences in its availability or acceptance or because of the effects of other uncontrolled environmental or social influences.

4c. Differential effects in subpopulations: Implications for prevention

Prevention programs are often labeled universal, selective, or indicated (Mrazek and Haggerty 1994), depending on the target population. Universal programs target whole populations, selective programs target high-risk populations, and indicated programs target those who have already evidenced early problem behavior. Most SBRTs in prevention involve universal programs, in which a single type and dose of program is delivered to all subjects. But is a single type and dose of a program effective for all participants, and if not, what implications does this have for SBRTs?

1982 recommendation. FandB's focus in 1982 was on ensuring that intervention and control groups are equivalent in terms of the average level of the problem behavior already evident among students or the average level of motivation to change behavior. Obviously, this is achieved by random assignment of sufficient numbers of schools to ensure statistical equivalence on all variables.

Our focus here will be on another issue that arises with universal programs, that of the likely differential effects on different subpopulations of the target population. Clearly, a program cannot prevent a behavior that will never occur. Thus, low-risk students do not really need the program, and no change in their behavior can be expected. On the other hand, the greatest program effects are possible among the highest-risk students, but can the highest-risk students be helped by a universal program, or will they need a more intensive selective or indicated program? Are there some students, such as those in a particular ethnic group, who would benefit more from different program content or different program delivery? Such questions suggest conducting analyses of the interaction between variables such as risk level, pretest status, and ethnicity with experimental condition.

History. In their earliest studies of smoking prevention programs, Best et al. (1984) recognized the possibility of differential effects on subsets of students. They found that the largest effects occurred for students at the highest risk of becoming smokers. Few other researchers have presented such analyses until recently.

In recent years, Sheppard Kellem and Hendricks Brown have advocated for such analyses, using growth curve approaches (e.g., Curran and Bollen 2001; Muthén 2001). They reported larger effects of the Good Behavior Game for the highest-risk group of students (Kellam et al. 1998). Segawa et al. (forthcoming) also found that the Aban Aya program had its greatest effects among males at highest risk. Others have found the largest effects for students in the middle of the range of risk, suggesting that their program was not powerful enough to affect those students at highest risk (Graham et al. 1990).

The success of adaptive interventions depends on several factors, including identification of appropriate tailoring variables, precise measurement of these variables, identification of appropriate rules for assigning intervention dosage, and careful adherence to these rules.

As our understanding of differential program effects on subpopulations grows, it becomes evident that in some cases, a "one size fits all" approach may not be the most effective prevention strategy. Increasingly, prevention scientists are turning to an adaptive intervention strategy (e.g., Conduct Problems Prevention Research Group 1992, 1999a, 1999b) as an alternative. In an adaptive intervention, the content and/or dose of the intervention is varied in response to characteristics of the designated recipient. The characteristics that form the basis for assignment of intervention content and/or dose are called tailoring variables. For example, in the Fast Track intervention, only students who demonstrated poor reading ability were provided with reading tutoring. Thus, reading ability served as a tailoring variable. Other components of the Fast Track intervention were similarly assigned based on other tailoring variables.

Collins, Murphy, and Bierman (2004) outlined methodological considerations relevant to the design and evaluation of adaptive interventions. They pointed out that adaptive interventions have the potential to reduce negative effects that may result from intervention doses that are too large or too small; to increase participant compliance; to reduce waste, by avoiding spending program resources on those not expected to benefit; and to increase the potency of interventions, if the resources saved are reallocated to individuals who can benefit from them. The success of adaptive interventions depends on several factors, including identification of appropriate tailoring variables, precise measurement of these variables, identification of appropriate rules for assigning intervention dosage, and careful adherence to these rules. More research is needed on the circumstances under which adaptive interventions may represent a viable and desirable alternative to the standard approach to prevention.

E. Conclusions

We derive six major conclusions from this review.

1. *Sequence planning is important*. This is true at the level of initial intervention development and testing, as Collins et al. (forthcoming) have outlined, and at the level of moving through the cycle of intervention development, efficacy trials, effectiveness trials, and broad-scale dissemination (Flay 1986). The Society for Prevention Research has recently developed criteria for assessing the efficacy, effectiveness, and disseminability of prevention interventions that address most of the issues discussed in this article (Flay, Biglan, et al. 2004).
2. *Time is important*. Prevention interventions can have immediate effects on cognitive or affective outcomes, and even on some behavioral outcomes, but the ultimate effects of importance to society often occur over the long term. It is important to determine whether school-based interventions have effects that last into and beyond high school and whether they significantly alter life course trajectories. The need for long-term follow-up of school-based interventions has many implications for research and measurement design.
3. *Keeping up with, and remaining open to, methodological advances is important*. School-based prevention researchers have, on the whole, been leaders in prevention and educational science because they have kept up with methodological advances and, in many cases, contributed directly to them. In the past twenty years, multilevel data analysis approaches, growth curve analysis, and modern missing data methods have greatly improved statistical analysis of SBRTs. Methodological research is being conducted in a number of areas that promise to make the next fifteen years equally exciting.
4. *Publication of all results is important*. Without publication of results, even from less than perfect studies, the field cannot learn. Publication of only partial results also is limiting to the field. Peer-review publication plays a particularly important role in the accumulation of a coherent body of knowledge. Sometimes, it is difficult to place a report of null results in the peer-review literature. Such reports should be placed where they can be easily accessed, such as a well-maintained Web site.
5. *Accumulation of knowledge is important*. The true measure of advancement in knowledge is not the individual study but the accumulation of findings from reviews and meta-analyses. Unlike many other areas of school-based research, there has been a clear accumulation of knowledge in school-based prevention research. Multiple meta-analyses have been possible and have contributed to knowledge accumulation. However, many preventive interventions remain "black boxes." More can and should be done to look inside these black boxes, particularly when new interventions are being developed.
6. *The devil is in the details*. Methodologically sound school-based research is not easy. It requires lots of institutional relationships and on-the-ground work relating to school

administrators and teachers; obtaining of archival data or pretest data to enable screening, matching, and assignment to conditions; ongoing attention to implementation fidelity; careful measurement; advanced data analysis; and thoughtful consideration of results before any conclusions are drawn. Despite the difficulties, we argue that it is possible to conduct high-quality SBRTs and to use this research to make progress in reducing the prevalence of problem behaviors.

Notes

1. Some of these programs (e.g., DARE) included some social influences awareness, normative education and skills training, but the overall emphasis was much more on information and affective issues.

2. Used random assignment, had at least four hours of programming, posttest at least three months, was not a placebo program, was not compared to another program (i.e., control was no treatment), was longitudinal, and had a measure of control for preexisting differences.

References

Aguinis, Herman, Charles A. Pierce, and Brian M. Quigley. 1993. Conditions under which a bogus pipeline procedure enhances the validity of self-reported cigarette smoking: A meta-analytic review. *Journal of Applied Social Psychology* 23 (5): 352-73.

Bandura, Albert. 1977. *Social learning theory.* Englewood Cliffs, NJ: Prentice Hall.

Best, J. Allan, Brian R. Flay, Shelagh M. J. Towson, Katherine B. Ryan, Cheryl L. Perry, K. Stephen Brown, Mary W. Kersell, and Josie R. d'Avernas. 1984. Smoking prevention and the concept of risk. *Journal of Applied Social Psychology* 143:257-73.

Best, J. Allan, Shirley J. Thomson, Susanne M. Santi, Edward A. Smith, and K. Stephen Brown. 1988. Preventing cigarette smoking among school children. In *Annual review of public health*, vol. 9, ed. Lester Breslow, Jonathan E. Fielding, and L. B. Lave. Palo Alto, CA: Annual Reviews Inc.

Biglan, Anthony, Patricia J. Mrazek, Douglas Carnine, and Brian R. Flay. 2003. The integration of research and practice in the prevention of youth problem behaviors. *American Psychologist* 58 (6-7): 433-40.

Biglan, Anthony, Herbert Severson, Dennis V. Ary, Carol Faller, Cheri Gallison, Robert Thompson, Russell Glasgow, and Edward Lichtenstein. 1987. Do smoking prevention programs really work? Attrition and the internal and external validity of an evaluation of a refusal skills training program. *Journal of Behavioral Medicine* 102:159-71.

Bloom, Howard S., Johannes M. Bos, and Suk-Won Lee. 1999. Using cluster random assignment to measure program impacts: Statistical implications for the evaluation of education programs. *Evaluation Review* 234:445-69.

Boruch, Robert F. 1975. On common contentions about randomized field experiments. In *Evaluation studies review annual*, vol. 1. Beverly Hills, CA: Sage.

Boruch, Robert G., and Ellen Foley. 2000. The honestly experimental society: Sites and other entities as the units of allocation and analysis in randomized trials. In *Validity and social experimentation: Donald Campbell's legacy*, vol. 1, ed. L. Bickman. Thousand Oaks, CA: Sage.

Botvin, Gilbert J. 2000. Preventing drug abuse in schools: Social competence enhancement approaches targeting individual-level etiologic factors. *Addictive Behaviors* 256:887-98.

Botvin, Gilbert J., Eli Baker, Linda Dusenbury, Elizabeth M. Botvin, and Tracy Diaz. 1995. Long-term follow-up results of a randomized drug abuse prevention trial in a white middle-class population. *Journal of the American Medical Association* 273 (14): 1106-12.

Botvin, Gilbert J., Eli Baker, Linda Dusenbury, Stephanie Tortu, and Elizabeth M. Botvin. 1990. Preventing adolescent drug abuse through a multimodal cognitive-behavioral approach: Results of a 3-year study. *Journal of Consulting and Clinical Psychology* 58 (4): 437-46.

Botvin, Gilbert J., and Kenneth W. Griffin. 2001. Life Skills Training: Theory, methods, and effectiveness of a drug abuse prevention approach. In *Innovations in adolescent substance abuse interventions*, ed. Eric F. Wagner and Holly B. Waldron. Amsterdam: Pergamon/Elsevier Science.

Botvin, Gilbert J., Kenneth W. Griffin, Tracy Diaz, N. Miller, and Michelle Ifill-Williams. 1999. Smoking initiation and escalation in early adolescent girls: One-year follow-up of a school-based prevention intervention for minority youth. *Journal of the American Medial Women's Association* 54:139-43.

Box, G. E. P., W. G. Hunter, and J. S. Hunter. 1978. *Statistics for experimenters: An introduction to design, data analysis, and model building.* New York: John Wiley.

Brooks-Gunn, J., and Mary Jane Rotheram-Borus. 1994. Rights to privacy in research: Adolescents versus parents. *Ethics and Behavior* 42:109-21.

Bryk, Anthony S., and Steven W. Raudenbush. 1992. *Hierarchical linear models: Applications and data analysis methods.* Newbury Park, CA: Sage.

Campbell, Donald T., and Robert F. Boruch. 1975. Making the case for randomized assignment to treatments by considering the alternatives: Six ways in which quasi-experimental evaluations in compensatory education tend to underestimate effects. In *Evaluation and experiment: Some critical issues in assessing social programs*, ed. C. Bennett and A. Lumsdaine. New York: Academic Press.

Campbell, Donald T., and Julian C. Stanley. 1967. *Experimental and quasi-experimental designs for research.* Chicago: Rand McNally.

Collins, Linda M., and John W. Graham. 2002. The effect of the timing and spacing of observations in longitudinal studies of tobacco and other drug use: Temporal design considerations. *Drug and Alcohol Dependence* 68 (Suppl. 1): S85-96.

Collins, Linda M., Susan A. Murphy, and Kathy L. Bierman. 2004. A conceptual framework for adaptive preventive interventions. *Prevention Science* 5:181-92.

Collins, Linda M., Susan A. Murphy, Vijay N. Nair, and Victor Strecher. Forthcoming. A strategy for optimizing and evaluating behavioral interventions. *Annals of Behavioral Medicine.*

Collins, Linda M., Joseph L. Schafer, and C. M. Kam. 2001. A comparison of inclusive and restrictive strategies in modern missing data procedures. *Psychological Methods* 64:330-51.

Conduct Problems Prevention Research Group. 1992. A developmental and clinical model for the prevention of conduct disorders: The Fast Track Program. *Development and Psychopathology* 4:509-28.

———. 1999a. Initial impact of the Fast Track prevention trial for conduct problems: I. The high-risk sample. *Journal of Consulting and Clinical Psychology* 67:631-47.

———. 1999b. Initial impact of the Fast Track prevention trial for conduct problems: II. Classroom effects. *Journal of Consulting and Clinical Psychology* 67:648-57.

Cook, Thomas D. 1999. Considering the major arguments against random assignment: An analysis of the intellectual culture surrounding evaluation in American schools of education. Presented at the Harvard Faculty Seminar on Experiments in Education, Harvard University, Cambridge, MA.

Cook, Thomas D., and Donald T. Campbell. 1979. *Quasi-experimentation: Design and analysis issues for field settings.* Chicago: Rand McNally.

Cook, Thomas D., and Monique R. Payne. 2000. Objecting to the objections to using random assignment in educational research. In *Evidence matters: Randomized trials in education research*, ed. Frederick Mosteller and Robert F. Boruch. Washington, DC: Brookings Institution Press.

Curran, Patrick J., and Kenneth A. Bollen. 2001. The best of both worlds: Combining autoregressive and latent curve models. In *New methods for the analysis of change of behavior*, ed. Linda M. Collins and Aline G. Sayer. Washington, DC: American Psychological Association.

Cushman, Mary, Lewis H. Kuller, Ross Prentice, Rebecca J. Rodabough, Bruce M. Psaty, Randall S. Stafford, Steven Sidney, and Frits Rosendaal. 2004. Estrogen plus progestin and risk of venous thrombosis. *Journal of the American Medical Association* 292 (13):1573-80.

Dent, Clyde W., J. Galaif, Steve Sussman, Alan Stacy, Dee Burton, and Brian R. Flay. 1993. Demographic, psychosocial, and behavioral differences in samples of actively and passively consented adolescents. *Addictive Behaviors* 28:51-56.

Derzon, James H., and Sandra J. Wilson. 1999. An empirical review of school-based programs to prevent violence: Report to the Hamilton Fish National Institute on School and Community Violence. Presented at the annual meeting of the American Society of Criminology, Toronto, Canada.

Dielman, Ted E., Sharon L. Leach, Ann L. Lyons, Amy T. Lorenger, D. M. Klos, and William J. Horvath. 1985. Resisting pressures to smoke: Fifteen-month follow-up results of an elementary school based smoking prevention project. *International Journal of Health Education* 4:28-35.

Donaldson, Stewart I., John W. Graham, and William B Hansen. 1994. Testing the generalizability of intervening mechanism theories: Understanding the effects of adolescent drug use prevention interventions.
Journal of Behavioral Medicine 17:1-22.

Durlak, Joseph A., and Anne M. Wells. 1997. Primary prevention mental health programs for children and
adolescents: A meta-analytic review. *American Journal of Community Psychology* 252:115-52.

Ellickson, Phyllis L. 1994. Getting and keeping schools and kids for evaluation studies. *Journal of Community
Psychology*, CSAP Special Issue, pp. 102-16.

Ellickson, Phyllis L., Domenica Bianca, and Diane C. Schoeff. 1988. Containing attrition in school-based
research: An innovative approach. *Evaluation Review* 124:331-51.

Ellickson, Phyllis L., and Jennifer A. Hawes. 1989. An assessment of active versus passive methods for obtaining parental consent. *Evaluation Review* 132:45-55.

Evans, Richard I. 1976. Smoking in children: Developing a social psychological strategy of deterrence. *Preventive Medicine* 5:122-27.

Field, Marilyn J., and Richard E. Berman, eds. 2004. *The ethical conduct of research involving children*.
Washington, DC: Institute of Medicine.

Flay, Brian R. 1985. Psychosocial approaches to smoking prevention: A review of findings. *Health Psychology*
45:449-88.

———. 1986. Efficacy and effectiveness trials and other phases of research in the development of health promotion programs. *Preventive Medicine* 15:451-74.

———. 1987. Social psychological approaches to smoking prevention: Review and recommendations. In
Advances in health promotion and education, vol 2., ed. W. Ward, S. Simonds, P. D. Mullen, and M. H.
Becker. Greenwich, CT: JAI.

———. 2000. Approaches to substance use prevention utilizing school curriculum plus social environment
change. *Addictive Behaviors* 256:861-85.

———. 2002. Positive youth development requires comprehensive health promotion programs. *American
Journal of Health Behavior* 266:407-24.

Flay, Brian R., Carol G. Allred, and Nicole Ordway. 2001. Effects of the Positive Action Program on achievement and discipline: Two matched-control comparisons. *Prevention Science* 22:71-90.

Flay, Brian R., and J. Allan Best. 1982. Overcoming design problems in evaluating health behavior problems.
Evaluation and the Health Professions 5:43-69.

Flay, Brian R., Anthony Biglan, Robert F. Boruch, Felipe G. Castro, Denise Gottfredson, Shepard Kellam,
Eve K. Moscicki, Steven Schinke, Jeffery Valentine, and Peter Ji. 2004. *Standards of evidence: Criteria
for efficacy, effectiveness and dissemination*. Washington, DC: Society for Prevention Research.

Flay, Brian R., Bonnie R. Brannon, C. Anderson Johnson, William B. Hansen, Arthur L. Ulene, Deborah A.
Whitney-Saltiel, Laura R. Gleason, Steve Sussman, Michael D. Gavin, Kimarie M. Glowacz, Debra F.
Sobol, and Dana C. Spiegel. 1988. The television, school and family smoking prevention/cessation pro-
ject: I. Theoretical basis and program development. *Preventive Medicine* 175:585-607.

Flay, Brian R., Josie R. d'Avernas, J. Allan Best, Mary W. Kersell, and Katherine B. Ryan. 1983. Cigarette
smoking: Why young people do it and ways of preventing it. In *Pediatric and adolescent behavioral medicine*, ed. P. J. McGrath and P. Firestone. New York: Springer.

Flay, Brian R., Sally Graumlich, Eisuke Segawa, James L. Burns, Michelle Y. Holliday, and Aban Aya Investigators. 2004. Effects of two prevention programs on high-risk behaviors among African-American youth:
A randomized trial. *Archives of Pediatric and Adolescent Medicine* 158:377-84.

Flay, Brian R., David Koepke, Shirley T. Thomson, Susanne Santi, J. Allan Best, and K. Stephen Brown. 1989.
Six-year follow-up of the first Waterloo school smoking prevention trial. *American Journal of Public
Health* 79 (10): 1371-76.

Flay, Brian R., Todd Q. Miller, Donald Hedeker, Ohid Siddiqui, Cynthia F. Britton, Bonnie R. Brannon, Carl
Anderson Johnson, William B. Hansen, Steve Sussman, and Clyde Dent. 1995. The television, school and
family smoking prevention and cessation project: VIII. Student outcomes and mediating variables. *Preventive Medicine* 24:29-40.

Flay, Brian R., and John Petraitis. 1994. The theory of triadic influence: A new theory of health behavior with
implications for preventive interventions. In *Advances in medical sociology*, vol. IV, *A reconsideration of
models of health behavior change*, ed. Gary S. Albrecht. Greenwich, CT: JAI.

Flay, Brian R., Katerine B. Ryan, J. Allan Best, K. Stephen Brown, Mary W. Kersell, Jose R. d'Avernas, and Mark P. Zanna. 1985. Are social psychological smoking prevention programs effective? The Waterloo study. *Journal of Behavioral Medicine* 81:37-59.

Frost, Jennifer J., and Jacqueline D. Forrest. 1995. Understanding the impact of effective teenage pregnancy prevention programs. *Family Planning Perspectives* 275:188-95.

Glasgow, Russell E., Kevin D. McCaul, V. B. Freeborn, and H. K. O'Neill. 1981. Immediate and long-term health consequences information in the prevention of adolescent smoking. *The Behavior Therapist* 4:15-16.

Goldstein, H. 1995. *Multilevel statistical models.* 2nd ed. London: Edward Arnold.

———. 1987. *Multilevel models in educational and social research.* London: Oxford University Press.

Goodstadt, Michael. 1978. Alcohol and drug education: Models and outcomes. *Health Education Monographs* 6:263-79.

Gottfredson, Denise C., Gary D. Gottfredson, and S. Skroban. 1996. A multimodal school-based prevention demonstration. *Journal of Adolescent Research* 111:97-115.

Graham, John W., P. E. Cumsille, and E. Elek-Fiske. 2003. Methods for handling missing data. In *Research methods in psychology*, ed. J. A. Schinka and W. F. Velicer, 87-114. Vol. 2 of *Handbook of psychology*, editor-in-chief, I. B. Weiner. New York: Wiley.

Graham, John W., Brian R. Flay, C. Anderson Johnson, William B. Hansen, and Linda M. Collins. 1984. Group comparability: A multiattribute utility measurement approach to the use of random assignment with small numbers of aggregated units. *Evaluation Review* 8 (2): 247-60.

Graham, John W., C. Anderson Johnson, William B. Hansen, Brian R. Flay, and Mimi Gee. 1990. Drug use prevention programs, gender, and ethnicity: Evaluation of three seventh grade Project SMART cohorts. *Preventive Medicine* 193:305-13.

Green, Dorothy E. 1979. Youth education. In *Smoking and health: A report of the Surgeon General.* DHEW Publication no. (PHS) 79-50066. Washington, DC: U.S. Public Health Service, Office on Smoking and Health.

Greenwald, Peter, and Joseph W. Cullen. 1984. The scientific approach to cancer control. *CA: A Cancer Journal for Clinicians* 34:328-32.

Hallfors, Denise, and Karen D. Godette. 2002. Will the "principles of effectiveness" improve prevention practice? Early findings from a diffusion study. *Health Education Research* 174:461-70.

Hansen, William B. 1992. School-based substance abuse prevention: A review of the state of the art in curriculum, 1980-1990. *Health Education Research* 73:403-30.

Hansen, William B., Linda M. Collins, Kevin C. Malotte, Carl Anderson Johnson, and Jonathan E. Fielding. 1985. Attrition in prevention research. *Journal of Behavioral Medicine* 8:261-75.

Hansen, William B., and John W. Graham. 1991. Preventing alcohol, marijuana, and cigarette use among adolescents: Peer pressure resistance training versus establishing conservative norms. *Preventive Medicine* 203:414-30.

Hansen, William B., John W. Graham, Bonnie H. Wolkenstein, Beth Z. Lundy, Jill L. Pearson, Brian R. Flay, and C. Anderson Johnson. 1988. Differential impact of three alcohol prevention curricula on hypothesized mediating variables. *Journal of Drug Education* 18 (2): 143-53.

Hansen, William B., C. Anderson Johnson, Brian R. Flay, John W. Graham, and Judith L. Sobel. 1998. Affective and social influences approaches to the prevention of multiple substance abuse among seventh grade students: Results from Project SMART. *Preventive Medicine* 17:135-54.

Hansen, William B., Nancy S. Tobler, and John W. Graham. 1990. Attrition in substance abuse prevention research: A meta-analysis of 85 longitudinally followed cohorts. *Evaluation Review* 146:677-85.

Hawkins, J. David, Richard F. Catalano, R. Kosterman, R. Abbott, and K. G. Hill. 1999. Preventing adolescent health-risk behaviors by strengthening protection during childhood. *Archives of Pediatrics and Adolescent Medicine* 153 (3): 226-34.

Hedeker, Donald, and Robert D. Gibbons. 1997. Application of random-effects pattern-mixture models for missing data in longitudinal studies. *Psychological Methods* 2:64-78.

Hedeker, Donald, Robert D. Gibbons, and Brian R. Flay. 1994. Random-effects regression models for clustered data: With an example from smoking prevention research. *Journal of Consulting and Clinical Psychology* 624: 757-65.

Hedeker, Donald, and Jennifer S. Rose. 2000. The natural history of smoking: A pattern-mixture random-effects regression model. In *Multivariate applications in substance use research*, ed. Jennifer S. Rose, Laurie Chassin, Clark C. Presson, and Steven J. Sherman. Hillsdale, NJ: Lawrence Erlbaum.

Holder, Harold, Gayle Boyd, Jan Howard, Brian R. Flay, Robert Voas, and Michael Grossman. 1995. Alcohol-problem prevention policy: The need for a phases of research model. *Journal of Public Health Policy* 163:324-46.

Holder, Harold, Brian R. Flay, Jan Howard, Gayle Boyd, Robert Voas, and Michael Grossman. 1999. Phases of alcohol problem prevention research. *Journal of Alcoholism: Clinical and Experimental Research* 231:183-94.

Jessor, Richard, and Shirley L Jessor. 1977. *Problem behavior and psychosocial development*. New York: Academic Press.

Ji, Peter, Steve Pokorny, and Leonard Jason. 2004. Factors influencing middle and high schools' active parental consent return rates. *Evaluation Review* 286:578-91.

Kellam, Shepard G., X. Ling, R. Merisca, C. Hendricks Brown, and Nicholas Ialongo. 1998. The effect of the level of aggression in the first grade classroom on the course and malleability of aggressive behavior into middle school. *Development and Psychopathology* 102:165-85. (Erratum appears in *Development and Psychopathology* 121 [2000]: 107.)

Kirby, Douglas. 2001. Understanding what works and what doesn't in reducing adolescent sexual risk-taking. *Family Planning Perspectives* 336:276-81.

Kirby, Douglas, and Ralph J. DiClemente. 1994. School-based interventions to prevent unprotected sex and HIV among adolescents. In *Preventing AIDS: Theories and methods of behavioral interventions. AIDS prevention and mental health*, ed. Ralph J. DiClemente and John L. Peterson, 117-39. New York, Plenum.

Koepke, David, and Brian R. Flay. 1989. Levels of analysis. *New Directions in Program Evaluation* 43:75-88.

Laird, Nan M. 1988. Missing data in longitudinal studies. *Statistics in Medicine* 7:305-15.

Little, Roderick, and Linda Yau. 1996. Intent-to-treat analysis for longitudinal studies with drop-outs. *Biometrics* 52:3124-3133.

———. 1998. Statistical techniques for analyzing data from prevention trials: Treatment of no-shows using Rubin's causal model. *Psychological Methods* 3:147-59.

MacKinnon, David P., C. Anderson Johnson, Mary Ann Pentz, James H. Dwyer, William B. Hansen, Brian R. Flay, and Eric Yu Wang. 1991. Mediating mechanisms in a school-based drug prevention program: First-year effects of the Midwestern Prevention Project. *Health Psychology* 103:164-72.

MacKinnon, David P., and Chondra L. Lockwood. 2003. Advances in statistical methods for substance abuse prevention research. *Prevention Science* 43:155-71.

MacKinnon, David P., Marcia P. Taborga, and Antonio A. Morgan-Lopez. 2002. Mediation designs for tobacco prevention research. *Drug and Alcohol Dependence* 68:S69-S83.

McCaul, Kevin D., and Russell Glasgow. 1985. Preventing adolescent smoking: What have we learned about treatment construct validity? *Health Psychology* 44:361-87.

McGuire, William J. 1964. Inducing resistance to persuasion. In *Advances in experimental social psychology*, vol. 1, ed. Leonard Berkowitz. New York: Academic Press.

———. 1985. Attitudes and attitude change. In *Handbook of social psychology*, vol. 2, 3rd ed., ed. G. Lindsey and E. Aranson. Reading, MA: Addison-Wesley.

McKinlay, John B. 1981. From "promising report" to "standard procedure": Seven stages in the career of a medical innovation. *The Milbank Memorial Fund Quarterly. Health and Society* 59:374-411.

Moberg, Paul D., and Douglas L. Piper. 1990. Obtaining active parental consent via telephone in adolescent substance abuse prevention research. *Evaluation Review* 143:315-23.

Mrazek, Patricia J., and Robert J. Haggerty, eds. 1994. *Reducing risks for mental disorders: Frontiers for preventive intervention research*. Washington, DC: National Academy Press.

Murray, David M. 1998. *Design and analysis of group-randomized trials*. New York: Oxford University Press.

Murray, David M., and Cheryl L. Perry. 1987. The measurement of substance use among adolescents: When is the "bogus pipeline" method needed? *Addictive Behaviors* 12:225-33.

Murray, David M., Brenda L. Rooney, Peter J. Hannan, Arthur V. Peterson, Dennis V. Ary, Albert Biglan, Gilbert J. Botvin, Richard I. Evans, Brian R. Flay, Robert Futterman, Greg J. Getz, Patrick M. Marek, Mario Orlandi, Mary Ann Pentz, Cheryl L. Perry, and Steven P. Schinke. 1994. Intraclass correlation among common measures of adolescent smoking: Estimates, correlates and applications in smoking prevention studies. *American Journal of Epidemiology* 140 (11): 1038-50.

Muthén, Bengt O. 2001. Second-generation structural equation modeling with a combination of categorical and continuous latent variables: New opportunities for latent class-latent growth modeling. In *New methods for the analysis of change*, ed. Linda M. Collins and A. G. Sayer. Washington, DC: American Psychological Association.

National Heart, Lung and Blood Institute. 1983. *Guidelines for demonstration and education research grants*, vol. 12, no. 9. Washington, DC: National Heart, Lung and Blood Institute.

O'Donnell, Lydia N., Richard H. Duran, Alexi San Doval, Michael J. Breslin, Greg M. Juhn, and Ann Stueve. 1997. Obtaining written parental permission for school-based health surveys of urban young adolescents. *Journal of Adolescent Health* 21:376-83.

Office of Technology Assessment. 1978. *Assessing the efficacy and safety of medical technologies*. NTIS Order no. PB-286929. September. Washington, DC: Government Printing Office.

Patrick, Donald L., Allen Cheadle, Diane C. Thomspon, Paula Diehr, Thomas Koepsell, and Susan Kinne. 1994. The validity of self-reported smoking: A review and meta-analysis. *American Journal of Public Health* 847:1086-93.

Peterson, Authur V., Jr., K. A. Kealey, S. L. Mann, P. M. Marek, and I. G. Sarason. 2000. Hutchinson Smoking Prevention Project: Long-term randomized trial in school-based tobacco use prevention—Results on smoking. *Journal of the National Cancer Institute* 92 (24): 1979-91.

Petraitis, John, and Brian R. Flay. 2002. Bridging the gap between theory and practice. In *Handbook for drug abuse prevention*, ed. William J. Bukoski and Zili Slaboda, chap. 14, 282-98. New York: Kluwer Academic/ Plenum.

Petraitis, John, Brian R. Flay, and Todd Q. Miller. 1995. Reviewing theories of adolescent substance abuse: Organizing pieces of the puzzle. *Psychological Bulletin* 1171:67-86.

Pirie, Phyllis L., David M. Murray, and Peter Jacobs. 1988. Smoking prevalence in a cohort of adolescents, including absentees, dropouts and transfers. *American Journal of Public Health* 782:76-178.

Presti, David E., Dennis V. Ary, and Ed Lichtenstein. 1992. The context of smoking initiation and maintenance: Findings from interviews with youths. *Journal of Substance Use* 4:35-45.

Protection of Human Subjects, 45 C.F.R. 46. 2001. http://ohrp.osophs.dhhs.gov/humansubjects/guidance/ 45cfr46.htm (accessed November 22, 2002).

Protection of Pupil Rights Amendment, 2002. 20 U.S.C. 1232h.

Riecken, Henry W., and Robert F. Boruch. 1978. Social experiments. *Annual Review of Sociology* 4:511-32.

Roese, Neal J., and David W. Jamieson. 1993. Twenty years of bogus pipeline research: A critical review and meta-analysis. *Psychological Bulletin* 114:363-75.

Rohrbach, Louise Ann, Carol S. Hodgson, Benjamin I. Broder, Susanne B. Montgomery, Brian R. Flay, William B. Hansen, and Mary Ann Pentz. 1995. Parental participation in drug abuse prevention: Results from the Midwestern Prevention Project. In *Alcohol problems among adolescents*, ed. Gayle M. Boyd, Jan Howard, and Robert A. Zucker. Hillsdale, NJ: Lawrence Erlbaum.

Rooney, Brenda L., and David M. Murray. 1996. A meta-analysis of smoking prevention programs after adjustment for errors in the unit of analysis. *Health Education Quarterly* 231:48-64.

Rosnow, R. L. 2002. The nature and role of demand characteristics in scientific inquiry. *Prevention and Treatment* 502. http://gateway.ut.ovid.com/gw2/ovidweb.cgi (accessed January 7, 2005).

Schafer, Joseph L. 1997. *Analysis of incomplete multivariate data*. London: Chapman and Hall.

Schafer, Joseph L., and John W. Graham. 2002. Missing data: Our view of the state of the art. *Psychological Methods* 72:147-77.

Sechrest, Lee, Stephen West, Meredith A. Phillips, R. Redner, and W. Yeaton. 1979. Some neglected problems in evaluation research: Strength and integrity of treatments. In *Evaluation studies review annual*, vol. 4, ed. Lee Sechrest, Stephen B. West, Meredith A. Phillips, R. Redner, and W. Yeaton. Beverly Hills, CA: Sage.

Segawa, Eisuke, Job E. Ngwe, Yan Li, Brian R. Flay, and Aban Aya Co-Investigators. Forthcoming. Evaluation of the effects of the Aban Aya Youth Project in reducing violence among African American adolescent males using latent class growth mixture modeling techniques. *Evaluation Review*.

Severson, Herbert, and Anthony Biglan. 1989. Rationale for the use of passive consent in smoking prevention research: Politics, policy and pragmatics. *Preventive Medicine* 18:267-79.

Shadish, William R., Thomas D. Cook, and Donald T. Campbell. 2002. *Experimental and quasi-experimental designs for generalized causal inference.* New York: Houghton Mifflin.

Siddiqui, Ohid, Donald Hedeker, Brian R. Flay, and Frank B. Hu. 1996. Intraclass correlation estimates in a school-based smoking prevention study: Outcome and mediating variables by gender and ethnicity. *American Journal of Epidemiology* 1444:425-33.

Society for Adolescent Medicine. 1995. Guidelines for adolescent health research. *Journal of Adolescent Health* 17:264-69.

Spitzer, Walter O., Alvan R. Feinstein, and David L. Sackett. 1975. What is a health care trial? *Journal of the American Medical Association* 233 (2): 161-63.

Stacy, Alan W., Steve Sussman, Brian R. Flay, K. Stephen Brown, Susan Santi, and J. Allan Best. 1990. Validity of alternative self-report indices of smoking among adolescents. *Journal of Consulting and Clinical Psychology* 24:442-46.

Sussman, Steve, and Susan L. Ames. 2001. *The social psychology of drug abuse.* Philadelphia: Open University Press.

Sussman, Steve, Clyde W. Dent, Bonnie R. Brannon, Karen Glowacz, Laura R. Gleason, William B. Hansen, C. Anderson Johnson, and Brian R. Flay. 1989. The Television, School and Family Smoking Prevention/Cessation Project: IV. Controlling for program success expectancies across experimental and control conditions. *Addictive Behaviors* 146:601-10.

Sussman, Steve Y., Clyde W. Dent, Dee Burton, Alan W. Stacy, and Brian R. Flay. 1995. *Developing school-based tobacco use prevention and cessation programs.* Thousand Oaks, CA: Sage.

Sussman, Steve, Ginger Hahn, Clyde W. Dent, Alan W. Stacy, Dee Burton, and Brian R. Flay. 1993. Naturalistic observation of adolescent tobacco use. *International Journal of the Addictions* 289:803-11.

Thompson, Eva Lynn. 1978. Smoking education programs, 1960-1976. *American Journal of Public Health* 68:257.

Tigges, Beth Baldwin. 2003. Parental consent and adolescent risk behavior research. *Journal of Nursing Scholarship* 353:283-89.

Tobler, Nancy S. 1986. Meta-analysis of 143 adolescent drug prevention programs: Quantitative outcome results of program participants compared to a control or comparison group. *Journal of Drug Issues* 164:537-67.

―――. 1992. Drug prevention programs can work: Research findings. *Journal of Addictive Diseases* 113:1-28.

Tobler, Nancy S., Michael R. Roona, Peter Ochshorn, Diana G. Marshall, Andrei V. Streke, and Kimberly M. Stackpole. 2000. School-based adolescent drug prevention programs: 1998 meta-analysis. *Journal of Primary Prevention* 204:275-336.

Tobler, Nancy S., and Howard H. Stratton. 1997. Effectiveness of school-based drug prevention programs: A meta-analysis of the research. *Journal of Primary Prevention* 181:71-128.

Tolan, Patrick H., and Nancy G. Guerra. 1994. Prevention of delinquency: Current status and issues. *Applied Preventive Psychology* 3:251-73.

Turner, Charles F., Heather G. Miller, and Lincoln E. Moses, eds. 1989. *AIDS: Sexual behavior and intravenous drug use.* Washington, DC: National Academy Press.

U.S. Department of Health and Human Services. 1991. *Title 45 Code of Federal Regulations Part 46, Protection of Human Subjects. Subpart A: Federal Policy for the Protection of Human Subjects DHHS Policy for Protection of Human Research Subjects. 56 FR 28003.* June 18. Washington, DC: U.S. Department of Health and Human Services.

Webb, Eugene J., Donald T. Campbell, Richard D. Schwartz, and Lee Sechrest. 1966. *Unobtrusive measures: Nonreactive research in the social sciences.* Skokie, IL: Rand McNally.

Weber, Mark D., C. Anderson Johnson, Sandra Carter, Barbara Dietsch, Lynn Caldwell-Stacy, Raymond Palmer, Brian R. Flay, and William B. Hansen. 1989. Project SMART Parent Program: Preliminary results of a chronic disease risk reduction trial. *Annals of Medicine* 21:231-33.

West, Steven G., and Leona S. Aiken. 1997. Toward understanding individual effects in multicomponent prevention programs: Design and analysis strategies. In *The science of prevention: Methodological advances from alcohol and substance abuse research,* ed. Kendall J. Bryant, Michael Windle, and Stephen G. West. Washington, DC: American Psychological Association.

Place-Based Randomized Trials to Test the Effects on Instructional Practices of a Mathematics/ Science Professional Development Program for Teachers

By
ANDREW C. PORTER,
ROLF K. BLANK,
JOHN L. SMITHSON,
and
ERIC OSTHOFF

A professional development model was designed for and is being tested in approximately fifty U.S. middle schools in five large urban districts, with half in each district randomly assigned to receive the two-year treatment. Each school forms a mathematics/science leadership team of five to seven members, including at least one administrator. Teams receive professional development in district-level workshops, then work with all math and science teachers in their school. The core idea is to provide teachers with data on their instructional practices and student achievement, then teach them how to use that data to improve their effectiveness. This article documents the successes and failures of treatment implementation and the collection of baseline and outcome data. The focus is on learning about doing place-based randomized trials to test the efficacy of education programs. At the time of this writing, treatment is not yet complete and study results are not available.

Keywords: professional development model; place-based randomized trials; instructional practices; data-based decision making; school leadership team; urban middle schools

This article describes the conduct of a place-based randomized-trial study of a teacher professional development program designed for and implemented in middle-school math and science programs in large urban districts. There is an urgent need in the United States to improve the quality of mathematics and science instruction, especially in middle schools. Data to

NOTE: This article was prepared following a presentation at the Rockefeller Foundation Bellagio Study and Conference Center at a meeting on "Progress and Prospects for Place-Based Randomized Trials," organized by Robert Boruch and Dorothy de Moya for the Campbell Collaboration. Support for the work came from the National Science Foundation (REC no. 0087562); the Wisconsin Center for Education Research, School of Education, University of Wisconsin–Madison; and the Council of Chief State School Officers. The opinions expressed in this publication are those of the authors and do not necessarily reflect the views of the National Science Foundation, the Wisconsin Center for Education Research, or the Council of Chief State School Officers.

DOI: 10.1177/0002716205274743

support this contention come from the National Assessment of Educational Progress (NAEP) (U.S. Department of Education 2000, 2002), as well as the Third International Mathematics and Science Study (now called the Trends in International Mathematics and Science Study) and its repeat (TIMSS and TIMSS-R) (Martin et al. 2001; Mullis et al. 2001). In international comparisons, U.S. students do fairly well at the fourth-grade level, but by the eighth grade, they have fallen behind other countries in both mathematics and science. NAEP data make clear that the achievement of students in urban areas is lower than that of students in the rest of the country—thus this study's focus on middle-school math and science in large urban districts.

Andrew C. Porter is Patricia and Rodes Hart Professor of Educational Leadership and Policy and director of the Learning Sciences Institute at Vanderbilt University. He has published widely on psychometrics, student assessment, education indicators, and research on teaching. Currently he has research support from the National Science Foundation (codirector, System-Wide Change for All Learners and Educators Math and Science Partnership [SCALE]; principal investigator, Improving Effectiveness of Instruction in Mathematics and Science with Data on Enacted Curriculum) and ED's Office of Educational Research and Improvement (CPRE—Consortium for Policy Research in Education). He is an elected member and former officer of the National Academies, and past-president of the American Educational Research Association.

Rolf K. Blank is director of Education Indicators at the Council of Chief State School Officers, where he has been a senior staff member for seventeen years. He is responsible for developing, managing, and reporting a system of state-by-state and national indicators of the condition and quality of education in public schools. He directs the council's work with the U.S. Department of Education on State Education Indicators and Accountability Systems (providing annual trends for each state on student outcomes, school programs, and staff and school demographics) as well as a three-year National Science Foundation–funded experimental design study on Improving Effectiveness of Instruction in Mathematics and Science with Data on Enacted Curriculum. He also coordinates two state collaborative projects—one on accountability systems and a second on surveys of enacted curriculum—that provide technical assistance and professional development to state education leaders and staff. He holds a Ph.D. from Florida State University and an M.A. from the University of Wisconsin–Madison.

John L. Smithson is a research associate at the Wisconsin Center for Education Research, where he directs the Measures of the Enacted Curriculum and related projects, including development, maintenance, and hosting of the SEC Online Web site. He has worked for the past ten years developing and using measures of instructional practice and content to investigate the impacts of education reform efforts. Previous studies include Reform Up Close: A Classroom Analysis; the Upgrading Mathematics Project; and the Data on Enacted Curriculum Study. He is currently a co–principal investigator on the Longitudinal Design to Measure Effects of MSP Professional Development in Improving Instruction.

Eric Osthoff is an associate researcher at the Wisconsin Center for Education Research at the University of Wisconsin–Madison. He is currently conducting a case study of systemwide mathematics and science reform in the Los Angeles Unified School District. Publications include "Support from External Agencies" (with Andrew Porter and G. Wehlage) in Authentic Achievement: Restructuring Schools for Intellectual Quality, *edited by Fred M. Newmann and Associates (Jossey-Bass, publisher); and "Standard Setting as a Strategy for Upgrading High School Mathematics and Science" (with Andrew Porter and John Smithson) in* The Governance of Curriculum, *edited by R. F. Elmore and S. H. Fuhrman (Association for Supervision and Curriculum Development, publisher).*

The core idea of the professional development program is to provide teachers with data on their instructional practices and student achievement and then to teach them how to use that data to improve their effectiveness. There are several reasons why we elected to study a professional development program of this nature, and to do so using place-based randomized trials. Over the past decade or so, a

---

In the 1970s, 1980s, and 1990s, experiments all but disappeared from the education research landscape. But with President Bush's administration has come great enthusiasm for using research-based education programs and procedures.

---

great deal of research has established the characteristics of effective professional development, especially in math and science (Cohen and Hill 2001; Desimone et al. 2002; Garet et al. 2001; Loucks-Horsley et al. 1998; Porter et al. 2003). Without elaboration, effective professional development (1) engages participants in active learning, giving them the opportunity to construct their own knowledge; (2) is designed for groups of participants (e.g., a team of teachers or all teachers in a given grade from a school); (3) is coherent (i.e., tailored to the teachers' level of experience and aligned with the content standards, assessments, and other policy instruments of the system within which the teachers teach); (4) focuses on the content of instruction, and especially knowledge of how students learn that content; and (5) is sustained over time (in contrast to one-shot workshops).

Second, we now have available several tools for studying teachers' decisions about what to teach, and increasingly practitioners find these tools useful for reflecting on their practice (Porter 2002). We describe these tools in greater detail below (see "The DEC Treatment"). For now, it is sufficient to know that they include surveys of teachers' instructional practices, both pedagogy and content; procedures for content-analyzing curriculum materials, including content standards, assessments, and textbooks; and finally, tools for analyzing and graphically portraying teachers' instructional practices and their alignment with student achievement tests and content standards. We hypothesize that these tools, and the data and reports they generate, can make powerful contributions to teacher professional development designed to help teachers better understand their instructional practice and how it might be strengthened.

Third, there is currently a great deal of interest in data-based decision making in education (Creighton 2001; Smith and Freeman 2002; Streifer 2001; Yeagley 2001). Nancy Love (2002) and her colleagues have developed a promising professional development program aimed at helping teachers and administrators learn to use data and analyses of data, especially student achievement data, to make decisions and to improve their practice.

Finally, there is currently a great deal of interest in and support for doing randomized experiments in education. In the 1970s, 1980s, and 1990s, experiments all but disappeared from the education research landscape. But with President Bush's administration has come great enthusiasm for using research-based education programs and procedures. In particular, the No Child Left Behind Act (2002) places great emphasis on research-based practices in education. Methodologists have long known that experiments are the "gold standard" for establishing cause-and-effect relationships in any field, and education is no exception (Boruch 1997; Boruch, De Moya, and Snyder 2002; Cook 2002). Thus, the time was right to do an experiment; both funding sources and the field were more inclined to be supportive than they had been for decades.

In sum, math and science instruction in urban middle schools needs to improve. High-quality professional development seems an important lever for making that happen. Data-based decision making is hypothesized to be an important focus for professional development, and professional development programs on data-based decision making have been designed and piloted. Finally, powerful tools are available for collecting data on instructional practices and their alignment with student achievement tests—data that can be used to complement the more readily available data on student achievement.

Our study, "Assisting Teachers in Using Data on Enacted Curriculum (DEC) to Improve Effectiveness of Instruction in Mathematics and Science Education," began with baseline surveys administered in the spring of 2001 (Council of Chief State School Officers 2002). The treatment began late in the summer of 2001 and extended through the 2001-2 school year and halfway through the 2002-3 school year. Thus, at this writing, the study has not been completed (the final data are just now being collected). The focus of this article is on the design and implementation of the place-based randomized trial. In particular, we seek to answer the following questions: What is the nature of the treatment? What are the difficulties in its implementation? How faithfully were we able to implement the experimental design? What did we learn in the process of conducting the experiment? and What do we judge to be its strengths and weaknesses to date?

The Design

The study design consists of place-based randomized trials, with middle schools in large urban districts randomly assigned to the treatment or control condition. Originally, the sample consisted of forty middle schools located in the Charlotte-Mecklenburg, Chicago, Miami-Dade, and Philadelphia school districts. Ten schools were recruited in each of two districts, twelve in another, and eight in the fourth. Four schools dropped out before random assignment, primarily due to teachers' low response to a baseline survey. Within the first three months of working with the treatment schools, an additional three schools dropped out. In Philadelphia, one of the control schools was randomly assigned to the treatment condition, making sixteen treatment schools and seventeen control schools, for a total of thirty-three schools in the study. To compensate for attrition, an additional district was recruited, Winston-Salem, with fifteen schools, eight of which were randomly assigned to treatment. The Winston-Salem site began treatment one year later than schools in the other four districts and so is not discussed further in this chapter.

We collected teacher survey data (described in detail later under "The DEC Treatment") from 559 math and science teachers in the treatment and control middle schools in the four original districts, representing just more than 75 percent of all math and science teachers in those schools. Seventy percent were female, 40 percent White, 33 percent African American, and 20 percent Hispanic. The majority of teachers were generalists, with just 9 percent having mathematics education as their major and 6 percent science education as their major. Twenty-seven percent of the teachers reported that they had received more than one hundred hours of professional development in the preceding two years. Twenty-three percent reported having received less than thirty hours, and 8 percent reported having received no professional development in the preceding two years.

The independent variable is the treatment versus the control condition. Of course, in education there is no such thing as a strict control. The control-school teachers continued to participate in professional development, and the teachers in the treatment schools participated in professional development other than the treatment. Thus, we are collecting data not only on the quality of the treatment implementation but also on the other professional development experiences of both the treatment- and the control-school teachers.

The treatment is interesting in that it does not prescribe what is to happen in each participating teacher's classroom. Rather, it specifies professional development in which leadership teams participate. The team members, in turn, provide professional development to their colleagues in their schools. The professional development is aimed at helping teachers reflect on their individual and collective practices, and from that reflection they are to decide how their instruction might be strengthened. Clearly, schools may choose to focus their energies in different places, as may individual teachers.

The lack of prescriptiveness for classroom practice makes defining valid and sensitive dependent variables difficult. One dependent variable is the degree of alignment between the content of each teacher's instruction and the content of the state or district test most frequently used for accountability purposes. We hypothesize that the tests and content standards are aligned so that the greater the effect of the treatment, the greater will be the alignment of teachers' content practices with the accountability test used with their students. In addition, we have formulated uniquely targeted dependent variables for each school, focusing on the types of changes in instruction that each school decided were most needed, based on the treatment-facilitated teacher reflection. The problem with these targeted dependent variables is that they are aligned with the intended changes in one school, rather than with intended changes across all treatment schools. Still, we will be able to see whether particular schools made more progress toward their unique targets than other schools did toward theirs.

Ideally, gains in student achievement would have been another dependent variable. Unfortunately, the National Science Foundation (NSF) limited funding to a three-year period in its call for proposals. We do not believe that three years is long enough for the treatment to have strong effects on student achievement. Thus, we did not institute a student achievement testing program of our own. Nevertheless, we are collecting student achievement data from the districts. Of course, each district has a different testing protocol, using a different test and different testing times, and even different criteria for deciding who is and who is not tested. We will do our best to use these achievement data, but if we find no effects, we will not conclude that the treatment is unable to affect student achievement. Again, if there are to be effects on student achievement, we would expect them in the out years; and we intend to ask NSF to continue our funding so that we can look at this possibility.

The DEC Treatment

The DEC professional development model

The professional development model for the DEC project is based on the following:

1. standards-based improvement of instruction;
2. continuous improvement of practice using data and formative evaluation; and
3. school-based collaboration and networking to foster the sharing of teaching ideas, models, and strategies for improvement.

DEC treatment schools are asked to form a five- to seven-member mathematics and science leadership team (referred to hereafter as the *school leadership team*) at the outset of the project. The teams include at least one administrator—the principal or the assistant principal for curriculum—mathematics and science department chairs, lead or master mathematics and science teachers, and other math and science teachers such that a range of grades and subjects are represented. The teams participate in all project professional development workshops and meetings throughout the treatment.

In addition to the school leadership teams, the DEC treatment calls for each district contact person to involve district-level instructional support staff by inviting them to participate in all the workshops. Districts have the option of scheduling separate workshops for entire district groups in supporting mathematics and science instruction in the schools. The rationale for involving a larger support network is to ensure that everyone working in the schools has knowledge of the processes, techniques, and goals of the DEC work.

The steps in the DEC treatment are

- Baseline surveys of instructional practice and student achievement.
- *Two-day professional development workshop.* Working in school leadership teams, teachers and administrators learn to use rich, in-depth data to inform decisions about curriculum and improved practice, gain skills in analyzing survey data and organizing data-driven dialogue, and learn how to set measurable student learning goals and use curriculum data in school improvement plans. The data include student achievement data from the district and/or state, analyses of teacher responses to the baseline survey, and content analyses of the achievement tests (described in a later section).
- *Follow-up technical assistance in schools.* School leadership team members use their new skills with curriculum data to work with math and science teachers in their schools. The DEC project team provides assistance with data applications on-site, as well as by phone and e-mail. District math and science specialists incorporate data into their ongoing work with teachers.
- *Professional development follow-up workshop.* An additional one-day workshop is held for school leadership teams. The focus is on analysis of data, especially analysis of the alignment of assessments, standards, and teaching practices. The goal is to move from inquiry about data into action for improving teaching.
- *Evaluation of progress; refocusing of assistance.* At the end of year one, the DEC project team meets with staff from each school to help determine progress, identify problems, and focus on further action steps for the next school year. In year two, new staff members in schools are brought into the treatment, and assistance continues through midyear.
- Follow-up survey is conducted to measure results. (Table 1 provides a timeline of activities.)

Each member of each school's mathematics and science leadership team receives materials relevant to the DEC treatment (Council of Chief State School Officers 2002).

A major intent of the DEC treatment is to involve mathematics and science leadership teams directly in the processes and techniques for using their data to highlight important questions and to discover tentative causal factors. A second and equally important purpose is to use the professional development workshops to model "best practices" in professional development.

The DEC approach to technical assistance is based on the prior work of Schmocker (2002) and Fullan (2002) on effective strategies for improving student achievement. The content and processes introduced in the DEC treatment through hands-on activities, simulations, and direct engagement with instructional and curriculum data have been adapted from the book *Using Data/Getting Results: A Practical Guide for School Improvement in Mathematics and Science*, developed by Nancy Love (2002). Another source that has added greatly to the overall design of the workshop process and activities is *The Adaptive School: Developing and Facilitating Collaborative Groups* (Wellman and Garmston 1999). Further guidance for the DEC professional development design has come from Loucks-Horsley et al. (1998), Cohen and Hill (2001), and Porter et al. (2003).

Another goal of the DEC treatment is to develop the capacity of school leadership teams to engage a larger group of their own staff in dialogue about their data

TABLE 1

TIMELINE OF ACTIVITIES FOR DATA ON ENACTED CURRICULUM (DEC)
PROFESSIONAL DEVELOPMENT (PD) AND TECHNICAL ASSISTANCE (TA)

Date	Event and Purpose	Participants
March 2001	Introduction to DEC goals, design, and requirements (three-hour session)	District curriculum staff, principals, department heads
March-April 2001	Site visits to all participating schools (two to three hours)	Principals and other staff
April-May 2001	Complete Surveys of Enacted Curriculum	All mathematics and science teachers
August 2001	Intro. Leader PD Workshop on Using Data & Collaborative Inquiry (two full days)	School leadership teams and district support staff
October-November 2001	TA (three-hour sessions in phase 1 schools)	School leadership teams
January-February 2002	PD Workshop on Investigating Instructional Practice, Content, and Cognitive Demand Aligned to State Assessment. Outcome to identify student learning goals (one day)	School leadership teams
March-April 2002	PD Workshop on Using Data, Collaborative Inquiry, and a grounding in the DEC project	District support staff and instructional specialists
March-April 2002	TA to establish measurable goals and to design structure for ongoing data analysis by the staff on a regular basis (three-hour sessions in phase 1 schools)	School leadership teams
May, June, and August 2002	PD Workshop on Analyzing Student Work as a means of monitoring progress (one day)	School leadership teams and district support staff
September-October 2002	TA: Analysis/comparison of newest student achievement data (three hours)	School leadership teams
January-February 2003	Workshop or TA as needed	School leadership teams
March-April 2003	Complete Surveys of Enacted Curriculum	All mathematics and science teachers

and inquiry into their own teaching and learning. The school leadership teams participate directly in the professional development workshops, where they work on plans and strategies for involving all of their math and science teachers in developing skills with data analysis and data-driven dialogue about improving instruction.

The DEC treatment is based on the expectation that schools will enter the project from many different perspectives with different sets of individual challenges. Meeting with the leadership teams individually allows project staff to adapt and modify information and resources to meet the needs of individual schools while at the same time attempting to move them along a continuum toward establishing student learning goals and continuing their investigation of factors related to reaching those goals.

Tools for describing content and alignment

As stated earlier, one of the factors motivating us to build the treatment and conduct the study was the existence of several research-based tools for describing instructional practices (both pedagogy and content), describing the content of curriculum materials (e.g., content standards, assessments), and measuring the nature and degree of alignment between instructional practices and curriculum materials (Porter 2002). These tools have proven useful not only to researchers but also to practitioners, through the collaboration between the University of Wisconsin–Madison and the Council of Chief State School Officers. Thus, our treatment can be understood in part by the nature of the data provided to school leadership teams and other teachers in the treatment schools. The nature of these data is described below.

Survey of enacted curriculum (SEC)

An SEC, developed with NSF support and used in more than four hundred schools across eleven states, represents one tool. The SEC designed for use with math and science teachers provides data on pedagogical practices (how both teachers and students spend their time), homework, student grouping, classroom assessment strategies, technology use, teachers' beliefs about what content is important to teach and what their students are capable of learning, professional development, and the content teachers cover. The items are grouped into a dozen scales. In addition, a school administrator survey is administered to school principals to collect data on schools' (1) strategies for standards-based reform, (2) professional development, (3) sources of data used, and (4) purposes for data use.

The SEC uses a two-dimensional grid for collecting information about teachers' content decisions. One dimension lists topics (in mathematics or science). For example, mathematics content areas are (1) number sense, (2) measurement, (3) data analysis/probability/statistics, (4) algebraic concepts, (5) geometric concepts, and (6) instructional technology. Each of these general content areas is broken down into a dozen or so specific topics. For example, under geometric concepts are such specific topics as angles, symmetry, and theorem. The second dimension of the grid relates to expectations for students (referred to here as *cognitive demand*).

FIGURE 1
CONTENT MATRIX

Topics	Categories of Cognitive Demand				
	Memorize	Perform Procedures	Demonstrate Understanding	Conjecture Generalize Prove	Solve Nonroutine Problems
Multiple-Step Equations					
Inequalities					
Literal Equations					
Lines/Slope and Intercept					
Operations on Polynomials					
Quadratic Equations					

Categories of cognitive demand in mathematics are (1) memorize facts, definitions, formulas; (2) perform procedures; (3) demonstrate understanding of mathematical ideas; (4) conjecture, analyze, prove; and (5) solve nonroutine problems/make connections.

Completion of the two-dimensional grid entails the following three steps:

1. The teacher works through the specific topics, reporting for each whether it was taught.
2. For those topics taught, the teacher describes degree of coverage on a 3-point scale, indicating whether the coverage represented (1) less than one class/lesson, (2) one to five classes/lessons, or (3) more than five classes/lessons.
3. For each topic covered at least to some extent, the teacher indicates which of the five categories of cognitive demand were taught, and for those that were taught, the degree of emphasis. The 3-point emphasis scale distinguishes (1) slight emphasis (less than 25 percent of the time spent on the topic), (2) moderate emphasis (25 to 33 percent of the time spent on the topic), and (3) sustained emphasis (more than 33 percent of the time spent on the topic).

A greatly simplified example of the grid is found in Figure 1.

The same two-dimensional grid is used to conduct content analyses of the student achievement test used in the district or state. To perform content analyses, three or more experts are convened, introduced to the two-dimensional grid, and

FIGURE 2
CONTENT MAPPING

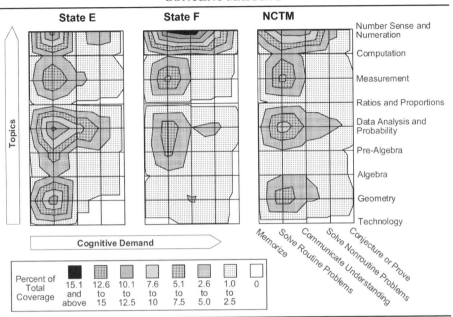

asked to practice using the grid by content analyzing items on a sample test. Each expert independently judges for each item which cells in the two-dimensional grid represent the content a student must know to answer the question. To standardize the process across experts, each item can be placed in up to three cells of the grid. If the item has one score point for a correct answer, as in multiple-choice items, the score point is divided evenly among the cells identified by the expert. When short-answer or extended-response items are analyzed, the score points attached to the item are allocated across the cells identified. Results for each cell are averaged across experts, with each expert weighted equally.

Content mapping

Whether the two-dimensional grid is used by teachers to analyze instructional content or by experts to analyze test content, the raw data are converted into proportions of emphasis such that the proportions sum to one across all the cells in the grid. The data can be presented in a graphic form similar to a topographical map, where north and south represent topics and east and west represent cognitive demand. The third dimension represents relative emphasis. Figure 2 illustrates a topographical map using the content standards of two states and those of the National Council of Teachers of Mathematics (NCTM) for seventh-grade mathematics. These displays are at the coarse-grain level. More fine-grained analyses can

FIGURE 3
NUMBER SENSE AND NUMERATION

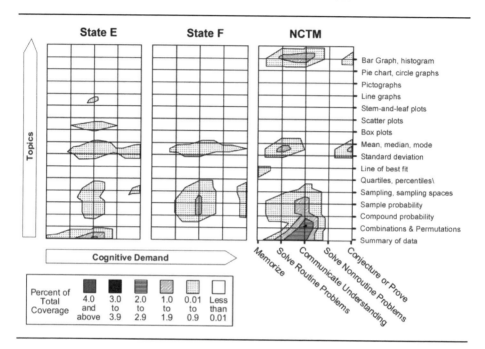

be presented by using more micro-level topics within, say, number sense and numeration (see Figure 3). Especially powerful presentations of these topographical maps can be made using a presentation graphics program such as PowerPoint, which makes it possible to point and click at a result in the coarse-grained map and immediately display the underlying fine-grained maps.

By displaying the content map for State E next to the content maps for State F and NCTM (Figures 2 and 3), it is possible to compare and contrast the content emphasized by one state's standards to that emphasized by another state's standards or by the NCTM. It is easy to see both similarities and differences in content emphasis. The methodology is quite general, allowing comparisons among standards, assessments, and instruction. In DEC, content maps were available for each teacher and one math and one science achievement test for each participating city.

Alignment indices

The degree of alignment can be measured in an alignment index. Essentially, a comparison is made between the cells of two content grids (see Figure 4). If the proportions in one grid exactly parallel the proportions in another grid, alignment is perfect. The alignment index, also displayed in Figure 4, is a function of the sum

FIGURE 4
COGNITIVE DEMAND

Assessment

.3	0	.1
0	.1	0
0	.2	.1
0	.1	.1

Instruction

.2	0	.1
0	.2	0
.1	.2	.1
0	0	.1

Topics

$$\text{Alignment Index} = 1 - \frac{\Sigma \mid X\text{-}Y \mid}{2}$$

X=Assessment Cell Proportions
Y=Standards Cell Proportions

across cells in the grid of the absolute difference in proportions, say, between a particular assessment and a particular teacher's instruction. When divided by 2 and subtracted from 1, the alignment index ranges from 1 (perfect alignment) to 0 (no alignment).

There is real power to the alignment index because it allows practitioners to examine patterns of alignment among teachers' instructional content. For example, teachers in a school can be compared pairwise to each other with regard to their instructional content. The alignment data are assembled in something like a correlation matrix, with individual teachers representing both the rows and columns of the matrix. The off-diagonal elements in the matrix represent the degree of alignment between one teacher's instruction and another teacher's instruction. Table 2 illustrates this idea by showing the alignment of instruction in eighth-grade mathematics among ten states (where each state is represented by the average across a sample of teachers). In the DEC work, analyses are used to show whether alignment among teachers' content emphases is greater within a grade level than between grade levels to look at grade-to-grade articulation in content taught. The illustrations in Figures 1 through 4 are not from DEC schools because we agreed to use those data only for feedback as a part of the study treatment.

Summary

It was the potential power of these tools for describing the content of instruction and the content of student achievement assessments, together with the earlier

TABLE 2

ALIGNMENT OF INSTRUCTION WITH INSTRUCTION:
EIGHTH-GRADE MATH: STATE COLLABORATIVE ON ASSESSMENT AND STUDENT STANDARDS (SCASS) STUDY

State	H	J	K	L	E	O	G	I	M	N
H	1.0									
J	.73	1.0								
K	.59	.66	1.0							
L	.56	.64	.67	1.0						
E	.65	.71	.78	.70	1.0					
O	.71	.80	.63	.65	.70	1.0				
G	.71	.81	.66	.67	.71	.84	1.0			
I	.73	.82	.63	.66	.68	.79	.80	1.0		
M	.68	.77	.61	.62	.66	.73	.76	.79	1.0	
N	.62	.69	.58	.61	.62	.71	.70	.67	.65	1.0

NOTE: Average Alignment = .69.

work on data-based decision making (focusing primarily on student achievement), that led to the design of the DEC treatment. The amount of data provided to schools is substantial. Each treatment school receives a customized school-based report within three months after the initial administration of the teacher surveys. These reports contain more than 150 pages of school-specific data organized into charts covering twenty categories of survey results. Each category of charts is disaggregated based on seven grouping variables (e.g., grade level, achievement level, percent minority). The training provided to school leadership teams makes use of these data as a starting point for conversations and activities by the teams during workshops and technical assistance visits.

Implementation

Survey response rates

Treatment implementation began with the administration of teacher surveys in the spring of 2001 (with a follow-up administration in the fall of 2001 at the request of some treatment schools that wanted to include new teachers and/or increase the response rate among veteran teachers). One index of the quality of treatment implementation is the response rate to the survey, which required an hour to an hour and a half of a teacher's time to complete. Across thirty-six schools that participated in the first-year baseline survey, the response rate from teachers was 77 percent for mathematics and 76 percent for science teachers. These rates are similar to those found in other studies using the survey of enacted curriculum or similar instruments (Gamoran et al. 1997; Garet et al. 2001; Porter et al. 1993).

School-by-school response rates varied considerably, ranging from 17 to 100 percent, with twenty-one schools having 90 percent or greater response rates. Response rates also differed by district, with Miami-Dade having the highest rate (90 percent).

The response rate to the principal survey was 79 percent, with no differences noted across districts.

Participation in the professional development program

Another measure of treatment implementation is the participation of school leadership teams in the professional development program (see Table 3). There are four dimensions to this participation. The first of these is the total number of professional development/technical assistance sessions attended by one or more members of a school's leadership team. The total number of sessions attended by schools ranges from 3 to 6, with an average of 4.56 sessions attended per school. As of the date of this report, all schools have had an opportunity to participate in 5 sessions.

Some schools in the Charlotte-Mecklenburg and Philadelphia districts have attended as few as three sessions. The Philadelphia school that has participated in

TABLE 3

SCHOOL-LEVEL PARTICIPATION IN DATA ON ENACTED CURRICULUM (DEC) PROFESSIONAL DEVELOPMENT AND TECHNICAL ASSISTANCE

District	School ID	Total Sessions Attended	Average Number Attending	Sessions Attended by Administration	Participation Stability Index
Charlotte-Mecklenburg	66	3	1.67	100%	55.33%
	68	3	2.33	100%	58.25%
	62	3	2.67	100%	66.75%
Chicago	91	5	4.80	80%	65.71%
	92	5	2.20	60%	73.33%
	93	4	3.25	100%	54.42%
	97	5	3.20	80%	45.71%
Miami-Dade	80	6	4.33	67%	48.16%
	811	5	4.20	100%	62.88%
	87	6	4.00	17%	44.44%
	810	5	4.40	100%	73.33%
	85	6	3.67	83%	48.85%
	88	4	2.75	75%	60.00%
Philadelphia	72	5	4.40	100%	30.91%
	70	3	5.00	67%	55.52%
	76	5	2.60	60%	60.00%
Overall average	NA	4.56	3.47[a]	78.12%[a]	57.32%[a]

a. Overall average weighted to reflect number of sessions attended by schools.

only three sessions to date joined the study late, after a school that had already participated in two sessions dropped out because it ceased to be a middle school. Participation by the Charlotte-Mecklenburg schools was impeded by two events. First, North Carolina decided to renorm its end-of-grade tests (used to determine whether students are able to advance in grade levels and course sequences). Many schools felt it would be impractical to proceed with data-driven decision making until the state provided them with the results for the end-of-grade tests. Second, the Charlotte-Mecklenburg district embarked on a massive reorganization of schools, students, and teachers upon getting out from under a federal court desegregation order. In particular, the district responded by instituting a wide-open school choice program, resulting in the reassignment of more than two-thirds of all students and staff. The logistical challenges of the reorganization overwhelmed school and district staff, making it difficult to schedule DEC training during the last several months of the 2001-2 school year.

Although Miami School 87 (see Table 3) participated in six sessions, two of these were abbreviated repeat sessions conducted with a newly constituted leadership team. It became necessary to restart the initiative at this particular school when administrative and staff turnover resulted in near total attrition of the original school leadership team.

The second dimension of participation is the average number of persons attending professional development sessions as part of a school's leadership team. School averages range from 1.67 to 5, with an overall weighted sample average of 3.47 persons. To date, the Charlotte-Mecklenburg schools have averaged 2.22 persons; Chicago, 3.37; Philadelphia, 3.85; and Miami, 3.94.

The third participation dimension is the percentage of sessions at which a school's representatives have included the principal or an assistant principal. Charlotte-Mecklenburg stands out for having an administrator present at 100 percent of its schools' sessions. The administrative participation from other districts has been fairly similar: Miami-Dade, 71 percent; Philadelphia, 77 percent; and Chicago, 79 percent. Differences in principal participation rates are much larger

---

When the postintervention survey has been administered and analyzed, we will be able to examine the relationship between the participation stability index and the schoolwide impact of the DEC [Data on Enacted Curriculum] treatment— a promising avenue of inquiry.

---

within than across districts. One Miami-Dade school that changed principals several times during the 2001-2 school year had an administrator present at only one of six sessions. Meanwhile, two other Miami-Dade schools had administrative representation at all sessions. Philadelphia and Chicago schools ranged from 60 to 100 percent administrator participation. In schools that had 100 percent administrator representation at DEC sessions, administrators generally attended most if not all of each session. In schools that had less than 100 percent administrator participation at DEC sessions, administrators sometimes further reduced actual participation by coming just for the beginning of sessions or circulating in and out of sessions.

The fourth dimension of school participation is captured in the participation stability index. This index reflects how consistent schools were in whom they selected to participate. To calculate the index, we listed every school staff person who attended a session. The percentage of all sessions attended by each individual is then calculated, and the percentages summed and divided by the total number of staff members attending one or more sessions. Thus, the index reflects the average rate of participation by the individuals in the school who attended one or more sessions. The greater the number of sessions and the number of individuals sent, the lower the index. An index of 20 percent is very low. Such a score would be given, for example, to a school that sent a total of twenty different people to five sessions, with no individual attending more than once.

The stability index for treatment schools has ranged from 31 to 73 percent. When the postintervention survey has been administered and analyzed, we will be able to examine the relationship between the participation stability index and the schoolwide impact of the DEC treatment—a promising avenue of inquiry.

Factors affecting participation in the DEC treatment

Five factors have affected the extent and quality of school participation in the treatment.

Time for school leadership teams

Securing meeting time for school leadership teams has been perhaps the single greatest challenge. Leadership teams need substantial time as a group to have the kind of interactions conducive to the formation of a robust professional community. Teams need time not only to attend DEC sessions but also to jointly explore relevant student achievement data, SEC data on classroom practices, research and practitioner knowledge of best instructional practices, and issues of curriculum alignment and assessment.

Support for school leadership teams has come from principals and district administrators alike. Many principals in the study have seen the DEC initiative as providing a timely source of instructional guidance that can play an important role in helping their schools achieve greater alignment to state and district standards and assessments. Accordingly, they have hired substitute teachers to cover for school leadership team members while they attend DEC sessions, and they have released members from schoolwide or districtwide activities to participate in DEC sessions. In Miami-Dade, the district provided stipends for teachers participating in DEC activities held on noncontract days.

The most serious obstacle to finding time for school leadership teams to meet, as well as for other teachers to participate in DEC-related activities, is the general scarcity of teacher meeting time. This problem is structural. Resource constraints have led many urban school districts to cut back on the amount of time teachers have for planning, staff meetings, professional development, and in-services. In Miami-Dade, a severe shortage of certified mathematics and science teachers, combined with a shortage of classroom space, has led the district to offer teachers salary bonuses to increase their class load from six to seven. The vast majority of mathematics and science teachers have opted for the increased class load and made room by dropping their one daily planning period. In Miami School 811, the principal took the unusual step of using categorical program money to purchase an additional hour of teachers' time each day to restore a daily planning period.

Miami-Dade is fortunate that teachers have the first thirty-five minutes of every day available for meetings of their departments, instructional teams, grade-level teams, and the whole faculty. In contrast, resources in Philadelphia were spread so thin that a decision was made to eliminate teacher planning and meeting time, including time for school faculty meetings.

Another structural impediment to team meetings in all districts is the shortage of substitute teachers. Most schools report difficulty securing substitutes, especially getting four or more to cover simultaneously for members of DEC school leadership teams. Achieving coverage for DEC team meetings usually requires a combination of substitutes and other school staff (teachers with planning periods, classroom aides, curriculum specialists, etc.). However, issues remain, even when coverage is secured. Teachers worry that substitutes will not be able to maintain classroom control and that little teaching or learning will occur in their absence.

Stability of school leadership teams

The DEC schools that have moved furthest and fastest to integrate DEC methods into school improvement are the ones that have been able to keep a core group involved in DEC professional development and technical assistance. In other schools, staff turnover has led to changes in school leadership team membership. Such changes have resulted in teams' having to go back over old ground instead of sustaining forward movement. In addition, some schools with stable DEC team membership have alternated members' participation instead of having all team members participate in every DEC professional development or technical assistance event. This reduction in the stability of team participation has slowed team progress as well.

Structural factors in the Charlotte-Mecklenburg district are likely to pose substantial challenges to maintaining continuity in the district's school leadership teams. As noted above, Charlotte-Mecklenburg has undergone extensive staffing changes during the 2001-2 and 2002-3 school years, including the reassignment of up to two-thirds of all middle-school mathematics and science teachers. Staffing changes are only half the story in Charlotte-Mecklenburg, however; a substantial majority of students also changed schools. Some schools have taken on huge enrollment increases, while the enrollment in other schools has plummeted. For example, one school went from 1,100 students in 2001-2 to 1,650 in 2002-3. The school has added dozens of portable trailer classrooms, many teachers float among classrooms, there is a new principal, and the school went from serving primarily low-income and minority students to serving primarily wealthy white students.

In Philadelphia, by contrast, it appears that staffing in the district's DEC schools has remained relatively stable despite major changes in district administration and student assignment. Staffing in the Miami-Dade district has also proven fairly stable, with the exception of School 87. In Chicago, at least two school leadership team members retired at the conclusion of the 2001-2 school year.

Maternity leave creates another structural obstacle to continuity in school leadership team membership. Seventy percent of DEC survey respondents were female. A number of school leadership teams were affected when members left for maternity leave.

Most teachers who participated as leadership team members appeared to appreciate the opportunity and value of continued participation. However, in each of two Chicago schools, one or two teachers expressed some misgivings about participating in DEC. In Chicago School 97, the principal appeared to have made a decision early on to accommodate the DEC project's presence without giving the project a high priority. This principal was among those who participated the least in DEC sessions, typically leaving for portions of sessions after helping them get under way. The school was a "no-show" for Professional Development Session 3, and new faces came and went from the DEC meetings in which the school did participate.

Given the numerous structural obstacles to school leadership team stability discussed above, the participation stability index (see Table 3) indicates that schools placed a high priority on enabling core team members to participate consistently in DEC activities. If we were to exclude cases in which school leadership team instability arose from structural factors, such as teacher reassignment and medical leave, the overall index would rise substantially.

Schoolwide use of the DEC treatment

There are two basic models for professional development delivery: (1) direct delivery by professional providers and (2) indirect delivery using a training-of-trainers approach. Direct delivery would not have been logistically feasible for the DEC project. It has been difficult enough getting the leadership team members released for activities. Further expanding sessions to include all mathematics and science teachers in all DEC schools would have been impossible. Thus, the project elected to form school leadership teams and use them to reach the remainder of math and science teachers at their schools.

This training-of-trainers approach has posed several challenges. First, the focus of DEC training had to be split between (1) issues directly related to classroom teaching and learning and (2) issues related to schoolwide collaborative efforts to improve instructional practice. Second, it is difficult to ensure the quality of treatment delivered by the school leadership teams who have been trained by the DEC project. Third, one must be alert to the possibility that using school faculty to deliver training may come into conflict with school cultural norms and be resisted by some staff members. To date, however, we have observed that the turnkey approach has resulted in fairly broad exposure of mathematics and science teachers to the DEC treatment.

Several principals did not appear to readily grasp the nature of DEC data; nor, once the data had been clarified, did they appear to have strategies for exploring its implications for instruction in their schools. Principals' scant prior knowledge of data analysis and interpretation is not in itself a barrier to successful implementation of the DEC model. However, if principals who lack prior knowledge in this area feel they cannot afford to appear to be learning alongside other school leadership team members, then decreased participation in, and schoolwide commitment to, the initiative seems a predictable result.

Principal participation

DEC implementation has moved fastest and furthest in schools where principals have consistently attended and fully participated in DEC activities. Our observations indicate it is optimal for principals themselves to participate in all sessions, though several schools have made good progress with an assistant principal representing school administration on the leadership team.

[I]f principals who lack prior knowledge in this area feel they cannot afford to appear to be learning alongside other school leadership team members, then decreased participation in, and schoolwide commitment to, the initiative seems a predictable result.

We have identified several possible reasons for the impact principal participation has on the rate and quality of implementation. First, when principals, who invariably have crowded schedules, invest their own time and energy in an activity, it sends a signal to staff that the activity is important and teachers' own participation is consequential. Although principal participation may have symbolic implications, we believe teachers also know from experience that principals generally do not have time for things that they think will not make a difference.

A second way principal participation enhances implementation is by enabling school leadership teams to work with greater confidence and dispatch because teams get instant feedback from principals about alternative improvement goals and strategies. When principals do not attend DEC sessions, only so much can be accomplished before suspending activities to get principal input.

Third, principals who attend DEC sessions have more opportunities to see firsthand how the DEC treatment can dovetail with existing school improvement goals. For example, the impact of DEC initiatives depends considerably on the extent to which the initiatives become integrated into local school improvement plans.

District priorities and policies

District priorities and policies have had considerable impact on how readily schools entered into and progressed with DEC-related activities. The standards-based orientation of DEC makes it complementary to federal and state standards-based initiatives. Three of four districts participating in DEC in the 2001-2 school year also had an NSF Urban Systemic Initiative (USI). DEC staff members have communicated frequently with USI staff to focus more energy on mathematics and science improvement than could be accomplished by either initiative acting in isolation.

In addition to providing a generally favorable climate for data-driven instructional improvement, districts have taken specific steps to provide concrete support. In many cases, district staff have attended DEC sessions to express their support for the initiative and to keep apprised of how it is being implemented so that they can justify the use of district resources to further DEC activities. For example, in many cases district administrators have asked principals to excuse school leadership team members from in-services otherwise required of all teachers so that the team members could attend DEC sessions or meet to plan DEC project–related activities. District administrators have also arranged for teachers to receive continuing education credits for DEC participation and, as previously mentioned, have occasionally paid stipends to teachers for participating in DEC on noncontract days.

An extremely important way that district administrators in two sites supported DEC was by including appropriate district staff in DEC sessions for participating schools and by arranging for extra sessions for groups of district staff. In Miami-Dade, special sessions were provided as appropriate for district mathematics and science specialists (who are dedicated full-time to helping schools improve mathematics and science teaching and learning), district mathematics and science curriculum supervisors, assessment and accountability personnel, USI staff, and others. In Chicago, several district representatives attended the initial two-day professional development session, and a one-day special session was held for USI and other district staff at a later time. A special session was also conducted for USI staff in Philadelphia.

If the reluctance of some schools to make a commitment to the DEC treatment is based on a desire to see evidence of success, then DEC may now be poised to win some converts. This is especially true in Miami-Dade where three DEC schools made big gains on state school accountability scores. The state grade for Miami Schools 810 and 811 moved from a D to a C, and School 85 went from a C to an A. In the summer of 2002, school leadership team members from Schools 810 and 811 repeatedly told other principals, teachers, and district administrators that DEC had been the main reason for their improved performance. School 85 indicated that DEC was one of several equally important factors in their progress.

An obstacle encountered in Chicago was an edict issued by district administration at the beginning of the 2001-2 school year directing schools to give maximum effort to increasing reading scores. Though there seemed to be some confusion about exactly what schools were being told to do, the principals in DEC schools told us that many principals in the district instructed all teachers to give top priority to teaching reading skills and worry less about other subjects. Time dedicated to math instruction was perhaps the least affected, but time spent on science was substantially cut. The edict also tended to make subjects other than reading a low priority for principals when planning professional development and in-service activities.

Critiquing the Experiment

Four decades ago, Campbell and Stanley (1963) provided a powerful template for critiquing experiments in education. They identified the concepts of *internal validity*—the extent to which an experiment provides unbiased estimates of treatment main effects—and *external validity*—the extent to which the results from an experiment can be generalized. These two types of validity form the cornerstone for designing and critiquing experiments in any field. To internal and external validity can be added issues of precision—that is, the extent to which the effect size is estimated with a small standard error (Porter 1997). Analysis of precision must wait until dependent variable data are available for analysis. Discussion of internal and external validity follows.

Internal validity

Within districts, schools were randomly assigned to the treatment or control condition. Of course, random assignment does not guarantee unbiased estimates of treatment main effects. For example, there was modest differential attrition between the treatment and control schools, with three schools lost from the treatment condition.

In the Charlotte-Mecklenburg district, substantial reorganization caused problems of "crossover." Massive movement of teachers from one school to another has created a situation in which teachers who received treatment have moved to control schools, and vice versa. This is primarily a problem of implementation, but it also means that, to some extent, control schools may have benefited from being joined by teachers who have received the treatment.

A randomized experiment can also be compromised by dependence among the units receiving treatment. For example, if students are randomly assigned to the treatment or control condition and all students in the treatment condition experience the treatment as a group, then there is only one replicate of the treatment, and that is confounded with the comparison of treatment versus control. Within our study of professional development, school leadership teams received their training together in a central place. Furthermore, the trainer, a charismatic individual, provided all of the training to all of the leadership teams in all of the districts. Still, the bulk of the treatment took place in each school separately. First, each school had to form a leadership team, and that leadership team had to take action in the school.

Second, each leadership team needed to provide training to all of the other math and science teachers in the school.

In sum, we conclude that the internal validity of the experiment is strong, though not perfect. One site was compromised with crossover effects but has been replaced by an additional site one year late in the study. Other threats to internal validity seem, for the most part, to have been controlled.

External validity

Having a single trainer limits external validity. Ideally, there should have been a different trainer for each school, but this arrangement simply would not have been feasible. In our next study, however, we will explore the feasibility of training trainers, who, in turn, will train school leadership teams, which, in turn, will train teachers at their school.

There are several other limits to the external validity of the study. The focus is on urban schools serving high concentrations of students of color and students from low-income families. The work is in middle-school math and science. Schools within each district were recruited, so they are volunteers. Four schools dropped out of the study before random assignment, due to low teacher response to the baseline survey. Clearly, generalization of results must be limited in all of these ways.

A not-quite-so-obvious threat to external validity comes from the timing of the study and the context in which it was conducted. The treatment took place at a time when there was a huge emphasis in the United States on standards-based reform and a concomitant interest in improving math and science achievement of students, especially students of color and students from low-income families. The reauthorization of Title I (No Child Left Behind Act 2002) immediately increased student achievement testing in math, with science to follow. All of these factors may have added to districts' and schools' receptiveness to our professional development program. Furthermore, as mentioned above, three of the four districts had an NSF-funded USI, with a similar interest in providing professional development to strengthen the teaching of mathematics and science. USIs could have been competitors, but field data suggest they were allies.

The unique context may explain in part why we experienced relatively little trouble recruiting schools. Moreover, the enthusiasm for data-based decision making may have further strengthened the attractiveness of our intervention. Clearly, the results of the study can best be generalized to other generally favorable climates.

Unfortunately, our study is limited to three years. As noted earlier, this was a condition NSF placed in its call for proposals. The three-year limitation has had several negative effects on the external validity of the study. First, it meant that a delayed test of effects on instructional practices was not possible. Nor is it possible to see the extent to which our treatments stay in place over time. Second, effects on student achievement are unlikely in such a short period. Thus, our work does not have the benefit of a student achievement test administered by our project. Although we will look at student achievement data available from the schools and districts, the utility of those data are severely limited. Consequently, whatever treatment effects we do find will be limited to the set of dependent variables analyzed.

We would be remiss if we did not mention one other threat to the validity of our study. Clearly, the designers of the intervention were the designers of the experiment. Ideally, our intervention would be evaluated by a third party. However, a third-party evaluation, though ideal, is not easy to secure. NSF may have funded our proposal in part because we proposed to develop a promising intervention. Of course, we needed to evaluate that intervention. Even if we had hired a third party to do the evaluation, they would have been reporting to us. Still, the fact that our project lacks a third-party evaluation may cause unknown compromises to the validity, both internal and external, of the study.

Issues in Doing Place-Based Randomized Trials in Education

We close this article by reflecting on our experience thus far in conducting a place-based randomized-trial study of professional development for middle-school math and science teachers in large urban school districts. Much of what we have learned through our experience is well known. Still, since experiments have been rare in education over the past several decades, it may be worth sharing insights from a recent experience.

A fundamental issue in considering an experiment in education is knowing whether an experiment is warranted. Experiments are not cheap; nor are they easy to conduct. Moreover, many questions in education research cannot be answered by experiments. But some can, and some should. Exactly what kinds of education questions are amenable to experimental research?

First, one must have a promising intervention—an intervention that is theoretically motivated and addresses an important outcome of education practice. We believe our treatment meets both of these criteria. Second, the treatment needs to be reasonably straightforward if there is any hope that it can be implemented. Of course, what is straightforward in one person's mind may be highly nuanced and complicated in another's. Our treatment borders on the complicated. Some schools and districts implemented the treatment much more faithfully and fully than others. Part of the variance in implementation may be due to differing degrees of commitment, but part of it may be attributable to varying degrees of capacity, as well. Education interventions that are highly complex might have important effects when fully implemented, but if they can rarely be fully implemented, they are not valuable. Third, and tightly connected with the preceding point, the treatment should have been pilot-tested to get an early indication of its feasibility and promise. Here again, the treatment we are testing meets the crite-

172   THE ANNALS OF THE AMERICAN ACADEMY

rion, having been used in a number of sites, in a form not exactly like the current form, but close enough to be useful.

Another issue to consider is the hypothesis being tested. To what should the treatment be compared? We chose to compare our treatment schools, in which our professional development intervention was implemented, to a set of control schools, in which no specific professional development intervention was implemented. Ours was not a strict control in the sense that teachers in the control schools received no professional development. In that sense, strict controls in education are rarely possible. Schools are responsible for providing the best possible education to their students. Teachers in schools are professionals who should participate in professional development on a regular basis.

We could have selected an alternative intervention for comparison, but we did not elect this option for two reasons. First, data-based decision making is a relatively new enthusiasm in education, and we knew of no good alternative to our data-based decision-making professional development program. Second, our professional development program focuses as much, if not more, on providing data on instructional practices as it does on providing data on student achievement. Again, we knew of no good alternative. Finally, the modal school in the United States is receiving no professional development on data-based decision making, and the effect size we wished to estimate was our program's effect in comparison to that of the modal school.

Selecting a comparison group is one of the most important decisions to be made in an experiment. After all, the comparison defines the effect that will be estimated. A couple of related issues are worth mentioning. First, does our professional development program supplement or supplant professional development that otherwise would have gone on in the treatment schools? That is, in our treatment schools, are we looking at the effects of all of the ongoing professional development that the control groups are experiencing, *plus* our program, or has our program taken the time and energy of treatment school teachers such that they are less likely to continue to participate in other professional development? Another related issue is maintaining the control group schools. They need to fully cooperate with, and participate in, measures of the study's dependent variables. We are not certain yet what difficulties lie ahead for our study. Baseline measures went well, but when we go back for posttest measures, will we find the same level of cooperation? Will the control schools be eager to receive the delayed treatment, or will they have forgotten about the opportunity for that treatment and be unwilling to cooperate? Our current expectation is that they will be cooperative, but that remains to be seen.

Yet a third issue concerns the level of implementation. At least in education research, Berman and McLaughlin (1975) are credited with identifying the importance of studying implementation, a point that has since been made by many others as well (Pressman and Wildavsky 1984; Stebbins et al. 1976; Stringfield et al. 1994). We are investing considerable resources in measuring implementation, especially in the Miami-Dade and Chicago sites. Thus far, we are convinced that a treatment took place in virtually all of the schools, but in varying degrees. As described earlier, the degree of implementation appears to depend on a number of factors, including (1) principal leadership, (2) district support, and (3) teacher and principal mobility.

Perhaps not surprisingly, the degree of treatment implementation has depended to a considerable extent on the vagaries of the school districts and states. We essentially lost our Charlotte-Mecklenburg site when the district reorganized after coming out from under court-ordered desegregation. Our Philadelphia site somehow remained in the study despite the state's takeover of that district, but it was not easy.

[T]he degree of implementation appears to depend on a number of factors, including (1) principal leadership, (2) district support, and (3) teacher and principal mobility.

We are committed to using our measures of degree of implementation to study the effect sizes of our treatment. Of course, this will be a nonexperimental study of natural variation, so the arguments for cause-and-effect relationships will be difficult. Still, the question is simply too important to ignore: do there appear to be larger treatment effects for schools in which implementation was most complete? We are also interested in using level of implementation as a dependent variable, trying to link variance among treatment schools in implementation to factors that could be, at least to some extent, manipulated. Principal leadership may not be particularly manipulable, although we might add a component to our intervention to test this question. District support, in contrast, might be more susceptible to influence, and we are already at work on approaches that would allow us to look at this factor. At least at this time, teacher and principal mobility seems largely outside our control. We hope to learn more about factors that influenced the level of implementation in our study so that we can (1) revise and strengthen our intervention and (2) better understand how to generalize our treatment effect.

One extremely important, yet fairly simple, index of implementation is whether schools can be recruited to try the treatment in the first place. Here, we have had considerable success, despite what some might view as rather modest incentives. These incentives—a free, hopefully high-quality professional development program, delivered immediately to the treatment schools and on a delayed basis to the control schools—may have been particularly effective because of the timeliness of our program's focus on improving math and science in middle schools through data-based decision making.

We close with one last issue. If our treatment works—if it has important positive effects on instructional practice (and on student achievement, if we are able to introduce that dependent variable)—then what will we have learned about bringing the treatment to scale? The answer is, *very little*. To bring the treatment to scale, should it be found effective, we would need to address at least three key challenges. First, we would have to find a way to produce more trainers on a par with the one used in this experiment. Second, we would need to build an infrastructure for "selling" the treatment to hundreds, if not thousands, of schools across the country. Third, we would need to find a way to maintain the fidelity and integrity of the treatment as it was scaled up through multiple trainers in multiple, geographically dispersed sites over an extended period of time. These challenges were not addressed in this experiment; nor should they necessarily have been. First things first. Our ambition was to address the most fundamental question: is the treatment any good? Still, once that initial question has been answered in the affirmative, questions about taking the treatment to scale, which are in some ways analogous to concerns about external validity, must be addressed if an intervention is ultimately to be found worthy.

References

Berman, Paul, and Milbrey W. McLaughlin. 1975. *Federal programs supporting educational change: Vol. 4. The findings in review*. R-1589/4-HEW. Santa Monica, CA: RAND.

Boruch, R. F. 1997. *Randomized experiments for planning and evaluation: A practical guide*. Thousand Oaks, CA: Sage.

Boruch, Robert, Dorothy De Moya, and Brooke Snyder. 2002. The importance of randomized field trials in education and related areas. In *Randomized trials in education research*, ed. Frederick Mosteller and Robert Boruch. Washington, DC: Brookings Institution.

Campbell, David T., and J. C. Stanley. 1963. Experimental and quasi-experimental designs for research teaching. In *Handbook of research on teaching*, ed. N. L. Gage, 171-246. Chicago: Rand McNally.

Cohen, David K., and Heather C. Hill. 2001. *Learning policy: When state education reform works*. New Haven, CT: Yale University Press.

Cook, Thomas D. 2002. Randomized experiments in educational policy research: A critical examination of the reasons the educational evaluation community has offered for not doing them. *Educational Evaluation and Policy Analysis* 24 (3): 175-99.

Council of Chief State School Officers. 2002. *Experimental design to measure effects of assisting teachers in using data on enacted curriculum to improve effectiveness of instruction in mathematics and science education*. DEC Project: Year 2 Report to the National Science Foundation on Grant REC no. 0087562. September. Washington, DC: Council of Chief State School Officers.

Creighton, Theodore B. 2001. Data analysis in administrators' hands: An oxymoron? *The School Administrator* 4 (58): 6-11.

Desimone, Laura, Andrew C. Porter, Michael Garet, Kwang Suk Yoon, and Bea Birman. 2002. Effects of professional development on teachers' instruction: Results from a three-year longitudinal study. *Educational Evaluation and Policy Analysis* 24 (2): 81-112.

Fullan, Michael. 2002. The three stories of education reform. *Phi Delta Kappan* 81 (8): 581-84.

Gamoran, Adam, Andrew C. Porter, John L. Smithson, and Paula A. White. 1997. Upgrading high school mathematics instruction: Improving learning opportunities for low-achieving, low-income youth. *Educational Evaluation and Policy Analysis* 19 (4): 325-38.

Garet, Michael S., Andrew C. Porter, Laura Desimone, Bea F. Birman, and Kwang Suk Yoon. 2001. What makes professional development effective? Results from a national sample of teachers. *American Educational Research Journal* 38 (4): 915-45.

Loucks-Horsley, Susan, Peter W. Hewson, Nancy Love, and Katherine E. Stiles. 1998. *Designing professional development for teachers of science and mathematics*. Thousand Oaks, CA: Corwin.

Love, Nancy. 2002. *Using data/getting results: A practical guide for school improvement in mathematics and science*. Norwood, MA: Christopher Gordon.

Martin, Michael O., Ina V. S. Mullis, Eugenio J. Gonzalez, Kathleen M. O'Connor, Steven J. Chrostowski, Kelvin D. Gregory, T. A. Smith, and R. A. Garden. 2001. *Science benchmarking report TIMSS 1999—Eighth grade: Achievement for U.S. states and districts in an international context*. Boston: Boston College, Lynch School of Education.

Mullis, Ina V. S., Michael O. Martin, Eugenio J. Gonzalez, Kathleen M. O'Connor, Steven J. Chrostowski, Kelvin D. Gregory, R. A. Garden, and T. A. Smith. 2001. *Mathematics benchmarking report TIMSS 1999—Eighth grade: Achievement for U.S. states and districts in an international context*. Boston: Boston College, Lynch School of Education.

No Child Left Behind Act of 2001, Pub. L. No. 107-110, 115 Stat. 1425. 2002. http://www.ed.gov/legislation/ESEA02/107-110.pdf (accessed April 29, 2003).

Porter, Andrew C. 1997. Comparative experiments in education. In *Complementary methods for research in education*, 2nd ed., ed. Richard M. Jaeger, 523-85. Washington, DC: American Educational Research Association.

———. 2002. Measuring the content of instruction: Uses in research and practice. *Educational Researcher* 31 (7): 3-14.

Porter, Andrew C., Michael S. Garet, Laura M. Desimone, and Bea F. Birman. 2003. Providing effective professional development: Lessons from the Eisenhower Program. *Science Educator* 12 (1): 23-40.

Porter, Andrew C., Michael W. Kirst, Eric J. Osthoff, John L. Smithson, and Steven A. Schneider. 1993. *Reform up close: An analysis of high school mathematics and science classrooms*. Final Report to the National Science Foundation on Grant no. SAP-8953446 to the Consortium for Policy Research in Education. Madison: University of Wisconsin–Madison, Consortium for Policy Research in Education.

Pressman, Jeffrey L., and Aaron Wildavsky. 1984. *Implementation*. 3rd ed. Berkeley: University of California Press.

Schmocker, Michael. 2002. Up and away. *Journal of Staff Development Council* 23 (2): 10-13.

Smith, Christopher L., and Rachel L. Freeman. 2002. Using continuous system level assessment to build school capacity. *American Journal of Evaluation* 23 (3): 307-19.

Stebbins, Linda B., Robert G. St. Pierre, Elizabeth C. Proper, Richard B. Anderson, and Thomas R. Cerva. 1976. *Education as experimentation: A planned variation model*. Vol. III, U.S. Office of Education Contract no. 300-75-0134. Cambridge, MA: Abt Associates.

Streifer, Phillip A. 2001. The "drill down" process. *The School Administrator* 4 (58): 16-19.

Stringfield, Samuel, Linda F. Winfield, Mary Ann Millsap, M. Puma, B. Gamse, and B. Randall. 1994. *Urban and suburban/rural special strategies for educating disadvantaged children: First year report*. Baltimore: Johns Hopkins University Press.

U.S. Department of Education, National Center for Education Statistics. 2000. *NAEP 1999 trends in academic progress: Three decades of student performance*. NCES 2000-469. Washington, DC: Government Printing Office.

———. 2002. *The condition of education 2002*. NCES 2002-025. Washington, DC: Government Printing Office.

Wellman, Bruce M., and Robert J. Garmston. 1999. *The adaptive school: Developing and facilitating collaborative groups*. Norwood, MA: Christopher-Gordon.

Yeagley, Raymond. 2001. Data in your hands. *The School Administrator* 4 (58): 12-15.

Emergent Principles for the Design, Implementa-tion, and Analysis of Cluster-Based Experiments in Social Science

By
THOMAS D. COOK

In experimentally designed research, many good reasons exist for assigning groups or clusters to treatments rather than individuals. This article discusses them. But cluster-level designs face some unique or exacerbated challenges. The article identifies them and offers some principles about them. One emphasizes how statistical power and sample size estimation depend on intraclass correlations, particularly after conditioning on the use of cluster-level covariates. Another stresses assigning experimental units at the lowest level of aggregation possible, provided this does not subtly change the research question. A third emphasizes the utility of minimizing and measuring interunit communication, though neither is easy to achieve. A fourth advises against experiments that are totally black box and so leave program implementation and process unstudied, though such study often makes the research process more salient. The last principle involves the utility of describing treatment heterogeneity and estimating its consequences, though causal conclusions about the heterogeneity will be less well warranted compared to conclusions about the intended treatment, every experiment's major focus.

Keywords: cluster random assignment; cluster level; allocation principle; interventions; unit of assignment; statistical power; treatment contamination; causal chain

Purposes

This article discusses some of the rationales, problems, and solutions associated with randomized experiments that assign groups to treatments rather than individuals. These groups might be entire schools, communities, or work sites, and typically, every individual within such a unit is assigned to the same treatment status, though individuals could also be randomly chosen within groups. Experiments of this form

Thomas D. Cook is a professor in the Institute of Policy Research, Northwestern University. He received his Ph.D. from Stanford University in 1967. His areas of interest include social psychology, social science of human development, evaluation research, and education. He is interested in social science methods for inferring causation, and through this interest he examines

DOI: 10.1177/0002716205275738

are often called group-, cluster- or place-based, since the unit of assignment is a cluster of individuals who share space.

Systematic social forces operate so that neighborhoods tend to vary in their constellation of residents just as schools vary in their profiles of students and teachers. That people fill space in systematic ways is a major finding of demography and sociology and is central to studying the determinants, processes, and consequences of who lives where or who attends a particular type of institution. However, such systematic selection is a problem for other research purposes and leads to most of the problems associated with using cluster random assignment to learn about how a given intervention affects groups of people who share space.

Social scientists have had considerable experience with randomly assigning individuals to treatments and even more with randomly selecting individuals to be in surveys. But experience with the design, implementation, and analysis of cluster-based experiments is more recent and limited. This is unfortunate since social scientists often identify the nature of methodological problems, and some possible solutions to them, in the crucible of experience—by doing a particular type of research and reflecting on it. Since multilevel experiments are rare, the wisdom about how to do them well is less developed than the corresponding wisdom about individual-level experiments. And it is certainly less than the wisdom about implementing random selection in survey research, where seventy years of relevant experience have accumulated on improving some discrete aspect of survey research. This experience even comes from experiments on, say, how to word items, to record responses, to do face-to-face or telephone interviews, or how interviewer and interviewee race or gender should be managed. My main purpose here is to increase the relevant wisdom about successfully implementing cluster-level randomized experiments, even if only at the margin.

While I will consider theoretical work on cluster-based studies in statistics and research design, my main emphasis is on lessons I have learned over the past decade in implementing experiments with schools as the unit of analysis (Cook et al. 1999; Cook, Hunt, and Murphy 2000), in consulting about experiments designed to prevent cardiovascular disease in smaller cities (Farquhar et al. 1990; Blackburn et al. 1984), and in doing work on neighborhood social relations and their effects on family life (Cook, Shagle, and Degirmencioglu 1997; Cook et al. 2002; Furstenberg et al. 1999). In education, many different units of assignment are possible, including districts, schools, grade levels, classrooms, or individuals. In disease prevention and urban improvement, different units are again possible— cities, planners' neighborhoods, census tracts, block groups, or individuals. However, school-based prevention studies assign schools and classrooms, not neighbor-

issues in evaluation research, primarily in the areas of education and community health. Works include Quasi-Experimentation Design and Analysis Issues for Field Settings, Qualitative and Quantitative Methods in Evaluation Research *and* The Foundations of Evaluation Theory. *He is a fellow of the American Academy of Arts and Sciences and a Margaret Mead Fellow of the American Academy of Political and Social Science. At Northwestern University, he it the Joan and Serepta Harrison Professor of Ethics and Justice and a professor of sociology.*

hood spaces, to the treatment groups used to explore ways of reducing violence, drug use, or smoking among students.

I want to be clear up front about some limitations to this article. Many of the problems I consider do not have empirically and consensually validated solutions of which I am aware. This forces me to consider incomplete solutions, both contingent ones that work under special circumstances and partial ones that ameliorate a problem without solving it. Of the problems I consider, some are unique to cluster-based designs because they are products of social clustering. Others are germane to experiments that assign individuals but are exacerbated in the group context. Also, I limit the analysis to single experiments that probe whether a causal relationship is plausible with the specific populations, settings, historical periods, manipulations, and measures sampled in that study. Examining the many other factors that moderate such a cause-effect relationship is better accomplished by synthesizing results across many experiments. But space precludes examining the special issues entailed in synthesizing cluster-based experiments rather than individual-level ones, a topic that is even less developed than thinking about single cluster-level experiments.

Why Assign at the Cluster Level?

It is intrinsic to some interventions that they are based on superindividual concepts. For instance, whole school reform seeks to modify the academic and social climate of a school building and to improve teacher practice norms throughout the whole school. Program developers vary in how they want to achieve such goals. But most efforts include giving staff more responsibility for the choices that affect their practice, including a role in setting the school's annual objectives and goals. Professional development is also typically provided to enhance specific practice skills, to build commitment to the reform effort, and to get staff to accept their interdependence with colleagues and parents in furthering students' development. The relevant theories regularly invoke constructs like school governance, culture, climate, norms, teams, and networks, each a concept that cannot be reduced to individual behavior. The hope is even to create a new culture whose norms will affect the behavior of current teachers and students and also future ones.

Interventions can also be designed to target individual staff members and students and yet require a school level of assignment. For instance, program designers can pay special attention to those individuals who function as building-level opinion leaders by virtue of their social networks and power to influence, using these individuals to catalyze building- or classroom-level change. As an explanatory construct, social network is also inherently superindividual.

But social communication processes can occur in contexts where classrooms are not selected because of special network or normative links to the rest of the school. Interventions designed to be self-contained within smaller groups like classrooms can still be talked about in other classrooms, with the result that program details can percolate from classes receiving a particular intervention into classes designed to receive a different intervention. Since this treatment dissemination clouds interpretation of any study results, whenever unplanned treatment dissemination is plausible schools need to be the unit of assignment rather than classrooms or grade levels. In this case, the unit of assignment is chosen to protect against a potential source of bias rather than to support an intervention that is specifically designed to activate a superindividual process like norm creation or dissemination through an existing social network.

Another argument for cluster-based assignment has to do with desired impact. The hope is that individual change will be greater in size, permanence, and generalization if it is achieved through group- rather than individual-level processes. One reason for this hope is that larger units like schools entail reaching more individuals when compared to efforts designed to reach only individuals. Another is that novel norm and network changes can emerge when larger groups are targeted, changes that then come to characterize the setting as a whole, serving not just to maintain change in those originally exposed to an intervention but also to influence the next cohorts who enter a school or community even after the intervention has been removed. A third reason for hope is that intervention with larger aggregates promises change that is stubborn and resistant to counterforces because it is anchored in multiple rather than single influences. It is one thing for a principal to urge teachers to change, and it is another thing for principals, fellow teachers, school boards, and parents to urge the same thing at different times, in different venues and perhaps even modeling the change in different ways. An educational intervention aimed at individual teachers would not reach as many children or entail as many potentially convergent influences for creating and maintaining new individual and group behaviors.

The hope is to reach more individuals, to change local norms and networks, and to link healthy living to multiple source and times.

The same potential advantages hold in public health. An intervention designed to promote a heart healthy lifestyle might affix heart healthy signs to specific commodities in local grocery stores. It might involve blood pressure screening stations at convenient locations. It might include community-wide races and walks to promote exercise as well as outreach activities to teach students about nutrition, exercise, and stress reduction. Even the local media might be solicited to focus on healthy living. The hope is to reach more individuals, to change local norms and networks, and to link healthy living to multiple source and times.

One should also not forget an important political reason for assigning clusters rather than individuals. Assignment to different treatments inevitably creates a source of inequality and potential resentment among those assigned to the less desirable treatment. Depending on the nature of the intervention, these inequalities and resentments can be especially large and pointed if they involve individuals who are in contact with each other. So it gets administrators off unpleasant hooks if, instead of assigning different treatments within the same class and so making inequalities particularly salient, the treatments are instead assigned between classes or—even better—between schools. The assumption is that individuals are less likely to react negatively to differences that are not under their very noses.

The rationales above reflect the loose way experiments are discussed in ordinary language. Discourse centers on testing the causal influence of some named X. But experiments test the effects of a contrast between what happened in the intervention group exposed to X relative to some other group, often a no-treatment control group. In formal thinking about experiments, the causal agent is always a comparative entity, whereas in public discourse, it tends to be an absolute one. In ordinary language, the treatment is considered to be invariable, as though X were implemented at the same strength in all the units. Variation within each treatment group is common, though, some of it due to differences in treatment exposure. So the real experimental question is whether X has a marginally greater influence than its comparison *despite* this within-group variation. However, variation in treatment implementation invites questions about the effects of the treatment implemented at its best rather than its average, a question that particularly interests theorists, program designers, and policy makers desperate to find something that works. This "treatment on treated" question is not technically experimental because assignment to implementation levels is not random. Experiments test whether the average difference in implementation between an X and comparison group has an effect over and above the noise from within-group variation. This experimental "intent to treat" conception is more nuanced than the ordinary language understanding that an experiment tests the effects of X; and it is not a direct test of the effects of X when implemented at its best.

Why the *Random* Assignment of Larger Units?

I offer here a structural rationale for assigning clusters at random that alternatively describes the traditional statistical rationale. The starting point is the sociological reality that societies are structured in complex ways. The American educational system includes a federal level within which states are nested and a state level within which districts are nested. Within these districts are schools, and within these schools are grade cohorts. Within these grade cohorts are classrooms, and within these classes are individual students and teachers. So the nesting is hierarchical, multilayered like a Russian matryoshka doll.

However, the nesting is rarely balanced. A student can be with one set of fellow students in English and another in math. Also, the nesting is often multidimensional. For instance, schools are complexly related in space both to neighborhoods and families. Every student lives in a family and neighborhood that has links to schools and that can also affect educational performance either independently of schools or in complex interaction with them (Cook et al. 2002). And the cross-classification of social contexts is itself unbalanced since some children from a particular neighborhood attend one school and others another, the children in one class or school come from many different neighborhoods, and siblings can attend different schools or even live apart in different neighborhoods and homes (Cook 2003). Thus, to state that social structures are hierarchically ordered only scratches the surface of the myriad forms of this ordering.

To add to the complexity, social structures are not fixed in time. Individual students can change tracks (classes) within high school, both within and between school years. They can also leave their school for reasons other than formal graduation. Furthermore, new schools are founded and old ones shut down; schools regularly change their senior personnel; and where they exist, neighborhood schools sometimes redraw their receiving boundaries. Individuals are contextually embedded in ways that are synchronously multilevel, multidimensional, and imbalanced, and these complex relationships vary with time. This is a daunting structure to understand and model.

Fortunately, well-implemented cluster-based random assignment makes fewer demands on the analyst to know and model the structural complexity of society. When schools are randomly assigned in sufficient numbers, concerns about specific state and district confounds should be minimal since any one state or district factor should be equally represented in each of the treatment groups being compared. At most, one needs to describe these larger contexts and speculate about whether the causal results obtained might have varied with them. Also of little concern are school differences in how classrooms are constituted or otherwise used pedagogically and whether school-correlated neighborhood or family factors may have operated as confounds. Again, such factors should be equally distributed across the various treatment groups. Even temporal shifts in structure are only a causal concern if schools (or students) leave the study in patterned ways that differ by treatment condition. This can be easily checked, of course, and it is a consequence of the treatment even if it bedevils the understanding of other treatment consequences. Nor need one worry about imbalanced context crossings since these also should not vary by condition.

Without random assignment, any school-based causal study would have to struggle to rule out the possibility that these various interdependent structural realities function as causal confounds. With correctly implemented random assignment, the threats emanating from how society is organized and changes over time are dealt with by design and not by any ancillary information and assumptions the analyst is forced to use (and measure where possible). If the art of research design is to make the fewest and most transparent assumptions possible whose behavior is also the best known, then for answering a causal question the random assignment of clusters meets this bill better than its quasi-experimental and nonexperimental alternatives.

Principles of Improved Cluster-Level Design

Principle 1: Know the size of unconditional and conditional intraclass correlations, what determines them, and how they affect statistical power and hence sample size estimation

The systematic ways in which individuals cluster within space means that the observations they provide for data analysis are rarely independent. The degree of nonindependence is indexed by the intraclass correlation (ICC). In its unconditional form, this measures what fraction of the total variance in a variable lies between higher-order units and how much is due to individual differences within them, including error. In its conditional form, it indexes what fraction of the variance is between higher-order units after statistical adjustments have been made for other variables. When the ICC is zero, observations are independent and statistical power and statistical tests can be computed using traditional, individual-level methods. But in my experience, few unconditional ICCs are zero, and inventories of ICCs for a variety of different types of clusters and variables show this across many fields. Such systematic clustering creates problems of two kinds.

The first concerns statistical power and hence sample size estimation. The needed sample size of clustered units is sensitive to the magnitude of ICC, and even very small correlations can increase the sample size needed (Raudenbush and Bryk 2002). Moreover, in most (but not all) circumstances, the number of clusters affects power much more than the number of units within a cluster. So cluster-level experiments should be designed to minimize the ICC by using legitimate statistical adjustments. To understand this, consider academic achievement where, at the school level, unconditional ICC values on nationally available tests usually vary between .05 and .15 (Raudenbush 1997). The rule of thumb has developed from these values that school sample sizes of forty to fifty are usually needed to attain the statistical power traditionally needed to test intercept differences in balanced school-level experiments with two treatment conditions. This is a large number of schools, given the usual financial costs and especially if several school districts have to be sampled, forcing researchers to struggle with different school boards, time schedules, institutional review board procedures, and the like.

Individual- or cluster-level covariates are useful in this context because statistical power and sample size depend on the conditional rather than the unconditional ICC and covariates can reduce the unconditional ICC. The more the covariates do this, the more the study approximates an individual-level analysis. One type of covariate stands out for its ability to minimize the conditional ICC, a cluster-level covariate that is highly correlated with the outcome. Consider school-level achievement means from before and after an intervention and the correlation between them. Being larger units, schools are very reliably measured because individual differences are averaged out and this high reliability will increase correlations. Both measures are on the same test, probably measured in the same way, thus also increasing the correlation between the covariate and outcome. Indeed, one-year school-level achievement correlations typically range between .70 and .90, and correlations at the higher end of this range can reduce the conditional ICC to close to zero and so require fewer schools. Gargani and Cook (2005) showed this using two reading measures a year apart that were correlated .85, that reduced the ICC from .11 to .02 and that, in a balanced two-group design, required only 22 schools to detect an effect as small as .20, with alpha = .05 and beta = .80. Also relevant is that, when the conditional ICC is so close to zero, within-cluster sample sizes and the number of repeat measures then count more for power compared to when the ICC is higher. So very powerful cluster-level covariates are important for reducing the number of clusters needed and hence for getting more experiments done on the same fixed budget.

Knowing unconditional and especially conditional ICC values and their determinants is vital for the design of multilevel experiments and for analyzing the data from them. And they are important in their own right as descriptions of the extent to which spatially separated units vary on a given attribute.

Nonetheless, the ideal experiment selects more clustered units than the minimum necessary. This is to protect against the attrition of clusters. When this happens, the loss in power can be considerable in small-N designs. And cluster attrition does sometimes happen, as when new principals are appointed during a study and want nothing to do with their predecessors' initiatives. The technical ideal in this situation is to keep their schools in the measurement framework even if not in the treatment framework. Retaining them respects the original treatment assignment and intent-to-treat conception and permits unbiased estimates, though these are likely to be smaller because schools with only partial treatment exposure are included in the treatment group. But keeping schools that have dropped out of treatment in the measurement framework is not always possible, and so sample sizes need to be calculated with some slack, slack that can be financially burdensome when entire schools or communities are under study.

But consider the alternative by examining the community heart healthy studies of the 1970s and 1980s. The financial cost of organizing entire communities of at least forty thousand inhabitants for five years or more meant that the largest study randomly assigned but six communities, three to each treatment condition (Blackburn et al. 1984). Realizing this was a hopelessly underpowered study, the researchers sought to bolster it by measuring many individual-level covariates and up to nine years of annual outcome measurement, but the drag from so few communities was still too great. The next wave of studies was more focused, on, say, just smoking prevention, and the sample size of communities was increased to about twenty spread over two conditions, Project COMMIT having eleven pairs of matched settings (Gail et al. 1992). Since then, the sample size requirements have continued to creep up, with the median target being thirty-five, a number that Eldridge et al. (2004) bemoaned as too low in light of the often binary nature of outcomes in public health. In whole school reform, the experiments have not been much bigger, with the two Comer evaluations having twenty-three and nineteen schools, each equally distributed over two conditions (Cook, Hunt, and Murphy 2000; Cook et al. 2002). While these last studies also utilized school-level covariates, their correlation with the outcome was not at the level that Gargani and Cook (2005) showed were needed.

There are other things that can also be done to increase statistical power at the cluster level when powerful covariates are not available. Increasing sample size is obviously one. The most interesting version of this is when the costs of adding treatment units far exceeds that of adding control ones and so controls are oversampled, as in a third Comer study that had thirty-six schools sampled 2:1. However, the power increment associated with design imbalance depends on the harmonic mean of the two treatments (Raudenbush 1997), making the total effect less than if the thirty-six schools had been equally assigned to treatment and control. But still, power does increase over having twenty-four schools equally balanced. To add clusters, it is also sometimes possible to sample fewer individuals within a school, using the resources saved to add more schools. However, it is usually much more expensive to add a single school than to add many students within a school that is already in the research design. So this option usually adds few schools. But when studying achievement with school sample sizes between twenty and forty, even a small change in the number of schools can make a big difference to power. So the option should not always be rejected out of hand.

The second problem that follows from nonindependent, clustered observations is that statistical tests of the hypothesized causal relationship will be biased unless the ICC is taken into account. If it is not, standard errors will be based on the (inappropriate) large number of units within clusters rather than on the smaller number of clusters. Since standard errors will be inappropriately small, effect sizes will be too large and causal conclusions will be too often positive. This is not a problem for researchers who rely on magnitude estimates that are independent of standard errors. But the vast majority of social scientists use statistical tests, and they have a problem because their hypothesis tests are too liberal.

Sensitivity to the downward bias in standard errors in multilevel designs has increased over the past decade. Researchers are more and more using texts and software programs that explicitly model dependencies in multilevel contexts (e.g.,

Raudenbush and Bryk 2002). So ignorance of ICCs and of their relevance for valid statistical tests is a declining problem. It is still a problem, though, in interpreting past research where published reports failed to take data dependencies into account—for example, in studies of peer tutoring that involve groups of two or more students and so require a group-level unit of analysis and in other forms of peer research where many ICC values are in the .20 to .35 range (Cook, Deng, and Morgano 2005) and so much higher than in school or neighborhood research. Unfortunately, sensitivity to clustering is rare in both of these research traditions, though probably increasing. Knowing unconditional and especially conditional ICC values and their determinants is vital for the design of multilevel experiments and for analyzing the data from them. And they are important in their own right as descriptions of the extent to which spatially separated units vary on a given attribute.

Principle 2: Assign units to treatments at the lowest level of aggregation possible, as long as this does not change the research question

On many practical grounds that I later elaborate, the results from cluster-based randomized experiments tend to be more difficult to interpret than the results from experiments with individuals. Thus, it is imperative to ask whether a causal question about an aggregate process absolutely requires assigning clusters rather than individuals. This is actually a special case of an even broader principle—that units should be assigned to treatment at the lowest level possible in the hierarchy from school districts, schools, grade levels, classrooms, and individuals or in the hierarchy from states, cities, city planning areas, census tracts, census blocks, households, and individuals.

To understand why lower levels of assignment are more desirable ceteris paribus, begin by considering quantitative research on neighborhood effects (Wilson 1987). As explicated by Jencks and Mayer (1990), the dominant research question is, Do neighborhoods affect children or adults for reasons that are more than the sum of individual differences? Of course, neighborhoods inevitably differ in composition, in the average of their individual difference profiles. But Jencks and Mayer's framing equates neighborhood effects with "emergent properties," with social processes that emerge from social interaction and that involve superindividual explanatory concepts like norms, networks, cultures, or institutions. In this formulation, summing individual differences cannot suffice to create a neighborhood effect because it does not speak to a collective process or structure.

A specific research strategy is associated with this "emergent properties" conception of a neighborhood effect. It depends on correlating neighborhood attributes selected for their theoretical interest with a particular outcome that has been statistically adjusted for all the measured individual difference attributes that vary with it and with the neighborhood differences under analysis. These individual differences are typically measured from surveys. The individual outcome data also often come from surveys but sometimes from administrative records too. And the geo-coded neighborhood attributes come either from the decennial census or from individual survey responses about neighborhood conditions aggregated across residents to the neighborhood level.

This strategy has revealed neighborhood "effects" that have been interpreted as modest (Brooks-Gunn, Duncan, and Aber 1997). The implication is that the unadjusted neighborhood differences one observes in daily life and descriptive statistics reflect who lives where and not what happens to them where they live. That is, they would have behaved similarly had they lived in affluent or in impoverished neighborhoods, suggesting that place does not matter much to individual welfare. Another possibility, though, is the methodology generating this momentous conclusion has serious limitations. So some scholars went a step further and sought to examine how spontaneous *changes* in one's neighborhood were related to *changes* in individual outcomes, again after statistically controlling for many measured and neighborhood-correlated individual differences. But this new strategy also failed to show large and systematic neighborhood effects and still leaves sophisticated readers wondering whether all selection effects have been controlled and whether the treatment contrast is not unduly restricted since most spontaneous moves are to neighborhoods whose attributes are not very different from the neighborhoods one just left. What to do, then, given that it is not really feasible to randomly assign whole neighborhoods to some kind of dramatic economic, social, and psychological upgrading, which analysts do not know how to do well in theory, let alone in practice?

The decision was made to do a randomized experiment on the topic, but assigning smaller intact households rather than larger neighborhoods. If I can oversimplify the experiment, called Moving to Opportunity (MTO) (Orr et al. 2003), it took volunteer families living in the inner part of five cities and randomly assigned them either to staying there or to getting housing vouchers and other forms of assistance permitting them to live in the suburbs. The causal question was, How does moving to a neighborhood with greater resources change the behavior of family members? Selection does not now seem to be a problem; nor does restriction on the independent variable; and the research question is still about the superindividual concept of a neighborhood. Yet families are randomly assigned to treatments, not neighborhoods.

Now carry through in greater detail the thought experiment begun earlier in which neighborhoods are the unit of treatment assignment, not households. Poor neighborhoods might be randomly assigned to improvements in the types of material, political, social, and institutional resources that are thought to cause better family outcomes in the suburbs. As desirable as upgrading inner-city neighborhoods might be, the prospects for it are not bright. It would be extremely expensive to sample the number of neighborhoods required for an experiment. It would also require a broad social buy-in that would not be easy to achieve since upgrading some city neighborhoods but not others will likely engender a bruising and high-profile public discussion that many governments would prefer to avoid. Anyway, city planners do not know how to design and implement such simultaneous multi-dimensional upgrading. And materially upgrading existing communities does not answer quite the same question as moving individuals to the suburbs since only the latter requires a radical change in the neighborhood's social composition. Such change is central to the conception of MTO, but it need not happen when upgrading existing poor neighborhoods.

As expensive as the multicity MTO was, its research costs were probably less than the combined costs of its many nonexperimental predecessors. MTO also fulfilled better a core function of causal research—maximizing the contrast tested. If one compares the poverty level of the receiving suburbs in the experiment with the poverty level of the neighborhoods spontaneously moved to in prior nonexperiments, the difference is very large. In science, experiments have traditionally sought, in Francis Bacon's words, "to twist nature by the tail," not to mirror it as some policy analysts want them to do. The large treatment contrast suggests again that MTO answers a different question from its predecessors. It describes what radical, large neighborhood changes *can* do to individuals and families—the traditional efficacy question of public health research (Flay 1986). It does not answer questions about what neighborhood change routinely *does* to individuals and families within the range of change that typically takes place—the traditional effectiveness question.

The above discussion speaks to the rationales for MTO and to the advantages that occur from having many lower-order cases for assignment rather than fewer higher-order ones. It has nothing to say about how well MTO was implemented and the implications of variation in such implementation. As a matter of record, almost 50 percent of the treatment families were not in the neighborhood assigned to them after five years. This does not preclude an intent-to-treat analysis since most families were kept in the measurement frame. So one could learn what effect the program had on those who were assigned to a suburb as opposed to a question about the effects it had just on those who stayed in their assigned suburb or who finished up in a suburb "demographically like" the assigned one. Analysts now have promising procedures for providing unbiased estimates of this last type of "treatment on treated" question using the original random assignment as an instrumental valuable (Angrist, Imbrens, and Rubin 1996). But the method is a large sample test and so not feasible with a small number of large-sized clusters. However, it is more feasible with larger numbers of small-sized clusters like the families in MTO, and this type of statistical analysis was actually used in Orr et al. (2003). So an added advantage of smaller clusters is the increased chance to analyze both causal questions: about the intent to treat and the effects of treatment on the treated.

In designing an experiment about clustered entities like neighborhoods, one needs to ask what is the lowest unit at which clustering is necessary, though recourse to lower-order units can sometimes subtly shift the nature of the question. Much more can be gained by assignment at the individual or household level (as with MTO), in contrast to the block group or census tract or city planners' level. By the same principle, when an educational intervention can be assigned to districts, schools, classrooms, or individual teachers and students, the lower level is to be preferred. The same holds if a coronary disease prevention intervention can be assigned to cities, neighborhoods, blocks, families, or individuals. The main advantages are for statistical power, control over implementation, and a greater chance to learn about both the intent to treat and treatment on treated questions.

Principle 3: Minimize and measure interunit communication, though neither will be easy when schools or neighborhoods are the unit of assignment

Whatever the unit of assignment, interunit communication is a problem because it can modify the planned treatment contrast. Cook and Campbell (1979) have enumerated many different processes and consequences associated with interunit communication in experiments. Most likely is that comparison cases will borrow from treatment ones and so reduce the achieved contrast, thereby increasing the chances of incorrectly failing to reject the null hypothesis. However, it is also possible for control cases to become resentfully demoralized at not receiving the treatment, leading them to do less well than otherwise. Then, a false positive conclusion can result if the controls have done worse and not because the experimentals have done better.

While these processes also operate at the individual level, my speculation is that they are exacerbated at the group level because of the larger numbers of individuals involved in toto—given the sample size requirements for and within groups—and also because group-level interventions are likely to be more socially salient and discussed than individual-level ones.

The best way to prevent interunit communication about treatment details is to assign units at such a social remove that they hardly communicate, and if they do, it is not about treatment details. Assigning treatment and control status to individual students or teachers within the same school means they can potentially compare experiences more readily than if intact schools were randomly assigned. If it is true that teachers generally communicate less about treatment details between grade levels than within them, then within-school treatments should be assigned across grades rather than within them. This suggests the utility of randomly assigning schools so that, say, all second-grade teachers are in one treatment and all the third-grade teachers are in another, while the opposite is the case in the other set of randomly assigned schools. This within-school design has obvious advantages over a complete between-school design, especially as regards the number of schools needed and hence financial cost. But interpreting the results depends heavily on teachers not sharing experiences across grades within a school. They are less likely to do so if a manipulation is not salient; but low-profile interventions are not that common in education, especially if academic achievement is the principal outcome and if teachers are called upon to implement the intervention. So I think that treatment contamination is a *potential* major problem in cluster-based experiments and serves as a rationale for often assigning entire schools to treatments rather than grade levels or classrooms within a school.

If such advantages accrue as the unit of assignment increases in size, why stop with aggregates like schools or cities? Why not go to even higher levels, to the district in the case of education or to the state or region in the case of cardiac health?

The brief answer is that increasing the size of the unit increases financial costs, on one hand, and also adversely affects the trade-off between an intervention's intensity and coverage, on the other. Although larger units usually entail greater coverage and less treatment contamination, they can often reduce treatment fidelity because monitoring by research staff tends to decline the more geographically dispersed units are. Also, most professionals in education and health know more about targeting their work to single identified individuals or small groups like classrooms than they know about targeting whole schools and entire communities. Moreover, teachers are probably motivated more by calls for change from their immediate colleagues as opposed to senior staff in school district headquarters. Since clusters are composed of individuals, the fear is that a treatment's average fidelity will drop off as unit size increases and that variation in implementation will increase both within schools and communities and across the group of schools and communities constituting a treatment or control group.

[T]eachers are probably motivated more by calls for change from their immediate colleagues as opposed to senior staff in school district headquarters.

Of course, it is not always possible to know in advance if there will be interunit communication or whether it will be of enough power to imperil causal conclusions. Most interventions have a theory (or logic model) specifying the causally potent components of the intervention, and it is exposure to these components that should be measured in assessments of interunit communication. Thus, Cook, Hunt, and Murphy (2000) showed that interunit communication took place in only three of their eleven control schools. In one instance, a principal from one condition was married to a teacher from another. In another school, a control group teacher was the daughter of a senior official at the program central office and she invited her father to come speak about his work. And in the final case, a control principal read up on the intervention by himself and tried to implement some of its particulars. In addition, the program coordinator in the district did some districtwide professional development and mentioned aspects of the program to teachers from control schools. So interunit communication took place but was restricted to a minority of schools. Moreover, the control schools never had the salaried program staff in them who were responsible for coordinating the program in treatment schools. Nor did any control teachers go to within-district or out-of-town retreats at the developers' headquarters to learn about program implementation. So measures of what was implemented in the control schools showed few of the specific structural changes the program design called for. To record some interunit communication does not mean that it is widespread or involves central details from the program theory.

But why should one ever incur the risk of treatment contamination? Why not simply add more units deliberately chosen so as to be more physically remote from each other? One way to do this would be by randomly assigning district schools to a second- and third-grade intervention or no intervention at all instead of randomly assigning them to have the intervention in their second or third grade, as in the earlier example. Another way would be to select schools for intervention that are in different school districts rather than all coming from the same district. In the first case, the main hypothesis is now a between-school one rather than a within-school one and so will require more schools. The second case entails schools from many districts, and so they will be more different from each other and more of them will be required for the same level of statistical power. Dealing with possible contamination by increasing physical distance will very often entail greater expense and logistical headaches. Just try, for instance, getting permission to do research from many school districts, going through each one's institutional review board with its unique requirements! So the hope is to assign grades or teachers within schools rather than entire schools.

But moving to the lower level leads to a dilemma that the following example highlights. Currently under way is an educational experiment on whole school reform that centrally features a literacy curriculum with grade-specific materials. In this study, schools are randomly assigned to getting a grade-specific curriculum in one grade, with another grade serving as a control. So all schools get one version of the same theoretical intervention, but it randomly varies as to which one they get. Under these conditions, how plausible is it to assume that teachers at the control grade level are unaware of what their language arts' colleagues are doing in different classes? In my judgment, some interunit communication about the intervention seems likely. After all, the comparison is with what fellow language arts teachers in the other grades are doing, not with what PE or sixth-grade teachers are doing. And since most of the control teachers voted for the new curriculum as a precondition for it entering their school, will they not be curious about it?

The researchers will doubtless measure interunit communication about treatment particulars, though this is difficult to do well; and they will likely construct arguments using these data about how likely such communication was to have biased results. But these arguments are bound to sound defensive or incomplete, and readers will likely vary in how plausible they judge them to be. Although the within-school strategy has considerable statistical advantages, it is a disadvantage that one cannot judge in advance how much serious interunit communication is likely and how convincing measures of such communication will be in arguments about the extent to which treatment contamination is a problem. Still, the measurement of such interunit communication is taking place, and that is all to the good.

The researchers' problem could have been avoided in the first place, albeit at extra cost, by assigning intact schools to the treatments so that, within each school, all the relevant grades received the intervention. The investigators tried this initially, inviting schools that desired the intervention to participate as treatment or control schools depending on the coin toss. But nearly all refused. Since wholesale refusal has not been common in the brief history of experiments on school reform, it is instructive to ask why it occurred this time.

I assume that acceptance of the invitation to random assignment is more likely when those soliciting the assignment are genuinely unsure about the efficacy of the intervention and state this as the major rationale for assigning at random. In the example under analysis, the program developer was the solicitor, and the schools his staff solicited were those that had already agreed to the intervention. In this circumstance, can one readily imagine the program developer asserting that an experiment was needed because the program of his design for which they had already signed up was not demonstrably effective? To make this argument would also have meant abjuring the results of his own prior quasi-experimental research that he had used for years to market the program to schools and funders. Can one easily imagine the developer using the best arguments for randomization, particularly since the schools solicited for the experiment had already voted to accept the program. Was it now being intimated after the fact that their vote only entitled them to be in a lottery to be in the program as opposed to being in the program proper? Were they given a guarantee of getting into the program in future years? What was said about what changes they could and could not make while serving as a control group? Were they asked to introduce nothing new in reading, or were they free to do whatever they wanted after learning they did not get into the treatment group? Schools are continuously evolving organizations and can never be asked to entomb themselves in usual practice. The implication of all this is that program developers should never be in charge of soliciting participation to be in an experiment. Their role is to advocate for their program, not to be brokers of the best approximation to the truth about their own program's effectiveness.

In their evaluation of *Sesame Street*'s second viewing season, Bogatz and Ball (1972) devised an innovative strategy that exemplifies the flexible thinking required to reduce interunit communication when assigning higher-order aggregates to treatments. At the time, the show was available in some markets only on cable. So the evaluators went to poorer neighborhoods without cable, and in families with a child of target age, they offered to provide cable to the home on a random assignment basis, together with books, toys, and games designed to raise the profile of *Sesame Street*. The fear was that children from control-group homes without cable would visit their friends nearby and ask to see *Sesame Street*. So Bogatz and Ball decided that all the families with a child of target age living within a block were to be assigned, thus making the unit of assignment a street block and not a home. And to reduce visiting across contiguous blocks, the sampling strategy excluded all blocks that touched on a block that was to be randomly assigned to the experimental or control condition. This created a cordon sanitaire around the study blocks. While it did not rule out all visiting between treatment and control homes, it surely reduced it and exemplifies what it takes to reduce this threat that will often not be completely ruled out.

It is obvious that the second and third principles are at odds because selecting the lowest unit for assignment usually increases the likelihood of the very communication between treatments that threatens interpretation. The connection is not inevitable, of course. But selecting units that are distant can increase costs and choosing interventions that are nonsalient—and hence not talked about—can decrease treatment impact. So, the solutions themselves entail other tradeoffs. Indeed, they are only the most striking of a large and complicated network of tradeoffs that currently make the design of cluster-level experiments as much an art as a science—notwithstanding the reality of scientific features like statistical power calculation and data analysis through hierarchical linear modeling. As the years of experience doing experiments accumulate, we will gain more reliable data and insights into these tradeoffs and will doubtless make better choices than today. But today, underinformed guesses will be required about the likelihood of treatment-correlated communication, about how many of the treatment or control units will be affected by such communication, about the communication being about theoretically and empirically significant components of what are usually complex multidimensional treatment packages, and about the quality with which such communication can be measured. Depending on the underinformed judgments that inevitably have to be made, a smaller or larger unit will be selected. At this early moment in the history of cluster-level experiments, traditional scientific conservatism suggests larger units—even though this strains budgets. But resources will force many researchers into the riskier choice of smaller units. So, some scholars are needed who will track—as well and as honestly as possible—just what amount and type of inter-unit communication occurs about treatment particulars.

Principle 4: Avoid black box experiments despite their policy relevance; instead explore implementation and causal mediating processes

When process measurement is made within an experiment, the conclusions cannot be generalized beyond contexts that include such measurement. Yet social policy rarely stipulates such measurement as part of an ongoing program. So if research is to have high fidelity to policy, it should be of a black box type, shorn of all unnecessary measurement. Science assigns measurement a different priority; for assessments of treatment implementation, unit characteristics and causal mediation are important for explaining why a cause-effect relationship occurs (or is not observed). This measurement-related trade-off between policy and science needs affects every experiment, whatever the unit of assignment.

But the trade-off is particularly acute when experimenting with clusters. In part, this is because the sources of variation are particularly complex in multilevel experiments. If schools are assigned to condition, there will be both general and time-varying implementation differences between schools, between grade levels within schools, and between classrooms within grade levels, not to speak of between teachers and between students within classrooms. Moreover, experimenter-based attempts to enhance implementation quality will nearly always be less effective when dealing with all these levels simultaneously than when dealing only with, say, teachers. It is from the many sources of implementation variance and the presumption of diminished ability to ensure quality implementation that the need springs to check that the planned intervention occurs at an intensity that is considered "adequate" for bringing about effects. And it is impossible to do this without measuring those processes that occur between manipulating the independent variable and measuring the outcome.

In cluster-based experiments, treatment heterogeneity is the norm, not the exception; and it is likely greater than in most individual-level experiments.

A second rationale for measuring implementation processes is to probe the substantive theory through which influence is supposed to be transmitted from the intervention to the outcome. Such theory is usually laid out as a time-flow chart with boxes and arrows that illustrate the expected pathways of influence. Measuring the elements in this logic model is always important but is particularly problematic in multilevel studies because the theory tends to be more complex and more multidisciplinary as one moves through the various organizational levels to finish up at the individual. Also, the time lines might be more unclear as one struggles with causal paths both within and between levels. After all, one needs theories, not just of what happens at the individual level, but also at the classroom and individual levels at different times—a necessary but daunting task.

Experiments that fail to reject the null hypothesis are unhelpful if one cannot assess where the planned sequence of change broke down. And in experiments that do reject the null hypothesis, it is useful for both theory and practice to learn why the effect came about. One might discover, for instance, that classrooms are the major contributors to change and that schools merely provide the physical shell within which classrooms are found and through which children change. Knowing this simplifies the policy and theory implications of an experiment, reducing the role of the school level in this case and simplifying which program elements to emphasize to achieve successful transfer to other locations.

Heterogeneity of implementation usually increases with the size of clusters. Some community-based experiments have targeted cities of forty to one hundred thousand inhabitants. In one case, after five years of implementation targeted at physicians, physician associations, hospitals, grocery stores, schools, adult voluntary associations, the media, and athletic clubs, about half the inhabitants could not recognize the Minnesota Heart Health Project's logo or remember having come in direct contact with the program (Blackburn et al. 1984). Moreover, many city inhabitants did not immediately need the program services since they already led heart healthy lives. The implication is that mobilizing large communities around heart healthy living is difficult, given competing influences in the lives of many local people and their associations. So the National Heart, Lung, Blood Institute halted this kind of study, preferring to fund preventive work with individuals from populations known to be predisposed to poor cardiac health to whom treatment materials could be better targeted because of their presumed homogeneity, at least relative to whole cities where implementation quality was a real issue, as was targeting those truly in need.

Measures of intervening processes are used in three main ways. One is to describe their relationship to the randomly manipulated independent variable. In this kind of analysis, the intervening variable is an outcome in its own right. One can and should ask how the treatment affected a given intervening process, and answers to questions like this will be unbiased. Second, if the intervening measures are made at several time points they can be used as probes of the hypothesis about the temporal sequencing of change—what changes first and then later. Third, the measures can be used to test the entire causal chain. However, a selection problem arises when testing how one intervening variable affects another. Exposure to the first intervening variable in the causal chain is not random. As noted earlier, statisticians are now working on ways to deal with this using the random assignment as an instrumental variable (Angrist, Imbrens, and Rubin 1996) but assuming large samples that are not relevant to experiments with few clusters, each of large size. Nor are they relevant to models with multiple intervening variables changing at different times. Nonetheless, I think it still worth empirically probing each link in the postulated causal chain as long as the results are presented cautiously and with less certainty than the intent-to-treat results.

Nowhere is this tentative and dangerous analysis more needed than when large-sized clusters are involved. Then, the causal chain tends to be longer, increasing the chances of incorrectly specifying and inadequately measuring any one causal link. Moreover, effects later in the causal chain are likely to be more weakly related to the manipulation because they depend on more prior causal relationships being true when they are, almost certainly and at best, only probabilistically related to each other. Multiplying out all these probabilities highlights how tenuous is the molar causal link between the intervention and the outcome. This is why measurement of causal processes is a necessity at this early stage in the evolution of experience with cluster-based experiments, even if such measurement does go against the policy need to have experiments re-create the conditions of practical policy implementation that rarely include measuring intervening processes.

Principle 5: Explicitly acknowledge the great heterogeneity in treatment implementation in cluster-level designs and analyze its likely consequences even though these causal conclusions will be inferior to conclusions about the intended treatment

Descriptive studies of the outcomes most used in neighborhood and school research show few ICC values greater than .25—even in national studies and after corrections for unreliability (Cook, Shagle, and Degirmencioglu 1997). This implies that neighborhoods and schools are internally heterogeneous; the same is even true at the lower level of classrooms or street blocks through internal homogeneity is understandably greater at these lower levels.

Yet group-level interventions are often introduced into such heterogeneous settings under the implicit assumption that the intervention is equally meaningful and relevant to all residents or students. They are generally not, of course, as was seen with the heart healthy experiments in very large communities. It is naïve to believe that a treatment will be implemented in standard fashion across all the units within a treatment group. Nonstandardization is the reality both from one cluster to the next in a given treatment group and also, as I am discussing here, from one cluster to another within the same treatment group. In cluster-based experiments, treatment heterogeneity is the norm, not the exception; and it is likely greater than in most individual-level experiments.

The situation is exacerbated where local reinvention of the intervention is encouraged. For instance, the School Development Program (Comer 1988) specifies some procedures that should be followed within each school, but the school governance committee is encouraged to decide for itself which goals the school should pursue and how these goals might be realized. As a result, the program differs considerably from one school to the next within a district. To add to the complexity, district officials can add program factors at their more central level. Thus, the program in Prince George's County emphasizes mental health issues (Cook, Hunt, and Murphy 2000); the program in Chicago began emphasizing parent involvement and then switched to stimulating reading (Cook et al. 2002); and the program in Detroit emphasized coordination with outside consultants trying to stimulate reading and math. I surmise that local reinvention is more likely with clusters than individuals because clustered units are usually more physically dispersed, more used to exercising collective responsibility and tailoring materials to their needs and, anyway, researchers can control them even less than they can control individuals. But there is more to it than this. Advantages of ownership and maintenance occur if collectives are actively engaged in an intervention and generate marginal increments that make it more responsive to local circumstances.

This heterogeneity of treatment implementation problem is reduced when an intervention is linked to a detailed and well-articulated protocol and when homogenizing conditions are set for entry into a study. If 80 percent of the teachers have to agree to an intervention before it can be introduced into a school, this weeds out sites with minimal or highly variable interest in implementing a planned change including those where there is active dispute about the intervention's value. The flip side of this, of course, is that generalization is only warranted to such primed places. Another useful strategy is to monitor implementation at the earliest treatment stages and to use this feedback to tighten up on those aspects of implementation that are within the researchers' control. And of course, implementation should always be carefully and exhaustively measured.

The classical statistical response to incomplete and variable implementation at any level is to increase the sample size of units. This should be done where feasible, notwithstanding the many practical difficulties in finding willing clusters, in funding implementation at these sites, and in maintaining implementation quality as sites are added. I also think that a statistical strategy should be followed that is often considered to be ill advised. In addition to the necessary intent-to-treat analysis, a subsidiary analysis of the treatment on the treated should be done that uses measures of implementation from each unit at each level to provide quality of implementation scores. These should then be used in a quasi-experimental analysis of how variation in implementation quality affects the major outcomes. Since the analysis is biased, it is worth analyzing the data under several different assumptions about the direction of bias, and conclusions should be stated with less confidence than those from the unbiased intent-to-treat analysis. It strikes me as unproductively puritan to collect but not use implementation data when implementation quality so obviously varies from person to person within schools or neighborhoods and, particularly, between schools and neighborhoods assigned to the same treatment. The question of the treatment's effectiveness at its best is centrally important to many actors, including theorists, program developers, and some policy makers. It seems odd to neglect it completely in favor of a question about the effects of a treatment at its average that is conditional on the particular comparison groups chosen and on the level of uncontrolled background noise.

Conclusion

All things being equal, it is much more difficult to do an experiment that simultaneously deals with units at two or more levels—usually the individual and some higher-order level like a school or community. Social scientists have not yet acquired much experience in implementing cluster-based experiments, and the knowledge to be gained by emulating medicine's more evolved tradition of multisite randomized clinical trials is limited. In that tradition, individuals are assigned to treatments from within sites rather than between sites so that sites serve to increase power and generalization and not to be units of assignment per se. Social scientists will have to learn most of their lessons about cluster-based experiments in the crucible of their own experience. Solutions will also have to come from reflections on such experiences as well as from developments in statistical theory.

I have tried here to synthesize some of that experience, both as I have learned it in my own cluster-based experiments and in considering the work of others. The major problems are few, but quite messy. Cumulatively, they probably seem daunting to anyone who has not done experiments or has only done them with individuals. And they are indeed daunting. I make no pretence to having perfect solutions that can be plugged in across all types of clustering and all types of independent and dependent variables. But I do claim to have explicated the problems as I experienced them, and that is a modest start.

References

Angrist, J. D., G. W. Imbrens, and D. B. Rubin. 1996. Identification of causal effects using instrumental variables. *Journal of the American Statistical Association* 91:444-55.

Blackburn, H., R. Luepker, F. G. Kline, N. Bracht, R. Carlaw, D. Jacos, M. Mittelmark, L. Stauffer, and H. L. Taylor. 1984. The Minnesota Heart Health Program: A research and demonstration project in cardiovascular disease prevention. In *Behavioral health*, ed. J. D. Matarazzo, S. Weiss, J. A. Herd, N. E. Mller, and S. M. Weiss. New York: Wiley.

Bogatz, G. A., and S. Ball. 1972. *The impact of "Sesame Street" on children's first school experience*. Princeton, NJ: Educational Testing Service.

Brooks-Gunn, J., G. J. Duncan, and J. L. Aber, eds. 1997. *Neighborhood poverty: Context and consequences for children*. Vol. 1. New York: Russell Sage Foundation.

Comer, J. P. 1988. Educating poor minority children. *Scientific American* 259:42-48.

Cook, T. D. 2003. The rationale for studying multiple contexts simultaneously. *Addiction* 98 (Suppl. 1): 151-55.

Cook, T. D., and D. T. Campbell. 1979. *Quasi-experimentation: Design and analysis issues for field settings*. Chicago: Rand-McNally.

Cook, T. D., Y. Y. Deng, and E. Morgano. 2005. Peer group effects in early adolescence: The role of friends' average grade point average. Manuscript, Northwestern University, Evanston, IL.

Cook, T. D., F. Habib, M. Phillips, R. A. Settersten, S. C. Shagle, and S. M. Degirmencioglu. 1999. Comer's School Development Program in Prince George's County: A theory-based evaluation. *American Educational Research Journal* 36 (3): 543-97.

Cook, T. D., M. Herman, M. Phillips, and R. J. Setterston Jr. 2002. Some ways in which neighborhoods, nuclear families, friendship groups and schools jointly affect changes in early adolescent development. *Child Development* 73 (4): 1283-1309.

Cook, T. D., H. D. Hunt, and R. F. Murphy. 2000. Comer's School Development Program in Chicago: A theory-based evaluation. *American Educational Research Journal* 37 (2): 535-97.

Cook, T. D., S. C. Shagle, and S. M. Degirmencioglu. 1997. Capturing social process for testing mediational models of neighborhood effects. In *Neighborhood poverty: Context and consequences for children*, vol. 2, ed. J. Brooks-Gunn, G. J. Duncan, and J. L. Aber. New York: Russell Sage Foundation.

Eldridge, S. M., D. Ashby, G. S. Feder, A. R. Rudnicka, and O. C. Ukoumunne. 2004. Lessons for cluster randomized trials in the twenty-first century: A systematic review of trials in primary care. *Clinical Trials* 1:80-90.

Farquhar, J. W., S. P. Fortmann, J. A. Flora, C. B. Taylor, W. L. Haskell, P. T. Williams, N. Maccoby, and P. D. Wood. 1990. The Stanford Five-City Project: Effects of community-wide education on cardiovascular disease risk factors. *Journal of the American Medical Association* 26:359-65.

Flay, B. R. 1986. Efficacy and effectiveness trials (and other phases of research) in the development of health promotion programs. *Preventive Medicine* 15:451-74.

Furstenberg, F. F., Jr., T. D. Cook, J. Eccles, G. H. Elder, and A. Sameroff. 1999. *Managing to make it: Urban families in high-risk neighborhoods*. Chicago: University of Chicago Press.

Gail, M. H., D. P. Byar, T. F. Pechacek, and D. K. Corle. 1992. Aspects of statistical design for the Community Intervention Trial for Smoking Cessation (COMMIT). *Controlled Clinical Trials* 13 (1): 6-21

Gargani, J., and T. D. Cook. 2005. How many schools? The limits of the conventional wisdom about sample size requirements for cluster randomized trials. Manuscript, Graduate School of Education, University of California, Berkeley.

Jencks, C., and S. Mayer. 1990. The social consequences of growing up in a poor neighborhood. In *Inner city poverty in the United States*, ed. L. Lynn. Washington, DC: National Academy Press.

Orr, Larry, Judith D. Feins, Robin Jacob, Erik Beecroft, Lisa Sanbonmatsu, Lawrence F. Katz, Jeffrey B. Liebman, and Jeffrey R. Kling. 2003. *Moving to Opportunity: Interim impacts evaluation*. Cambridge, MA: Abt Associates.

Raudenbush, S. W. 1997. Statistical analysis and optimal design for cluster randomized design. *Psychological Methods* 2:173-85.

Raudenbush, S. W., and A. S. Bryk. 2002. *Heirarchical linear models: Applications and data analysis methods*. Thousand Oaks, CA: Sage.

Wilson, W. J. 1987. *The truly disadvantaged: The inner city, the underclass, and public policy*. Chicago: University of Chicago Press.

Randomization and Social Program Evaluation: The Case of Progresa

SUSAN W. PARKER
and
GRACIELA M. TERUEL

In this article, the authors analyze the development of Progresa, a Mexican antipoverty program that conditions monetary transfers to human capital investment of its beneficiary families. The program is the principal antipoverty strategy of the Mexican government and has served as a model for similar programs in a number of countries in Latin America. Progresa is also noteworthy because it was subject to a rigorous evaluation effort in rural areas, which included an experimental design. The authors first describe the rationale behind the design of Progresa, in particular, the conditioning of monetary transfers to children's school attendance and regular health clinic visits. The authors then turn to the evaluation effort, analyzing the randomized trial, the evaluation results, and the effect of the evaluation on the evolution of the program. Finally, the authors consider the limitations of the evaluation as well as areas where more research is needed.

Keywords: randomization; experimental design; Progresa; Mexico

Introduction

We analyze in this article the development of Progresa (the Education, Health and Nutrition Program),[1] a Mexican antipoverty program that conditions monetary transfers to human capital investment of its beneficiary families. The program is the principal antipoverty strategy of the Mexican government, representing in 2003, 46.5 percent of the federal government's annual poverty budget. The program began operating in 1997 in poor rural areas and has recently expanded to cover urban areas. By the end of 2003, more than 4.2 million families were receiving benefits, with the goal of 5 million families by the end of 2004. The program has captured attention at the international level and

NOTE: The authors gratefully acknowledge support for the development of this article from the Campbell Collaboration. They also benefited from comments received at the Campbell Collaboration/Rockefeller Foundation Conference on Place-Randomized Trials in Bellagio, Italy (2002) and in New York City (2003).

DOI: 10.1177/0002716205274515

has served as a model for similar programs in several other countries in Latin America. The Inter-American Development Bank recently gave Mexico its largest loan ever with the objective of extending Progresa to urban areas. Leading economists have also praised its success and advocated its expansion in other contexts (see Becker 1999; and Krueger 2002).

The program, while providing cash transfers, is aimed at increasing families' investment in human capital as defined by education, health, and nutrition. To achieve this objective, Progresa conditions cash transfers on children's enrollment and regular school attendance as well as clinic attendance. These transfers correspond on average to a 22 percent increase in the income levels of the beneficiary families and are given directly to the mother of the family. The program also includes in-kind health benefits and nutritional supplements for children up to age five and pregnant and lactating women.

The program is noteworthy because it was subject to a rigorous evaluation effort in rural areas that included an experimental design. A subset of communities eligible to receive Progresa was randomly assigned to a treatment (320 communities) or control (186 communities) group. For the approximately twenty-four thousand households living in these communities, household interviews were carried out both prior and after program implementation over a period of three years. An organization, the International Food Policy Research Institute, was hired to provide an external evaluation on the impacts of Progresa. These impacts included direct impacts (e.g., education, health, and nutrition) as well as other potential impact indicators, including child and adult work, consumption patterns, women's status, and transfers.

In what follows, we describe and analyze the design of Progresa, in particular, the rationale for conditioning monetary transfers to children's educational attendance and regular health clinic visits and the fact that benefits are given directly to the woman head of the household. We then turn our attention to the evaluation effort, analyzing the randomized trial, the evaluation results, and the effect of the evaluation on the evolution of the program. Finally, we consider the limitations of the evaluation and areas where more research should be focused, for instance,

Susan W. Parker (Ph.D.), professor of economics at Centro de Investigación y Docencia Económicas, A.C. (CIDE) in Mexico City, is an expert in program design and family behavior. Since its inception, she has played a central role in the evaluation of Progresa, a large-scale nationwide cash transfer program that now serves as a model for many countries around the world. She has extensive fieldwork experience including innovative work tracking movers within Mexico and to the United States. Her recent work has been published or is forthcoming in the International Economic Review, *the* Journal of Population Economics, *and the* Review of Economic Development.

Graciela M. Teruel (Ph.D.) is professor of economics at Universidad Iberoamericana in Mexico City. She is an expert on poverty and household welfare in Mexico and is a leading expert in the design of innovative research surveys. She codirects the Mexican Family Life Survey, an extremely innovative, ongoing, longitudinal survey of individuals, households, families, and communities in Mexico. Her recent work has been published in the Journal of Development Economics, Economics and Human Biology, *and the* Journal of Population Economics.

TABLE 1

BENEFICIARY HOUSEHOLDS:
PROGRESA, BY DATE OF INCORPORATION AND GEOGRAPHIC AREA

	Rural	Semiurban	Urban
Aug-Sep 1997	113,995	9,854	68
Nov-Dec 1997	91,323	4,571	133
Jan-Feb 1998	134,341	6,090	360
Jul-Aug 1998	766,874	68,508	2,643
Sep-Oct 1998	53,343	3,612	1,254
Nov-Dec 1998	315,096	41,765	4,706
Mar-Apr 1999	63,212	16,765	191
Jul-Aug 1999	175,218	55,175	1,430
Sep-Oct 1999	18,102	2,485	58
Nov-Dec 1999	163,881	49,258	2,151
Mar-Apr 2000	4,909	3	19
Jul-Aug 2000	15,453	2,841	33
Mar-Apr 2001	116,816	8,627	334
Jul-Aug 2001	302,435	202,123	66,241
Nov-Dec 2001	74,434	27,846	30,105
Jul-Aug 2002	504,567	134,802	365,715
Sep-Oct 2002	8,912	2,354	2,065
Jul-Aug 2003	116,304	32,271	24,749
Sep-Oct 2003	20,506	6,901	2,173
Total	3,059,721	675,851	504,428

SOURCE: Progresa program personnel.

whether the grant amounts represent the "correct" amounts (in terms of maximizing impact for a given cost), the effect that sample attrition may have on the evaluation results, and the implications of the relatively short duration of the experimental design.

A Description of Progresa

Progresa began operating in 1997, as a program aimed at poor households living in marginalized rural communities. The program was at first implemented in communities with fewer than 2,500 inhabitants, although a small number of communities with between 2,500 and 14,999 inhabitants (called semiurban) were also included. Urban communities, defined as areas with 15,000 inhabitants or more, began to be incorporated in the year 2001.

Table 1 shows the incorporation of beneficiary families in Progresa by geographic area over time through the end of 2003. Currently, the majority of beneficiary families are found in rural areas. Semiurban areas account for almost seven hundred thousand families, and the remainder, about five hundred thousand, are found in urban areas.

TABLE 2
MONTHLY AMOUNT OF EDUCATIONAL GRANT (PESOS),
SECOND SEMESTER 2003

Grade	Boys	Girls
Primary		
Third year	105	105
Fourth year	120	120
Fifth year	155	155
Sixth year	210	210
Secondary		
First year	305	320
Second year	320	355
Third year	335	390
High school		
First year	510	585
Second year	545	625
Third year	580	660

NOTE: 10 pesos = US$1.

It is important to note that the same general package of benefits is provided in both rural and urban areas. We now turn to a description of these benefits.

Specific benefits

Perhaps the first innovation of Progresa is the fact that it combines three different components, that is, education, health, and nutrition, in one program. The reason for linking these three components in one program, as stated in the original document proposing Progresa (Poder Ejecutivo Federal 1997), was based on the philosophy that the interactions between the components would enhance the effectiveness of an integrated program over and above the separate benefits from each component. For instance, children who suffer from malnutrition are more likely to drop out of school or repeat years of school, implying that attempts to ensure that children go to school will be more effective if combined with adequate nutrition and health programs, thereby helping to break the vicious cycle of intergenerational poverty transmission (Poder Ejecutivo Federal 1997).

Under the education component, Progresa currently provides monetary educational grants for each child younger than twenty-two years of age enrolled in school between the third grade of primary and the third grade of high school. It is important to note, however, that grants were originally only provided through secondary school. The addition of education grants at the high school level was implemented in the year 2001. These grants (Table 2) increase as children progress to higher grades and, beginning at the secondary level, are slightly higher for girls than for boys. The amounts of the monthly grants range from about US$10.50 (105 pesos)

TABLE 3

INTERVENTIONS IN THE BASIC HEALTH SERVICES PACKAGE

Basic sanitation at the family level
Family planning
Prenatal, childbirth, and puerperal care
Supervision of nutrition and children's growth
Vaccinations
Prevention and treatment of outbreaks of diarrhea
Antiparasite treatment
Prevention and treatment of respiratory infections
Prevention and control of tuberculosis
Prevention and control of high blood pressure and diabetes mellitus
Accident prevention and first aid for injuries
Community training for health care self-help

in the third grade of primary to about US$58 (580 pesos) for boys and US$66 (660 pesos) for girls in the third year of high school.

The second component, health, provides basic health care for all members of the family, with a particular emphasis on preventive health care (Table 3). These services are provided by public health institutions in Mexico. The third component, nutrition, includes a fixed monetary transfer equal to about $US15.50 (155 pesos) monthly for improved food consumption, as well as nutritional supplements, which are principally targeted to children between the ages of four months and two years and pregnant and lactating women. They are also given to children aged two to four if any signs of malnutrition are detected.

Perhaps the first innovation of Progresa is the fact that it combines three different components, that is, education, health, and nutrition, in one program.

Receipt of the benefits is contingent on fulfillment of certain obligations by the beneficiary families. The monetary educational grants are linked to the school attendance of children so that if a child misses more than three school days in a month (for unjustified reasons), the family will not receive the grant that month. Similarly, families must complete a schedule of visits to the health care facilities in order to receive the monetary supports for improved nutrition (Table 4). The

TABLE 4

ANNUAL FREQUENCY OF HEALTH CARE VISITS REQUIRED BY PROGRESA

Age Group	Frequency of Checkups
Children	
Younger than 4 months	3 checkups: 7 and 28 days, and at 2 months
4 to 24 months	8 checkups: 4, 6, 9, 12, 15, 18, 21, and 24 months, with 1 additional monthly weight and height checkup
2 to 4 years old	3 checkups a year: 1 every 4 months
5 to 16 years old	2 checkups a year: 1 every 6 months
Women	
Pregnant	5 check-ups: prenatal period
During purpureum and lactation	2 checkups: in immediate purpureum and 1 during lactation
Adults and youths	
17 to 60 years old	1 checkup per year
Older than 60 years old	1 checkup per year

school attendance of children and family health visits are verified through school and clinic records. Progresa has a maximum limit of monthly benefits for each family currently equivalent to about $US90 for families with children in primary and secondary school and $US160 for those with children in high school.

All of the monetary benefits are given directly to a woman of the family, most frequently the mother. Benefits are provided directly to the female beneficiary by wire transfer in offices and modules that are installed nearby the communities. In some urban areas, Progresa is using bank accounts to transfer money to its beneficiaries.

The targeting mechanism differs between rural and urban areas. In rural areas, Progresa selects its beneficiary families through a three-stage targeting mechanism. In the first stage, Progresa uses geographic targeting to select poor regions and communities. Communities with a high level of marginality, as measured by aggregate socioeconomic community characteristics, are selected to participate in the program. Next, to identify the beneficiary families, Progresa carries out a survey of socioeconomic conditions for all households in the selected communities. With this data, discriminant analysis is used to identify beneficiary households from nonbeneficiary households. Households are evaluated to be in extreme poverty not just on the basis of income but on the basis of a number of other characteristics as well, such as dwelling characteristics in the household, dependency ratios, ownership of durable goods, animals and land, and the presence of disabled individuals.

Once beneficiary households have been identified, an assembly is arranged in the community where the list of selected families is made public and an agreement is reached among all families in the community. It is worth noting that in practice, this last step rarely resulted in significant changes to the list of beneficiary families.

In urban areas, the targeting mechanism is substantially different, and there is an element of self-selection in that potential beneficiaries must show up to a Progresa module in their geographic area of residence (local advertising is used to make potential beneficiaries aware of the opportunity to receive Progresa). At the module, their basic socioeconomic levels are assessed; for those that pass this initial qualifying test, a home visit is programmed to verify socioeconomic information; and based upon this information, a similar discriminant analysis as in rural areas is used to decide whether the household is eligible for Progresa.

An Analysis of the Design of Progresa

Progresa represents a significant change in the provision of social programs in Mexico. In this section, we analyze in detail some of the more innovative design features of the program, in particular those relating to (1) the conditionality of the benefits to human capital investment and (2) gender aspects.

Human capital and conditionality

Among the most important aspects of the program is its focus on investment in human capital. Whereas Progresa was designed with the objective of providing some immediate monetary assistance to families in extreme poverty, an equally important objective is that of increasing the human capital of its beneficiaries in the future. In this way, Progresa sees the lack of human capital in the poor population as a central cause of poverty and hopes that by increasing investment in human capital, above all, in children, the future poverty of these individuals (e.g., when they become adults) will be reduced. In accordance with the views of most economists, Progresa considers that the returns to investing in human capital, as measured by education, health, and nutrition are important. Greater investment in human capital is expected to have permanent effects in increasing future income of beneficiaries (Becker 1993; Mincer 1974). The theory of human capital, and the measurement of "returns to education" or the lifetime increase in income that can be expected through an increase in schooling years has been verified in numerous empirical studies in developing and developed nations. Furthermore, recent studies have indicated that both health and nutrition also have important returns in terms of future income (Strauss and Thomas 1995, 1998). Thus, economic theory and empirical economic studies were clearly instrumental in the design of Progresa.

One might ask why poor families do not invest "enough" in human capital. Progresa's answer is that families may be aware of the benefits of human capital investment but cannot afford to invest as much as they would like (Poder Ejecutivo Federal 1997). The costs of school attendance are not just monetary costs associated with attending school but the opportunity costs of sending children to school. The opportunity cost of sending children to school is the income or value of income that children would earn if they were working rather than attending school. Since families need this income for current consumption, they take their children out of school at early ages and send them to work. Progresa substitutes for the income children would earn if they were working and thus, theoretically at least, permits parents to send their children to school. Again, this is a vision clearly influenced by economists (see Becker 1993).

Progresa requires children to miss no more than three days a month or lose the education grant in that month. This conditionality is one aspect that has received most attention at the international level. However, the rationale for conditioning benefits to human capital investment is not clearly stated in the original document explaining the motivation for Progresa. If the problem is that parents do

---

[The decision to send monetary benefits to the mother] was motivated by the social science literature that argues that resources under the control of women tend to have a greater impact on the well-being of children than resources under the control of men.

---

not have the current income to finance their children's school enrollment, this would imply, in the words of economists, a credit constraint. And while it might imply that the policy of giving monetary transfers is appropriate, it is not obvious why the transfers should be conditional on behavior such as sending children to school. Many economists might argue that conditionality requirements are paternalistic (e.g., the implication is that government knows better than the parents how they should invest and allocate resources to their children) and therefore not necessarily welfare improving relative to unconditional transfers. Under this scenario, it might be preferable (e.g., better for the family) to give unconditional transfers. One potential motivation for conditioning benefits is the assumption that there are some social returns to investing in education that are not reaped by the individual, for example, social returns are higher to private returns. If individuals only take into account private returns when deciding their (or their children's) investment in human capital, they will underinvest relative to the social optimum. A review of the literature, however, was unable to find empirical studies that demonstrated that social returns were significantly higher than private returns. Martinelli and Parker (2003) explored alternative reasons why a welfare-minded government might condition transfers, focusing on conditionality as a way to implement outcomes closer to the mother's preference in the context of intrahousehold bargaining.

A final point related to the conditionality is that the program assumes that the returns to education are likely to be high, even in the relatively isolated areas where Progresa began operating and where it is likely that school quality is low. Resources such as libraries or computers are notably lacking in schools in rural areas. Many communities do not even have secondary schools within easy commuting distance (Coady and Parker 2004). Many of the secondary schools in rural areas are *tele-secundarias*, which provide televised classes, as well as a single instructor who helps children with exercises in all different materials. In contrast, urban areas have general secondary schools, with a different teacher for each class material. It is dubious whether the returns to schooling are as high in rural areas as in urban areas. This is an area that has not been sufficiently studied. A study of school quality and the returns to education as well as other forms of human capital would be extremely valuable in terms of predicting the long-term effects of the program in rural Mexico.

Gender aspects

In addition to the emphasis placed on prenatal and postnatal care, Progresa has two gender aspects that have received international attention. The first is the point that the monetary benefits are received by the mother of the household. This design feature, as stated in program documents, was motivated by the social science literature that argues that resources under the control of women tend to have a greater impact on the well-being of children than resources under the control of men. Again, this is a literature dominated predominantly by economists (see, e.g., Thomas 1990). At the time Progresa was developed, there were no studies in the context of Mexico that would validate the relevance of this assumption. The implicit assumption was that Mexico is similar to Brazil and other countries for which empirical evidence did exist. Recent studies (Rubalcava, Teruel, and Thomas 2004; and Attanasio and Lechene 2002) support the point, in Mexico as elsewhere, that resources under the control of women have greater positive impacts on children than resources under the control of men.

The second important gender aspect is that, beginning with the education grants at the level of junior high, the grant levels are higher (about 10 to 15 percent) for girls than boys. This feature was originally motivated, according to Progresa, by the observation that in rural areas, girls tended to have a higher dropout rate than boys after finishing primary school. Thus, the higher grant levels were aimed at compensating for this lower achievement.

Nevertheless, as shown in Behrman, Sengupta, and Todd (2000a) and Parker and Pederzini (2001), actual attainment of girls in terms of years of completed schooling in rural areas is quite similar to that of boys. The seeming paradox between lower enrollment and similar attainment in years of schooling can be explained by the point that boys tend to have higher repetition rates than girls. That is, when girls enroll in school, they tend to do better than boys, that is, finish school levels faster.[2]

The Evaluation of Progresa

The randomized trial

We turn now to a description of the randomized trial that Progresa carried out as part of its evaluation strategy. It is worth emphasizing that the evaluation of Progresa was quite novel in Mexico in many respects. Progresa was the first social program in Mexico to carry out a rigorous evaluation of program impacts. Program officials emphasized from the beginning of the program the importance of developing a rigorous evaluation; in general, it represented a strategy to try to ensure that the program would not be eliminated with changes in the government. As part of the strategy to provide credible results of program impacts, Progresa officials hired the International Food Policy Research Institute (IFPRI) to carry out an extensive external evaluation of program impacts between 1998 and 2000 (Skoufias 2001).

One of the advantages of the Progresa evaluation is that it was planned in conjunction with the program. The evaluation was implemented at an early stage, a point where the program was not yet so large that it would be difficult to construct a control group for a randomized evaluation.

The evaluation design was heavily influenced by the works of economists in the field of evaluation, who have generally argued that a randomized design, although not without potential difficulties, can have great advantages over nonexperimental methods in obtaining unbiased estimates of program impact (Heckman 1992). The Progresa evaluation can be considered to be somewhere in between a randomized experiment and a quasi-experimental evaluation. The general principle behind the evaluation was to use randomization to the extent that it was feasible. In this case, for a sample of communities eligible to participate in Progresa, the evaluation strategy was to carry out a randomization between control and treatment communities.

Initially, in the case of Progresa, randomization at the household level was considered but judged to be infeasible by program officials. The reasoning here was that randomizing households within communities, in a context where communities are quite small and "everyone knows everyone" would have created problems between those in the treatment group and those in the control group. Program officials feared that it would create the perception of discretionality in the selection process (e.g., households equally poor in the community where some are receiving benefits and others are not) (Gomez de Leon, Parker, and Hernandez 1999).

The alternative chosen was to select a sample of Progresa communities and *randomize communities* between the treatment group and the control group. This was a perhaps natural level at which to randomize as it fits well with the actual selection mechanism of Progresa beneficiaries where in the first stage localities are selected before passing to a second stage where households within communities are determined to be eligible. A potential limitation of randomizing at the community level, however, was the likelihood of observing less randomness at the individual level (discussed below). Behrman and Todd (1999) noted that randomizing at the community level implied that one was unable to analyze locality-specific treatment effects. This is the case if one uses a dummy variable to represent the impact of Progresa; nevertheless, if one uses amounts received by Progresa as the impact variable, one can obtain locality-specific impacts.

Progresa selected a sample of 506 communities in seven states as its "evaluation" sample, which corresponded to 24,077 households. These seven states were among the first states to receive Progresa benefits.[3] Of the 506 communities, 320 communities correspond to the treatment group and 186 correspond to the control group. The 320 treatment communities were randomly selected using probabilities that were proportional to the size distribution of communities from a universe of 4,546 communities in the seven states. Using the same method, a sample of 186 control communities were drawn from a sample of 1,850 communities within the seven states that were scheduled by Progresa to receive benefits at a later time. Treatment beneficiary household began to receive benefits in May 1998, whereas control households began to receive benefits in December 1999.

Thus, the "experiment" lasted only for a year and a half. This is clearly a short time period and implies that the sorts of impacts that could be evaluated under Progresa include only variables likely to be affected in the short run, such as school attendance, expenditure patterns, health clinic attendance, and so on. The evaluation of longer-term variables, for instance, on actual years of completed schooling and future employment of Progresa beneficiaries, marriage and fertility patterns (variables not included in the IFPRI evaluation), will be more difficult to analyze given this short period. Future evaluations of the rural evaluation population using an experimental methodology will only be able to carry out the experiment of comparing, say, effects on families/individuals who received benefits for six years versus the control group of four and a half years, clearly a much weaker comparison than between a family receiving Progresa for six years versus a family who had never received Progresa. For the evaluation of these longer-term variables, some non-experimental methods will also be necessary. This is an important limitation, which we return to at the end of the article.

Constructing a control group is clearly an ethical issue in the context of a program aimed at the poorest members of the population. The point that it might be perceived that eligible communities were being kept out of Progresa for the sake of the evaluation was of great concern to program officials. The argument internally put forth by Progresa officials was that the evaluation was carried out at an early phase where budget limitations implied that not all eligible families could be incorporated. Thus, there were many eligible households who were not receiving benefits during this time period; the actual control group would be no different from these other eligible households; they were simply being monitored (e.g., applied questionnaires) meanwhile. Indeed, one could argue that in a situation of insufficient funds, the fairest determinant of which families received benefits first would be through a lottery or randomization.

While this argument would seem to be fairly sensible, program officials did not publicize the design of the evaluation until the program evaluation had been concluded in the year 2000 and results were made public. At this point, however, when the evaluation results were released, one prominent newspaper, *Reforma*, included a number of articles in December 2000 (Torre 2000) criticizing the experimental nature of the evaluation and, in particular, arguing that poor families had been kept out only for the sake of evaluation. The cost of the evaluation (e.g., the contract given to IFPRI) was also criticized, under the argument that the cost of the contract (2.5 million dollars) could have been used to incorporate additional families into the program.

Information gathering in the evaluation

In this section, we briefly describe the information that Progresa collected for both the treatment and control group and comment on some issues with the fieldwork.

The first information that Progresa has for both the control group and the treatment group is the survey that is used to identify beneficiary households (Survey of Household Socio-Economic Characteristics [ENCASEH]). For the treatment and control group, it was carried out in October and November 1997. The baseline[4] round of the Evaluation Questionnaire (ENCEL) was carried out in March 1998, approximately one month before the treatment group was incorporated. Follow-up surveys were carried out in November 1998, May 1999, and November 1999.[5] The ENCEL includes extensive information on numerous individual, household, and community characteristics including all sources of income levels, labor market participation, demographic and socioeconomic information, children's school attendance, health utilization, community characteristics, women's status indicators, consumption, asset ownership, and agricultural participation, among others (see Skoufias [2001] for a more detailed description of the data in the different rounds of analysis). Some special interest modules were also carried out, usually on a one-time-only basis, and include such topics as time allocation among different activities and family background of women to measure their bargaining power within the household.

Within each community, all households, regardless of poverty status, were interviewed. This was done partly for evaluation purposes and partly due to the fact that most of the cost of interviewing in communities lies in actually getting to the community. Once there, the marginal cost of carrying out extra interviews is relatively low. This is another important feature of the evaluation design, and it implies that within each treatment community, data exists for both beneficiary and non-beneficiary households; and within each control community, there are data for households who are eligible for Progresa (that is, in extreme poverty) and those who are not eligible for Progresa (Table 5). This is an interesting feature of the data,

TABLE 5

THE SAMPLE OF ALL HOUSEHOLDS
IN TREATMENT AND CONTROL VILLAGES

Household Eligibility Status	Treatment Locality Where Progresa Is in Operation $(T = 1)$	Control Locality Where Progresa Operations Are Delayed $(T = 0)$
Eligible for Progresa benefits $(E = 1)$	A. $E = 1, T = 1$	B. $E = 1, T = 0$
Noneligible for Progresa benefits $(E = 0)$	C. $E = 0, T = 1$	D. $E = 0, T = 0$

which allows one to verify that nonbeneficiary households living in Progresa communities were not subject to spillover aspects (for instance, if they were less likely to receive health services as a result of congestion from Progresa). The nonbeneficiaries can also potentially serve as a control group, particularly in the period after which the control group is incorporated to receive benefits. Nevertheless, there were few evaluation studies in the IFPRI evaluation that actually used the nonbeneficiaries as a control group.

There were a number of issues that Progresa faced in terms of carrying out repeated interviews of the control group. First, the period of the experiment covered a period of huge growth in the number of beneficiaries. Whereas the number of beneficiaries was less than four hundred thousand at the time the experimental period began, there were 2 million households by the time that the experiment was ended. This growth in beneficiaries likely did not go unrecognized by the control communities. Particularly as localities close by (and with quite similar characteristics) began to receive program benefits, interviewers reported more and more complaints within control communities expressed to interviewers there while carrying out follow-up interviews of the ENCEL. In spite of efforts of the interviewers to not reveal that the surveys were related to Progresa, it became quite clear that the control communities were certain that the evaluation surveys were related to Progresa. Pressure applied by control communities through local and state government officials very likely, in combination with the fast growth of Progresa, contributed to the decision by program officials to end the experiment earlier than planned (e.g., at the end of 1999 rather than in the year 2000, which was the original intention). The rapid growth of Progresa implied that the argument that maintaining a control group was not unethical given that many other eligible families were not receiving benefits due to budget constraints was no longer sustainable. This situation is perhaps not unusual, so that one possible lesson here is that randomized designs of evaluations in the case of social programs are unlikely to be able to last for a long period of time, particularly when the constructed control group does not receive any program benefits, as opposed to control groups that might receive some other alternative program during the experimental period.

Evaluation Results
and Their Impact on Public Policy

In this section, we turn to the results of the evaluation. We describe the extent to which the randomization was effectively done and how these results affected the estimators used to generate impact results. We also comment on the impact at a public policy level that the evaluation has had, both on policy making in Mexico as well as in other countries. Note that we provide only a brief description of the various impact results of Progresa; an excellent summary of the results is contained in Skoufias (2001). Additionally, the actual evaluation reports can all be found at www.ifpri.org.

Quality of experiment and estimators used in the evaluation

The first aspect of relevance to discuss is the quality of the randomization. That is, are any observed differences between the characteristics of individuals between the two groups statistically significant? This subject is the topic of the first evaluation report carried out by IFPRI, done by Jere Behrman and Petra Todd (1999).

Behrman and Todd (1999) compared characteristics in the treatment and control group for a wide variety of indicators prior to program implementation. In general, they concluded that at the community level, treatment and control groups appear to be random. Nevertheless, at the individual level, they found some small significant differences in preprogram characteristics between the treatment and control group. Behrman and Todd argued that this may largely reflect the large sample size (twenty-four thousand households and more than one hundred thousand individuals).

As a response to the analysis of Behrman and Todd (1999), many of the evaluation reports use the evidence of these differences to justify using regression methods, with control variables, as opposed to simply comparing mean values between the control and treatment group. Additionally, in general, the reports tend to assume that double difference methods are adequate to control for potential preprogram differences in the impact variables of interest, although it is important to note that no report analyzes the extent to which this assumption is justified. Double difference estimators are, in fact, used by almost all of the reports. The only cases in which they are not used are where the relevant impact variables were not included in the baseline. In this case, cross-sectional estimators are generally used to estimate program impacts, that is, comparing differences between the treatment and control group after program implementation. These evaluations, given the evidence of preprogram differences just cited, are the weakest of those carried out in the evaluation.

The standard equation used to estimate double difference impact estimates in almost all of the reports is of the following type:

$$Y_{it} = \sum_{r=1}^{4} \alpha_{0i} R + \alpha_1 T_i + \alpha_2^* T_i R_2 + \alpha_3^* T_i R_3 + \alpha_4^* T_i R_4 + \sum_{j=1}^{J} \beta_j X_{jit} + \varepsilon_{it},$$

where Y_{it} reflects the impact variable of interest, R refers to the round of the ENCEL, T refers to whether the individual/household lives in a treatment or control community, and X_{jit} refers to the vector of j control characteristics for individual/household i in period t.

Note that this framework in effect provides double difference estimators of the impact of Progresa. The coefficient α_1 is expected to be statistically insignificant from 0 and provides an indication of whether preprogram differences exist between the treatment group and the control group. The coefficients α_2 through α_4 represent the impact estimates, that is, they provide an estimate of the differences between the treatment and control group in the relevant round after program implementation relative to α_1. Note that this framework allows the estimated impacts to differ over time. A final point is that the above equation was generally restricted to the sample of households/individuals eligible for Progresa, that is, most analyses excluded the noneligible from the analysis.

Results of the IFPRI evaluation

The results of the IFPRI evaluation can only be characterized as extremely positive. In the words of the Foreword by Coordinator of the Progresa-IFPRI evaluation, Emmanuel Skoufias,

> In summary, the results of the evaluation of IFPRI show that after only three years, poor Mexican children living in the rural areas where Progresa operates have increased their school enrolment, have more balanced diets, are receiving more medical attention, and are learning that the future can be very different from the past. (Skoufias and McClafferty 2001, 3)

Important positive impacts were reported in school enrollment, health clinic attendance, nutrition, and expenditures. In the case of education, the largest impacts were reported on children who enter secondary school, where impacts represent a percentage increase of enrollment of more than 20 percent for girls and 10 percent for boys. The research revealed that much of the positive impact on enrollment was due to increasing continuation rates rather than on getting children who were out of school to return. Little effect of Progresa on enrollment in primary school was found; this, however, reflects the point that most (more than 95 percent) children in rural areas, even before Progresa, enroll in primary school; therefore, the scope for improving enrollment at this level was limited (Schultz 2004; Behrman, Sengupta, and Todd 2000b).

Important health and nutrition effects were also reported. Progresa children aged one to five years have a 12 percent lower incidence of illness than non-Progresa children (Gertler 2000). Additionally, data suggest that Progresa has had large impact on increasing child growth and in reducing child stunting. Behrman and Hoddinott (2000) reported an impact of Progresa equivalent to an increase of 16 percent in mean growth rate per year (corresponding to one centimeter) for children who received treatment between twelve and thirty-six months of age.

Finally, Progresa has also had important effects on expenditure patterns: overall median food expenditures were 13 percent higher in Progresa households when compared with control households. Perhaps just as important, this increase was primarily due to higher expenditures on fruit, vegetables, meats, and animal products, suggesting that beneficiaries are eating a healthier diet under Progresa (Hoddinott, Skoufias, and Washburn 2000).

With respect to the continuation of Progresa, the evaluation likely played an important role in ensuring that the program was not eliminated with the change of government.

Perhaps the only important potentially negative impact found by the IFPRI research team relates to the impacts of Progresa on community relations (Adato 2000). Progresa, as described earlier, in rural areas, targets benefits first at the geographical level and then to households within these eligible communities. This implies that within the same community, there are Progresa beneficiaries and nonbeneficiaries. The IFPRI evaluation reports that this distinction within the community has created some tensions between the two groups.

Impacts of the evaluation on public policy

What impact have these results had on public policy in Mexico? First, with respect to the continuation of Progresa, the evaluation likely played an important role in ensuring that the program was not eliminated with the change of government. In the past few governments, it has been common for each administration, even when the political party of the president is the same, to want to distinguish their years with their own particular social program. In the case of Progresa, whereas there was some ambiguity in the beginning of the Fox administration (the first, by the way, non-PRI (International Revolutionary Party) president in more than seventy years) on Progresa, ultimately, Progresa was not only maintained but expanded to urban areas. In addition, the education grants it provides were extended to the high school level. Note that this particular policy extension was directly recommended in one of the IFPRI documents summarizing the evaluation results. (Skoufias and McClafferty 2001). Thus, the results of the IFPRI evaluation have had an important impact on the direction of the evaluation. This is not to say, however, that Progresa has followed all of the recommendations made by

IFPRI. For instance, the same summary report recommends considering eliminating primary grants and using the money to increase grant levels at the secondary level (where program impacts are much higher). This particular recommendation has not been followed.

With respect to the design of overall social policy in Mexico, the IFPRI evaluation has also had an impact. As mentioned earlier, the IFPRI evaluation was the first rigorous evaluation of a social policy in Mexico. In particular, the year after the IFPRI evaluation was released to the public, Congress issued a new law requiring *all* social programs to carry out external evaluations of their impacts every year. It is also the case that in the language of this new law, Congress stated that preferably "national institutions" be hired to do the external evaluations, which may have also been a reaction to the IFPRI evaluation.

Finally, at the international level, there have also been important effects of the evaluation. In particular, a number of Latin American countries, such as Colombia, Jamaica, Honduras, and Argentina, have not only implemented Progresa-like programs; they have also implemented the model of external evaluation, in many cases with financing by institutions such as the World Bank and the Inter-American Development Bank.

Limitations of the Evaluation and Areas for Future Research

The sources of the impacts of Progresa

One serious limitation of the evaluation is that all beneficiaries are offered the same package of benefits. It would be useful to estimate the impact of variation in grant amounts, such as equalizing grants for boys and girls or increasing benefits at the secondary level while removing entire grants from elementary level. Another important question is the effect that the conditionality requirements might have on program impacts, versus a similar program with no conditionality requirements. Moreover, an integrated program of benefits such as the one offered by Progresa makes it difficult to isolate the effect of the different components on relevant outcomes. If an increase in school attendance is witnessed as a result of Progresa, it is of interest to know whether the increase was due entirely to the educational grants received or whether there was also an impact from the health component (because healthier children are more likely to attend school). The design of the evaluation makes it difficult to answer this question (see, however, Rubalcava, Teruel, and Thomas [2004] for an effort to isolate the impact of the mother rather than the father collecting the grant).

A potential, exciting alternative for predicting the impact of potential changes in program design is the use of structural estimation. Todd and Wolpin (2004) estimated a behavior model of parental decisions of child schooling using the Progresa data. They were able to validate the model's predictions by seeing how well the model predicts the experimental impact of the program. They then simulated policy interventions that were not part of the randomized design, for instance, varying subsidy amounts. This would seem a promising approach, especially given that even when experimental designs are possible, as in the current case, it is generally infeasible to vary program benefits in many different dimensions to evaluate alternative designs of the program.

Take-up of benefits

Another issue that has forth not been studied is that of non-take-up of benefits. Non-take-up here can be broadly defined to include families who do not participate in the program; an alternative indicator would be to focus on children who are eligible for grants but choose not to receive them. Non-take-up overall of families appeared in the evaluation to be initially low at about 3 to 4 percent; nevertheless, for these families, there is no information on reasons for failure to take up the benefits, for instance, whether they moved out of the community or simply refused the program benefits.

Perhaps an even more critical issue is that of non-take-up of children for the education grants in beneficiary families. Whereas there are substantial positive impacts of Progresa on secondary enrollment, there still remain 40 percent of children who are eligible for grants but choose not to receive them. The reasons for this nonparticipation are clearly complex and have not, to our knowledge, been studied. One potential reason is that the size of the education grants is insufficient to motivate the return to school of youth who had potentially already dropped out of school prior to Progresa and thus would have to reenroll in a classroom with much younger classmates.

Attrition

Fieldwork protocols in Progresa dictated revisiting only the original dwellings, proceeding to interview whoever was there, if anyone. As a consequence, attrition has turned out to be a serious problem in the ENCEL surveys. For example, by the end of the November 2000 ENCEL round, approximately 16.01 percent of households and 21.89 percent of individuals originally interviewed in the fall of 1997 were no longer in the survey. Most of this attrition is caused by apparent changes of residence or migration (close to 80 percent), and the rest is related to nonresponse and deaths (Teruel and Rubalcava 2003).

Thomas, Frankenberg, and Smith (2001) have highlighted the point that movers may be very different than stayers in the context of longitudinal surveys and stressed the importance of following movers. For the current evaluation, there are two related issues. First, if attrition in the ENCEL surveys differs between treatment and control groups as Teruel and Rubalcava (2003) suggested, this attrition may bias the estimated impacts of the program, and thus it would be useful to have information on the attritors to correct any bias. Second, with high percentages of migrant individuals, it is obviously of interest to know the impacts of the program not only on the population remaining in their home communities but also for the population that leaves. This is likely to be particularly true for youth, who are the most likely to leave their household and community of origin, and also presumably the group most likely to be impacted by the program benefits.

In the IFPRI evaluation, none of the evaluation studies considered the possible biasing effects of attrition on estimated program impacts. Note that following and locating movers is no trivial exercise, particularly in the Mexican case, where a fair proportion of movers migrate to the United States. There are now some tentative plans for the program to follow up a subsample of movers in 2005 or 2006; thus far, a pilot project has been carried out by Parker (2005) in the state of Queretaro on following youth aged fifteen to twenty-one who have left their household. The pilot has been successful at interviewing 70 percent of those moving to a nearby area in the same state and about 55 percent of those moving to the United States. The information should be useful for addressing possible program biases and allow longer-term impacts to be analyzed.

Outlook

Perhaps the most important and lasting limitation of the evaluation relates to the duration of the experimental design, which as described earlier, lasted only about 1.5 years. While this was adequate for the purposes of evaluating short-term indicators such as school enrollment or household expenditure—indeed, the evaluation was by all indicators quite successful—the longer-term perspective is more complicated. Given the interest in estimating medium-term impacts of the program, a set of new communities that had previously not been eligible for benefits (because of not satisfying program requirements on having schools and health clinics close by) has been chosen to constitute a new comparison group. A new follow-up round in 2003 has been carried out, following up the original 506 ENCEL communities as well as interviewing those in the new comparison communities. In addition to comparisons based on the experimental design, which are generally restricted to estimating impacts with respect to differential exposure to benefits (6 versus 4.5 years of benefits), two alternative estimators are now being assessed for potentially estimating program impact. These include both regression discontinuity analysis with the original ENCEL households and matching between the ENCEL households and the new comparison group. Whereas the experimental design has been a critical factor to the program's initial success, it appears that estimation of the longer-term impacts of the program will need some nonexperimental estimators or structural estimation such as that carried out in Todd and Wolpin (2004).

Notes

1. The name of Progresa was changed to Oportunidades by President Fox; in this article, nevertheless, we continue to refer to the program as Progresa.

2. Given this, the rationale for maintaining higher grant levels for girls than boys would seem to be suspect. It is interesting to note that the feature of higher grants for girls than boys was maintained when the program was extended in 2001 to urban areas. This is in spite of the fact that girls in urban areas are currently doing slightly better in terms of overall achievement than boys (Parker and Pederzini 2001). In fact, in some Latin American countries, there is a concern of a potential "reverse" gender gap in education (Duryea and Arends-Kuenning 1999), which may also be relevant for Mexico.

3. The states include Guerrero, Hidalgo, Michoacan, Puebla, Queretaro, San Luis Potosí, and Veracruz.

4. Note that in effect there are two baseline surveys that can be used as part of the evaluation, the Survey of Household Socio-Economic Characteristics (ENCASEH) and the first round of the Evaluation Questionnaire (ENCEL).

5. Additional rounds of the ENCEL were carried out in May and November 2000. Both these rounds took place after the control group began to receive benefits and were not used in the evaluation carried out by the International Food Policy Research Institute (IFPRI).

References

Adato, Michelle. 2000. *Final report: The impact of PROGRESA on community social relationships.* September. Report submitted to PROGRESA. Washington: DC: International Food Policy Research Institute.

Attanasio, Orazio, and Valerie Lechene. 2002. Tests of income pooling in household decisions. *Review of Economic Dynamics* 5 (4): 720-48.

Becker, Gary S. 1993. *Human capital.* Chicago: University of Chicago Press.

———. 1999. "Bribe" third world parents to keep their kids in school. *Business Week*, November 22.

Behrman, Jere R., and John Hoddinott. 2000. *An evaluation of the impact of PROGRESA on pre-school child height.* July. Report submitted to PROGRESA. Washington, DC: International Food Policy Research Institute.

Behrman, Jere R., Piyali Sengupta, and Petra E. Todd. 2000a. *Final report: The impact of PROGRESA on achievement test scores in the first year.* September. Washington, DC: International Food Policy Research Institute.

———. 2000b. *Progressing through PROGRESA: An impact assessment of a school subsidy experiment.* Washington, DC: International Food Policy Research Institute.

Behrman, Jere R., and Petra E. Todd. 1999. *Randomness in the experimental samples of PROGRESA (education, health, and nutrition program).* February. Report submitted to PROGRESA. Washington, DC: International Food Policy Research Institute.

Coady, David P. 2000. *Final report: The application of social cost-benefit analysis to the evaluation of PROGRESA.* November. Report submitted to PROGRESA. Washington, DC: International Food Policy Research Institute.

Coady, David P., and Susan W. Parker. 2004. A cost-effectiveness analysis of demand and supply side education interventions: The Case of Progresa in Mexico. *Review of Development Economics* 8 (3): 440-51.

Duryea, Suzanne, and Mary Arends-Kuenning. 1999. New gender gaps in schooling: Adolescent boys at risk in Latin America. Paper presented at the annual meeting of the Population Association of America, New York.

Gertler, Paul J. 2000. *Final report: The impact of PROGRESA on health.* November. Report submitted to PROGRESA. Washington, DC: International Food Policy Research Institute.

Gomez de Leon, Jose, Susan W. Parker, and Daniel Hernandez. 1999. The design and methodology of the impact evaluation of the Education, Health and Nutrition Program (PROGRESA) in Mexico. Photocopy.

Heckman, James J. 1992. Randomization and social policy evaluation. In *Evaluating welfare and training programs*, ed. C. Manski and I. Garfinkel. Cambridge, MA: Harvard University Press.

Hoddinott, John, Emmanuel Skoufias, and Ryan Washburn. 2000. *The impact of PROGRESA on consumption: A final report.* September. Report submitted to PROGRESA. Washington, DC: International Food Policy Research Institute.

Krueger, Alan B. 2002. Economic scene: A model for evaluating the use of development dollars, south of the border. *The New York Times*, May 2.

Martinelli, Cesar, and Susan W. Parker. 2003. Should transfers to poor families be conditional on school attendance? A household bargaining approach. *International Economic Review* 44 (2): 523-44.

Mincer, Jacob. 1974. *Schooling, experience and earnings*. New York: National Bureau of Economic Research.

Parker, Susan W. 2005. Following up PROGRESA migrants: Evidence from the Mexican state of Queretaro. Photocopy, Mexico City.

Parker, Susan W., and Carla Pederzini. 2001. Gender differences by education in Mexico. In *The economics of gender in Mexico: Work, family, state, and market*, ed. Elizabeth Katz and Maria Correia. Washington, DC: World Bank.

Poder Ejecutivo Federal. 1997. *Progresa: Programa de Educacion, Salud y Alimentacion*. Mexico City: Office of the President.

Rubalcava, Luis N., Graciela M. Teruel, and Duncan Thomas. 2004. Spending, saving and public transfers paid to women. California Center for Population Research, On-Line Working Paper Series, Paper CCPR-024-04. http://repositories.cdlib.org/ccpr/olwp/CCPR-024-04/.

Schultz, T. Paul. 2004. School subsidies for the poor: Evaluating a Mexican strategy for reducing poverty. *Journal of Development Economics* 74 (1): 199-250.

Skoufias, Emmanuel. 2001. PROGRESA and its impacts on the human capital and welfare of households in rural Mexico: A synthesis of the results of an evaluation by IFPRI. Washington DC: International Food Policy Research Institute.

Skoufias, Emmanuel, and Bonnie McClafferty. 2001. *Is PROGRESA working? Summary of the results of an evaluation by IFPRI*. Report submitted to PROGRESA. Washington, DC: International Food Policy Research Institute.

Strauss, John A., and Duncan Thomas. 1995. Human resources: Empirical modeling of household and family decisions. In *Handbook of development economics*, ed. T. N. Srinivasan and J. Behrman. Amsterdam: North Holland.

―――. 1998. Health, nutrition, and economic development. *Journal of Economic Literature* 36 (2): 766-817.

Teruel, Graciela M., and Luis N. Rubalcava. 2003. The effect of PROGRESA on the demographic structure of the household. Photocopy, Universidad Iberoamericana, Mexico City.

Thomas, Duncan. 1990. Intrahousehold resource allocation: An inferential approach. *Journal of Human Resources* 25 (4): 635-64.

Thomas, Duncan, Elizabeth Frankenberg, and James P. Smith. 2001. Lost but not forgotten: Attrition in the Indonesian Family Life Survey. *Journal of Human Resources* 36 (3): 556-92.

Todd, Petra E., and Kenneth I. Wolpin. 2004. Using experimental data to validate a dynamic behavioral model of human capital investments in children: Evaluating the impact of Mexico's PROGRESA program. Photocopy, University of Pennsylvania, Philadelphia.

Torre, Wilbert. 2000. Mural. *Reforma*, December 26.

Hot Spots Policing Experiments and Criminal Justice Research: Lessons from the Field

By
DAVID WEISBURD

In this article, more general lessons are drawn from two randomized experiments in hot spots policing that the author helped design and implement in the 1990s: the Minneapolis Hot Spots Experiment and the Jersey City Drug Market Analysis Experiment. Using a case study approach, factors that facilitate and inhibit development and implementation of randomized trials are identified with particular focus on the special problems and/or advantages of place-based experiments. While the author's main comments focus on the success of place-based randomized trials in evaluating hot spots policing approaches, he draws insight as well into the reasons why the successful example of experiments in hot spots policing has not inspired similar place-based experimentation in other areas of policing or criminal justice. Eight specific lessons regarding the implementation and development of place-based randomized trials and experimental methods more generally are identified.

Keywords: hot spots policing; experimental criminology; place-based experiments; policing; crime at place; cluster randomized trials

Introduction

There is widespread acceptance today that randomized experiments provide more valid answers to policy questions than do nonexperimental studies (e.g., see Boruch, Snyder, and DeMoya 2000; Campbell and Boruch 1975; Cook and Campbell 1979; Farrington 1983;

David Weisburd is a professor of criminology in the Hebrew University Law School and professor of criminology and criminal justice at the University of Maryland. He is one of the early proponents of place-based experimental research in criminology and was a principal investigator on a series of place-based experimental studies supported by the National Institute of Justice. Professor Weisburd is cochair of the Campbell Crime and Justice Group and president of the Academy of Experimental Criminology. He is also the founding editor of the Journal of Experimental Criminology.

NOTE: This article was prepared for the Campbell Collaboration/Rockefeller Foundation meeting on "Progress and Prospects for Place Based Randomized Trials," Bellagio, Italy, November 11-15, 2002.

DOI: 10.1177/0002716205274597

Feder, Jolin, and Feyerherm 2000; Shadish, Cook, and Campbell 2002; Weisburd 2003). As Feder and Boruch (2000, 292) wrote, "There is little disagreement that experiments provide a superior method for assessing the effectiveness of a given intervention." Nonetheless, experiments remain the oddity rather than the norm in evaluations of criminal justice practice. Comparing criminal justice to medicine, Jonathan Shepherd (2003) described a "comparative famine" of randomized trials. And Garner and Visher (2003) and Nuttall (2003) documented the failure of the major American and British criminal justice funding agencies to concern themselves with randomized experimental approaches to program or treatment evaluations.

The marginal status of criminal justice experimentation is all the more remarkable given the growing evidence that experiments can be carried out in a number of different criminal justice settings (Boruch, Snyder, and DeMoya 2000; Dennis 1988; Petrosino 1988; Weisburd 1993). While the number of randomized experiments in criminal justice is still very small compared to the hundreds of thousands of randomized trials in medical research, researchers have documented as many as three hundred randomized studies that are relevant to criminal justice problems (Petrosino 2000). It is just no longer possible to argue that randomized experiments cannot be carried out in criminal justice. Indeed, randomized experiments have been conducted regarding the full range of criminal justice institutions and across a wide array of criminal justice subjects.

What then explains the "famine" of criminal justice experimentation and the failure of randomized experiments to move into the mainstream of criminal justice evaluations? One common explanation for the failure to widely implement experimental study is that randomization presents serious ethical problems that are difficult to overcome in most areas of criminal justice practice (Clarke and Cornish 1972). Even if experiments can overcome ethical barriers, it is often noted that experiments are very difficult to implement in crime and justice and often lead to implementation failures so significant that the advantages of experimental study are brought into question (Clarke and Cornish 1972; Petersilia 1989; Weisburd 1993). Finally, and perhaps most important, critics of experimental approaches have argued that implementation of the experimental method imposes so many limitations on criminal justice practice that even if ethical barriers can be overcome and experiments carried out successfully, they are not likely to have much policy relevance (Eck 2002; Pawson and Tilley 1997).

Place-based randomized trials in the area of hot spots policing appear very much at odds with these common assumptions regarding experimentation in criminal justice. Hot spots policing refers to the concentration of police resources in small discrete areas such as addresses, street blocks, or clusters of addresses or street blocks (Sherman and Weisburd 1995; Weisburd and Braga 2003). It has become a core strategy in American police agencies, and there is good reason to believe that research played an important role in its wide adoption (Weisburd and Lum forthcoming). Importantly, given our discussion of the marginal status of experimentation in criminal justice, randomized experiments have played a central role in the evaluation of hot spots policing strategies (Braga 2001; see also Braga et al. 1999; Sherman and Rogan 1995; Sherman and Weisburd 1995; Weisburd and Eck 2004; Weisburd and Green 1995).

In the case of hot spots policing, the cluster randomized approach was developed not because of ethical or practical concerns but rather as a direct response to theoretical innovations in criminology and criminal justice.

Why has experimentation in hot spots policing succeeded in playing a central role in research and policy in criminal justice when experimentation more generally has played a marginal role? How were common ethical dilemmas overcome? How were common implementation problems resolved? What accounts for the widespread policy relevance of these studies, despite the fact that they were implemented within the constraints of an experimental design? To try to gain insight into these questions, I draw upon lessons from two specific randomized experiments in hot spots policing that I helped design and implement in the 1990s: the Minneapolis Hot Spots Experiment (Sherman and Weisburd 1995) and the Jersey City Drug Market Analysis (DMA) Experiment (Weisburd and Green 1995). Using a case study approach, I identify factors that facilitate and inhibit development and implementation of randomized trials with particular focus on the special problems and or advantages of place-based experiments. While my main comments will focus on the success of place-based randomized trials in evaluating hot spots policing approaches, I will draw insight as well into the reasons why the successful example of experiments in hot spots policing has not inspired similar place-based experimentation in other areas of policing or criminal justice.

The Emergence of Place-Based Randomized Experiments in Crime Hot Spots

In many cases of cluster randomized trials, the choice of "place" as a unit of analysis develops from ethical or practical concerns (Boruch et al. 2004). Randomization, for example, may be carried out at the institutional level because researchers can find no ethically acceptable way of distributing resources randomly at the individual level. Randomization may also be carried out at the place level because of the practical difficulties of randomization at the individual level. Interventions for children, for example, may be very hard to randomize successfully within a classroom but may be possible to randomize across schools. In the case of hot spots policing, the cluster randomized approach was developed not because of ethical or practical concerns but rather as a direct response to theoretical innovations in criminology and criminal justice. Focus on place was part of a paradigm shift in the ways that criminologists understood the nature of crime problems (see Weisburd 2002; Weisburd and Braga 2003).

Everett Rogers (1995) noted in his seminal work on diffusion of innovation that the emergence of innovation is generally preceded by the wide recognition of a need for change, often provoked by some type of crisis. Without that recognition or crisis, institutions and individuals will often find it simpler to continue just as they were. This model is very much consistent with the emergence of hot spots policing and its diffusion in police agencies.

The crisis of confidence in American policing

The 1970s and 1980s were decades of shock and crisis for American policing and for American police scholars. By the early 1990s, it appeared that every major police strategy to prevent or control crime had come to be "unmasked" by scientific evaluation. For example, there was no more visible approach to crime prevention in policing, or one that involved greater cost, than preventive patrol in cars. The idea that police presence spread widely across the urban landscape was an important method for preventing crime and increasing citizen feelings of safety was a bedrock assumption of American policing. But in a major evaluation of preventive patrol in Kansas City, Missouri, the Police Foundation concluded that increasing or decreasing the intensity of preventive patrol did not affect either crime, service delivery to citizens, or citizen feelings of security (Kelling et al. 1974). Similarly, rapid response to emergency calls to the police was considered to be a crucial component of police effectiveness. Yet in another large-scale study, Spelman and Brown (1984) concluded that improvement in police response times had no appreciable impact on the apprehension or arrest of offenders.

These and other studies in the 1970s and 1980s led scholars to challenge the fundamental premise of whether the police could have a significant impact on crime (see also Greenwood, Petersilia, and Chaiken 1977; Levine 1975). While the police had long considered their role as "crime fighters" as central to the police function (Klockars 1988), the scientific evidence seemed to suggest otherwise. Michael Gottfredson and Travis Hirschi (1990, 270), for example, wrote in their classic book on the causes of crime that "no evidence exists that augmentation of patrol forces or equipment, differential patrol strategies, or differential intensities of surveillance have an effect on crime rates." David Bayley, a distinguished police scholar, wrote even more strongly in 1994,

> The police do not prevent crime. This is one of the best-kept secrets of modern life. Experts know it, the police know it, but the public does not know it. Yet the police pretend

that they are society's best defense against crime. . . . This is a myth. First, repeated analysis has consistently failed to find any connection between the number of police officers and crime rates. Secondly, the primary strategies adopted by modern police have been shown to have little or no effect on crime. (p. 3)

As predicted by Rogers's (1995) model of diffusion of innovation, this period of challenge to the effectiveness of traditional models of American policing was followed by a new openness to police innovation in the 1990s. In part, this openness was reflected in what might be termed an expansion of the police function. For example, community policing defined new tasks for the police, often extending much beyond the traditional crime control function (Goldstein 1987; Greene and Mastrofski 1988; Rosenbaum 1994). While new roles for the police were an important part of police innovation in the 1990s, neither scholars nor practitioners abandoned the idea that police could be more effective in preventing and controlling crime (e.g., see Goldstein 1979, 1990). The emergence of hot spots policing represents one attempt to develop more effective police practices. It can be traced directly to emerging theoretical perspectives in criminology that suggested the importance of place in understanding crime.

Crime places as a focus of police crime prevention efforts

The traditional focus of research and theory in criminology has been upon individuals and communities (Nettler 1978; Sherman 1995). In the case of individuals, criminologists have sought to understand why certain people as opposed to others become criminals (e.g., see Akers 1973; Gottfredson and Hirschi 1990; Hirschi 1969; Raine 1993) or to explain why certain offenders become involved in criminal activity at different stages of the life course or cease involvement at other stages (e.g., see Moffitt 1993; Sampson and Laub 1993).

In the case of communities, criminologists have often tried to explain why certain types of crime or different levels of criminality are found in some communities as contrasted with others (e.g., see Agnew 1999; Bursik and Grasmick 1993; Sampson and Groves 1989; Shaw and McKay 1972), or how community-level variables, such as relative deprivation, low socioeconomic status, or lack of economic opportunity, may affect individual criminality (e.g., see Agnew 1992; Cloward and Ohlin 1960; Merton 1968; Wolfgang and Ferracuti 1967). In most cases, research on communities has focused on the "macro" level, often studying states (Loftin and Hill 1974), cities (Baumer et al. 1998), and neighborhoods (Bursik and Grasmick 1993; Sampson 1985).

Nonetheless, criminologists have almost from the outset recognized that the situational opportunities provided at the "micro" level of place can affect the occurrence of crime. Edwin Sutherland (1947), for example, whose main focus was upon the learning processes that bring offenders to participate in criminal behavior, noted in his classic criminology textbook that the immediate situation influences crime in many ways. For example, "A thief may steal from a fruit stand when the owner is not in sight but refrain when the owner is in sight; a bank burglar may attack a bank which is poorly protected but refrain from attacking a bank protected by watchmen and burglar alarms" (p. 5). Nonetheless, Sutherland, as other criminologists, did not see "crime places"—small discrete areas within communities (Eck and Weisburd 1995)—as a relevant focus of criminological study. This was the case, in part, because crime opportunities provided by places were assumed to be so numerous as to make concentration on specific places of little utility for theory or policy. In turn, criminologists traditionally assumed that situational factors played a relatively minor role in explaining crime as compared with the "driving force of criminal dispositions" (Clarke and Felson 1993, 4; Trasler 1993). Combining an assumption of a wide array of criminal opportunities, and a view of offenders that saw them as highly motivated to commit crime, it is understandable that criminologists paid little attention to the problem of the development of crime at place.

The period of challenge to police practice noted above was also a period of more general challenge to traditional understandings of the crime problem. Beginning with C. Ray Jeffery (1971) and Robert Martinson (1974), a series of major reviews of criminal justice interventions and treatments supported a more general view that "nothing works" in criminal justice. Summarizing the overall standing of what they defined as traditional "offender centred" crime prevention, Patricia and Paul Brantingham wrote in 1990, for example, "If traditional approaches worked well, of course, there would be little pressure to find new forms of crime prevention. If traditional approaches worked well, few people would possess criminal motivation and fewer still would actually commit crimes" (p. 19).

One influential critique of traditional criminological approaches to understanding crime that was to have strong influence on the development of interest in crime places was brought by Cohen and Felson (1979). They argued that the emphasis placed in criminological theory on the developmental factors that affect criminal motivations failed to recognize the importance of other elements of the crime equation. In their theory of "routine activities," criminal events required not simply a "motivated offender" but also the presence of a "suitable target" and the absence of a "capable guardian" such as a police officer on the street or a doorman in an apartment building. They showed that crime rates could be affected by changing the nature of targets or of guardianship, irrespective of the overall level of predispositions to crime found in society. That Cohen and Felson suggested that crime could be affected without reference to the motivations that individual offenders bring to the crime situation was a truly radical idea in criminological circles in 1979. The "routine activities" perspective they presented established the context of crime as an important focus of study.

Drawing upon similar themes, British scholars led by Ronald Clarke began to explore the theoretical and practical possibilities of situational crime prevention (Clarke 1983, 1992, 1995; Cornish and Clarke 1986). Their focus was on criminal contexts and the possibilities for reducing the opportunities for crime in very specific situations. Their approach, like that of Cohen and Felson (1979), turned traditional crime prevention theory on its head. At the center of their crime equation was opportunity. And they sought to change opportunity rather than reform offenders. In situational crime prevention, more often than not "opportunity made the thief" (Felson and Clarke 1998). This was in sharp contrast to the traditional view that the thief simply took advantage of a very large number of potential opportunities. In a series of case studies, situational crime prevention advocates showed that reducing criminal opportunities in very specific contexts can lead to crime reduction and prevention (Clarke 1992, 1995).

The idea of focusing police patrol on crime hot spots represented a direct application of the empirical findings regarding the concentration of crime in discrete places.

One natural outgrowth of these perspectives was that the place where crime occurs would become an important focus for crime prevention researchers. In the mid- to late 1980s, a group of criminologists began to examine the distribution of crime at places. Their findings were to radically change the way many criminologists understood the crime equation, drawing them into a new area of inquiry that was to have important implications for police practice. Perhaps the most influential of these studies was conducted by Lawrence Sherman and his colleagues (Sherman, Gartin, and Buerger 1989). Looking at crime addresses in the city of Minneapolis, they found a concentration of crime at place that was startling. Only 3 percent of the addresses in Minneapolis accounted for 50 percent of the crime calls to the police. Similar results were reported in a series of other studies in different locations and using different methodologies, each suggesting a very high concentration of crime in very specific places (e.g., see Pierce, Spaar, and Briggs 1988; Weisburd, Maher, and Sherman 1992; Weisburd and Green 1994). Such concentrations did not necessarily follow traditional ideas about crime and communities. There were often discrete places free of crime in neighborhoods that were considered troubled and crime hot spots in neighborhoods that were seen generally as advantaged and not crime-prone (Weisburd and Green 1994). This empirical research reinforced theoretical perspectives that emphasized the importance of crime places. It also redirected the attentions of crime prevention scholars to small areas often encompassing only one or a few city blocks that could be defined as hot spots of crime.

Cluster Randomized Trials
at Crime Hot Spots:
Two Examples

These emerging theoretical paradigms and empirical findings led Lawrence Sherman and I (Sherman and Weisburd 1995) to explore the practical implications of the hot spots approach for policing. With cooperation from the Minneapolis Police Department, we developed a large experimental field study of "police patrol in crime hot spots." The study sought to challenge the conclusions of the Kansas City Preventive Patrol Experiment noted earlier, then well established, that police patrol has little value in preventing or controlling crime. But the study also sought to show that the focus of police efforts on crime hot spots presented a new and promising approach for police practice.

The idea of focusing police patrol on crime hot spots represented a direct application of the empirical findings regarding the concentration of crime in discrete places. The Kansas City Preventive Patrol Experiment had looked at the effects of police patrol in large police beats. However, if "only 3 percent of the addresses in a city produce more than half of all the requests for police response, if no police are dispatched to 40 percent of the addresses and intersections in a city over one year, and, if among the 60 percent with any requests the majority register only one request a year, then concentrating police in a few locations makes more sense that spreading them evenly through a beat" (Sherman and Weisburd 1995, 629).

Applying these findings to police practice raised significant questions for police and for criminologists about the overall crime control benefits of a hot spots approach. How would one know if crime prevention benefits gained at hot spots would not simply be displaced to other areas close by? Sherman and Weisburd (1995) noted that displacement was a potential but not necessarily certain occurrence. They argued, moreover, that the first task for researchers was to establish that there would be any deterrent effect of police presence at the hot spots themselves:

> The main argument against directing extra resources to the hot spots is that it would simply displace crime problems from one address to another without achieving any overall or lasting reduction in crime. The premise of this argument is that a fixed supply of criminals is seeking outlets for the fixed number of crimes they are predestined to commit. Although that argument may fit some public drug markets, it does not fit all crime or even all vice. . . . In any case, displacement is merely a rival theory explaining *why* crime declines at a specific hot spot, if it declines. The first step is to see whether crime can be reduced at those spots at all, with a research design capable of giving a fair answer to that question. (p. 629)

The results of the Minneapolis Experiment stood in sharp distinction to those of the earlier Kansas City study. The Minneapolis Experiment included randomization of 110 crime hot spots, each "hot spot" about one city block in length, to intervention and control conditions. The intervention sites received on average between two and three times as much preventive patrol as the control sites. For the ten months in which the experiment was properly implemented, there was a significant and stable difference between the two groups of hot spots in terms of crime calls to the police and observations of disorder in those areas. Crime, or at least crime calls and disorder, appeared to be prevented in the intervention as opposed to the control locations. Sherman and Weisburd (1995, 645) concluded that their results show "clear, if modest, general deterrent effects of substantial increases in police presence in crime hot spots." They noted that it was time for "criminologists to stop saying 'there is no evidence' that police patrol can affect crime" (p. 647).

Before the results of the Minneapolis Hot Spots Experiment were available, the National Institute of Justice (NIJ) decided to support a series of studies that would examine the problem of drug markets in American cities. This Drug Market Analysis Program (DMAP) was developed in good part as a response to the more general concern regarding drug crime that was very much on the public agenda at the time. But it was also strongly influenced by the hot spots findings and the implementation of the Minneapolis experiment.

One of the studies supported by DMAP drew heavily from the methods of the Minneapolis experiment, but its focus was on whether applying a "problem-oriented policing strategy" in drug markets would lead to more effective drug policing than that of more traditional methods. Fifty-six hot spots of drug activity were randomized to experimental and control conditions. The drug hot spots themselves varied in size: most were composed of just one or a group of two to four street segments (see Weisburd and Green 1995).[1] The intervention strategy followed a stepwise approach that sought to engage business owners and citizens in crime control efforts, to apply pressure to reduce drug and drug-related activity through police crackdowns, and to initiate a maintenance program with the assistance of the patrol division of the police department. In line with tactics employed by street-level narcotics units in many other American cities, the strategy used in control group hot spots involved unsystematic arrest-oriented narcotics enforcement based on ad hoc target selection.

Comparing seven-month preintervention and postintervention periods, Lorraine Green and I found consistent and strong effects of the experimental strategy on disorder-related emergency calls for service (Weisburd and Green 1995). We also found little evidence of displacement of crime to areas near the experimental hot spots. Indeed, data suggested a phenomenon opposite to that of displacement, which Ronald Clarke and I have termed "diffusion of crime control benefits" (Clarke and Weisburd 1994). In the case of specific crime call categories (public morals and narcotics), areas immediately surrounding the experimental drug hot spots were found to have significantly lower counts (comparing preintervention and postintervention periods) than areas around the control drug hot spots. We concluded that while there is little evidence that "strategies of crime control broadly defined, do much to solve crime problems," the "police can be effective when they take a more specific approach to crime and disorder" (Weisburd and Green 1995, 717).

Why Randomized Experiments?

The fact that hot spots policing emerged from innovations in crime prevention theory does not in itself explain why the first major hot spots studies were conducted as cluster randomized trials. As noted earlier, randomized experiments have, for the most part, remained on the margins of criminal justice evaluation. Why then, do we have a push for randomized experimental evaluation of hot spots practices? Indeed, of nine hot spots policing studies identified in a review by Braga (2001), fully five have been cluster randomized trials. Only one other area of criminology— mandatory arrest policies for domestic violence (see Garner, Fagan, and Maxwell 1995)—has had this type of concentration of experimental studies. I think it not coincidental that they were developed close in time and under the same federal funding agency and administration as the Minneapolis and Jersey City experiments.

In good part, the development of cluster randomized trials in hot spots policing, as the more general innovation of hot spots policing itself, can be traced to the crisis in criminal justice practice of the 1970s and 1980s. As scholars began to assess why so much of the evidence regarding criminal justice practice was negative, they looked not only to the failures of conventional theories and approaches in terms of what works in crime prevention but also to the methods that were used to assess crime prevention programs. A number of critics began to question whether the approach to evaluation taken by criminal justice researchers was itself a major factor explaining why so many programs were found ineffective (Visher and Weisburd 1998). These scholars called for more rigorous evaluation methods in criminal justice.

Perhaps the most influential of these critiques was brought by David Farrington, Lloyd Ohlin, and James Q. Wilson. In a seminal book titled *Understanding and Controlling Crime* (1986), they placed strong emphasis not only on what we know about the crime problem but also on the ways in which we come to gain knowledge. They argued that randomized experiments must be conducted if criminal justice is to draw valid policy conclusions about what works. The fact that Ohlin and Wilson were two of the leading figures of the elder generation of American criminologists, and Farrington one of the leaders of the then-younger generation, added significant weight to the book's conclusions.

In trying to revisit a core police practice—preventive patrol—in hot spots, Lawrence Sherman and I were strongly affected by this critique. We agreed from the outset that a randomized experiment was necessary if we were to develop a study with real authority for influencing what were then commonly held beliefs about the ineffectiveness of police patrol. Our main problem was to gain the cooperation of a major police agency that would be willing to randomly allocate preventive patrol to police hot spots.

This meant that we needed to identify a police executive who not only was committed to innovation and research in policing but who also had sufficient trust in Sherman and me to allow a major intervention in normal patrol operations based on a scientific research design. Sherman had already developed a strong relationship with Anthony Bouza, who had become chief of the Minneapolis Police Department, in the 1980s. He had previously supported the Minneapolis Domestic Violence Experiment (Sherman and Berk 1984), a groundbreaking study in the application of randomized experimental methods in policing. He recognized the possibilities of hot spots approaches as well as the desirability of randomized evaluations. The relationship between Bouza and Sherman, as well as the support of an innovative mayor and City Council, made the proposal of a randomized study possible.

The choice of an experimental design did not necessarily facilitate the funding of the Minneapolis project. An original proposal for the hot spots study was submitted to the NIJ under the policing and crime control areas. Shortly after the peer review was completed, I had an informal meeting with a NIJ grant monitor who sat in on the review of the Minneapolis Hot Spots Experiment. She noted that reviewers were impressed by the proposal but thought that it led to many unanswered questions regarding the methods and the program. The peer review committee had suggested that we revise and resubmit the proposal for the next NIJ funding cycle. Importantly, as noted in the original proposal, we had only a short time to implement the study before the present chief of police would retire. A revise and resubmit in which we would have to wait for the next funding cycle would have effectively "killed" the study.

My experience suggests that the peer review response to the proposal for the Minneapolis experiment is not uncommon in review of experimental studies in criminal justice. One of the distinct advantages of experimental study is that the methods are transparent and the achievement of confidence in the validity of the comparisons made is based on aspects of design rather than statistical manipulation. But the fact that so much needs to be laid out clearly in terms of design and implementation at the outset in an experiment naturally leads to loose ends in the description of a study. In contrast, nonexperimental studies rely upon statistical approaches to deal with problems such as dosage or subject variability after the study is completed. Nonexperimental studies can be more "cleanly" described in a proposal since the investigator can claim that problems will be addressed "post facto." Irrespective of whether the nonexperimental approach is in fact convincing in a statistical sense, it is less awkward in description in a proposal. Joel Garner, a former deputy director of research at the NIJ, explains:

> I agree that peer review panels may want more details in a proposed experimental design than in a proposed nonexperimental design. . . . In an experimental design, certain features are fixed forever. In a non-experimental design, nothing is fixed, so they can be changed later. If you can't change features later, you want to be sure that they are right at the beginning. (Personal communication 2002)

Consequently, if there is not a "bias" in favor of randomized experiments because of their advantage in terms of ensuring high internal validity, peer reviewers will tend to favor nonexperimental designs. In the case of the Minneapolis Experiment, and I suspect in other experimental studies in criminal justice as well, the choice of experimental methods likely hindered rather than facilitated funding. This is a point I will return to at the end of the article. But at this juncture, it is important to note the irony that scientific review of experimentation in criminal justice may often serve as a barrier to experimental study.

In response to this serendipitous meeting with an NIJ program manager, Sherman met with the then-director of the NIJ, James K. Stewart. Sherman explained the time constraints relevant to the experiment, a point that Stewart, a former police officer, understood. It is also important to note that Stewart had become a strong advocate of the experimental method. Stewart established a special peer review panel for the study. The design was approved with modifications, and the experiment was able to be implemented while Anthony Bouza served as chief of police.

The Jersey City DMA Experiment provides an almost mirror image to that of the Minneapolis Hot Spots study. This experiment was developed in response to a specific solicitation that called for the use of hot spots approaches to examine the problem of drug markets. The original DMAP solicitation encouraged experimental methods as part of James K. Stewart's more general support for randomized studies. It supplied funding both to researchers and to the police agency involved. The proposed funding level of $450,000 per site in a first wave, to be supplemented in a second wave of funding, made this a major research/program effort in criminal justice at the time.

In the Jersey City Experiment, there was no special relationship between the researcher and practitioner, though the connection to the police department was made through individual officers whom I had come to know. Nor was the Jersey City Police Department's management known for its commitment to innovation in police practices. The police department's choice to participate in the study was based primarily on its desire to become more innovative and to gain recognition through the receipt of federal funding. Moreover, after a decade of increasing drug problems in the city, commanders in the department were interested in reform in their approach to drug markets. More generally, the openness of police agencies to researchers and innovation during this period can also be seen as linked to the crisis in policing described earlier. The agreement to implement a randomized study was made at the outset and was a precondition that I set for a partnership with Rutgers University in the development of an application to the NIJ.

The NIJ had established a special peer review committee for the DMA funding program. While the peer review committee strongly endorsed the Jersey City experiment, it was not one of those sites initially chosen for funding. Ironically, it was NIJ's concern that the Jersey City Police Department was not nationally prominent enough to warrant a major national research effort that held up research funding. Only after a series of discussions with NIJ staff and the director were they convinced that the site would be worthwhile to include among the DMAP participants.

This example suggests that "ordinary" police agencies can be brought on board to participate in experimental study if there is strong governmental encouragement and financial support that rewards participation. A similar experience in the Spouse Assault Replication Program (SARP) reinforces these observations. Joel Garner (2002), who served as program manager for SARP, noted in a personal communication that he knew that the program was a success the "day that we got 17 proposals with something like 21 police agencies willing to randomly assign offenders to be arrested."

Ironically, however, if there is not a presumption for experimentation, researchers proposing experimental studies will often find themselves in an inferior position in scientific peer review—in good part because of the necessity of defining clearly a host of practical and methodological questions that are difficult to identify neatly at the outset.

Why experimentation? Examination of these studies suggests an initial observation regarding the successful development and funding of randomized studies. In a discipline where there is not a presumption for experimentation, experiments are more likely to be proposed when there is strong attack upon conventional practices. In this sense, practitioners and researchers bring out their strongest "weapons" when they are most on the defensive. Ironically, however, if there is not a presumption for experimentation, researchers proposing experimental studies will often find themselves in an inferior position in scientific peer review—in good part because of the necessity of defining clearly a host of practical and methodological questions that are difficult to identify neatly at the outset.

Place-Based Approaches and Ethical Concerns: Avoiding Traditional Pitfalls and Encountering New Ones

Boruch et al. (2004) suggested that it may be possible to avoid many ethical and moral dilemmas commonly associated with experimentation by randomly allocating at the organizational or place level, rather than randomly allocating individuals.

At first glance, one might question why the change in unit of analysis should affect ethical concerns. Why should it matter, for example, whether students in a specific school are allocated to treatment and control conditions versus all students in specific schools? The end result is the same. Some individuals will gain treatment and others not. However, where subjects do not experience the inequality of treatment directly (e.g., by seeing other students in their school being treated differently), ethical dilemmas may just not be raised. In this context, it may be politically more feasible to conduct cluster or place-based randomized trials rather than individual-level randomized studies.

The general proposition that place-based studies are likely to be faced with relatively fewer ethical objections applies to both the Minneapolis and Jersey City experiments. I do not recall any of the city officials that we were in contact with in these studies raising significant ethical concerns during negotiations over randomly allocating either crime hot spots or drug markets to treatment and control conditions. In recent correspondence with Sherman (2002), he noted as well that "no one ever raised ethical objections" to the Minneapolis Hot Spots Experiment. Moreover, as neither study collected information directly from human subjects, but relied rather on official police data and observations of the sites, they were not subject to significant human subjects review. This contrasts strongly with controversies often surrounding the random allocation of individuals in criminal justice settings.

While the location of treatment at the level of places rather than individuals certainly contributed to an environment in which ethical concerns were not central, the nature of the treatment and control conditions were also an important feature limiting ethical objections. In both studies, accepted police practices were employed. Preventive patrol was a standard strategy in policing, and though applied at an unusual dosage in the Minneapolis Hot Spots Experiment, its use was not controversial. In turn, the basic features of the strategy used in the experimental sites in the Jersey City DMA Experiment were based on well-established principles of problem-oriented policing (see Goldstein 1990).

Moreover, in both studies, the experimental treatment was not compared to a "placebo" condition. In the Minneapolis experiment, the control hot spots continued to receive emergency service from the police; When citizens called the police for service, squad cars were dispatched as was standard practice. The goal in the Minneapolis study was to increase police presence at hot spots to three hours per day and to maintain a ratio between experimental and control sites of at least two to one in patrol presence. Accordingly, what was compared in the experiment was a very high dosage of preventive patrol in the intervention sites to a relatively lower dosage in the control sites. Similarly, in the Jersey City DMA study, the control condition also received "treatment," though in this case it was the standard package of practices used by the Jersey City narcotics squad. A fair playing field for the study was provided by dividing up the narcotics squad into two separate units of equal size, an experimental unit and a control unit. The experimental unit was charged with "treatment" of the experimental or intervention drug markets and the control unit with "treatment" of the control drug markets.

By not withdrawing all intervention from the control locations, we avoided many of the ethical objections that practitioners and the public ordinarily raise in randomized field trials. This was especially the case in the Jersey City experiment, where the level of police service in terms of officers assigned was equivalent for the two groups. As Frank Gajewski (personal communication 2002), the senior police commander who served as a principal investigator for the study, explained, "We only had a few problems with this since we were not withholding treatment from any of the markets. Arrests were being made citywide and the detectives could still show that they were 'doing something.' " Even in the Minneapolis experiment, neither police nor researchers expected that the level of police service at the control hot spots would change dramatically from prior patterns. Spreading preventive patrol throughout the city naturally led to a relatively small dosage of police presence in any specific location. The hot spots approach allowed the concentration of resources in specific environments at a relatively high level of dosage.

While common ethical objections to random allocation did not surface in the hot spots studies, different types of objections were raised by citizens and the police. The objections are suggestive of more serious problems that might develop in place-based experiments. For example, in Minneapolis, the City Council was asked to approve the reallocation of police resources in the hot spots experiment. One city councilman in a low crime area would not give his approval unless "an early warning crime trend analysis plan" would monitor burglary trends and send more patrols back into his neighborhood if "burglary rashes developed" (Sherman, personal communication, 2002). Monitoring did not reveal such increases in burglary, and thus the experiment was not affected.

In the Jersey City experiment, when a citizens group in one area of Jersey City found out that their neighbors were getting extra police attention, they demanded to be made part of the hot spots study. The police convinced the citizens group that they continued to get good police service but that their problem (to their benefit) was not sufficiently serious to make them eligible to join the experiment. In Jersey City, all of the drug areas that showed consistent and serious activity were included in the study. This coverage, combined with the "equality of police resources" in the experimental and control areas, made it possible to avoid objections that some serious drug markets were receiving more police attention than others. Nonetheless, the rule that "experiments with lower public visibility will generally be easier to implement" (Weisburd 2000, 186) appears particularly relevant to cluster randomized trials.

A more complex problem was raised by police officers participating in the Minneapolis study. Many patrol officers objected to the hot spots approach of "sitting" in or riding though specific areas. My comments here are based on "ride-alongs" in Minneapolis and comments from field researchers. While we tried to draw support from rank-and-file police officers for the experiment through briefings, pizza parties, and the distribution of t-shirts bearing the project logo ("Minneapolis Hot Spot Cop"), many officers argued that the hot spots approach was unethical and violated their obligations to protect the public. In particular, they argued that the approach simply allowed crime to shift around the corners from the hot spots. In practice, there were not any wide-scale attempts by officers to undermine the experiment, but these objections appear similar to the practitioner concerns that undermined the Kingswood study that forms the basis for Clarke and Cornish's (1972) well-known critique of experimentation in the Home Office. In that study, practitioner beliefs about appropriate treatment led them to divert potential subjects from participation in the experiment. Clarke and Cornish defined this as an ethical dilemma in experimentation. I think it important to note that place-based studies may face similar ethical dilemmas.

Implementing Place-Based Randomized Trials: The Importance of Monitoring Experimental and Control Conditions and the Problem of Complexity

Boruch et al. (2004) suggested that it may be difficult to monitor "implementation fidelity" in a cluster randomized trial, especially when integration or coordination of a wide variety of services across agencies is required. While cluster randomized trials certainly raise new complexities in terms of the monitoring of treatments, the experience of the hot spots studies is that monitoring may be facilitated by focusing on clearly defined places and the application of treatments in a visible social environment.

Both the Minneapolis and Jersey City experiments placed strong emphasis on monitoring treatment integrity. Earlier reviews had suggested that failures to ensure delivery of treatment, or to ensure differences in treatment dosage between treatment and control conditions, were common in criminal justice (e.g., see Weisburd 1993). In the Minneapolis Hot Spots Experiment, a major effort was made to observe activity at the hot spots during the study: almost sixty-five hundred observations of the intervention and control hot spots were conducted, each of seventy minutes' duration. While one main purpose of the observations was to develop a measure of disorder that was independent of official police data, these social observations were also used to document and describe the level of dosage of police presence in the experimental hot spots and the ratio of that dosage between intervention and control hot spots. In the Jersey City study, day-to-day activities of the narcotics experimental and control units were monitored using several sources. First, weekly random ride-alongs were conducted by project staff. Second, both the control and experimental squads were required to complete daily activity logs. Third, detectives assigned to the intervention sites were required to complete a solo surveillance form that documented their attendance at their individual hot spots. Finally, narcotics arrest reports were monitored to keep track of the places where enforcement action was taken.

The importance of monitoring in both studies was confirmed by identification of "breakdowns" in the application of treatment. In the Minneapolis project, a ratio of greater than two to one in police presence between experimental and control hot spots was maintained until July (the experiment began in December of the previous year). But in August, a full breakdown of the experimental treatment was identified, with there being no difference in the observed ratio of patrol in the experimental versus control hot spots. The failure to maintain treatment dosage during the summer months is understandable, given the increase in citizen calls and street-level activity in the hotter weather and when children are on summer vacation. Nonetheless, had treatment fidelity not been monitored using observational methods, our findings would have been confounded by a long period in which treatment was not maintained. This confounding would have led us to mistakenly conclude that specific comparisons were not statistically significant (Sherman and Weisburd 1995). Because of monitoring, we decided to structure our analysis to take into account the breakdown of the experiment during the summer months.

In the Jersey City DMA study, the problem observed through monitoring was not a decline in activity over time but rather a failure on the part of the experimental unit to fully implement treatments at the outset of the study. During the first nine months of the study, only nine experimental hot spots received all of the basic components of the experimental intervention. To fully implement the study, the intervention period was increased from twelve to fifteen months. Additionally, a detailed implementation schedule for each site was developed, and the narcotics squad commander was replaced and put under the direct line of command of then-captain and co–principal investigator of the study, Frank Gajewski (later to be appointed chief of police in Jersey City). During the last five months of the study, all of the hot spots received the basic components of the experimental strategy as originally proposed.

Both the Minneapolis and Jersey City place-based trials illustrate the importance of monitoring experimental studies. They also suggest that monitoring place-based studies may be easier than individually based randomization, in part because places are constant, do not move as do individual subjects, and provide a clear locus for assessing treatment implementation. But these examples also illustrate another important component of maintaining the integrity of experiments more generally. Practitioner involvement in the experimental process is crucial for successfully maintaining treatment fidelity.

Given resistance among rank-and-file police officers to the hot spots approach in Minneapolis, one might ask how treatment fidelity was maintained at a high level up until the summer months. I have suggested elsewhere that "it will be easier to develop randomized experiments in systems in which there is a high degree of hierarchical control" (Weisburd 2000, 188). In Minneapolis, for example, the experiment was "facilitated" by a change in the case law that gave the chief of police more control over the four patrol precinct commanders (see Sherman and Weisburd 1995). Whatever the attitudes of individual officers, the hierarchical structure of the Minneapolis Police Department facilitated the chief's imposition of an experimental design.

In Jersey City, the strong involvement of a senior police commander as a principal investigator in the study played a crucial role in preventing a complete breakdown of the experiment after nine months. As noted above, he took personal authority over the narcotics unit and used his command powers to carefully monitor the daily activities of detectives in the experiment. This suggests the importance of the integration of clinical work and research work in criminal justice, much as they are integrated in medical experiments (see Shepherd 2003). It also reinforces the importance of practitioner "belief" in the importance and necessity of implementing a randomized study. In the Kingswood experiment described by Clarke and Cornish (1972), they illustrated how doubts regarding the application of the experimental treatment led practitioners to undermine the implementation of the study. In the Jersey City experiment, Captain Frank Gajewski was strongly convinced of the failures of traditional approaches and the necessity of testing new ones. Indeed, he described the traditional narcotics enforcement approach more as a method of maintaining drug markets than closing them down:

> One can look at these drug markets as vineyards. The arrests made within their borders can be symbolized as the fruit from the vine. Each vineyard is capable of producing a continual supply of "fruit" as long as the vine is left intact. Some vineyards are larger than others. The arrest strategy sees the pickers (the police) traveling from vineyard to vineyard harvesting the fruit. There are many vineyards so the pickers never stay too long at any particular site. As demand increases from irate citizens . . . the police respond by picking more fruit. Police administrators seeking to assuage the public, display the high harvest numbers as evidence of their commitment and the efficiency of their organization. But the vines are never uprooted, indeed police activity may contribute to their health. (Gajewski 1994, 20)

The extent to which coercive power is needed to ensure treatment fidelity may depend on the complexity of treatments that are brought in a cluster randomized trial. While the Minneapolis experiment involved the entire police force, what was required for successful implementation of the study was very simple: officers were expected to be present at the experimental sites whenever possible. As Sherman and Weisburd (1995) noted,

> What the officers did while present at the sites varied widely by officer. During an inspection visit at our invitation, Kelling [the principal investigator of the earlier Kansas City Preventive Patrol Experiment] observed that some were reading newspapers or sunning themselves while sitting on the patrol car, while others were engaging citizens in friendly interaction in community-policing style. The experiment was clearly no test of the content of police presence, only of the amount. (p. 634)

In contrast, the Jersey City DMA Experiment demanded a complex staged treatment for each experimental site:

> In step one of the strategy, the officers analyzed the nature and form of the drug problem at experimental sites in order to identify and develop effective strategies for closing down drug locations. In step two they coordinated their enforcement efforts, which culminated in an intensive crackdown on the drug hot spots. In the final stage of the program, officers tried to maintain gains made earlier through continued monitoring of activity in treated locations. (Weisburd and Green 1995, 731)

One lesson that can be drawn from a comparison of the two studies is that when treatments are more complex, it is likely to be necessary to use more coercive mechanisms for maintaining treatment fidelity. In both studies, efforts were made

---

One lesson that can be drawn from a comparison of the two studies is that when treatments are more complex, it is likely to be necessary to use more coercive mechanisms for maintaining treatment fidelity.

---

to gain officer cooperation in the experiment. Indeed, in the Jersey City DMA study, narcotics officers were invited to planning meetings held at conference hotels and were included in site visits to examine "successful" examples of narcotics enforcement in other jurisdictions. Attempts were made to solve basic grievances that were related to implementation of the study in ways that were sympathetic to the detectives. For example, early on in the experiment, the detectives complained that the use of strategies that were not focused on arrests in the experimental squad would reduce their overtime. Since overtime accounted for as much as 50 or 100 percent increases in salary, this was a particularly difficult issue. However, to facilitate support for the experiment, it was agreed that overtime would be maintained at equal levels in both squads. Despite these attempts to encourage commitment to the experiment, in the end treatment fidelity was only maintained by the establishment of strong coercive control over the experimental squad.

Offsetting Sample Size Limitations in Cluster Randomized Trials

One potential disadvantage of cluster randomized trials is that the choice of organizational or institutional units of analysis may restrict the number of cases available for randomization as compared with trials randomly allocating individuals. It was recognized at the outset that there would be a limited number of hot spots that could be studied in both the Minneapolis and Jersey City experiments. In the Jersey City DMA Experiment, the number of hot spots was limited by the restricted number of drug markets in the city. After placing a considerable degree of effort in defining drug hot spots, only fifty-two were identified that met the criteria established. In Minneapolis, a much larger number of potential sites could be identified, but the police department did not feel it could maintain a high level of patrol activity at a large number of places. Eventually, after negotiation with the police department, an experiment with fifty-five experimental or intervention hot spots and fifty-five control hot spots was approved.[2]

As Boruch et al. (2004) noted, the fact that a limited number of cases can be included in many cluster randomized trials raises significant concerns regarding the ability of randomization to provide for equivalent groups (see also Farrington, Ohlin, and Wilson 1986). To overcome the statistical limitations created by the small number of units in both the Minneapolis and Jersey City experiments, randomization was restricted to create as much equivalence as possible between the experimental and control conditions. It was decided at the outset that not enough was known about the relationship between characteristics of places and the experimental outcomes to match hot spots in pairs. Such matching would have meant a significant loss of degrees of freedom for the analysis without a known proportional benefit in terms of equivalence of the groups. Instead, a compromise solution was taken, in which the hot spots were grouped into statistical blocks (Fleiss 1986; Lipsey 1990; Weisburd 1993). In the Minneapolis Hot Spots experiment, the 110 hot spots were grouped into five statistical blocks of unequal size based on natural cutting points within the distribution of more serious crime calls to the police. In the Jersey City DMA Experiment, the 52 hot spots were divided into four unequal groups based on reported arrests and emergency calls to the police. These are the first criminal justice studies that we could identify that randomized within statistical blocks. Randomization was also restricted to create an equal number of experimental and control units within each block.

Block randomization was also used as a method of increasing the statistical power of the two studies. Sherman and I noted in the design of the Minneapolis study that the "major statistical limitation in all experiments in patrol or neighborhood-level crime reduction is lack of power" (Sherman and Weisburd 1995, 627). In part because of limitations in sample size, in both experiments considerable efforts were made to increase statistical power using other methods. By making the intervention and control groups as similar as possible in terms of official crime data, we sought to increase the ability of each study to distinguish the effects of the intervention from potential error variability.[3]

Statistical power was also a factor in the selection of the hot spots. Analysis of earlier data in Minneapolis suggested that some hot spots showed extreme fluctuations in crime calls year to year. If such fluctuations were indicative of future trends at those places, the inclusion of such "unstable" units in the study would again increase the error variance of the outcomes examined. The fact that a limited number of cases could be included in the study meant that the effects of such "unstable hot spots" might obscure treatment effects. For this reason, hot spots with greater than a 150 percent increase or 75 percent decrease in serious crime calls in a two-year period before the selection year were excluded. In the Jersey City DMA Experiment, it was required that there be evidence of repetitive drug activity over a six-month period for a street segment or intersection to be included in the selection process.

Why Have Hot Spots Experiments Failed to Inspire?

Place-based randomized trials have played a leading role in the development of innovation in hot spots policing (Weisburd and Lum forthcoming). This article describes the crisis in American policing and criminal justice more generally that led scholars to focus on the problem of place and how that crisis also encouraged the development of experimental methods to test hot spots approaches. Contrary to the position that experimentation is likely to be blocked by major ethical objections, these studies encountered few ethical barriers either from the institutions charged with carrying out the experiment or the citizens in the communities in which they were implemented. This seems to have been due in part to the use of places as a unit for random allocation, in part to the testing of police strategies that had already gained some legitimacy, and in part to the fact that a placebo control group was not used. The place-based unit of analysis also facilitated careful monitoring of the experiments. This monitoring in turn allowed for a high level of treatment fidelity, therefore enabling successful implementation of treatment and a fair test of the treatments examined.

Recent studies suggest that hot spots policing approaches have become widely diffused in police practice. For example, a recent Police Foundation study found that more than seven in ten police departments with one hundred or more sworn officers reported using crime mapping to identify "crime hot spots" (Weisburd et al. 2001). Examining the diffusion of crime mapping technologies in police agencies, Weisburd and Lum (forthcoming) found that the rapid adoption of computerized crime mapping in police agencies is closely linked to the implementation of hot spots policing programs and that the timing of this adoption in the 1990s follows closely the dissemination of the findings of the hot spots policing experiments.

One might assume from this "success story" that the model of hot spots policing experiments would have been replicated in other criminal justice areas. In practice, the hot spots experiments did not lead to the large-scale adoption of cluster randomized methods either in policing or in criminal justice more generally. Why, then, have the hot spots studies, which appear to have been influential both in defining the effectiveness of a major new policing approach and in encouraging its widespread adoption, failed to inspire the use of experimental methods more broadly for place-based evaluations of police or criminal justice programs?

One explanation can be drawn directly from this review. There must be a predisposition from the outset for the application of experimental methods in field settings. As illustrated above, randomized experiments may face special difficulties in gaining peer review approval. For experiments to succeed in the peer review process, there must be a recognition of the particular advantages of randomized experiments, much as there is today in medical trials, and much as there was in the case of the Jersey City DMA Experiment. As long as the playing field remains even for experimental and nonexperimental methods, experiments will find it more diffi-cult to transverse the peer review process. But we might ask why criminal justice funders have not chosen to exhibit such a preference for experimental studies given the clear benefits of experimental methods in deciding upon the effective-ness of treatments and programs.

Garner and Visher (2003) suggested one general explanation for the failure to encourage randomized experiments in their review of NIJ funding patterns over the past decade. They found that randomized experiments cost about 30 percent more on average than nonexperimental studies. These costs are understandable in the context of the discussion above, where the processes of monitoring treatment fidelity were clearly expensive and at the same time crucial to the success of the experimental methods used. Nonetheless, when funders feel pressured to provide a wide coverage of many different topic areas, they are certainly likely to look to fund efforts that are less costly and allow them to do more. Analyses of existing data, for example, are much less costly than field experiments though their results may be equivocal.

Conclusions

Place-based randomized trials in hot spots policing provide a promising model for application of experimental methods in criminal justice. Not only have experi-mental methods been developed successfully, but they have also provided strong policy-relevant findings that have been applied widely in practice. Using a case study approach to examine two of these studies, the Minneapolis Hot Spots Exper-iment and the Jersey City DMA Experiment, I draw eight specific lessons regard-ing the implementation and development of place-based randomized trials and experimental methods more generally:

1. A crisis in the legitimacy of conventional practices is likely to facilitate the development of randomized controlled experiments.
2. The final number reflected both the police department's capabilities in bringing ade-quate dosage to the sites as well as a power analysis suggesting that this number was ade-quate for the purposes of the experiment.
3. There must be a predisposition toward randomized trials if experimental designs are to succeed either in scientific review or in the political processes that lead to funding allocations.
4. Random allocation of places can lead to fewer ethical objections to experimental study.
5. Monitoring treatment fidelity is essential to successful experimentation. Such monitoring may be facilitated by the use of place as a unit of analysis in cluster randomized trials.
6. Strong hierarchical controls within the institution administering treatment, and a collab-orative involvement of an individual able to utilize such authority, are likely to facilitate the implementation of a place-based randomized trial.
7. The more complex the treatment or intervention, the more coercive the mechanisms that are likely to be necessary for maintaining treatment integrity.

8. Place-based randomized trials are likely to face strong limitations in the number of sites that can be identified or treated. Block randomization provides a method for overcoming some problems related to restrictions in sample size, including ensuring the equivalence of groups and maximizing statistical power of tests employed.

Notes

1. Two main criteria were used for defining the drug hot spots after identifying street segments and intersections with repetitive drug activity: (1) street segments and intersections were linked that evidenced similar types of drug activity, and (2) active segments and intersections were linked only if they were within one block and one intersection of one another. See Weisburd and Green (1995) for details regarding the approach used.

2. The final number reflected both the police department's capabilities in bringing adequate dosage to the sites as well as a power analysis suggesting that this number was adequate for the purposes of the experiment.

3. Block randomization also allowed for the specification of block and block-by-treatment interactions in the models within an experimental context. In this way, error variance in assessing treatment outcomes would be further reduced by distinguishing error variance used for testing treatment impacts from block and block-by-treatment effects. Block-by-treatment interactions were included only if they were found to be statistically significant as suggested by Fleiss (1986).

References

Agnew, Robert. 1992. Foundation for a general strain theory of crime and delinquency. *Criminology* 30:47-84.

———. 1999. A general strain theory of community differences in crime rates. *Journal of Research in Crime and Delinquency* 36:123-55.

Akers, Ronald. 1973. *Deviant behavior: A social learning approach*. Belmont, CA: Wadsworth.

Baumer, Eric, Janet Lauritsen, Richard Rosenfeld, and Richard Wright. 1998. The influence of crack cocaine on robbery, burglary, and homicide rates: A cross-city, longitudinal analysis. *Journal of Research in Crime and Delinquency* 35 (3): 316-40.

Bayley, David. 1994. *Police for the future*. New York: Oxford University Press.

Boruch, Robert, Henry May, Herbert Turner, and Julia Lavenberg (with Anthony Petrosino, Dorothy DeMoya, Jeremy Grimshaw, and Ellen Foley). 2004. Estimating the effects of interventions that are deployed in many places: Place randomized trials. *American Behavioral Scientist* 47 (5): 608-33.

Boruch, Robert, Brooke Snyder, and Dorothy DeMoya. 2000. The importance of randomized field trials. *Crime and Delinquency* 46:156-80.

Braga, Anthony. 2001. The effects of hot spots policing on crime. *Annals of the American Academy of Political and Social Sciences* 578:104-25.

Braga, Anthony, David Weisburd, Elin Waring, Lorraine Green-Mazerolle, William Spelman, and Francis Gajewski. 1999. Problem oriented policing in violent crime places: A randomized controlled experiment. *Criminology* 37 (3): 541-80.

Brantingham, Patricia L., and Paul J. Brantingham. 1990. Situational crime prevention in practice. *Canadian Journal of Criminology* 32 (1): 17-40.

Bursik, Robert J., Jr., and Harold G. Grasmick. 1993. *Neighborhoods and crime*. San Francisco: Lexington.

Campbell, Donald, and Robert Boruch. 1975. Making the case for randomized assignment to treatments by considering the alternatives: Six ways in which quasi-experimental evaluations in compensatory education tend to underestimate effects. In *Evaluation and experiment: Some critical issues in assessing social programs*, ed. Carl A. Bennett and Arthur Lumsdaine. New York: Academic Press.

Clarke, Ronald V. 1983. Situational crime prevention: Its theoretical basis and practical scope. In *Crime and Justice: An Annual Review of Research 4*, ed. Michael Tonry and Norval Morris. Chicago: University of Chicago Press.

———. 1992. *Situational crime prevention: Successful case studies*. Albany, NY: Harrow and Heston.

————. 1995. Situational crime prevention: Achievements and challenges. In *Building a safer society: Strategic approaches to crime prevention, crime and justice: A review of research 19*, ed. Michael Tonry and David Farrington. Chicago: University of Chicago Press.

Clarke, Ronald, and Derek Cornish. 1972. *The controlled trial in institutional research: Paradigm or pitfall for penal evaluators?* London: Her Majesty's Stationery Office.

Clarke, Ronald V., and Marcus Felson, eds. 1993. Routine activity and rational choice. *Advances in Criminological Theory* 5:1-14.

Clarke, Ronald V., and David Weisburd. 1994. Diffusion of crime control benefits: Observations on the reverse of displacement. *Crime Prevention Studies* 2:165-84.

Cloward, Richard, and Lloyd Ohlin. 1960. *Delinquency and opportunity*. Glencoe, IL: Free Press.

Cohen, Lawrence E., and Marcus Felson. 1979. Social change and crime rate trends: A routine activity approach. *American Sociological Review* 44:588-605.

Cook, Thomas, and Donald Campbell. 1979. *Quasi-experimentation: Design and analysis issues for field settings*. Chicago: Rand McNally College Publishing Company.

Cornish, Derek B., and Ronald V. Clarke. 1986. *The reasoning criminal: Rational choice perspectives on offending*. New York: Springer-Verlag.

Dennis, M. L. 1988. Implementing randomized field experiments: An analysis of criminal and civil justice research. Unpublished Ph.D. diss., Northwestern University, Department of Psychology, Evanston, IL.

Eck, John E. 2002. Learning from experience in problem-oriented policing and situational crime prevention: The positive functions of weak evaluations and the negative functions of strong ones. In *Evaluation for crime prevention. Crime prevention studies 14*, ed. Nick Tilley, 93-119. Monsey, NY: Criminal Justice Press.

Eck, John E., and David Weisburd, eds. 1995. *Crime and place: Crime prevention studies: 4*. Monsey, NY: Willow Tree Press.

Farrington, David P. 1983. Randomized experiments in crime and justice. In *Crime and justice: An annual review of research*, ed. Norval Morris and Michael Tonry. Chicago: University of Chicago Press.

Farrington, David, Lloyd Ohlin, and James Q. Wilson. 1986. *Understanding and controlling crime—Toward a new research strategy*. Secaucus, NJ: Springer-Verlag.

Feder, Lynette, and Robert F. Boruch. 2000. The need for experiments in criminal justice settings. *Crime and Delinquency* 46:291-94.

Feder, Lynette, Annette Jolin, and William Feyerherm. 2000. Lessons from two randomized experiments in criminal justice settings. *Crime and Delinquency* 46:380-400.

Felson, Marcus, and Ronald V. Clarke. 1998. *Opportunity makes the thief: Practical theory for crime prevention*. Police Research Series, Paper 98. London: Research, Development and Statistics Directorate, Home Office Policing and Reducing Crime Unit.

Fleiss, Joseph. 1986. *The design and analysis of clinical experiments*. New York: John Wiley.

Garner, Joel, Jeffrey Fagan, and Christopher Maxwell. 1995. Published findings from the Spouse Assault Replication Program: A critical review. *Journal of Quantitative Criminology* 11 (1): 3-28.

Garner, Joel, and Christy Visher. 2003. The federal role in experimentation. *Evaluation Review* 27:316-35.

Gajewski, Francis. 1994. Ethics in policing. Manuscript.

Goldstein, Herman. 1979. Improving policing: A problem oriented approach. *Crime and Delinquency* 25:236-58.

————. 1987. Toward community-oriented policing: Potential, basic requirements and threshold questions. *Crime and Delinquency* 33:6-30.

————. 1990. *Problem-oriented policing*. New York: McGraw-Hill.

Gottfredson, Michael, and Travis Hirschi. 1990. *A general theory of crime*. Stanford, CA: Stanford University Press.

Greene, Jack R., and Stephen D. Mastrofski. 1988. *Community policing: Rhetoric or reality*. New York: Praeger.

Greenwood, Peter J., Joan Petersilia, and Jan Chaiken. 1977. *The criminal investigation process*. Lexington, MA: D. C. Heath.

Hirschi, Travis. 1969. *Causes of delinquency*. Berkeley: University of California Press.

Jeffery, C. Ray. 1971. *Crime prevention through environmental design*. Beverly Hills, CA: Sage.

Kelling, George, Anthony M. Pate, Duanne Dieckman, and Charles E. Brown. 1974. *The Kansas City Preventive Patrol Experiment: Summary report*. Washington, DC: Police Foundation.

Klockars, Carl. 1988. The rhetoric of community policing. In *Community policing: Rhetoric or reality*, ed. Jack R. Greene and Stephen D. Mastrofski. New York: Praeger.

Levine, James P. 1975. Ineffectiveness of adding police to prevent crime. *Public Policy* 23:523-45.

Lipsey, Mark. 1990. *Design sensitivity: Statistical power for experimental research*. Newbury Park, CA: Sage.

Loftin, Colin, and Robert Hill. 1974. Regional subculture and homicide: An examination of the Gastil-Hackney thesis. *American Sociological Review* 39:714-24.

Martinson, Robert. 1974. What works? Questions and answers about prison reform. *The Public Interest* 35:22-54.

Merton, Robert K. 1968. Social structure and anomie. *American Sociological Review* 3:672-82.

Moffitt, Terrie. 1993. Adolescence-limited and life-course persistent antisocial behavior: A developmental taxonomy. *Psychological Review* 4:674.

Nettler, Gwynn. 1978. *Explaining crime*. 2nd ed. New York: McGraw-Hill.

Nuttall, Christopher. 2003. The Home Office and random allocation experiments. *Evaluation Review* 27:267-89.

Pawson, Ray, and Nick Tilley. 1997. *Realistic evaluation*. London: Sage.

Petersilia, Joan. 1989. Implementing randomized experiments: Lessons from BJA's Intensive Supervision Project. *Evaluation Review* 13 (5): 435-58.

Petrosino, Anthony. 1988. A survey of 150 randomized experiments in crime reduction: Some preliminary findings. *Forum: Justice Research and Statistics Association* 16 (1): 7-8.

———. 2000. What works to reduce offending? A systematic review of 300 randomized field trials. Manuscript.

Pierce, Glen L., S. Spaar, and L. R. Briggs. 1988. *The character of police work: Strategic and tactical implications*. Boston: Center for Applied Social Research, Northeastern University.

Raine, Adrian. 1993. *The psychopathy of crime*. New York: Academic Press.

Rogers, Everett. 1995. *Diffusion of innovations*. New York: Free Press.

Rosenbaum, Dennis P., ed. 1994. *The challenge of community policing: Testing the promises*. Thousand Oaks, CA: Sage.

Sampson, Robert. 1985. Neighborhood and crime: The structural determinants of personal victimization. *Journal of Research in Crime and Delinquency* 22 (1): 7-40.

Sampson, Robert, and W. Byron Groves. 1989. Community structure and crime: Testing social disorganization theory. *American Journal of Sociology* 94:774.

Sampson, Robert J., and John H. Laub. 1993. *Crime in the making: Pathways and turning points through life*. Cambridge, MA: Harvard University Press.

Shadish, W., Thomas Cook, and Donald Campbell. 2002. *Experimental and quasi-experimental designs for generalized causal inference*. Boston: Houghton Mifflin.

Shaw, Clifford, and Henry McKay. 1972. *Delinquency and urban areas*. Chicago: University of Chicago Press.

Shepherd, Jonathan. 2003. Explaining feast or famine in randomized field trials: Medical science and criminology compared. *Evaluation Review* 27:290-315.

Sherman, Lawrence. 1995. Hot spots of crime and criminal careers of places. In *Crime and place: Crime prevention studies: 4*, ed. John E. Eck and David Weisburd. Monsey, NY: Willow Tree Press.

Sherman, Lawrence, and Richard Berk. 1984. Specific deterrent effects of arrest for domestic assault. *American Sociological Review* 49 (2): 261-72.

Sherman, Lawrence, Patrick R. Gartin, and Michael E. Buerger. 1989. Hot spots of predatory crime: Routine activities and the criminology of place. *Criminology* 27:27-56.

Sherman, Lawrence W., and Dennis Rogan. 1995. Deterrent effects of police raids on crack houses: A randomized controlled experiment. *Justice Quarterly* 12:755-82.

Sherman, Lawrence, and David Weisburd. 1995. General deterrent effects of police patrol in crime "hot-spots": A randomized controlled trial. *Justice Quarterly* 12:626-48.

Spelman, William, and Dale K. Brown. 1984. *Calling the police: Citizen reporting of serious crime*. Washington, DC: Government Printing Office.

Sutherland, Edwin. 1947. *Principals of criminology*. Chicago: J. B. Lippincott Co.

Trasler, Gordon. 1993. Conscience, opportunity, rational choice, and crime. In *Routine activity and rational choice: Advances in criminological theory*, vol. 5, ed. Ronald Clarke and Marcus Felson, 305-22. New Brunswick, NJ: Transaction Press.

Visher, Christy A., and David Weisburd. 1998. Identifying what works: Recent trends in crime prevention. *Crime, Law and Social Change* 28:223-42.

Weisburd, David (with Anthony Petrosino and Gail Mason). 1993. Design sensitivity in criminal justice experiments. In *Crime and justice: A review of research 17*, ed. Michael Tonry. Chicago: University of Chicago Press.

———. 2000. Randomized experiments in criminal justice policy: Prospects and problems. *Crime and Delinquency* 46 (2): 181-93.

———. 2002. From criminals to criminal contexts: Reorienting crime prevention research and policy. In *Crime and social organization, advances in criminological theory 10*, ed. Elin Waring and David Weisburd. New Brunswick, NJ: Transaction Publishers.

———. 2003. Ethical practice and evaluation of interventions in crime and justice. *Evaluation Review* 27:336-54.

Weisburd, David, and Anthony Braga. 2003. Hot spots policing. In *Crime prevention: New approaches*, ed. H. Kury and J. Obergfell-Fuchs. Manz, Germany: Weisser Ring.

Weisburd, David, and John Eck. 2004. What can police do to reduce crime, disorder, and fear? *Annals of the American Academy of Political and Social Science* 593:42-65.

Weisburd, David, and Lorraine Green. 1994. Defining the drug market: The case of the Jersey City DMA system. In *Drugs and crime: Evaluating public policy initiatives*, ed. D. L. MacKenzie and C. D. Uchida. Thousand Oaks, CA: Sage.

———. 1995. Policing drug hot-spots: The Jersey City Drug Market Analysis Experiment. *Justice Quarterly* 12:711-35.

Weisburd, David, and Cynthia Lum. Forthcoming. The diffusion of computerized crime mapping policing: Linking research and practice. *Police Practice and Research*.

Weisburd, D., L. Maher, and L. W. Sherman. 1992. Contrasting crime general and crime specific theory: The case of hot-spots of crime. In *Advances in criminological theory*, vol. 4, 45-70. New Brunswick, NJ: Transaction Press.

Weisburd, David, Stephen Mastrofski, Ann Marie McNally, and Rosann Greenspan. 2001. *Compstat and organizational change: Findings from a national survey*. Washington, DC: Police Foundation.

Wolfgang, Marvin E., and Franco Ferracuti. 1967. *The subculture of violence, toward an integrated theory in criminology*. New York: Tavistock.

Introducing New Contraceptives in Rural China: A Field Experiment

By
HERBERT L. SMITH

The project on Introducing New Contraceptives in Rural China (INCRC) was carried out between 1991 and 1996 in four counties of rural north China. The experimental component involved the random assignment of a multipronged treatment to four townships in each county. Two townships per county served as controls. The scale of the project made it nearly impossible to maintain the integrity of the experimental model that was at the core of the project's design. In spite of the massive numbers of people in the catchment areas of the study (>100,000), the experimental design was of low power, with but eight controls on sixteen treatments; when random assignment is at higher levels of analysis, masses of individual observations only create greater precision in the estimation of higher-order observations. However, the study would not have been conducted, and valuable observations would not have been made, were it not conceived as an experiment.

Keywords: China; family planning; field experiment; randomized experiment; evaluation; place-based randomization

This article presents an overview of work during the 1990s on a demographic, family planning experiment in four counties in rural China. The purpose of the experiment is conveyed in part by its official title, Introducing New Contraceptives in Rural China (INCRC). The Chinese State Family Planning Commission (SFPC) allowed twenty-four townships, across four counties, to participate in the study, which involved the provision of better contraceptives (the TCu380A IUD and Norplant) to

Herbert L. Smith is a professor of sociology and director of the Population Studies Center at the University of Pennsylvania, where he teaches demography, research methods, and social statistics. He was a winner of the 2002 Clifford C. Clogg Award from the Population Association of America for early career achievement and is an elected member (1991) of the Sociological Research Association. This article blends his interests in the demography of China, the design of social experiments, and causal analysis—topics on which he has published in a variety of journals including Demography, Population and Development Review, *and* Sociological Methodology.

DOI: 10.1177/0002716205274513

women in these areas and, perhaps of greater importance, a choice of which method of contraceptive they wish to use. Such choice represented an innovation under the Chinese family planning system, where method use was typically a function of parity (Tu 1995).

Project Background

In the 1970s, the Chinese government identified "population growth" as a fundamental obstacle to economic and social development (Hua 1980; Winckler 2002, 381-82). This set the stage for large-scale state intervention in the process of human reproduction. The apotheosis of this intervention was the introduction, in 1979, of the One Child Policy (Wang 1996; Blayo 1997). The concept was breathtaking. Perhaps the only thing more amazing was the alacrity with which the Chinese government put this plan into effect. Hindsight is twenty-twenty. Predictions circa 1979 that China would reach below-replacement-level rates of fertility within fifteen years were in short supply.

However, the path to lower fertility in China was smooth only on a graph. During the early and mid-1980s, the SFPC learned three things: (1) There was a good deal of resistance to the One Child Policy (Aird 1986). (2) The costs of enforcing the policy were high, in all senses of the term—the amount of surveillance and coercion required, the bad feeling engendered between cadres and common folk, and (of least concern) the disapproval of the international community. But (3) relaxing the One Child Family policy led to episodic increases in fertility that jeopardized the achievement of aggregate population goals (Hardee-Cleaveland and Banister 1988).

The SFPC was amenable to a technocratic solution to these problems, in the form of the introduction of "better contraceptives." Some of the appeal doubtless derived from ideological association, among socialism, science, technology, and progress. But much of the appeal was also practical. Better contraceptives, with fewer side effects, might grate less on the population compelled to use them. They could conceivably cut down on "unplanned" pregnancies, hence abortions. From these benefits might follow better relations between cadres and populace, a smoother working family planning bureaucracy, and less criticism from international observers.

The utilitarian calculus implicit in these motives is not meant to deny the sincerity of many SFPC officials, from those in Beijing all the way down to the village-

NOTE: The research described here was supported by a series of grants from the Rockefeller Foundation, and I wish to thank Sheldon J. Segal, the late W. Parker Mauldin, Steven Sinding, and Evelyn Majidi, of the former Population Sciences Division of the Rockefeller Foundation, for their assistance and encouragement. My work on the INCRC project was abetted by a literal cast of thousands; here I can thank Mark Hereward, Qiu Shuhua, M. Giovanna Merli, Ni Jiajun, Zhenchao Qian, Cameron Campbell, and especially Tu Ping. Thanks also to the Campbell Collaboration for support for this article.

level family planning workers. Bureaucracy breeds cynicism, but this is an incomplete description of the view that the incumbents of the family planning apparatus have of their "clients." There was widespread recognition of the human cost entailed in restricting fertility, especially when the means of doing so were relatively crude (e.g., widespread use of the stainless steel single-ring IUD, with its concomitant high failure rate; abortions, especially in the second or third trimester). Nor is the efficiency of a method from the standpoint of the bureaucracy necessarily privileged over its efficiency from the standpoint of the user.

A case in point is the Norplant, whose availability under the INCRC project was novel in the study areas. The provision of Norplant was quite costly to the SFPC, even when the actual cost of the device was underwritten by an outside donor, as was the case with the INCRC study. Local doctors had to be trained in the insertion and removal of the implant. Local family planning workers had to be educated in the new method, including the recognition of side effects. Periodic checkups of Norplant users are also required.

And of greatest potential cost: the Norplant is reversible. A long-term contraceptive such as Norplant probably substitutes best for female sterilization, the most ubiquitous method of family planning in China and one that removes a great deal of the monitoring burden from local cadres. If interest in the INCRC project derived only from cynical or instrumental motives, it would hardly have featured the introduction of Norplant. This said, it must also be acknowledged that, in a situation where reproduction is still highly restricted by the government, Norplant may—from the standpoint of the women who use it—have turned out to be as much curse as blessing, since, relative to sterilization, it prolongs the reliance of women on agents of the state (i.e., local family planning services).

The SFPC and the outside donors supporting the INCRC project had some fundamental differences in their understanding of what family planning is about. They converged in their assessment that "better contraceptives" are of value, but each valuation has a different underlying calculus. They may have used the same terms, but these terms can have meanings as different from one another as night from day. In the demographic and international family planning community, a birth that is "unplanned" or "unwanted" is unplanned or unwanted from the standpoint of a woman, or perhaps a couple. In China, an unplanned birth is literally that—a birth that does not fit in within the plan for fertility, as determined by the state. Similarly, "method failure" is straightforward enough to calculate given information on method use and subsequent time until cessation or failure. However, in China, the distinction between cessation and failure is blurred. Since the former is not within the legitimate purview of most Chinese women, "failure" is a polite fiction for bureaucrat, cadre, and woman alike.

Notwithstanding certain differences in meaning and purpose, there was sufficient common ground, and enthusiasm, for the development of the INCRC project, which began (in phases) during the years 1991 and 1992. The project featured three interventions: (1) provision of better contraceptives, (2) better training of family planning workers, and (3) introduction of method choice. Motivations, goals, and basic issues in implementation are summarized in Table 1. The last of

TABLE 1

INTERVENTIONS, GOALS AND MOTIVATIONS, AND OBSERVATIONS AND
EMENDATIONS CONCERNING THE FIELD EXPERIMENT ON INTRODUCING
NEW CONTRACEPTIVES IN RURAL CHINA, 1990-1996

Intervention	Goals and/or Motivations	Observations and Emendations
Provision of newer, more effective contraceptives, specifically, the TCu38OA IUD and the Norplant levonorgestrel-releasing implant. These were purchased by the external donor.	A generalized belief that better, long-acting contraceptives are the hallmark of a good family planning program; a concomitant belief that women should have access to a wide range of contraceptives; and a desire to increase "user satisfaction" Better, copper IUDs should reduce the side effects associated with the older, stainless steel single-ring IUD. They should fail less often and reduce unplanned pregnancies, hence abortions. (But see text.) Norplants should substitute for female sterilization, especially among young (younger than thirty) women, Also, scientists both in China and abroad are interested in the efficacy of Norplant in field (as opposed to clinical) settings.	Although copper IUDs tended to be in short supply in China at the time that this study was designed (1990-91), some TCu220 IUDs (and their equivalents) could be found in project areas and elsewhere. Moreover, access to these IUDs increased during the life of the project, independent of the project. No attempt was made to restrict their availability in either treatment or control sites; the Tcu38OA was simply added to the mix. During 1995, it became apparent that the Sinoplant, a Chinese-manufactured analogue of the Norplant, was becoming available in areas near some of the project sites. It was agreed in November 1995 that eligible control sites, from which the State Family Planning Commission (SFPC) had been restricting the Sinoplant, could offer them as per "normal" policy.
Better training of family planning workers (carried out by the SFPC).	Engendered in part by a realization that new methods would require new skills and better education of provider and client alike. However, there was also a realization, emanating as much from China as abroad, that the skill and knowledge level of too many providers was inadequate, new contraceptives or not. Better, more systematic training should lead to greater user satisfaction, fewer side effects, and better relations between workers and clients.	In fall 1992, it became apparent that there was a misunderstanding within project areas in Shandong province that "better training" was one of the "treatments" in the experiment: cadres in "control" townships had been participating in special county- and provincial-level training courses. This reflects ignorance as well on the part of the study design team, regarding the interconnectedness of family planning work across townships within counties.

(continued)

TABLE 1 (continued)

Intervention	Goals and/or Motivations	Observations and Emendations
The introduction of method choice	Transplantation of a general family planning research finding: that access to and choice among a wide range of contraceptives leads to increases in user satisfaction and contraceptive prevalence; and a general Western ideology: that individual choice is a good thing, sui generis. The principle was embraced by the SFPC in the hope that greater user satisfaction would have positive clinical and demographic impacts (see above) and would make family planning work less onerous for cadre and populace alike.	The idea of choice was not an easy idea to implement. Scientists were used to the idea that a contraceptive trial involved assigning one method to some women and another to others. Bureaucrats and cadres were occasionally suspicious of the idea of implementing choice, given its destabilizing implications. In general, because the concept of method choice ran counter to prevailing practice and attitudes in the Chinese family planning system, it was a hard idea to assimilate.

these, method choice, underscores the great gap that exists between Chinese and Western understandings of family planning programs. From a Western standpoint, choice of contraceptive method is a poor second to a more fundamental choice—that of family size. In China, however, the choice of family size is not "on the table," at least not explicitly.[1]

Yet it would be unfortunate to underestimate how radical the notion of method choice is, or at least was, at the start of the project. The experience of the SFPC has been that the system functions best when the population has the fewest choices; and there was clearly some trepidation, at various levels of the SFPC, to allowing women to choose whether they wanted the new contraceptives (Merli, Qian, and Smith 2004). Certainly the biggest success of the project, in terms of influencing policy within the Chinese family planning establishment, has been to create a reservoir of bureaucrats and family planning cadres who have seen "choice" in family planning "work," and who can testify that it makes their jobs easier and is not inherently destabilizing to the country's overall population goals. Winckler (2002, 383) wrote that "after a few years of experiments starting in 1995, 'quality of care' quickly became a popular concern in service delivery," and noted other experimental programs in the works. The INCRC project was an antecedent of all of these initiatives.

Serious relaxation in family planning policies is likely to be gradual (Merli, Qian, and Smith 2004; Winckler 2002), in which sense "freedom of method choice" was a first step. The presumption is that, especially in rural areas, the family planning program is keeping fertility at lower levels than would occur if families could have as many children as they wished. Given the low targets of the program, this is almost certainly true; the big unknown is, by how much (Merli and Smith 2002)?

The twin effects of (1) economic liberalization and (2) family planning education have almost certainly raised the cost of children and lowered demand, even in rural areas. Although the worst ethical ills of constrained reproduction are typically laid at the doorstep of the SFPC (in particular, sex selective abortion), it is possible that there exists in rural China a sufficient demand for (1) sons but (2) small families as to create a problem even if the SFPC were to disappear tomorrow. Consider, for example, the experience of South Korea (Park and Cho 1995; Goodkind 1996).

Study Design

The INCRC project was primarily an effort of the SFPC, with technical support from the Population Research Institute of Peking University and the Population Studies Center of the University of Pennsylvania and with funding from the Rockefeller Foundation. The project was designed as a randomized experiment. Because the treatments are policies or "regimes"—better contraceptives, better training of personnel, "choice"—the experimental unit is not the individual woman ("client"), but rather the lowest organizational unit at which it was deemed feasible to operationalize these policies. In rural areas, this is the township. Townships are administrative units that comprise (on average) two to three dozen villages. They typically feature a family planning service station (Kaufman et al. 1989) and a concomitant family planning administrative apparatus. This apparatus is charged with the responsibility of overseeing family planning services in the constituent villages, including the storage and provision of contraceptives, gynecological and obstetric "checkups" and procedures (including abortions and sterilizations), and family planning and demographic record keeping. Townships are "nested" within counties (or districts), which in turn are under the aegis of a local municipality, the first government below the provincial level.[2]

It was determined by the SFPC that the project would take place in two counties (Huasheng and Pangxie) in the Tangshan municipality of Hebei province and a county (Shanshui) and a district (Ciqixian) in Zibo municipality of Shandong province (Figure 1).[3] Tangshan is east of Beijing and north of Tianjin and is best known as the site of perhaps the most destructive earthquake in human history. Zibo is east of Jinan, the capital of Shandong province, en route to Qingdao. The four counties are parts of the rural hinterlands of these cities.[4] They are described below in more detail.

Within each county, six townships were selected at random by the project's scientific personnel. Then, also at random, two of the six townships in each county were designated to serve as controls.[5] Control townships were to participate in the basic data collection activities of the project but were not to receive any of the project's interventions.[6] If townships are the study's basic unit of analysis, then a total of twenty-four townships constitutes a fairly small *n*. However, townships are really only one level of *analysis*, even if they are the basic level of *experimental manipulation*. Married women of reproductive age constitute another important level of analysis, albeit a *nonexperimental* one, since at the level of the individual, there was

FIGURE 1
APPROXIMATE LOCATIONS OF FOUR INTRODUCING NEW CONTRACEPTIVES
IN RURAL CHINA (INCRC) PROJECT COUNTIES IN NORTH CHINA

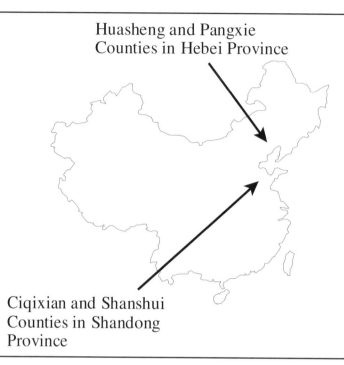

Huasheng and Pangxie
Counties in Hebei Province

Ciqixian and Shanshui
Counties in Shandong
Province

no random assignment of subjects to treatments. At the individual level, the INCRC project was rich in observational detail since there were in excess of 125,000 married women of reproductive age in the twenty-four townships.

The decision to do the project in twenty-four townships, with "treatments" dominating "controls" in the ratio of two-to-one, reflected the (inevitable?) cost-benefit compromise that attends social research. Having a greater number of townships in the study would have facilitated, in statistical terms, the measurement of "treatment effects" at the level at which the enhanced program was implemented. However, it would have been costly. First, the project was taking place at a time of rising prices in China, increased monetization of intragovernmental relations, and rising disparities between the incomes of those in the private and governmental sectors of the economy. Although there might have once been a time when a project such as this could have been carried out solely at the behest of the central government, with no considerations as to cost, that time had passed.

Second, twenty-four townships was at the limit of the number of field sites that a small group of investigators could expect to visit routinely. Management of more sites by the SFPC would have been possible, but it would have tipped the balance of the administration of the project, as between the bureaucratic and the scientific, in favor of the former.

Does it matter that the assignment of townships to treatment was at random, and so too was the selection of townships within county, but the choice of counties was not? This is a natural but ultimately misleading question, for the representativeness of the study's counties (and the external validity of the study) does not hinge on how the counties were selected. Even if four counties were selected "at random" from among all the counties of China, there would be scant hope, at least on statistical grounds, that they would somehow mirror the distribution of China along geographic, economic, ethnic, and demographic lines.[7] It became apparent that some of the counties selected by the SFPC have "special characteristics," but it is by no means clear how "special" they are in the overall Chinese context, where conformity is the norm, but institutionalized exceptionalism is important to administration at all levels.

In the demographic and international family planning community, a birth that is "unplanned" or "unwanted" is unplanned or unwanted from the standpoint of a woman, or perhaps a couple. In China, an unplanned birth is literally that—a birth that does not fit in within the plan for fertility, as determined by the state.

The point here is that the four INCRC counties were alternative *environments* (Kish 1987, 15) in which to measure the effects of change in local family planning programs on the contraceptive and demographic behavior of the populace. In studying the interactions of treatment-response relationships with environment, it is generally less essential that the environments be representative of populations than that they be representative of theoretically important conditioning variables (Smith 1990). The INCRC counties represented "the kind of model in family planning that the government has been trying to promote" (Tu 1993). Even within counties of this "kind," there was substantial variation in organizational and institutional relations that governed how family planning programs were put into practice. These ranged from the great enthusiasm for the project at the provincial level in Shandong but complete provincial inattention in Hebei,[8] to great turnover in personnel in one of the four counties, to the relative abilities of county- and township-level family planning workers to countenance having women choose their method of contraception, independent of their age and parity. In advising on the administration of the project, and in seeking to understand its results, we became very sensitized to the importance of "local conditions."

The Settings for the Study

From the earliest rounds of data collection, it became evident that there were interesting demographic and programmatic distinctions both within and between the study counties. We thus became increasingly interested in the politics, economics, and social organization of the system, including variations within our study sites. Although the formal INCRC project design took no account of the measurement of these phenomena, our field visits and field notes came to concentrate heavily on gleaning "side information" about local process, to better understand the data that were being collected by the INCRC project, and that were dominated by effects not attributable to the experimental interventions.

Huasheng is the closest county to Beijing, at about two- to three-hours' drive. Its per capita (p.c.) income in 1999 was 3,200 yuan, up from 570 yuan at the outset of the project in 1991. Huasheng is designated as a semimountainous county with a significant proportion of Man ethnic minority. This county was home to Wang Guofan, whose agricultural cooperative was singled out for praise by Mao Zedong in the early 1950s, and whose political connections made Huasheng a model county (Friedman, Pickowicz, and Selden 1991). Huasheng has experienced a certain amount of social and economic success, perhaps related to its connections, but there is also a sense in which local cadres may have been resting on their laurels. Year after year during the 1990s, Huasheng made no progress in industrial growth and city development while changes in the other project counties were much more evident.[9] A large proportion of women were having second births without meeting the policy requirements. How could this be? When we put this question to officials—local, municipal, or national—the stock answers are that minority populations are entitled to a second child, as are populations in mountainous areas, where life is hard. Indeed, these are principles enshrined in the national policy (e.g., Blayo 1997). In Huasheng, however, the Man minority is concentrated in only one of the six sample townships, and its villages all lie on a plain surrounded by mountains (hence the *semi*mountainous designation). We suspect that the two-child policy in Huasheng exists simply because of its favorable political connections.

Prior to the INCRC intervention, in Huasheng the probability of IUD removal and expulsion was the highest among all four counties (Tu 1995), and the probability of a pregnancy being aborted the lowest, regardless of the sex of the first birth (Tu and Smith 1995). Township cadres showed leniency and flexibility in implementing family planning rules and regulations, which made it easier for local women to remove themselves from the pervasive administrative scrutiny of their reproductive lives (Qian 1992). Penalties for out-of-plan births represented one portion of the family planning budget, and cadres in Huasheng acknowledged the financial benefits they gain from their collection (Qian 1997).

Pangxie is another two hours past Huasheng, on the coast. It has been a model county for family planning work since the *wan-xi-shao* campaign in the early 1970s. The county remains the best-performing county in Hebei province as regards family planning and provides a model for the rest of the province. Pangxie's economy still relies primarily on agricultural products. The p.c. income of Pangxie is reported as 3,560 yuan in 1999, up from 606 in 1991.[10] Maintaining the title of model county in family planning was a top priority at every administrative level. It led to an avidness in enforcement of regulations. Local authorities were quite reluctant to allow one-daughter families to have a second birth and were very strict with spacing and other requirements. The probability of IUD removal was low and the probability of abortion was high. Pangxie was the only one of the four counties to report normal sex ratios in the Baseline Survey for the period 1980 to 1991 (Smith and Tian 1993).

In spite of their formal "success" in family planning work in Pangxie, the morale of family planning workers was not high. Turnover of personnel was much higher than in the other three counties. Family planning cadres in all of Pangxie's study townships complained about their tight budget. Some even acknowledged they would rather see more out-of-plan births, as a way to raise revenue through fines (Qian 1994).

Ciqixian and Shanshui are two representative counties of Shandong, a province renowned for its speed in adjusting to central family planning directives and for the careful, effective management of its family planning program. The SFPC evidently chose Shandong over Hebei as the showcase for the INCRC project. The two Shandong counties received numerous visits from interested parties from other provinces and abroad. A national meeting on informed contraceptive choice was organized in the provincial capital, Jinan, and key officers of the state and various provincial Family Planning Commissions were invited to witness the INCRC project's implementation in selected Ciqixian and Shanshui townships. All levels of the Shandong's government and family planning hierarchy showed high administrative commitment to the INCRC project, and the pressure on county and township family planning cadres to implement the project "correctly" was great. For example, the speeches delivered by provincial and Zibo city government and family planning officials at the enumerators' training workshop for the Follow-Up Survey were dense with admonitions not to "disappoint the leaders' expectations for this project" (Merli 1994).

Ciqixian is two hours away from Jinan, the capital of Shandong province. It is the most urban and industrialized of the four counties.[11] In 2000, the p.c. income of its population was 3,328 yuan, up from 969 in 1991. Women in Ciqixian are better educated than women in other counties. Many of them work in nonagricultural jobs. Ciqixian's main industrial product is porcelain, which has made a good number of villages in the study quite prosperous.

Shanshui borders Ciqixian to the south; it is the most mountainous and rural county. National policy permits women living in mountainous areas to have two children regardless of the sex of the first child, yet in Shanshui the One-Son-Two-Child policy prevails. This is in line with the management of family planning in Shandong province, which has a history of particularly strict policy enforcement. Formerly classified as one of the nation's "poverty" counties *(pinkun xian)*, over the past few years Shanshui has experienced some economic growth and has become, in the words of local officials, a county of self-reliance *(zili gengsheng)*. Its p.c. income in 2000 was 2,324 yuan, up from 499 in 1991. Although proud of their achievements, local officials routinely inform foreign visitors (in the presence of national and provincial officials) of the county's backwardness, perhaps because being a "poor county" puts them in line for provincial subventions.

The households they selected for our visits all displayed the same composition—a mother with two children, one older daughter and a toddler son, and Norplant implanted—a likely indication of Shanshui officials' perceptions of the tastes and preferences of their Western interlocutors in matters of reproduction and contraceptive use.

Net of all other variables, Shanshui women were twice as likely prior to 1992 to have a second birth than were their Ciqixian counterparts, although the proportion of them progressing to a second birth was only 13 percent (Qian 1997). The Norplant termination rate during the study was the lowest of all counties, despite a comparatively high incidence of side effects (Zenger, Qiu, and Fang 1995). Was this an indication of difficult access to services in the most mountainous of the four counties? In spite of the remote location of some villages relative to the township family planning stations, our conversations with Shanshui county officials suggested a different explanation. In Shanshui, their "success" with Norplant is often measured against the comparatively lower number of acceptors in Ciqixian. In the minds of Shanshui officials, the concept of "free choice" is epitomized by the high number of Norplant acceptors among Shanshui women. The households they selected for our visits all displayed the same composition—a mother with two children, one older daughter and a toddler son, and Norplant implanted—a likely indication of Shanshui officials' perceptions of the tastes and preferences of their Western interlocutors in matters of reproduction and contraceptive use.

The access of the Western-based members of the investigative team to the four counties was facilitated by the INCRC project and the good relationship that was established with the SFPC during the course of the project. The purposes of our visits were, variously, to meet local officials and select study sites, to monitor the general course of the research, to participate in training of interviewers during the preparation of two surveys conducted for the project, to interview family planning workers and their clients, to set up a computerized record-keeping system, to maintain a demographic and contraceptive surveillance system, to examine related health system records, and to observe and evaluate the extent to which the innovations in family planning and reproductive health introduced by the INCRC project have been maintained as a functioning policy and have been extended beyond the project sites. We were, for better or worse, participant observers of the social organization of the system in these counties and the changes that it went through during the 1990s. It is difficult to imagine having similar access to these sites, especially during the first years of the project, when some of the areas were officially closed to Westerners, were we not technical advisers on "the experiment."

Data Collection

The INCRC project had three official data collection components. The first was a pair of linked sample surveys. The Baseline Survey was conducted in December 1991 and January 1992, prior to the implementation of new policies in the sixteen treatment townships (Tu et al. 1992; Tu and Hereward 1992). Within each of the twenty-four study townships, eight villages were selected at random; within each village, 50 married women under the age of thirty-five were randomly selected (all such women if there were 50 or fewer available), leading to a sample size of 8,603, uniformly distributed across the four counties. The Follow-Up Survey was conducted in July 1994 (Tu and Hereward 1994). Five villages were samples from each township, including three villages that had participated in the Baseline Survey. All married women ages thirty-eight and under were interviewed, unless the number of such women exceeded 150, in which case (approximately) 150 were sampled. The Follow-Up Survey yielded 11,759 interviews, including 2,735 women who had been interviewed in the Baseline Survey. For technical details, including sampling weights, see Smith (1999).

The second was the demographic and contraceptive surveillance system, or the Card System (Smith et al. 1997). Beginning in spring 1992, all twenty-four study townships set up a system with one card for each married woman of reproductive age. On this card was recorded the woman's date of birth, her parity, the number of children surviving, the date of birth of her youngest child, and her current contraceptive use. From that point forward, family planning workers entered subsequent pregnancies, their outcome, and any changes to contraceptive use, including the reason for method change or discontinuation. Beginning in 1994, the Card System records were computerized: each township was provided with a computer and a database program that simulated the physical card. The cards (and their computer representation) thus constituted an ongoing event history.

The third was a set of clinical records that maintain information, at regular intervals, on acceptors of the INCRC's new contraceptive methods (TCu380A and Norplant). This too was an ongoing data collection system (Zenger, Qiu, and Fang 1995; Tu et al. 1997).

Over the implementation of the project, we came to understand that our presence in the counties, and the emphasis on data quality, had the unanticipated effect of sensitizing those responsible for recording events to the problematic nature of such data. Attempts to rectify the problems did not help in the way that might be anticipated in a "normal" setting. The clearest case of this is provided by an analysis of abortions recorded by the Card System in Shanshui between 1992 and 1994 (Smith et al. 1997). The ratio of abortions to live births in the Card System dropped precipitously between 1992 and 1993, and abortions all but vanished in 1994. After excluding alternative hypotheses, we (Smith et al. 1997) argued that the drop-off in recorded abortions was directly attributable to a 1993 visit by a "human rights inspection team" to the four counties. The team questioned county and township family planning cadres at great length about coercive abortion practices. It was our direct observation in visits to Shanshui, following the visit of the inspection team, that the SFPC and local cadres were highly sensitized to the low impression now prevalent in the United States of abortion as a means of family planning.

Considerations in the Study's Experimental Design

Results from the INCRC project were reported at project-sponsored international conferences in Honolulu (1993), Seattle (1996), and Beijing (1998), not to mention various Chinese conferences in Jinan and elsewhere, plus the occasional meetings of the Population Association of American and the International Union for the Scientific Study of Population. A number of published papers feature results from the project, but only a couple—on receptivity to Norplant (Zenger, Qiu, and Fang 1995; Tu et al. 1998)—are specifically related to the "treatments" adumbrated in Table 1. Most (Smith 1994; Tu 1995; Tu and Smith 1995; Smith et al. 1997; Qian 1997; Merli 1998; Merli and Raftery 2000; Merli and Smith 2002) do not, and none take any real account of the experimental design. Yet the project is generally viewed as a success in China (Tu et al. 1998). What is going on here?

The answer, in experimental terms, is that the treatments were weak and ill defined, many investigators did not understand the experiment as designed, contamination was rife, and "history" (Campbell and Stanley 1963) intervened. It would be too strong to say that the experimental design of the INCRC project was a sham. It was not. I designed the study with the intent of comparing treatment and control townships, and the experimental aspects of the study were executed in good faith on all sides. The project was, however, infected from the start with a certain naïveté, a kind of collective myopia born of individual understandings and certitudes.

When I was asked in late 1989 to design a study that could be executed by the SFPC, I was inheriting a project that had been in gestation for several years between officials of the Rockefeller Foundation, their Western advisers, and representatives of the Chinese family planning establishment. The agenda of this last group was variously (1) to acquire hard currency funding from the West; (2) to convince the West that the one child policy was not being enforced in as draconian a manner as claimed, and that things were "loosening up," not "tightening up" (Zeng 1989); (3) to see whether better contraceptives would make the administration of

It was our direct observation in visits to Shanshui, following the visit of the inspection team, that the SFPC [State Family Planning Commission] and local cadres were highly sensitized to the low impression now prevalent in the United States of abortion as a means of family planning.

the family planning policy easier; (4) to improve the reproductive and health lives of Chinese women; and (5) to convince themselves (and state leadership) that ameliorative relaxations of strict policies would not foster mass resistance to the overall fertility-limiting goals of the regime. The donors and their advisers were especially keen on (4), did not need to be convinced of (2) (although it turned out not to be true), were used to (1), confused (3) with (4), and were anxious to help with (5), although they expected the relaxations (and "choice") would include the choice as to whether to use contraceptives—something that, a dozen years later, has not yet occurred in China (Merli, Qian, and Smith 2004; Winckler 2002). A further goal of some of the advisers—myself included—was to learn just what was going on with the Chinese family planning program. How did it work "on the ground" (e.g., Smith et al. 1996)?

At the point at which I became involved, plans for the project had been put on a temporary and embarrassing hold, a legacy of the events at Tiananmen Square earlier that year, which were a pointed indication that the reforms that were occurring in China during the 1980s had their limits. The plans for the SFPC/Rockefeller study, such as they existed, were on one hand those of a demonstration project (train these people better, give them some better contraceptives, pay more attention to what the women want, and watch how much better things will be) and a clinical experiment (randomly assign some women to receive the Norplant and others to serve as controls). The divide in perspective was not so much between Chinese and Westerners, but between those trained in a biomedical tradition, who tended to understand things in terms of a clinical experiment, and "policy people," who were more amenable to the idea of a demonstration project.

I embraced the experimental perspective but directed it away from the clinical model. First, the clinical efficacy of the Norplant was well documented. The real question was, How does it work in the field? Second, the idea of assigning women to contraceptives—something that turns out to have been standard prior to the inception of the INCRC project (Tu 1995), albeit at the behest of the state, and not a table of random numbers—was antithetical to the idea of "choice." I proposed instead that randomization take place at a higher level so that comparisons might focus on the difference between areas subject to the reforms proposed by the SFPC (including "choice," whatever that turned out to mean) and those that were left under the old system.

In concept, the design of the INCRC study was probably not a bad one. It was based on the distinction between *the unit of experimentation* and *the unit of analysis:*

> There is an intimate link between the unit of randomization in an experiment and the unit of analysis. Suppose one assigns programs to schools but one measures outcomes on students. What does the randomization justify as the level of analysis for internal variability? The usual social science and educational research textbooks are often silent on this issue.
>
> If one carries out the assignment of treatments at the level of schools, then that is the level that can be justified for causal analysis. To analyze the results at the student level is to introduce a new, nonrandomized level into the study. This means that if one does an experiment with 10 schools organized into 2 districts of 5 each and if one randomly assigns Program X to District 1 and Program Y to District 2, then there are just 2 observations at the level of assignment even though there were thousands of students participating in the study.
>
> The implications of these remarks are twofold. First, it is advisable to use randomization at the level at which units are most naturally manipulated. Second, when the unit of observation is "lower" than the unit of randomization or assignment of treatment, then for many purposes the data need to be aggregated in some appropriate fashion to provide a measure that can be analyzed at the level of assignment. (Meyer and Fienberg 1992, 21)

There was, however, a subtle difference between the INCRC design and the "classic" school-based assignment of treatments adumbrated by Meyer and Fienberg (1992). A new curriculum (for example) is something that is difficult to implement on a student-by-student basis. The "delivery device" is the teacher (or classroom); each unit of observation (student) within a classroom is supposed to be receiving the same treatment. In the INCRC study, the township level is supposed to provide a uniform policy, in the form of better-trained service personnel, a wider range of contraceptives, and choice among contraceptives. With respect to the last in particular—contraceptive method—the INCRC project is essentially an *encouragement design* (Holland 1988), with the actual contraceptive used by an individual being something that is determined (at least in part) by that individual; that is, it is not subject to randomization at either the individual or aggregated (township) level. Unlike the typical individual-level encouragement design, the INCRC project randomizes the treatment at the lowest level that a policy could conceivably be implemented. The "interference" (Rubin 1986) and interdependence in treatment assignment that makes causal inference so difficult at the micro (individual) level is simply a datum—an observational outcome—when randomization of policies (or "encouragements") takes place at a higher level (Smith 2003).

Some Experimental Results

Whatever might or might not have changed by dint of the weak INCRC interventions was swamped by the programmatic changes taking place across the entire system. To see this, consider the trends in the ratio of abortions to births in the project areas, as shown in Figure 2.[12] The INCRC project was supposed to cut down on the number of abortions. Better contraceptives were supposed to result in less contraceptive failure, although—as I have observed earlier—contraceptive failure can be a euphemism for pregnancies outside the plan: the vast majority of abortions that took place in the study areas during the 1980s could be attributed to violation of regulations regarding the spacing of children, the number of children, or the age of the mother (Tu and Smith 1995).

The control and treatment points and lines trace a rise in the ratio of abortions to births from the mid-1980s through 1991, that is, prior to the INCRC intervention. The y-axis of this figure is scaled logarithmically, so a constant slope can be read as a constant rate of increase. These data are based on retrospective pregnancy histories, as obtained in December 1991 during the Baseline Survey. There is a natural tendency to forget unpleasant events, such as abortions, that increases with duration from the event (Tu 1997). This could account for the decline in these ratios moving backward in time from 1991, except that we also know in retrospect that 1991 was a peak in tightening up on fertility via abortion campaigns (e.g., Winckler 2002, 385; and Figure 3).[13]

Although the trend in this period was the same, abortion to birth ratios were uniformly lower in the treatment townships. These are measurements of events taking place *before* the INCRC interventions. This apparent incomplete randomization is a result of the experimental design and the sampling plan. Each ratio has as a denominator of more than one thousand births, divided approximately between treatments and townships in the proportion 2:1. These births (and the abortions in the numerator) are spread across sixteen treatment townships and eight control townships. Each township is represented in the sample by eight villages. Variances for each annual difference between treatment and control townships thus have two

FIGURE 2
ABORTION-TO-BIRTH RATIOS FOR TREATMENT AND CONTROL AREAS IN
THE FOUR COUNTIES OF THE INTRODUCING NEW CONTRACEPTIVES IN
RURAL CHINA (INCRC) STUDY, 1983-1996

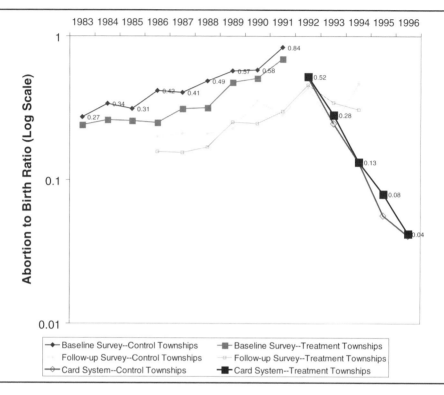

components: (1) differences between townships within treatment types, with 15
and 7 degrees of freedom, respectively; and (2) sampling variability in the estimate
of each township ratio, exacerbated by clustering (by village), which tends to inflate
design effects. In addition, each estimated variance for an annual difference is
(positively) correlated with all others since it is the same villages (if not the same
women) making the reports. The net effect is that even though the sample size at
the level of the *unit of observation* is fairly large, differences between treatment
and control townships of the magnitude of those found in Figure 2, from the Baseline Survey, are well within the margin of error accruing to randomization and
sampling.

In the Card System, there is no sampling error—all demographic events are
supposed to be recorded within the study townships. Either way, there is no ambiguity in Figure 2: there were no differences once the INCRC project began (in
1992); the treatment and control lines and points are all but indistinguishable.

FIGURE 3
ABORTION-TO-BIRTH RATIOS, CHINA, 1971-1997

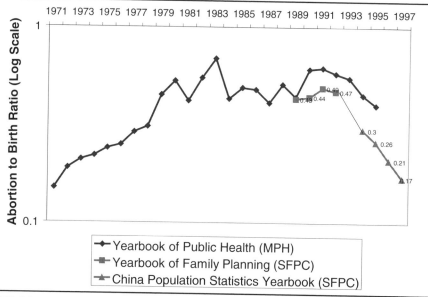

NOTE: MPH = Ministry of Public Health; SFPC = State Family Planning Commission.

There was a remarkable decline in the ratio of abortions to births, which were halved each year for four successive years. At the 1998 Beijing "wrap-up" conference for the project, Chinese officials touted this decline in abortions as an indicator of the project's success. Here, the experimental design was of some value since a comparison of treatment and control townships, as per Figure 2, quickly puts to lie such an attribution. I say "of some value" because the same point could have been made were the INCRC a demonstration project alone, and from a strictly observational viewpoint. Figure 4 shows official SFPC abortion to birth ratios for the same period in all of Hebei and Shandong, where it turns out that (reported) abortions were declining at a much faster rate than elsewhere in China. Although the four INCRC study counties were in no sense a random sample of all Hebei and Shandong counties (not to mention the weakness of random sampling with $n = 2$ or $n = 4$, as discussed previously), the decline in abortion rates in the INCRC study areas turns out to have mirrored closely those reported by the SFPC for both provinces—especially Hebei. This "side evidence" is of value to the experimental data since it suggests that the causes of the decline are not unique to the INCRC project.[14]

Prior to the inception of the INCRC study, women in the project counties were on a fairly strict regime regarding when they could have a child (Tu and Smith 1995) and what they should be doing about it (by way of contraception) in the interim (Tu 1995). Women were supposed to wait until ages twenty-three or

FIGURE 4
ABORTION-TO-BIRTH RATIOS, 1989-1997, HEBEI, SHANDONG, AND REST OF
CHINA (STATE FAMILY PLANNING COMMISSION [SFPC] STATISTICS)

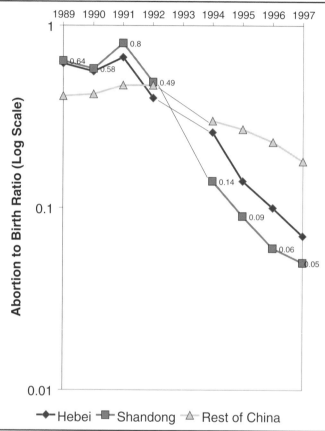

twenty-four to marry. At this point, they were allowed to have a first child, and they typically did so with alacrity (Merli and Raftery 2000). If the child were a boy, that was supposed to be it, except in Huasheng, where a second child was permitted regardless of the sex of the first child. If the child were a girl (or in Huasheng), a second child was permitted, but only after a delay of three or four years (and only if the woman were of sufficient age). Spacing between first and second children typically resulted from use of an IUD. After a second child, or after a first boy in most counties, women might use an IUD. But this raised the possibility of further contraceptive "failure." Tubal ligation—female sterilization—was preferable. It was cheaper and, from the standpoint of the family planning cadres, easier to manage.

Whether sterilization was equally desirable from the standpoint of rural women was something that could be examined from the standpoint of the experimental design of the INCRC. One of the key differences between treatment and control townships was the availability of the Norplant in the former. Norplant is long-acting and, unlike an IUD, not removable by the user (or an amateur medical technician). It was conceivable that women might prefer Norplant in lieu of sterilization since it did keep their reproductive futures "open" longer, and who knew when the opportunity might arise to have another child? And because Norplant took less month-to-month monitoring than did an IUD, the local family planning authorities might be more amenable to its use—a likely factor in the acceptability of Norplant in these rural setting, the choice of contraceptives afforded to women in the treatment townships notwithstanding.

Overall, there was a definite substitution effect of Norplant (or perhaps other methods) for sterilization. This can be seen by tracking differences in rates of sterilization between treatment and control townships. These can be summarized by comparing life table functions—specifically, Kaplan-Meier estimates of the cumulative proportion of women sterilized by age. (These are calculated from Card System data on age at sterilization, with women who were not sterilized by the end of the INCRC project [December 1996] constituting censored observations.) Figure 5 summarizes the differences across all study sites. The slope of the cumulative density function is steepest in the age range thirty to thirty-five, which corresponds to the years following a typical second birth. The curve for the treatment townships can be differentiated from that for the control townships from the very beginning of this interval, and the eventual difference in the proportion of women sterilized in a lifetime is projected to be around 10 percent, or the difference between roughly 60 percent (old system) and 50 percent (choice plus Norplant).

When randomized experimentation was invented, practitioners were advised to be sensitive to interactions (Fisher 1935/1971, 94). Attention to interactions in experiments involving social interventions has tended to be slight, in spite of the fact that—or, perhaps, *because*—interaction effects are not mitigated by random assignment (Smith 1990, sec. 2.2). Interactions need to be specified, on theoretical grounds. One of the hallmarks of the INCRC project was the recognition that population and family planning processes varied widely across study counties as a function of latent differences in the organization, motivation, and political centrality of the respective county family planning administrations. This is also evident in the effects of the INCRC initiatives on sterilization. The data in Figure 5 are an amalgam of the unique experiences of four different counties; see Figure 6 for Hebei and Figure 7 for Shandong. In Huasheng, which permits a second birth regardless of the sex of the first child, sterilization rates are quite high, reaching more than 75 percent in both control and treatment townships. In Pangxie, the proportion sterilized is closer to 50 percent, and there is more differentiation between control and treatment townships. General levels of sterilization in the two Shandong counties, Ciqixian and Shanshui, are similar to those in Pangxie. The interesting finding in Shandong is that the INCRC project led to a very substantial decline in sterilization in Ciqixian but had no effect in Shanshui. See Zenger, Qui, and Fang (1995) and Tu et al. (1997) for discussions of differences in adoption of Norplant in these counties.

FIGURE 5
KAPLAN-MEIER ESTIMATES OF CUMULATIVE PROPORTIONS STERILIZED,
BY AGE: TREATMENT VERSUS CONTROL TOWNSHIPS

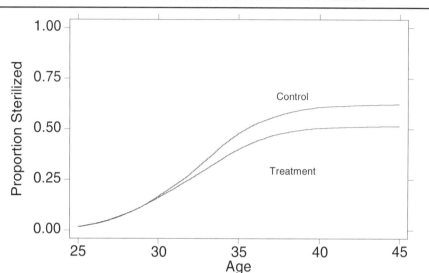

When the INCRC data are examined county by county, the benefits of randomization are substantially attenuated. Each county-specific pair of curves in Figures 6 and 7 has the same components of variance discussed in conjunction with the abortion-to-birth ratio data of Figure 2, except that the Card System is a virtual census of events, so stochastic variation within treatment (or control) townships is essentially nonexistent, absent some appeal to a universal physical process generating sterilizations from some superpopulation. As for the variation *between* treatment and control townships within a county, this is founded on two control townships and four treatment townships. With so few degrees of freedom, randomization does not afford much statistical power.[15] We are back at something like comparative case studies.

Conclusion

The literature on treatment effects investigates a class of interventions with partial coverage, so there is a "treatment" and "control" group. It is not helpful in evaluating interventions that apply universally within an economy unless there are data on separate economies experiencing different interventions and the economies are segregated from each other. . . .

The treatment effect literature approaches the problem of policy evaluation in the same way that biostatisticians approach the problem of evaluating a drug. Outcomes of persons exposed to a policy are compared to outcomes of those who are not. The analogy is

FIGURE 6
KAPLAN-MEIER ESTIMATES OF PROPORTION STERILIZED, BY AGE: HEBEI PROVINCE

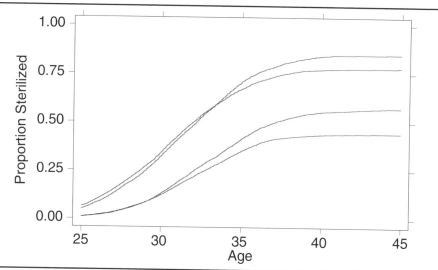

NOTE: Top two lines are Huasheng. Bottom two lines are Pangxie. Within each line pair, topmost line is for the control townships.

FIGURE 7
KAPLAN-MEIER ESTIMATES OF PROPORTION STERILIZED, BY AGE: SHANDONG PROVINCE

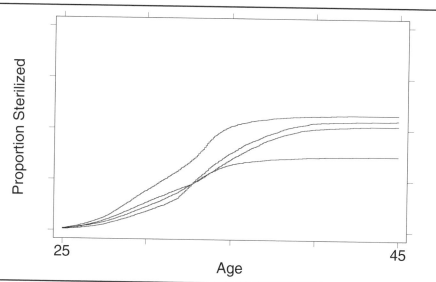

NOTE: Top and bottom lines are Ciqixian. Middle two lines are Shanshui. Within each line pair, topmost line is for the control townships.

more than a little strained in the context of evaluating many social policies because in a modern economy outcomes of persons are linked through markets and other forms of social interaction. This gives rise to the distinction between those who are "directly" affected and those only "indirectly" affected. (Heckman 2001, 713)

Heckman (2001) is dead on target in his criticisms of standard experimental design—random assignment of individual subjects to treatments—as a way of understanding the impact of policy interventions.[16] He is far from sanguine about the possibility of adapting the treatment model to experimentation (via randomization) at the level at which policy is actually implemented. The INCRC project was an attempt to examine the effects of a policy shift by manipulation of aggregated subjects—specifically, rural Chinese townships. Hindsight suggests that even at this level there is the possibility of serious interference between units—contamination—and I have already discoursed at length about the relative weakness of the policy intervention, especially as measured against a host of external factors influencing demographic change in these areas. There is also the problem of incomplete randomization as a function of the small number of experimental units, a problem that is exacerbated when treatment effects interact with population characteristics. So, it would be folly to argue that the INCRC study—although quite successful as a demonstration project—was a compelling counterexemplar to Heckman's skepticism regarding randomization at the level at which policy is being implemented. Future efforts in this direction will have to build constructively on the mistakes of the past.

Notes

1. One of the questions that arises in looking at data from the Introducing New Contraceptives in Rural China (INCRC) project is the extent to which there are unofficial accommodations to pressures for additional children.

2. In a country the size of China, there are bound to be exceptions to any organizational scheme, and thus the possibility of political-semantic confusion. For example, during the course of the INCRC project, one of our counties was proud to become a "city," or a "city county." This new status, however, did not remove it from the administrative apparatus of the Tangshan "municipality." For most purposes, however, it suffices to keep in mind the hierarchy that runs from nation to province to municipality to county to township to village.

3. Names of geographic entities at the county level and below are pseudonyms.

4. For economy of expression, I refer to the project's four counties, although one of them is, technically, a district.

5. Prior to the designation of townships as treatment or control, the six randomly selected townships were grouped geographically into blocks of three so that, for example, the control townships would not both be on one side of a county opposite the treatment townships.

6. But see "Observations and Emendations" corresponding to "better training of family planning workers" in Table 1.

7. China has, to an order of magnitude, the same number of "counties" as the United States of America, so a useful thought experiment is how four counties might be chosen to reflect the United States.

8. Visits to Shandong routinely included a stop in Jinan to meet with provincial-level officials, some of whom came along on visits to the counties or, when there was no stop in Jinan, were present beforehand in Zibo City. In Hebei, provincial authorities were most conspicuous in their absence. The reason for this may have be geographic: the capital of Hebei, Shijiazhuang, is southeast of Beijing and nowhere near the INCRC study sites. In the event, the inattention of the Hebei provincial State Family Planning Commission (SFPC)

to the project was mirrored in a palpable lack of enthusiasm at the municipal and county levels, at least as compared with Shandong.

   9. This did not get in the way of political advancement: Early in the decade, Huasheng's designation was upgraded from county *(xian)* to municipality *(shi)*, the absence of any evident ecological change differentiating Huasheng from other rural counties notwithstanding.

   10. I write "reported" because this would make Pangxie the county with the highest income among the four that were studied, and this is unlikely. Ciqixian is almost certainly better off economically; Huasheng, too. These income statistics evince a spurious precision and are better taken as (at best) order of magnitude estimates.

   11. Ciqixian is actually a district of Zibo city, but with the majority of its population (87 percent) classified as rural.

   12. Abortion-to-birth ratios are common demographic indicators of the extent of abortions. They are essentially a monotonic, nonlinear function of the probability that a given pregnancy is aborted.

   13. A further complication is that we discovered a tendency to underreport all kinds of pregnancies (Smith 1994), including births (Merli 1998; Merli and Raftery 2000). The underreporting of abortions was especially acute in the Follow-Up Survey, data from which appear as the light lines in Figure 2.

   14. Why did abortion decline? This is a question that I have not been able to answer to my satisfaction. One hypothesis is that the decline is real. But the overall number of births has not gone up. Thus, most of the decline in abortions is a decline in the number of pregnancies outside of the family planning policy. Why has this happened? Is it that there is less demand for children? There is slight evidence in favor of this (Merli and Smith 2002). Or have families given up trying to beat the system? The other hypothesis is that as the Chinese government—in particular, the SFPC—cottoned to the rising displeasure with abortions in the West, abortions began to disappear from the statistical system.

   15. Note departures in the curves for Huasheng and Shanshui prior to age thirty, which is typical of the kind of "pretest" imbalance that occurs when randomization is incomplete.

   16. My praise is superfluous. The remarks I have quoted come from his acceptance address upon receipt of the Nobel Prize in Economics.

References

Aird, John S. 1986. Coercion in family planning: Causes, methods, and consequences. In *China's economy looks toward the year 2000: The four modernizations*, vol. I, 184-221, Joint Economic Committee, Congress of the United States. Washington, DC: Government Printing Office.

Blayo, Yves. 1997. *Des politiques démographiques en Chine*. Paris: Presses Universitaires de France, Institut Nationale d'Études Démographiques.

Campbell, Donald T., and Julian C. Stanley. 1963. *Experimental and quasi-experimental designs for research*. Chicago: Rand McNally College Publishing Company.

Fisher, R. A. 1935/1971. *The design of experiments*. 9th ed. New York: Hafner.

Friedman, Edward, Paul G. Pickowicz, and Mark Selden. 1991. *Chinese village, socialist state*. New Haven, CT: Yale University Press.

Goodkind, Daniel. 1996. On substituting sex preference strategies in East Asia: Does prenatal sex selection reduce postnatal discrimination? *Population and Development Review* 22 (1): 111-25.

Hardee-Cleaveland, Karen, and Judith Banister. 1988. Fertility policy and implementation in China, 1986-1988. *Population and Development Review* 14 (2): 245-86.

Heckman, James J. 2001. Micro data, heterogeneity, and the evaluation of public policy: Nobel lecture. *Journal of Political Economy* 109 (4): 673-748.

Holland, Paul W. 1988. Causal inference, path analysis, and recursive structural equation models. In *Sociological methodology 1988*, ed. Clifford C. Clogg, 449-84. Washington, DC: American Sociological Association.

Hua Guofeng. 1980. Hua Guofeng on the promotion of family planning in China. *Population and Development Review* 6 (4): 685.

Kaufman, Joan, Zhang Zhirong, Qiao Xinjian, and Zhang Yang. 1989. Family planning policy and practice in rural China. *Population and Development Review* 15 (4): 707-29.

Kish, Leslie. 1987. *Statistical design for research*. New York: John Wiley.

Merli, M. Giovanna. 1994. *Report on a field visit to rural China, 9-30 July 1994*. Philadelphia: Population Studies Center, University of Pennsylvania.

———. 1998. Underreporting of births and infant deaths in rural China. Evidence from one county of northern China. *China Quarterly* 155:637-55.

Merli, M. Giovanna, Zhenchao Qian, and Herbert L. Smith. 2004. Adaptation of a political bureaucracy to economic and institutional change under socialism: The Chinese state family planning system. *Politics and Society* 31 (2): 231-56.

Merli, M. Giovanna, and Adrian Raftery. 2000. Are births underreported in rural China? Manipulation of statistical records in response to China's population policies. *Demography* 37 (1): 109-26.

Merli, M. Giovanna, and Herbert L. Smith. 2002. Has the Chinese family planning program been successful in changing fertility preferences? Evidence from linked records in four counties in rural northern China. *Demography* 39 (3): 557-72.

Meyer, Michael M., and Stephen E. Fienberg. 1992. *Assessing evaluation studies: The case of bilingual education strategies*. Panel to Review Evaluation Studies of Bilingual Education, Committee on National Statistics, Committee on Behavioral and Social Sciences and Education, National Research Council. Washington, DC: National Academy Press.

Park, Chai Bin, and Cho Nam-Hoon. 1995. Consequences of son preference in a low fertility society: Imbalance of the sex ratio at birth in Korea. *Population and Development Review* 21 (1): 59-84.

Qian, Zhenchao. 1992. *Report of field research in rural China*. Philadelphia: Population Studies Center, University of Pennsylvania.

———. 1994. *Revisiting [Huasheng] and [Pangxie]*. Philadelphia: Population Studies Center, University of Pennsylvania.

———. 1997. Progression to second birth in China: A study of four rural counties. *Population Studies* 51 (2): 221-28.

Rubin, Donald B. 1986. Comment: Which ifs have causal answers. *Journal of the American Statistical Association* 81 (396): 961-62.

Smith, Herbert L. 1990. Specification problems in experimental and nonexperimental social research. In *Sociological methodology 1990*, ed. Clifford C. Clogg, 59-91. Oxford: Basil Blackwell.

———. 1994. Nonreporting of births or nonreporting of pregnancies? Some evidence from four rural counties in north China. *Demography* 31 (3): 481-86.

———. 1999. *Notes on the design of the INCRC surveys*. Philadelphia: Population Studies Center, University of Pennsylvania.

———. 2003. Some thoughts on causation as it relates to demography and population studies. *Population and Development Review* 29 (3): 459-69.

Smith, Herbert L., M. Giovanna Merli, Mark Hereward, and Zhenchao Qian. 1996. Demographic research in rural China: Field observations from work in four counties in north China. Paper presented at the annual meeting of the Population Association of America, May, in New Orleans, LA.

Smith, Herbert L. and Linzhu Tian. 1993. Variations in sex ratios for first births in four counties: Where does the variation begin? Paper presented at the Conference on Introducing New Contraceptives in Rural China, June, in Honolulu, HI.

Smith, Herbert L., Tu Ping, M. Giovanna Merli, and Mark Hereward. 1997. Implementation of a demographic and contraceptive surveillance system in four counties in north China. *Population Research and Policy Review* 16:289-314.

Tu Ping. 1993. Contraceptive use patterns among young rural women in four counties of China. Paper presented at the First International Conference on Introducing New Contraceptives in Rural China, June, in Honolulu, HI.

———. 1995. IUD discontinuation patterns and correlates in four counties in north China. *Studies in Family Planning* 26 (3): 169-79.

———. 1997. *The inconsistency of retrospective report of pregnancies in four counties in north China*. Beijing: Institute of Population Research, Peking University.

Tu Ping, and Mark Hereward. 1992. *The Baseline Survey for the Project on Introducing New Contraceptives in Rural China. Part II. Tabulations of the data*. Beijing: State Family Planning Commission.

————. 1994. *The Follow-Up Survey for the Project on Introducing New Contraceptives with Enhanced Services in Rural China*. Beijing: State Family Planning Commission.

Tu Ping, Mark Hereward, Qiu Shuhua, and Ni Jiajun. 1992. *The Baseline Survey for the Project on Introducing New Contraceptives in Rural China. Part I. Preliminary findings of the survey*. Beijing: State Family Planning Commission.

Tu Ping, Qiu Shuhua, Fang Huimin, and Herbert L. Smith. 1997. Acceptance, efficacy, and side effects of Norplant implants in four counties in north China. *Studies in Family Planning* 28 (2): 122-31.

Tu Ping, Qiu Shuhua, Ni Jiajun, and Fang Huimin. 1998. A study on the introduction of new contraceptives with enhanced services in rural China. *Population Research* 4:6-14 (in Chinese).

Tu Ping, and Herbert L. Smith. 1995. Determinants of induced abortion and their policy implications in four counties in north China. *Studies in Family Planning* 26 (5): 278-86.

Wang Feng. 1996. A decade of the one-child family: Achievements and implications. In *China: The many facets of demographic change*, ed. Alice Goldstein and Wang Feng, 97-120. Boulder, CO: Westview.

Winckler, Edwin A. 2002. Chinese reproductive policy at the turn of the millennium: Dynamic stability. *Population and Development Review* 28 (3): 379-418.

Zeng Yi. 1989. Is the Chinese family planning program "tightening up?" *Population and Development Review* 15 (2): 333-37.

Zenger, Elizabeth, Qiu Shuhua, and Fang Huimin. 1995. Introduction of Norplant implants in four counties of rural China: A two-year evaluation. *Contraception* 52 (6): 349-55.

QUICK READ SYNOPSIS

Q R S

Place Randomized Trials:
Experimental Tests of Public Policy

Special Editor: ROBERT BORUCH
University of Pennsylvania

Volume 599, May 2005

Prepared by Herb Fayer (Consultant)

DOI: 10.1177/0002716205275835

Using Place-Based Random Assignment and Comparative Interrupted Time-Series Analysis to Evaluate the Jobs-Plus Employment Program for Public Housing Residents

Howard S. Bloom and James A. Riccio, MDRC

Background

This article describes a place-based research demonstration program to promote and sustain employment among residents in public housing.
- Because all residents were free to participate, it was not possible to randomly assign individuals to the program or a control group.
- Instead, the impact analysis is based on a design that selected matched groups of two or three public housing developments in each participating city and randomly assigned these developments to the program and or control group.
- In addition, an eleven-year comparative interrupted time-series analysis is being used to strengthen the design in order to provide credible estimates of program impacts.

NOTE: The program, Jobs-Plus Community Revitalization Initiative, is a place-based saturation-level employment demonstration tested in six cities. Instead of attempting to achieve a variety of community changes simultaneously, it focused on one goal: improving employment-related outcomes.

The Initiatives   With a goal of changing individuals and also of transforming the housing developments in which they live, the designers looked for guidance to a growing number of community change initiatives.
- Although their goals and tactics differ in details, these initiatives tend to share a common set of "community-building" principles that stress local control, collaborative decision making, resident empowerment, building on existing resident and community assets, and strengthening the capacity of residents and local institutions to promote and sustain community changes.
- The designers included a special component, which they called "community support for work," that helped residents to become sources of work promotion, encouragement, information, advice, and support to each other.
- They also saw the value of enlisting community stakeholders in designing, funding, and operating the project.
- This was a three-component intervention:
  - employment-related activities and support services,
  - financial incentives to work, and
  - community support for strengthening residents' work-focused social capital.

NOTE: Based on the above, Jobs-Plus was planned to be an unusually comprehensive and intensive community-focused employment intervention.

Saturation   Jobs-Plus is also distinctive because of its attempt to implement all program
Approach   components at saturation levels. It was targeted toward all working-age residents living in selected public housing developments.
- Thus, at the very least, all such residents were to be exposed to new work-promoting messages from staff and neighbors.
- The families who participated could benefit from the new financial incentives and a diverse array of services and supports.
- Saturation level is fundamental to the program's theory of change.
  - Targeting the intervention toward the entire working-age population was expected to produce a critical mass of residents whose experiences would generate momentum for change.
  - As these workers grew in number, it was expected that their visibility and influence would be enhanced.

Collaborative   The demonstrations' planners decided not to attempt to make detailed design
Process   choices centrally.
- They chose to leave these decisions to local collaboratives.
- Each collaborative was expected to include a broad group including the public housing authority, resident reps, the welfare department, and the workforce development system under the Workforce Investment Act—there were also lots of other agencies and providers.

Measuring   A central feature of the Jobs-Plus evaluation design is its focus on impacts from
Impacts   two different perspectives:
- Specific individual public housing residents—how did the program affect the future earnings, employment, and welfare receipt of its target individuals, even if they moved away?
- Specific public housing developments—How did the program affect levels of earnings, employment, and welfare receipt within its target developments, given that different people were living there at different times?

NOTE: The distinction between these two perspectives is key to any evaluation of a place-based initiative because sample members can move into or out of its target area.

Q
R
S

Program Impacts

In the field of employment and training research, random assignment experiments are now regarded as the best way to estimate program impacts.

- However, Jobs-Plus was not a program to which individuals or households could be assigned randomly—all able-bodied working-age adults in selected housing developments could participate.
- The random choice was thus among matched groups of two or three candidate housing developments.
- The remaining developments served as controls.
- Ethical concerns were handled by choosing groups to participate by lottery. Some residents who were interviewed noted that this was fairer than having the local public housing authority make the selection.

NOTE: It will be possible to estimate impacts by comparing outcomes of residents in the program group to those for residents in the control group. It will be possible to pool these estimates across sites by taking their average.

Statistical Power

Just how much statistical power is lost when moving from individual-level to group-level random assignment is an empirical issue that reflects three factors.

- The degree to which individual outcomes vary across groups.
- The number of groups being randomly assigned.
- The extent to which the variance of the outcome within and across groups is reduced by statistical controls for preexisting individual-level or group-level characteristics.

Lessons Learned

The experience with Jobs-Plus provided valuable lessons about using place-based random assignment to evaluate a comprehensive community initiative.

- It was possible to put such a research design into effect.
- It was necessary and possible to keep the research design in place for many years.
- A sustained and intensive effort was required to keep the research design in place and to maintain its integrity.
- When feasible, embedding a comparative interrupted time-series analysis within a place-based random assignment design can improve estimates of program impacts appreciably.

HIV Prevention among Women in Low-Income Housing Developments: Issues and Intervention Outcomes in a Place-Based Randomized Controlled Trial

Kathleen J. Sikkema, Yale University School of Medicine

Background

The scope and urgency of the HIV epidemic requires the development and evaluation of behavior change intervention strategies directed toward communities at risk for increased incidence of new infections.

- Large-scale trials that could reach greater numbers of people are needed.
- HIV prevention outcomes need behavior change supported by peer group norms consistent with risk reduction for best long-term impact.

- For better ways to intervene, we need to not only change the behavior of individuals but also to change social networks and communities to reinforce risk avoidance efforts of population members.

Diffusion

There has been a resurgence of social diffusion theory as a potential means to induce changes in communities and population member behavior.
- Mechanisms by which diffusion produces behavior change include
  - modeling and observational learning,
  - personal influence,
  - induction of beliefs that the innovative change brings benefits, and
  - creation of new social norms.
- How efficiently innovations diffuse depends on the nature of the innovation, characteristics of the early adopters, and characteristics of the population.
- For HIV prevention, the innovative trends include increased communication between sexual partners about AIDS and health concerns, adoption of safer practices, and deferral of sexual activity under risky circumstances when an individual does not want to have sex.

Modeling

Modeling processes influence behavioral learning and performance in a wide variety of areas.
- Peers who are liked, admired, and viewed as competent exert a strong influence on observer behavior.
- Perceptions about whether others in one's social group adopt, encourage, or support avoidance steps such as condom use can influence one's own sexual practices.

Gay Men Trials

The initial study focused on men in gay bars in sixteen small U.S. cities.
- Based on social diffusion theory, popular opinion leaders (POLs) were recruited.
- They were trained to model and endorse safer sexual behavior.
- There were eight trial groups and eight controls that received only educational information and condoms.
- After a year, risk behavior decreased significantly in the intervention cities.
NOTE: This study is believed to have been the first randomized, controlled trial of a community-level intervention to reduce HIV sexual risk behaviors.

Female Trials

The researchers extended the prevention models trials to poor, inner-city minority women living in low-income housing developments.
- Many women had low levels of risk sensitization, weak behavior change attitudes, limited use of condoms, and weak perceived norms concerning risk avoidance.
- The intervention needed to include AIDS preventive skills, attitudes, intentions, and efficacy beliefs and to provide normative and social supports— they also needed to identify social interaction and social influence patterns in the community.
- The intervention was done over a twelve-month period.
  - Opinion leaders helped develop the risk reduction workshop.
  - These women formed Women's Health Councils (WHCs) and invited women to participate in the two-month workshop.
  - Their goal was to reach all women tenants and to strengthen risk-avoidance behavior, attitudes, and normative perceptions about risk reduction.
- Community acceptance of the trials was enhanced by the offer of HIV risk reduction workshops to women in the control groups at the end of the study.

- After one year, there was a definite reduction in risk behavior in the intervention group compared to the control group. Several WHCs continued to offer community assistance including funding for additional HIV prevention efforts and programs for adolescents.

Other Projects The effectiveness and appeal of this community-level approach has resulted in a variety of ongoing research projects, including among adolescents.

Dissemination of Findings It is important to rapidly develop strategies for disseminating research findings and transferring evidence-based HIV interventions to those providing services in community-based and nongovernmental organizations.
- Further research is needed to identify innovative strategies to effectively transfer findings from research into prevention services with support of their implementation in at-risk communities.

Cluster Randomized Trials of Professional and Organizational Behavior Change Interventions in Health Care Settings

Jeremy Grimshaw, University of Ottawa; Martin Eccles,
University of Newcastle upon Tyne; Marion Campbell, University of Aberdeen;
Diana Elbourne, London School of Hygiene and Tropical Medicine

Background This article discusses the practical and ethical issues in the design, conduct, and analysis of cluster randomized trials.
- Cluster randomized trials are commonly used in health care. They raise ethical and methodological issues that have rarely been addressed.
- In spite of positive new evidence to improve patient care, patients, health services, and professionals are very slow to adopt it.
  - Typical approaches to promote findings have emphasized journals, lectures, and seminars, but providers and managers have little time to read literature or attend meetings.
  - They also encounter a range of barriers in areas of finance, organizational facilities, peer group standards, individual skills, and information overload.

NOTE: It is therefore not surprising that the uptake of research findings into health care appears slow and haphazard.

Implementation Research Implementation research looks at methods to promote the uptake of research findings into routine clinical practice by testing approaches to change professional and organizational behavior.
- We should expect the same strength of evidence when considering which strategies to use to improve uptake of research findings as we do when considering which antibiotic to use for each patient.
- The same arguments used to justify randomized controlled trials of clinical interventions are as salient to the evaluation of dissemination and implementation strategies:
  - The effects of interventions are likely to be modest.
  - The potential for bias is substantial.

- Our poor understanding of competing explanations for an observed effect makes it difficult to adjust for these in nonrandomized designs.
- Finally, most health care professionals and organizations have limited resources to support implementation initiatives.

Q R S

Design Issues Schwartz and Lellouch made a distinction between explanatory and pragmatic studies.
- Explanatory studies aim to test whether an intervention is beneficial under ideal conditions.
- Pragmatic studies aim to test whether an intervention is likely to be effective in routine practice by comparing the new procedure against the current regimen.
NOTE: Implementation research aims to develop a generalizable evidence base to support the choice of professional and organizational change strategies.

Level of Randomization Implementation researchers need to consider at what level to randomize units.
- This often involves considering the trade-off between contamination and feasibility.
- Consider a trial to evaluate professional behavior change strategies within hospital settings:
  - Potential levels of randomization (from "higher" to "lower") include the hospital, the clinical service or directorate, the ward, and the individual clinician.
  - Randomization at the level of the hospital will minimize the risk of contamination (e.g., members of the control group exchanging information with members of the treatment group) but dramatically increase the number of hospitals required in the study.
  - This could have substantial logistical and financial implications, limiting the study's feasibility.
- In contrast, randomization at the level of the individual ward will decrease the number of hospitals required but potentially increase the risk of contamination to an unacceptable level because of regular contact by professionals working within the same ward environment.
  - In our two case studies, we could have randomized at the level of the town, the health care center (where more than one family practice might be based), the family practice (most United Kingdom family practitioners work in group practices), or the individual family practitioners.
  - We chose to randomize at the level of the family practice, reasoning that the risk of contamination within a practice was high but that the risk of contamination across practices sharing the same premises was sufficiently low based upon our own clinical experiences and experiences of previous trials that had not demonstrated contamination at this level.

Sample Size Issues Within individual patient randomized trials, responses of patients are considered to be independent from each other.
- Patients within any one cluster are often more likely to respond in a similar manner and can no longer be assumed to act independently.
- This lack of independence in turn leads to a loss of statistical power in comparison with a patient randomized trial.
- To achieve the equivalent power of a patient randomized trial, standard sample size calculations need to be inflated by a factor based upon the degree of clustering.

Pretest Data   Relatively few clusters are allocated to control and study groups in cluster trials in implementation research.
- This causes an increased danger of imbalance in baseline performance of both groups.
- By adopting a pre-post design, the imbalance can be examined.
- Adjusting for baseline performance in the analysis stage can also increase statistical power if the premeasure is expected to be a good predictor of postperformance.
- In implementation research studies, baseline measures of performance are also useful in that they provide an initial estimate of the magnitude of the problem.

Intervention   Experimental interventions may be selected for a variety of reasons, including
Rationale
- the judgment of the researcher based upon a formal or informal assessment of the barriers to adopting an evidence-based practice,
- empirical evidence about the effectiveness of the intervention under similar (or different) conditions,
- theoretical considerations, and
- a proposed change in policy.

Control   Experiments may include a no-intervention control or an intervention control.
Interventions
- A no-intervention control will provide the best evidence about the likely counterfactual in the absence of the experimental intervention—this may not be informative if there is a well-established existing policy or intervention.

Ethical Issues   Researchers have not paid great attention to ethical issues arising in cluster randomized trials where professionals provide data about the care of individual patients.
- It is helpful to distinguish between ethical consent for study participation and consent for data collection.
- Individual consent is not the case for cluster-cluster trials, which are typical in implementation research—under such circumstances, professionals' usual ethical responsibilities should override the effects of anything the professional may consider harmful for a patient.

Data Collection Commonly, researchers have measured performance by asking the profes-
Issues   sional what they have done or intend to do in a specific set of circumstances.
- There is evidence that self-reports of activity tend to overestimate actual performance.
- There is a danger that the intervention may sensitize the professional in the experimental group about desired practice, potentially leading to an imbalance in the degree to which the experimental and control groups report their behavior.
- Given these concerns, researchers should measure actual performance and not rely on self-report.

Analytical   There are three general approaches to the analysis of cluster randomized
Issues   trials:
- analysis at cluster level,
- the adjustment of standard tests, and
- advanced statistical techniques using data recorded at both the individual and cluster level.

NOTE: The most appropriate analysis option will depend on a number of factors, including
- the unit of inference,
- the study design,
- whether the researchers wish to adjust for other relevant variables at the individual or cluster level,
- the type and distribution of outcome measure,
- the number of clusters randomized,
- the size of cluster and variability of cluster size, and
- statistical resources available to the research team.

Q
R
S

Economic Evaluation

The most informative evaluations to policy makers are those that incorporate concurrent economic evaluations of the relative efficiency of different implementation strategies in addition to their relative effectiveness.
- The evaluation can be used to judge whether costs are reduced and benefits increased, in which case the decision is straightforward, or if both costs and benefits have increased and if the benefits are worth the extra costs.

Process Evaluations

Randomized trials provide little information about the likely causal mechanisms of interventions and modifying factors.
- Process evaluations do provide insight into why an intervention was successful.

Reporting Issues

The need for clear reporting of randomized trials has been widely recognized.
- This has been highlighted through the publication of the CONSORT statement, which outlines the common standards for reporting of field trials.
- The CONSORT statement has been instrumental in improving the standards of reporting in clinical trials and has been widely adopted by medical journals.

Cluster Randomized Trials for the Evaluation of Strategies Designed to Promote Evidence-Based Practice in Perinatal and Neonatal Medicine

Laura C. Leviton, Robert Wood Johnson Foundation;
Jeffrey D. Horbar, University of Vermont

Background

Despite a large and growing body of evidence, the overuse, underuse, and misuse of therapeutic interventions are commonplace.
- New strategies designed to promote evidence-based practice must be identified, tested, and implemented.
- Using the illustrations of two cluster randomized trials, the authors discuss some of the theoretical, methodological, and practical issues of using these designs in a medical setting.
- Hospitals, long-term care settings, group practices, and health insurance plans all offer potential as the unit of assignment and intervention.
- There are many likely causes for the gap between evidence and practice.
  * Most obvious is that evidence continues to develop while practice changes less rapidly.

Q
R
S

◦ Print, electronic, and organizational strategies do not change practices very much.
◦

Interventions   Organizational interventions offer some promise.
- Decision and administrative supports enable the physician to change practice—things like hiring staff to counsel patients on self-management of chronic illness or a reminder in the medical chart.
- Several strategies mix the influences for change, such as local opinion leaders pushing innovations.

Rapid Cycle   A promising development in translating evidence into practice is the rapid cycle, collaborative improvement process.
- Quality teams first identify and plan an overall measurable aim.
- The teams develop a list of ideas.
- Through trial and learning cycles that introduce and test relatively small changes, adoption takes place and then another change is added.

Corticosteroid Trial   The aim of this trial was to test an intervention to encourage obstetricians and maternal-fetal specialists to adopt a practice guideline for using corticosteroid therapy when women go into premature labor.
- Despite strong evidence of this therapy's effectiveness, only 26 percent of eligible cases got the therapy.
- The study became a test of dissemination strategies—the usual methods would be contrasted with a more active effort.
- The American College of Obstetricians and Gynecologists endorsed the therapy; this helps effect change more rapidly.
- Treatment hospitals were exposed to active, low-cost dissemination:
  ◦ designation of a lead physician and nurse at each hospital,
  ◦ grand rounds by an eminent physician associated with the study,
  ◦ group discussions on uses of the therapy,
  ◦ chart reminders, and
  ◦ performance feedback at the hospital level.

Corticosteroid Trial Results   The intervention gave a statistically significant boost to the use of the therapy.
- The results were useful to show some conditions under which marginal increases in uptake of evidence-based practice could be achieved for relatively low cost.
- Although changes were already under way in the use of the therapy, the intervention speeded these changes.
- It confirmed the usefulness of a multifaceted approach.

Surfactant Trial   The aim of this trial was to evaluate a coordinated, multifaceted intervention designed to close the gap between research and practice in the use of surfactant therapy for preterm infants. There were three components:
- Hospitals in the intervention group received confidential feedback in their surfactant use.
- The researchers generated a review of the evidence on early surfactant therapy for use in a workshop.
- The workshop focused on evidence-based quality improvement.

Surfactant Trial Results   After the intervention, a significantly greater proportion of infants in the intervention hospitals received surfactant therapy in the delivery room.
- The median time an infant received the first dose was twenty-one minutes in intervention hospitals versus seventy-eight minutes in control hospitals.

- There were no significant differences, however, in the primary patient–level outcomes, infant mortality, and pneumothorax.
- Two "sea changes" in practice may have led the researchers to expect too large an effect on mortality.
  - Surfactant use time had already started to decrease.
  - Increased use of antenatal corticosteroids has led to a reduction in the mortality rate of preterm infants since the studies were conducted.

The Case for Cluster Randomized Studies

One way to frame the outcome measures for these studies is to track uptake of the practice at specific time points.
- Can intervention speed up the adoption of a practice?
- Taking into account features of an organization can help gain insight for more powerful interventions.
- The empirical argument for cluster random assignment is that medical practices vary substantially across organizations and localities, and powerful forces beyond individual beliefs and knowledge enable or prevent practice change.
  - Within a practice, change is best accomplished when systems and processes are retooled to enable change.
  - Outside the practice, forces affecting change include the standard of local care, the influence of peers, hospital admitting privileges, liability concerns, and the dominant health insurance plans.
  - Practitioners are embedded in organizations and networks that have strong influence on their behavior.
  - Secular trends can reduce or even wash out the effects of an intervention.
- Preexisting research networks offer economies of scale (in reduced cost and improved quality) in conducting cluster randomized studies.

Q
R
S

Historical Review of School-Based Randomized Trials for Evaluating Problem Behavior Prevention Programs

Brian R. Flay, University of Illinois at Chicago;
Linda M. Collins, Pennsylvania State University

Background

The design and statistical methodologies used in school-based intervention research have advanced greatly in the past twenty years. Methods have improved for
- randomization of whole schools and the resistance to randomization,
- choice of appropriate control groups,
- solutions when randomization breaks down,
- limiting and handling of variation in integrity of the intervention received,
- limiting biases introduced by data collection,
- awareness of the effects of intensive and long-term data collection,
- limiting and analysis of subject attrition and other missing data,
- parental consent approaches,
- design and analysis issues when only small numbers of schools are available or can be afforded,
- the choice of the unit of analysis,
- phases of research,
- optimizing and extending the reach of interventions, and

QRS

- differential effects in subpopulations.
NOTE: School-based prevention research still faces many significant method-ological challenges in the above areas.

Efficacy Trials

Most prevention studies have been efficacy trials.
- They have been conducted within the framework of models derived from the FDA's approach to the development of new drugs.
- Many researchers have bemoaned the lack of effectiveness trials, or other kinds of studies to assess the effects of proven interventions under real-world conditions—the need is for more randomized trials.

Efficacy and Effectiveness

Before the 1980s, there was little recognition of the desirability of a carefully designed sequence of studies to inform the development, testing, and adop-tion of effective prevention programs.
- Flay and Best advocated a careful distinction between formative and summative research, with the idea that interventions developed for early phases of research would not necessarily translate into effective programs in the real world.
- They also suggested the need for a thoughtful sequence of phases of research during the development of prevention programs.

Conclusions

There are six major conclusions.
- Sequence planning is important.
- Time is important—the ultimate effects of importance to society of an inter-vention occur over the long term.
- Keeping up with and remaining open to methodological advances is important.
- Publication of all results is important.
- Accumulation of knowledge is important—the true measure of advance-ment in knowledge is not the individual study but the accumulated findings from reviews and meta-analyses.
- The devil is in the details—methodologically sound school-based research is not easy; it requires lots of institutional relationships and on-the-ground work relating to school administrators and teachers.

Place-Based Randomized Trials to Test the Effects on Instructional Practices of a Mathematics/Science Professional Development Program for Teachers

Andrew C. Porter, Vanderbilt University;
Rolf K. Blank, Council of Chief State School Officers;
John L. Smithson, University of Wisconsin–Madison;
Eric Osthoff, University of Wisconsin–Madison

Background

A professional development model was designed for and is being tested in about fifty U.S. middle schools in five large urban districts.
- The focus of the article is on learning about doing place-based randomized trials to test the efficacy of education programs (treatment is not yet com-plete and study results are not available).

- Half the study schools in each district receive the intervention and half are controls.
- Each school forms a math/science leadership team including at least one administrator.
- Teams receive professional development workshops, then work with all math and science teachers in their school to teach them to use data on their practices to improve their effectiveness.

Reasons for the Study

There are several reasons to study a professional development program using place-based randomized trials.
- Over the past decade, a great deal of research has established the characteristics of effective professional development.
- We now have several tools for studying teachers' decisions about what to teach.
- There is now a great deal of interest in data-based decision making in education to help improve teacher practices.
- There is also interest in and support for doing randomized experiments in education.

NOTE: The focus of this article is on the design and implementation of the place-based randomized trial.

Independent Variable

The independent variable is the treatment versus the control condition—in education, there is no strict control.
- Control school teachers continued to participate in regular professional development.
- The teachers in intervention schools participated in professional development other than the treatment.
- The data were collected not only on the quality of the treatment implementation but also on the other professional development experiences of both the treatment and the control teachers.

NOTE: The professional development is aimed at helping teachers reflect on their individual and collective practices, and from that they are to decide how their instruction might be strengthened.

Dependent Variables

The lack of prescriptiveness for classroom practice makes defining valid and sensitive dependent variables difficult.
- One dependent variable is the degree of alignment between the content of each teacher's instruction and the content of the state or district test used for accountability purposes.
    - Uniquely targeted dependent variables were formulated for each school, focusing on the types of changes in instruction that each school decided were most needed.
    - The problem with these targeted variables is that they are aligned with the intended changes in one school rather than the intended changes across all schools.
- Ideally, gains in student achievement would have been another dependent variable, but due to a three-year limit on the program by the National Science Foundation, there are not strong enough effects to measure student achievement.

Data on Enacted Curriculum

The professional development model for the Data on Enacted Curriculum (DEC) project is based on
- standards-based improvement of instruction;
- continuous improvement of practice using data and formative evaluation;

- school-based collaboration and networking to foster the sharing of ideas, models, and strategies improvement;
- district contact persons to involve district-level instructional support staff by inviting them to participate in all workshops; and
- treatment steps that include
  - baseline surveys of instructional practice and student achievement,
  - a two-day professional development workshop,
  - follow-up technical assistance in schools,
  - a professional development follow-up workshop, and
  - evaluation of progress and refocusing of assistance.

NOTE: A major intent of the DEC treatment is to involve teams in the processes and techniques for using their data to highlight important questions and to discover tentative causal factors. Another goal is to develop the capacity of leadership teams to engage a larger group of their own staff in dialogue about their data and inquiry into their own teaching and learning.

Participation Factors

Five factors have affected the extent and quality of school participation in the treatment:
- time for meetings of the school leadership teams;
- stability of the teams;
- schoolwide use of the DEC treatment—it is difficult to ensure the quality of treatment due to variable team training and possible conflicts with school cultural norms;
- principal participation; and
- district priorities and policies.

Critiques

Campbell and Stanley provided a powerful template for critiquing experiments in education.
- They identified internal validity—the extent to which an experiment provides unbiased estimates of treatment main effects.
- They also identified external validity—the extent to which the results from an experiment can be generalized.
- To the above can be added issues of precision—the extent to which the effect size is estimated with a small standard error.

In this experiment,
- The internal validity is strong, though not perfect and the external validity has several limits:
  - The focus is on urban schools with students from low-income families.
  - The work is in middle school math and science.
  - Schools were volunteers.
  - A few schools dropped out.
  - The timing of the study and the context in which it was conducted—under a huge emphasis on standards-based reform and a push in math and science achievement.
- The three-year limitation had negative effects on external validity.
  - A delayed test of effects was not possible.
  - Effects on student achievement in such a short period are unlikely.
- The designers of the intervention were the designers of the study—a third-party evaluator would be preferred.

Insights

Since experiments have been rare in education, it is worth sharing some insights.
- A fundamental issue in considering an experiment in education is knowing if an experiment is warranted.

- First, there must be a promising intervention.
- Second, the treatment needs to be reasonably straightforward.
- Third, the treatment should be pilot-tested to get an indication of its feasibility and promise.
- Another issue is the hypothesis being tested.
  - To what should the treatment be compared? Selecting a comparison group is one of the most important decisions.
- The degree of treatment implementation is dependent to a considerable extent on the vagaries of the school districts and states.

Three Key Challenges

To bring the treatment to scale, should it be found effective, has three key challenges.
- A way would have to be found to produce more trainers on a par with the one used in this experiment.
- There is a need to build an infrastructure for "selling" the treatment.
- A way needs to be found to maintain the fidelity and integrity of the treatment as it is scaled up.

NOTE: These challenges were not addressed in this experiment but need to be once the effectiveness of the experiment is shown. Questions about taking the treatment to scale, which are in some ways analogous to concerns about external validity, must be addressed if an intervention is ultimately to be found worthy.

Emergent Principles for the Design, Implementation, and Analysis of Cluster-Based Experiments in Social Science

Thomas D. Cook, Northwestern University

Background

All things being equal, it is much more difficult to do an experiment that simultaneously deals with units at two or more levels—this is usually the individual and some higher-order level like a community or school.
- Social scientists have not yet acquired much experience in implementing cluster-based experiments, and the knowledge to be gained by emulating medicine's more evolved tradition of multisite randomized clinical trials is limited.
  - In the medical tradition, individuals are assigned to treatments from within sites rather than in between-site designs.
  - Thus, sites serve to increase power and generalization, not to be units of assignment per se.

NOTE: Social scientists will have to learn most of their lessons about cluster-based experiments in the crucible of their own experience. Solutions will also have to come from reflections on such experiences as well as from developments in statistical theory.

Cluster-Level Research

Why assign at the cluster level?
- Most concepts to be studied like school governance, culture, climate, norms, teams, and networks cannot be reduced to individual behavior—the

Q
R
S

hope is to create a new culture whose norms will affect the behavior of current (and also future) teachers and students.
- The unit of assignment level is chosen either because of theory or to protect against a potential source of bias.
- An argument for cluster-based assignment has to do with desired impact. The hope is that individual change will be greater if it is achieved through group- rather than individual-level processes.
- There is a political reason for assigning clusters rather than individuals. Assignment to different statuses inevitably creates potentially large inequality.

Random Assignment

Why the random assignment of larger units?
- To state that social structures are hierarchically ordered only scratches the surface of the myriad forms of this ordering.
- To add to the complexity, social structures are not fixed in time.
  - Students can change classes or leave school.

NOTE: Fortunately, well-implemented cluster-based random assignment simplifies structural complexity in ways that nonexperiments cannot. Without random assignment, any school-based causal study would have to struggle to rule out the possibility that various interdependent structural realities function as causal confounds.

Principles

Here are five principles of improved cluster-level design:
- *Principle 1:* Know the size of unconditional and conditional intraclass correlations, what determines them, and how they affect statistical power and hence sample size estimation.
- *Principle 2:* Assign units to treatments at the lowest level possible as long as this does not change the research question, for lower units entail many important advantages.
- *Principle 3:* Minimize interunit communication, though it will often be especially unclear how much to expect in designs where treatment assignment is within-school or within-neighborhood.
- *Principle 4:* Avoid black box experiments despite their policy relevance; instead, explore implementation and causal mediating processes.
- *Principle 5:* Explicitly acknowledge the great heterogeneity in treatment implementation and analyze its consequences confessing to the lower inferential quality of such conclusions.

Randomization and Social Program Evaluation: The Case of Progresa

Susan W. Parker, Centro de Investigación y Docencia Económicas;
Graciela M. Teruel, Universidad Iberoamericana

Background

This article analyzes the development of Progresa, the principal antipoverty strategy of the Mexican government.
- The program is aimed at increasing families' investment in human capital as defined by education, health, and nutrition and includes cash transfers linked to regular school attendance and family clinic visits. The program also

offers in-kind benefits including basic health care and nutritional supplements for children up to age five as well as pregnant and lactating women.
- It has served as a model for similar programs in several other Latin American countries.

NOTE: The program was subject to a rigorous evaluation effort in rural areas that included an experimental research design and impact studies conducted by an outside institution, the International Food Policy Research Institute (IFPRI).

Q R S

Program Benefits

Progresa combines education, health, and nutrition in one program to enhance the effectiveness.
- Cash benefits are conditional on children attending school and the family completing a schedule of regular clinic visits.
- Proxy means tests carried out for targeting.

NOTE: All the monetary benefits are given to a woman of the family based on research that women use more resources for children than do men.

Human Capital

The design of Progresa focuses on the lack of human capital as a central cause of poverty and hopes to reduce poverty by increasing investment in human capital, particularly that of children.
- It assumes that returns to education, health, and nutrition are likely to be high for its beneficiary population.
- The caveat is the little available information on returns to schooling and health in poor areas where Progresa operates.

Progress Evaluation

The Progresa evaluation includes a randomized design.
- The strategy was to select a sample of Progresa communities and randomize communities between the treatment and the control groups:
  - A potential limitation of randomizing at the community level was the likelihood of observing less randomness at the individual level.
  - A sample of 506 communities with 24,077 households in seven states was used.
- The experiment lasted only a year and a half, which makes longer-term impacts more difficult to analyze.
- Control group could not be maintained longer because of the rapid growth of the Program.

Evaluation Results

The results of the evaluation were extremely positive.
- In the words of the coordinator of the IFPRI evaluation, "The results show that after only three years, poor children have increased their school enrollment, have more balanced diets, are receiving more medical attention, and are learning that the future can be very different than the past."
- The only noted negative impact in the IFPRI evaluation was some increasing tension between Progresa beneficiaries and nonbeneficiaries in some communities.

Impacts on Public Policy

Some of the impacts of the evaluation include:
- The evaluation played an important role in ensuring that the program was not eliminated with the change of government.
- The year after the evaluation was released, Congress issued a new law requiring all social programs to carry out external evaluations of their impacts every year.
- Other Latin American countries have implemented similar programs and also implemented the model of external evaluation.

NOTE: Whereas the experimental design has been a critical factor in the program's initial success, it appears that estimation of the longer-term impacts will require nonexperimental estimators or structural estimation.

Hot Spots Policing Experiments and Criminal Justice Research: Lessons from the Field

David Weisburd, Hebrew University and University of Maryland

Background

There is widespread acceptance that randomized experiments provide more valid answers to policy questions than do nonexperimental studies.
- Experiments provide a superior method for assessing the effectiveness of a given intervention.
- Yet randomized studies are the oddity rather than the norm in spite of the fact that these experiments have been successfully carried out across a wide array of criminal justice settings. Explanations often given:
  - There are widespread ethical problems to overcome.
  - Experiments are difficult to implement.
  - Implementation imposes so many limitations on criminal justice practice that they are not likely to have much policy relevance.

NOTE: Place-based randomized trials in the area of hot spots policing appear at odds with the above assumptions—hot spot policing has become a core strategy and the research played an important role in its adoption.

Situational Causes of Crime

Criminologists recognize that the situational opportunities provided at the level of "place" can affect the occurrence of crime.
- Criminal events require not only a "motivated offender" but the presence of a "suitable target" and the absence of a "capable guardian."
  - Crime rates can be affected by changing the nature of the targets or of the guardianship regardless of the motivations that individual offenders bring to the crime situation.
- One natural outgrowth of these perspectives was that the place where crimes occur would become an important research focus.
  - Important research was done in Minneapolis and Jersey City that radically changed how criminologists understood the crime equation.
  - The findings showed that place crime can be reduced without displacing crime to other areas.

NOTE: It is important to recognize that randomized experiments must be conducted if criminal justice is to draw valid policy conclusions about what works. Ethical concerns, enforcement, and cost are factors that deter researchers from using this method.

Ethical Concerns

It may be possible to avoid many ethical dilemmas by randomly allocating at the organizational or place level, rather than by individuals.
- This was seen in both the Minneapolis and Jersey City studies.
  - No individuals were contacted for information, and all data came from police records and observation of the sites.
  - Accepted police practices were used.
  - There was no placebo—control sites also received some form of criminal justice treatment.

Importance of
Monitoring

Although monitoring may be difficult, the experience of the hot spots studies is that monitoring may be facilitated by focusing on clearly defined places and the application of treatments in a visible social environment.

- The importance of monitoring in both studies, Minneapolis and Jersey City, was confirmed by identification of breakdowns in the application of treatment.
- It is important to integrate clinical work and research work in criminal justice to get the practitioner to believe in the importance of implementing a randomized study.
- It is also important to consider coercive pressure from higher-ups to maintain treatment fidelity.

Concerns

The fact that a limited number of cases can be included in many cluster randomized trials raises concerns regarding the ability of randomization to provide for equivalent groups.

- Hot spots were grouped into statistical blocks made up of smaller components within the study—for example, the fifty-two hot spots were divided into four groups based on reported arrests and emergency calls to police.
- It appears that in spite of the successes using randomized trials in hot spot studies, there is reluctance to use these trials in other areas due probably to cost and difficulties in gaining approvals from funders who are not predisposed to this science.

Conclusions

There are eight specific lessons regarding the implementation and development of place-based randomized trials and experimental methods more generally:

- Crisis in the legitimacy of conventional practices may encourage randomized controlled experiments.
- There must be a predisposition toward randomized trials in political processes that lead to funding.
- There is a need for governmental support.
- Random allocation of places can lead to fewer ethical objections.
- Monitoring of the treatment fidelity is essential.
- Strong hierarchical controls within the institution administering treatment facilitates implementation.
- The more complex the treatment, the more the need for greater coercive controls of the treatment integrity.
- Block randomization provides a method for overcoming some problems related to restrictions in sample size.

Introducing New Contraceptives in Rural China: A Field Experiment

Herbert L. Smith, University of Pennsylvania

Background

This article presents an overview of work during the 1990s on a family planning experiment in four counties in rural China.

- The project featured three interventions:
  - provision of better contraceptives;
  - better training of family planning workers; and

Q
R
S

  ◦ offering a choice of contraception method—an innovation in the Chinese family planning system.
- The project was designed as a randomized experiment.
- The experimental unit was not the individual woman but rather the lowest organizational unit feasible for the design.
  ◦ Within each county, six townships were selected at random.
  ◦ Two of the six were randomly designated as controls.

NOTE: The decision to use twenty-four townships, with treatment groups in a two-to-one ratio to control groups, reflected the cost-benefit compromise that attends social research.

Study Settings   It became evident that interesting demographic and programmatic distinctions existed both within and between the counties in the study.
- The authors became interested in the politics, economics, and social organization of the system, including variations within the study sites.
- Although the formal design took no account of the measurement of these phenomena, field visits and notes came to rely heavily on gleaning "side information" about local process, to better understand the data that were dominated by effects not attributable to the experimental interventions.
- Visits to the sites were variously to
  ◦ meet local officials and select study sites,
  ◦ monitor the general course of the research,
  ◦ participate in training of interviewers,
  ◦ interview family planning workers and their clients,
  ◦ set up a record-keeping system,
  ◦ maintain a demographic and contraceptive surveillance system,
  ◦ examine related health system records, and
  ◦ observe and evaluate the extent to which innovations were maintained and expanded beyond the project sites.

Experimental   In experimental terms, the treatments were weak and ill defined; many inves-
Design   tigators did not understand the experiment as designed; contamination was rife; and "history" intervened.
- In concept, the design was probably not a bad one—it was based on the distinction between the unit of experimentation and the unit of analysis.
  ◦ It is advisable to use randomization at the level at which units are most naturally manipulated.
  ◦ When the unit of observation is "lower" than the unit of randomization or assignment of treatment, then for many purposes the data need to be aggregated to measure it at the level of assignment.
- Unlike the typical individual-level encouragement design, this project randomized the treatment at the lowest level that a policy could conceivably be implemented.
- Variations for each annual difference between treatment and control townships have two components:
  ◦ Differences between townships with treatment types, with fifteen and seven degrees of freedom, respectively.
  ◦ Sampling variability in the estimate of each township ratio, exacerbated by clustering (by village) which tends to inflate design effects.
- Even though the sample size at the level of the unit of observation is fairly large, differences between treatment and control townships from the Baseline Survey are well within the margin of error accruing to randomization and sampling.

- One of the hallmarks of the project was the recognition that population and family planning processes varied widely across study counties as a function of latent differences in the organization, motivation, and political centrality of the respective county planning administrations.

Statistics   When the data are examined, the benefits of randomization are substantially attenuated.
- As for the variation between treatment and control groups within a county, this is founded on two control townships and four treatment townships.
- With so few degrees of freedom, randomization does not afford much statistical power—we are back at something like comparative case studies.

Conclusion   The project was an attempt to examine the effects of policy shift by manipulation of aggregated subjects—the rural townships.
- Hindsight suggests that even at this level there is the possibility of serious interference between units (contamination).
- The policy intervention was weak as measured against a host of external factors influencing demographic change in these areas.
- There is the problem of incomplete randomization as a function of the small number of experimental units, a problem that is exacerbated when treatment effects interact with population characteristics.
- It would be folly to argue that the New Contraceptives in Rural China study, although quite successful as a demonstration project, was a compelling counterexemplar to skepticism regarding randomization at the level at which policy is being implemented.

QRS

A new and more powerful way to access SAGE Journals.

The content you want, the convenience you need.

SAGE Journals Online will offer a new and more powerful way to access SAGE journal content. The new online delivery platform will host SAGE journals and will represent one of the largest collections in the social sciences as well as an extensive STM list.

Powered by HighWire Press, the new SAGE platform will enable users to access content more easily and powerfully through

- Flexible browsing and searching capabilities
- Social science specific taxonomy
- User personalization (eTOCs, My Favorite Journals)
- Toll-free inter-journal reference linking
- External links (to/from ISI, CrossRef, MEDLINE)
- PDA downloading capabilities
- Pay per view options

Library friendly features:
- Familiar subscription and adminstration tools
- COUNTER compliant reports
- User-friendly usage statistics
- Subscription expiration notification services
- Enhanced subscription options – available in 2005. For more information visit http://www.sagepublications.com/2005subscriptioninfo.htm

SAGE Journals Online will be available in September 2004!

Bookmark www.sagepublications.com/sageonline for the latest details

⑤SAGE Publications www.sagepublications.com